DATE DUE			
Bolsh				he Soviet
Com				ions these
wom				lerground
befor				, and their
servic				more than
five h				he lives of
the n				at women
were				wer levels
durin				g leaflets,
speak				They also
creat				men from
tradit				aces their
fascir				novement
throu				zhnev.
GAYLORD			PRINTED IN U.S.A

Bolshevik women

Bolshevik women

Barbara Evans Clements

University of Akron

CAMBRIDGE
UNIVERSITY PRESS

PUBLISHED BY THE PRESS SYNDICATE OF THE UNIVERSITY OF CAMBRIDGE
The Pitt Building, Trumpington Street, Cambridge CB2 1RP, United Kingdom

CAMBRIDGE UNIVERSITY PRESS
The Edinburgh Building, Cambridge CB2 2RU, United Kingdom
40 West 20th Street, New York, NY 10011-4211, USA
10 Stamford Road, Oakleigh, Melbourne 3166, Australia

First published 1997

Printed in the United Kingdom at the University Press, Cambridge

Typeset in Plantin 10/12 pt

A catalogue record for this book is available from the British Library

ISBN 0 521 45403 4 hardback
ISBN 0 521 59920 2 paperback

VN

To Jerry, Pete, and Liv

That world of their youth – dark, ignorant, terrible with hate and disease – how was it that living in it, in the midst of corruption, filth, treachery, degradation, they had not mistrusted man nor themselves; had believed so beautifully, so . . . falsely?

"Aah, children," he said out loud, "how we believed, how we belonged." And he yearned to package for each of the children, the grandchildren, for everyone, *that joyous certainty, that sense of mattering, of moving and being moved, of being one and indivisible with the great of the past, with all that freed, ennobled.*

Tilly Olson, "Tell Me a Riddle" (1961)

Contents

Illustrations

Plates

Figures

Tables

Acknowledgments

I owe many thanks to the institutions and the people who have helped me over the years with this project. The University of Akron provided support in the form of faculty research grants, as did the National Endowment for the Humanities. Our interlibrary-loan librarians, particularly Sarah Lorenz Akers, patiently struggled with transliterated Russian in their search for my obscure sources. Greta Bucher diligently tracked down information on Bolshevichki hidden away in several Moscow archives. Leonid Nikolaevich Sidorov saved me from the daunting tasks of learning how to decipher prerevolutionary handwriting ("handscrawling" would be the better term) by translating some letters from the archives. Shelley Baranowski, Heather Hogan, William Rosenberg, and Lynne Viola, who generously agreed to read the book when it was still in its infancy, gave me the rigorous criticism that I sorely needed. Christine Worobec was, as always, a dear, supportive friend who gently corrected my mistakes (particularly on the peasants) and offered lots of encouragement as well as many constructive suggestions. Another friend, Priscilla Harding, made perceptive assessments of the manuscript and also listened to my thoughts about it for years over lunch. All these folks have my heartfelt thanks. I hope I can repay your many favors in the future.

I must also thank my family. My husband, Gerald Newman, read this book with the most unremittingly critical eye of all. His blood-red messages, written in Newmanic minuscule on the margins of my text, have forced me to clarify my thinking, have pointed me the way out of many a conceptual thicket, and have suggested more elegant ways of saying things. My stepchildren, Peter and Livia Newman, deserve many hugs and kisses for the forbearance, the love, the support, and the many good times they have always given me. I dedicate this book to Jerry, Liv, and Pete, and to many more days on the bird runs.

Introduction

The first great communist revolution of the twentieth century began in October 1917 when the Bolshevik faction of the Russian Social-Democratic Labor Party overthrew the Provisional Government led by Alexander Kerensky. Proclaiming itself Russia's new government, a rag-tag organization of revolutionaries, experienced mainly in writing polemics and dodging the police, brashly stepped into the spotlight on the world stage. The party's first leaders – Lenin, Trotsky, Stalin, Zinoviev, Kamenev, Bukharin – quickly rose to international fame, hailed by some as heroes, execrated by others as enemies of civilization. Less easily seen, as all eyes followed the men of the Council of People's Commissars, were the tens of thousands of female Bolsheviks who marched through the streets of Petrograd in 1917 or shouted fiery speeches to cheering regiments of mutinous soldiers. Ten percent of those audacious Reds who so terrified the capitalist world in the grim closing days of World War I were women.

There were several thousand Bolshevichki, that is, female Bolsheviks, in the party in March 1917, and more than 30,000 by December 1921. In the mid-1920s, after the organization had renamed itself the Communist Party of the Soviet Union and members had begun to refer to themselves as communists, the term "Bolshevik" came in the USSR to be an honorific, an appellation reserved for those people who had joined the party before 1921. The Bolsheviks were revered as revolutionary liberators and founders of the Soviet Union. Among them was an extraordinary collection of women, the Bolshevichki, who had worked alongside men in all the campaigns responsible for bringing the party to power. For two decades before the fall of the tsar in March 1917 they attempted to foment revolution by printing inflammatory leaflets and assembling bombs. After the tsar fell, they rushed into the milling crowds to become stump speakers and party recruiters (1917–18). During the civil war (1918–21), some of them led soldiers into battle; others began building the institutions of the new order. When at last the civil war was won, the Bolshevichki threw themselves no less energetically into the construction

1

of the Soviet regime, seeing in its establishment the opening of the final chapter in the history of human progress. These tens of thousands of women, the great majority of them born between 1870 and 1900, were lieutenants and foot soldiers within a radical movement that has had enormous importance in the history of the twentieth century.

Only two of them, Alexandra Kollontai, particularly famous as an outspoken advocate for women's emancipation, and Nadezhda Krupskaia, Lenin's wife, are well known today; the rest have been mostly forgotten in Russia and abroad.[1] This is unfortunate. In the first place, they deserve serious, detailed historical consideration in their own right, as a substantial and distinctive historical group. Secondly, since many of them were rank-and-file communists, no less involved than their male comrades in sustaining the party organization in its underground years, pushing it to power, defending it during the civil war, and employing it afterwards to build the Soviet system, study of them enhances our understanding of the development of the party as an institution. And thirdly, the Bolshevichki deserve attention because they were important members of a generation of activist women that transformed the situation of women across the European world in the early twentieth century. By leading Soviet efforts to establish political, civil, and economic equality for women, the Bolshevichki figured – though not always entirely willingly or self-consciously – as shock troops in one of the great social battles of the modern era, the attempted revision of ancient gender values and norms.

Before the Russian Revolution, female Bolsheviks had much in common with the female activists of other nations. They rejected lives of domesticity, sought work in the wider world, and drew on feminist and socialist texts for inspiration, as did the suffragettes in Britain and the temperance crusaders in the United States. They battled traditional restrictions on women that prevailed not only in the larger society but within their own movement, as did female trade unionists in Germany and

---

[1] A handful of studies deal with the Bolshevichki in detail. See Barbara Evans Clements, "The Enduring Kinship of the Baba and the Bolshevik Woman," *Soviet Union* 12 (1985): 161–84; Beate Fieseler, "The Making of Russian Female Social Democrats, 1890–1917," *International Review of Social History* 34 (1989): 193–226; Mark Chapin Scott, "Her Brother's Keeper: The Evolution of Women Bolsheviks," Ph.D. dissertation, University of Kansas, 1980. Richard Stites also discussed the Bolshevichki in *The Women's Liberation Movement in Russia: Feminism, Nihilism, and Bolshevism, 1860–1930* (Princeton, 1978), 269 -77. The biographies on leading Bolshevichki are the following: Barbara Evans Clements, *Bolshevik Feminist: The Life of Aleksandra Kollontai* (Bloomington, Ind., 1979); R. C. Elwood, *Inessa Armand* (Cambridge, 1992); Beatrice Farnsworth, *Alexandra Kollontai: Socialism, Feminism, and the Bolshevik Revolution* (Stanford, 1980); and Robert H. McNeal, *Bride of the Revolution: Krupskaia and Lenin* (Ann Arbor, Mich., 1972).

Austria. However, in the great debates over the means and objects of change for women, the Bolshevichki unswervingly took the socialist side, often denouncing feminism as a species of bourgeois reformism inadequate to meet the pressing needs of societies undergoing industrialization. They felt the same outrage as Jane Addams and Margaret Sanger when contemplating the evils of urban slums, but they concluded very differently that the pathways of reform and compromise were dead ends. The only true solution was root-and-branch destruction of the existing system, a thorough demolition which would be followed by the construction of a socialized, communalized society.

And then, lo and behold, that is precisely what history dealt them – a revolution that shook their nation to its foundations. Suddenly, they were attending, or so they believed, at the creation of a new world. The Bolshevichki were to have a hand in both the glories of the USSR and its horrors; and they would bear responsibility for both.

The context – the history of Bolshevism

The Bolshevichki considered themselves internationalists, and they professed to despise much of the culture that was their heritage. But it was Russia that had made them revolutionaries; and they repaid the favor by affecting Russian history, from the overthrow of the tsar to the establishment of the new regime to the building of the new society. It will help us to see them clearly if we review briefly the evolution of scholarship on the political movement to which they belonged. The Bolshevik Party began its life in 1903 as a faction of the Russian Social-Democratic Labor Party, it changed its name to the Russian Communist Party (Bolshevik) in 1918, and it rechristened itself again in the 1920s as the Communist Party of the Soviet Union. Before World War II, only a handful of scholars outside the borders of the USSR devoted themselves to the study of this organization, or indeed of Russia more generally. But the situation changed after the war, when the USSR claimed a major role in international relations. In the 1950s and 1960s in western Europe and North America, historians and political scientists produced a plethora of articles and books focusing on the Communist Party of the Soviet Union, and more particularly on the politics of its leaders.

Foremost in those days of Cold War confrontation was the question of why the Bolshevik Party developed into a powerful dictatorship. Scholars argued that the answer lay in the efforts of Lenin and his followers to build socialism through coercion. The Bolsheviks' determination to force Russia to comply with their own flawed reading of Marxism led ineluctably to dictatorship. This pioneering scholarship made much of the domineering temperaments of Bolshevik leaders, particularly Lenin, but it also considered the national context important. Russia's incompletely developed economy, its huge peasant population, and its autocratic traditions conditioned both the ideology of the Bolsheviks and the methods they employed.[2]

Later scholars considered as well the effects of the civil war of 1918–21. The Bolsheviks ousted the Provisional Government rather easily in October 1917 because other political parties were confused and indecisive, while they themselves were organized and responsive to the increasing impatience and anger of the population. Regular army units within striking distance of the capital, St. Petersburg, might have been able to block the coup, but their commanders, alienated from the Provisional Government and unsure of the loyalty of the troops, chose to sit on their hands in November 1917. "The Bolsheviks did not seize power in this year of revolutions," historian Adam Ulam wrote. "They picked it up."[3] Within a few months, however, their enemies had regrouped, armies led by officers from the tsarist military had formed in Ukraine and Siberia, and civil war broke out between the "Red" Bolshevik forces and their enemies, the coalition of monarchists, liberals, and socialists commonly known as the "Whites."

Scholars have argued that this brutal war was the crucible in which the Bolshevik dictatorship was made. To win it, the party abandoned the loose organization and egalitarian principles of its underground days and instead adopted the hierarchical structure and methods of command of an army, applying these not only to deploying troops, but to governing civilian society as well. Thus, the argument runs, the exigencies of a vicious conflict extinguished the democratic politics prized by the Bolsheviks before 1917 and brought to the fore instead dictatorial predilections which, although implicit in Bolshevik values from the beginning, had been held in check by the very different political circumstances of the past. Millions of wartime recruits to the party, acculturated to practices far more autocratic than those that had prevailed in the prerevolutionary years, then went on to rule the Soviet Union autocratically.[4]

[2] The scholarship on the early years of the Bolshevik Party is too voluminous to cite extensively here. For pioneering studies, see E. H. Carr, *The Bolshevik Revolution*, 3 vols. (New York, 1950–53); Robert V. Daniels, *The Conscience of the Revolution* (Cambridge, Mass., 1965); Isaac Deutscher, *The Prophet Armed: Trotsky, 1879–1921* (New York, 1954); Leopold H. Haimson, *The Russian Marxists and the Origins of Bolshevism* (Cambridge, Mass., 1955); Alfred G. Meyer, *Leninism* (New York, 1962); Leonard B. Schapiro, *The Communist Party of the Soviet Union* (New York, 1960); and Adam Ulam, *The Bolsheviks* (New York, 1965).

[3] Ulam, *The Bolsheviks*, 314.

[4] For discussions of the Bolsheviks in 1917, see Robert V. Daniels, *Red October* (New York, 1967); S. P. Melgunov, *The Bolshevik Seizure of Power* (Santa Barbara, Calif., 1972);

When historians turned their attention to the NEP years of the 1920s (named after the New Economic Policy announced in 1921) and to the Stalin era (1928–53), they formulated other useful questions. Could the party have built a more humane government if it had continued on the course of accommodation with the peasantry and the intelligentsia that it pursued from 1921 until the late 1920s? How did the revolution that began in 1917 change Russian society? What was the character of the changes that occurred in consequence of Stalin's economic initiatives, particularly the Five Year Plans for industrialization launched in 1928 and the collectivization of agriculture initiated in 1929? What were the connections between these great events? And how did Stalin's government, one of the most murderous of the century, function?

All these questions were in some sense implied by the first one: why did the Bolsheviks become dictators? But they productively led scholars away from the alliances and disputes of the leadership, and into the ways the party changed in membership, philosophy, and group dynamics as it grew from a tiny underground movement into a huge governing regime. Scholars began to connect the party's behavior to broad developmental patterns in the nation, particularly the ongoing effects of urbanization and industrialization. They argued that the party was as much acted on by these processes as acting to direct them. Seen from this perspective, Stalin's rise to power appeared to be due not only to the fact that he was a ruthless manipulator. It also occurred because he spoke to the basic understandings and aspirations of a political organization much affected by war, by power, and by the influx of millions of new members different in significant ways from the people who had founded the movement decades before.

Scholars also began to see that the party Stalin dominated was never as well controlled as he wished it to be, nor as well organized. Instead, it was broken down in the provinces into self-protective cliques. Indeed, close examination of party politics in the 1920s and 1930s called into question the very concept of totalitarianism. Investigations uncovered not a well-oiled machine but a jerry-built contraption driven by inexperienced people following confusing, even contradictory, road maps. Blunders

Alexander Rabinowitch, *Prelude to Revolution: The Petrograd Bolsheviks and the July 1917 Uprising* (Bloomington, Ind., 1968); and Rabinowitch, *The Bolsheviks Come to Power: The Revolution of 1917 in Petrograd* (New York, 1978). On the importance of the civil war in changing the party, see Stephen F. Cohen, *Bukharin and the Bolshevik Revolution*, rev. ed. (New York, 1980); Stephen F. Cohen, *Rethinking the Soviet Experience* (New York, 1985); Abbott Gleason, Peter Kenez, and Richard Stites, eds., *Bolshevik Culture: Experiment and Order in the Russian Revolution* (Bloomington, Ind., 1985); and Diane P. Koenker, William G. Rosenberg, and Ronald Grigor Suny, eds., *Party, State, and Society in the Russian Civil War* (Bloomington, Ind., 1989).

were the consequence, as was massive popular resistance that could thwart the government's well-laid plans – had there been any.[5]

Many of the Stalin regime's difficulties, it was perceived, flowed from the task the communist government had set for itself, that is, to engineer the nation's economic and social transformation according to vague guidelines sketched out by nineteenth-century socialists. Such an undertaking would not have gone smoothly even in a well-governed, homogeneous society – something which Russia had not been for centuries, and which it certainly was not in the first third of the twentieth century, an era of war, revolution, and bitter social division, presided over by inexperienced leaders. Against this background, the party's tendency to reach for the implements of force and terror as it struggled to impose control seemed increasingly understandable, if no more excusable.

While this interpretation was developing in the late 1970s and 1980s, scholars studying other aspects of Russia's revolutionary era, which they came to define as extending from the 1890s through into the 1930s, cast new light on party history, even though this was not their primary concern. Work on labor unions, the educational system, the fin-de-siècle intelligentsia, and the peasant village promoted a more complex view of Russia than had prevailed earlier, when so much attention was given to the problem of political leadership. Such studies looked away from the ambitious political state and toward the behavior of ordinary people who cultivated their own institutions and built their own beliefs, sometimes in open defiance of their political overlords. These social histories suggested, as had the political studies that preceded them, that the state was never as powerful as its managers imagined and that the people were never as passive as outsiders perceived them to be. The scholarship also debunked the venerable racist notion that Russia was the barbarous stepchild of Asian despotism. Russia, it was argued, was a European nation like any other, its history produced by the interaction of traditions, developmental processes, and influences from outside its borders.[6]

[5] Again the relevant scholarship is voluminous. For an early example of scholars moving away from the concentration on elite politics, see Sheila Fitzpatrick, *The Commissariat of Enlightenment* (Cambridge, 1970). For recent works on the NEP era, see Sheila Fitzpatrick, Alexander Rabinowitch, and Richard Stites, eds., *Russia in the Era of NEP* (Bloomington, Ind., 1991); and Lewis H. Siegelbaum, *Soviet State and Society Between Revolutions, 1918–1929* (New York, 1992). Important discussions of party politics appear in J. Arch Getty, *The Origins of the Great Purges* (New York, 1985); Moshe Lewin, *The Making of the Soviet System* (New York, 1985); Lewis H. Siegelbaum, *Stakhanovism and the Politics of Productivity in the USSR, 1935–1941* (New York, 1988); and Lynne Viola, *The Best Sons of the Fatherland* (New York, 1987). A major study of peasant resistance to party initiatives is Sheila Fitzpatrick's *Stalin's Peasants* (New York, 1994).

[6] On the working class, see William Chase, *Workers, Society, and the Soviet State* (Urbana, Ill., 1987); Heather G. Hogan, *Forging Revolution: Metalworkers, Managers, and the State in St. Petersburg, 1890–1914* (Bloomington, Ind., 1993); William Husband, *Revolution in the*

The context – the history of women in Russia

The study of women's history played another part in creating new perspectives onto Russia's past. Historians unearthed a wealth of information on Russian women, attesting to both similarities and profound differences between their lives and those of other Europeans. The similarities derived from the fact that all Europeans shared many of the same gender ideas, and organized their societies around the same basic divisions of labor and power between women and men. The patterned articulation of these arrangements is now referred to as that of "patriarchy," the name given to systems of social organization that distribute power through hierarchies of men ranked by age and social position. Patriarchy justifies male authority by arguing that it is ordained both by God ("our father which art in heaven") and by nature ("men are naturally fitter than women, for actions of labour and danger"). Women are situated in patriarchal systems according to their kinship to men; they gain authority from seniority within their families and from those families' rank in society.[7]

Historians of the women of Russia have spent a good deal of time examining Russian patriarchy. They have documented the way it was institutionalized in law, religion, and custom. They have argued that Russian women behaved rather like subordinate men, accommodating themselves to the social order and gaining its benefits by more or less willing subservience. Women avoided the alternative, direct resistance, because they knew that it was likely to be fruitless and might be severely punished by all the many authorities in their lives – their husbands, fathers, and landlords, as well as the minions of the tsar. Of course, historians have also found that women, like men, were acculturated to

Factory: The Birth of the Soviet Textile Industry, 1917–1920 (New York, 1990); Hiroaki Kuromiya, _Stalin's Industrial Revolution: Politics and Workers, 1928–1932_ (New York, 1988); and William Rosenberg and Lewis H. Siegelbaum, eds., _Social Dimensions of Soviet Industrialization_ (Bloomington, Ind., 1993). On the intelligentsia, see Laura Engelstein, _The Keys to Happiness: Sex and the Search for Modernity in Fin-de-Siècle Russia_ (Ithaca, N. Y., 1992). On education, see Jeffrey Brooks, _When Russia Learned to Read: Literacy and Popular Literature, 1861–1917_ (Princeton, 1986); and Ben Eklof, _Russian Peasant Schools_ (Berkeley, 1986). On the peasantry, see Teodor Shanin, _The Awkward Class. Political Sociology of Peasantry in a Developing Society: Russia, 1910–1925_ (Oxford, 1972); Shanin, _The Roots of Otherness: Russia's Turn of Century_ (New Haven, Conn., 1986); and Christine Worobec, _Peasant Russia: Family and Community in the Post-Emancipation Period_ (Princeton, 1991).

[7] The sources of quotations are the King James translation of "The Lord's Prayer," and Thomas Hobbes, _The Leviathan_, ed. C. B. Macpherson (Harmondsworth, UK, 1968), 250. For recent discussions of patriarchy, see Arthur Brittan, _Masculinity and Power_ (New York, 1989); Anna G. Jónasdóttir, _Why Women Are Oppressed_ (Philadelphia, 1994); and Mary Murray, _The Law of the Father? Patriarchy in the Transition from Feudalism to Capitalism_ (London, 1995).

their society and therefore accepted the legitimacy of many of its prescriptions, even those that strike late-twentieth-century people as discriminatory or demeaning.[8]

Scholars who have worked on the history of women in Russia in the late nineteenth and early twentieth centuries have documented the great disparities that prevailed between different ethnic and religious groups, between urban and rural dwellers, and between rich and poor. The vast majority of the women of the Russian Empire were poverty-stricken, illiterate peasants, subject to abuse from many directions – from the men in their families, from their mothers-in-law, and from the nobility in general. They married young, worked hard, bore many babies, and lost a goodly percentage of them to disease. They were religious: they cherished stories of the saints and of spirits who lurked in the rivers and forests. They made beautiful handicrafts and sang comforting lullabies. They maintained strong ties with other women. Those who survived into middle age could hope to become *khoziaiki* or *bolshukhi*, senior females with large, extended families, formidable women who sometimes enjoyed considerable authority over daughters, sons, and daughters-in-law.[9]

Scholars have also traced the ways in which change flowed back and forth between the villages and the cities in the late nineteenth century. Young peasant men at that time were leaving the countryside to work as artisans or factory hands in the rapidly growing urban areas. Moving in the other direction, toward the villages, came a host of educated people, especially doctors, teachers, and agronomists, who were intent on modernizing rural Russia. Peasant elders, male and female, eagerly bought urban manufactures – cloth, nails, cooking pots, lamps, brightly colored pictures – but they were far less enthusiastic about changing the customs of the village, particularly those that governed the position of women within the family and the community. Some parents permitted their daughters to attend primary school; a few women whose relatives could not provide work for them migrated to the cities; but until after the Russian Revolution most female peasants lived their lives much as their mothers and grandmothers had.

Meanwhile in the cities the situation of women was changing rapidly, in tune with similar developments rippling through the European world. Women of the nobility and the middling ranks of urban society were entering the paid-labor force, becoming educated, and joining various movements for reform. Scholars have probed much of this activity: they

---

[8] For a collection of articles that reflects these views, see Barbara Evans Clements, Barbara Alpern Engel, and Christine Worobec, eds., *Russia's Women: Accommodation, Resistance, Transformation* (Berkeley, 1991).

[9] For a thorough analysis of the lives of peasant women, see Worobec, *Peasant Russia*.

have examined the patterns of female migration to the city and the experiences of female factory and white-collar workers. They have analyzed the role of women in the professions and the crusades of the feminists, which began in the 1860s. Their work has uncovered the considerable similarities between the lives of urban women in Russia and elsewhere in the European world in the late nineteenth and early twentieth centuries. It has also revealed important differences that affected urban women's lives, particularly their efforts to improve their situation.[10]

In the main, these differences derived from Russia's political situation. The fact that before 1917 the recalcitrant tsarist government exercised far more control over society than did many governments in western Europe complicated all types of social activism. The government was strong, its liberal opposition was weak, and thus feminists and other female reformers were weak as well. Abroad, in Britain, the United States, and Scandinavia, the suffragists, temperance advocates, and other social activists found support within the increasingly powerful commercial and professional elites. Russia's business class was small because of the underdeveloped industrial economy. Professionals and intellectuals, known in Russia as the intelligentsia, were noted for their progressive views on women's emancipation, but they did not have the authority or independence of their counterparts in bourgeois democracies. Many of them, educators, doctors, lawyers, and engineers in particular, worked for the very government that resisted reform. The intelligentsia was also deeply split between radicals and liberals, a split that embraced as well deep divisions between female revolutionaries, among them the Bolshevichki, and the general spectrum of feminists, who were more reformist in their aspirations. In 1917, revolution swept away all the liberals, including the feminists, and empowered another group of female activists, the Bolshevichki. These women then played a central part in formulating and implementing Soviet programs of women's emancipation, with enormous consequences for the women of the USSR.

[10] On women's movement to the cities, see Barbara Alpern Engel, *Between the Fields and the City: Women, Work, and Family in Russia, 1861–1914* (New York, 1993). On the campaign to gain admission to higher education, see Christine Johanson, *Women's Struggle for Higher Education in Russia, 1855–1900* (Kingston, Ont., 1987). On factory workers, see Rose Glickman, *Russian Factory Women* (Berkeley, 1984). On teachers, see Christine Ruane, *Gender, Class, and the Professionalization of Russian City Teachers, 1860–1914* (Pittsburgh, 1994). On women in medicine, see Jeanette E. Tuve, *The First Russian Women Physicians* (Newtonville, Mass., 1984). On women of the intelligentsia, see Jane Costlow, Stephanie Sandler, and Judith Vowles, eds., *Sexuality and the Body in Russian Culture* (Stanford, 1993). On the feminists, see Linda Edmondson, *Feminism in Russia, 1900–1917* (Stanford, 1984). For studies of the city in the revolutionary era, see Daniel Brower, *The Russian City Between Tradition and Modernity, 1850–1900* (Berkeley, 1990); and Robert W. Thurston, *Liberal City, Conservative State: Moscow and Russia's Urban Crisis, 1906–1914* (New York, 1987).

The Bolshevichki and the history of the party

To see more clearly the role of the Bolshevichki in Russia's twentieth-century history should help to enlarge contemporary understanding in a variety of ways. First, it assists the study of the Communist Party. The Bolshevichki served not in the top leadership, on which attention has long been focused, but in the lower ranks of the organization. Their experience in the decades before 1917 is particularly illuminating, for it reveals differences between the rank and file and the leadership in these formative years that have been little analyzed. The theoreticians of the movement – Lenin, Trotsky, Martov, Dan, Plekhanov, Akselrod, and others – spent much of the prerevolutionary period in exile in western Europe, while the great majority of Russia's Social Democrats, male and female, lived on the run from the police inside Russia. Maintaining communications, finding the means to publish leaflets, bearing up in prison or in Siberian exile, keeping in touch with comrades, and preserving family ties were central preoccupations of the party rank and file, more important to them than the factional politics that obsessed the émigré leaders. The Bolshevichki worked diligently in this conspiratorial underground, learning skills that they later applied to winning the civil war and building the Soviet regime. And the underground experience shaped them and the party in ways that were fateful for both.

It is often helpful in the historical study of groups to scan their experience with tools garnered from other scholars' study of similar groups, modifying these as differing subjects require. To analyze data from the party's formative years, I have found it useful to employ concepts imported from sociological studies of social movements in the late twentieth century. Recent social-movement theory tends to project its generalizations from analysis of such contemporary organizations as Greenpeace and Mothers Against Drunk Driving, but many of the commonalities it has found in the behavior of the members of these activist and highly dedicated groups appear as well among the Russian Social Democrats of many decades earlier. Such parallels suggest that there were certain social dynamics at work in the formation of Russian Social Democracy that some scholars, especially those primarily engaged in assessing the ideas and personalities of the leaders, have not yet sufficiently considered. To see the Bolsheviks as people whose views and behavior were shaped by participation in the movement of which they were a part is not to deny that they were responsible political actors. It is, rather, to shift emphasis toward the idea that the Bolshevik Party developed its worldview and its collective consciousness in a process that was as much sociological and psychological as it was intellectual and political. The history of the Bolshevichki in the prerevolutionary underground provides a map of this process, revealing some of its complexity and multidimensionality.[11]

The history of the Bolshevichki during the 1917 revolution and the subsequent civil war deepens but also reinforces existing interpretations. Most Bolshevichki, like most Bolsheviks, accepted the necessity of militarizing the party in order to win the war. This pro-military response may seem curious, for one might have been tempted to assume that women would be more hostile than men to martial values. Such was not the case. There were Bolshevichki who protested the party's growing authoritarianism, and I will look at their criticism in some detail. But the evidence suggests that women, for reasons which I will consider, were no more likely than men to be critical of the party's growing heavy-handedness.

Although there was little gender difference in Bolshevik opinion over how to fight the civil war, there was a good deal of difference in the way the war affected male and female party members. Bolshevichki, always a small minority in the movement, had held a significant percentage of party offices before the revolution. Their office-holding peaked in 1917, and during the civil war it declined rapidly. I will argue that this decline resulted from the militarization of the party culture and from the accompanying transformation of the party into a governing regime. The civil war period thus figures as a central turning point in the careers of the Bolshevichki. Before 1918 they played an active role in the party leadership, especially at the local level. After 1921 they took government jobs in education, health care, journalism, editing, and economic management. This work was important, in fact crucial, to building the Soviet system. But moving away from political leadership marked a significant career shift for the women of the party, one that male Bolsheviks as a group did not make.

The history of the Bolshevichki from 1917 into the 1930s brings to central consideration the operation of gender ideas among Russia's communist revolutionaries. There are signs that this may soon become one of the most fruitful remaining lines of research into the history of the Communist Party. Gender is a relatively new category of analysis, and few

---

[11] For discussions of social-movement theory, see Enrique Laraña, Hank Johnston, and Joseph R. Gusfield, eds., *New Social Movements* (Philadelphia, 1994); and Aldon D. Morris and Carol McClurg Mueller, eds., *Frontiers in Social Movement Theory* (New Haven, Conn., 1992). The major studies of the underground are R. C. Elwood, *Russian Social Democracy in the Underground* (Assen, Netherlands, 1974); David Lane, *The Roots of Russian Communism* (Assen, Netherlands, 1969); and Allan K. Wildman, *The Making of a Workers' Revolution: Russian Social Democracy, 1891–1903* (Chicago, 1967). Of these scholars, Elwood looks most closely at the experiences of the rank and file.

scholars have applied it to the Bolsheviks; in the past, most historians did not consider gender questions important. The few who did found that the Russian Social Democrats had a good record on women's issues, particularly before the revolution: the party publicly renounced the sexism that was standard among European politicians in the early twentieth century, and allowed its female members to achieve a considerable degree of prominence and personal freedom. In addition, the reforms for women that the Bolsheviks enacted in the 1920s were decades ahead of their time. It is precisely because the Social Democrats in general and the Bolsheviks in particular were so emancipated from many of Europe's widely accepted ideas about woman's nature and her place in society that the influences of traditional values upon them have been difficult to analyze. There is evidence, however, that their proclamations on the subject were considerably more revolutionary than their practice.[12]

Studying the lives of the Bolshevichki helps to bring these gender issues into focus, for it reveals some of the differential patterns by which the revolutionaries actually created their party's collective belief system, assigned tasks, and parceled out authority. The operation of gender notions in this extremely radical movement provides a gauge to the depth of patriarchal beliefs in even these most liberated of Europeans. And it also calls unexpected attention to the durability of ancient connections between traditional gender ideas and political structures.

Women rose highest in the Bolshevik organization when it was at its most egalitarian, that is, before and during 1917. In the civil war that followed, as the Bolsheviks began building their party's dictatorship, they created and distributed power through networks of men, excluding Bolshevichki while at the same time proclaiming their commitment to women's equality. Bolshevichki who challenged this essentially hypocritical state of affairs were silenced, if not driven out. The Bolsheviks' reversion to tyrannical political habits deeply embedded in Russian culture was perforce a reversion to gender discrimination, because tyrannical politics, indeed the conventional politics of all political parties, were patriarchal to their very core everywhere in the European world.

---

[12] One of the first analyses of the masculinist political culture of Bolshevism was Elizabeth Waters, "The Female Form in Soviet Political Iconography, 1917–1936," in Clements, Engel, and Worobec, *Russia's Women*, 225–42. "Masculinism" has been defined as "the ideology that justifies and naturalizes male domination . . . the ideology of patriarchy" (Brittan, *Masculinity and Power*, 4). The Soviet program of women's emancipation has been the subject of a growing literature. For general histories, see Mary Buckley, *Women and Ideology in the Soviet Union* (Ann Arbor, Mich., 1989); Barbara Evans Clements, *Daughters of Revolution: A History of Women in the USSR* (Arlington Heights, Ill., 1994); Gail Warshofsky Lapidus, *Women in Soviet Society* (Berkeley, 1978); and Stites, *The Women's Liberation Movement in Russia*, 317–421. A more focused study is Wendy Z. Goldman's *Women, the State, and Revolution* (Cambridge, 1993).

Even these revolutionaries, I will argue, never seriously attempted to share political power between men and women. The marginalization of the Bolshevichki can be seen, therefore, as an important early part of the Communist Party's retreat from its democratic commitments.

The Bolshevichki and women's history

Study of the Bolshevichki may also help to broaden contemporary understanding of European female activists at the beginning of the twentieth century. There are few prosopographical studies of such activists, probably because adequate data are difficult to amass. Scholars have concentrated instead on individual leaders of the feminist and socialist movements, and on those movements generally. The histories they have written are instructive, for taken together they do suggest strong similarities between the Bolshevichki and their contemporaries, both inside Russia and across the continent. Such histories reveal that most politically active women came from middle-class families and were well educated, but also that a strong minority hailed from the urban working class. Virtually all such women became involved in social causes in late adolescence or early adulthood. Oftentimes the radicals began as reformers, then moved to a more thoroughgoing critique of the status quo, at which point they joined socialist movements. Reformers and radicals argued that change for women should be a central part of every movement's agenda. And women across the political spectrum contended with difficult ideological and personal demands placed on them by organizations deeply affected by patriarchal values.[13]

Thus a certain body of reliable information has been built up on leftist female activists throughout Europe in the late nineteenth and early twentieth centuries. And within the Russian context specifically, several scholars have labored to map the contours of the most visible and influential group of the period before 1890, the female populists of the

[13] For scholarship on socialist women, see Ronald Florence, *Marx's Daughters* (New York, 1975); Alfred G. Meyer, *The Feminism and Socialism of Lily Braun* (Bloomington, Ind., 1985); Marie Marmo Mullaney, *Revolutionary Women: Gender and the Socialist Revolutionary Role* (New York, 1983); and Jean Quataert and Marilyn Boxer, eds., *Socialist Women: European Socialist Feminism in the Nineteenth and Early Twentieth Centuries* (New York, 1978). Elzbieta Ettinger makes interesting comparisons between Rosa Luxemburg and Klara Zetkin in *Rosa Luxemburg: A Life* (Boston, 1986). On Luxemburg, also see J. P. Nettl, *Rosa Luxemburg*, 2 vols. (Oxford, 1966). On Goldman, see Candace Falk, *Love, Anarchy, and Emma Goldman*, rev. ed. (New Brunswick, N. J., 1990). On prominent Russian female revolutionaries, see Jay Bergman, *Vera Zasulich* (Stanford, 1983); Jane E. Good and David R. Jones, *Babushka: The Life of Russian Revolutionary Ekaterina K. Breshko-Breshkovskaia, 1844–1934* (Newtonville, Mass., 1991); and the works cited in note 14.

1870s. Barbara Alpern Engel was the first to analyze the ways in which these women constructed a revolutionary ethos by blending traditional Russian ideas with radical visions of social transformation. The revolutionary generation that came of age in the 1890s has received less attention, unfortunately. Turn-of-the-century Russia had by far the largest number of female revolutionaries of any country, and few investigators today would deny that detailed examination of any single group of them would make a useful contribution to women's studies in general. One may hope that this will be found even more true of the present work, a history of those revolutionary women who managed to come to power.[14]

The Bolshevichki in their own right

This study grew out of a far less ambitious endeavor. More than a decade ago, having completed a biography of Alexandra Kollontai, I decided to write a book that would consist of short portraits of communist women whose work and lives were historically significant and interesting, but little known. I chose as subjects two of the most important political leaders among the Bolshevichki – Elena Stasova, the secretary of the Central Committee from March 1919 to March 1920, and Evgeniia Bosh, a prominent member of the Ukrainian party organization in 1917 and 1918 – and the two women who, along with Kollontai, were the party's leading proponents of Marxist feminism – Inessa Armand and Konkordiia Samoilova.

As I researched the lives of Armand, Bosh, Samoilova, and Stasova, I came increasingly to realize the need for a full-scale study of the group of which they were a part, that is, the Bolshevichki. The Bolshevichki were, by their own and the party's definitions, female communists who joined the party before 1921. For purposes of analysis they can be divided into two generations, people who came into the movement before 1917 and those who became members during the period 1917–21, the period dominated by the civil war. This is a distinction that the Bolsheviks

---

[14] See Barbara Alpern Engel's *Mothers and Daughters: Women of the Intelligentsia in Nineteenth-Century Russia* (Cambridge, 1983); Barbara Alpern Engel and Clifford Rosenthal, eds., *Five Sisters: Women Against the Tsar* (New York, 1975). See also Vera Broido, *Apostles into Terrorists* (New York, 1977). On female Socialist Revolutionaries, see Margaret Maxwell, *Narodniki Women: Russian Women Who Sacrificed Themselves for the Dream of Freedom* (New York, 1990); Maureen Perrie, "The Social Composition and Structure of the Socialist-Revolutionary Party Before 1917," *Soviet Studies* 24 (October 1972): 223–50; and Isaac Steinberg, *Spiridonova, Revolutionary Terrorist*, trans. and ed. Gwenda David and Eric Mosbacher, intro. Henry W. Nevinson, originally published 1935 (Freeport, N. Y., 1971). There is a more general discussion in Robert H. McNeal, "Women in the Russian Radical Movement," *Journal of Social History* 2 (Winter 1971–72): 143–63, as well as in Stites, *The Women's Liberation Movement in Russia*, 115–54, 233–77.

themselves made, and it remains a meaningful one, for the people who joined the party before the revolution differed from the civil war generation in their formative experiences and presumably in their motives for becoming revolutionaries.

Uncovering the history of these women as a group appeared at first to be a daunting undertaking because there was so little written about them in the scholarship on the Communist Party. Fortunately, it turned out that the primary sources of party history – newspapers, periodicals, published collections of documents, and memoirs – contain a wealth of relevant information. Many Bolshevichki also wrote short autobiographies when they were living in honored retirement in the 1950s and 1960s. Their own memoirs, the documents of party history, and archival holdings that became available in the early 1990s proved to contain enough information to permit me to study the Bolshevichki collectively.

Indeed, they made it possible to construct a data base containing records on 545 Bolshevichki, 318 of whom joined the party before 1917, and 227 of whom joined during the civil war years. These two samples are sufficiently large to yield trustworthy generalizations about the Bolshevichki's personal lives and careers, particularly those of the women of the prerevolutionary generation. That entire group probably numbered no more than 2,500 people, so 318 may well be more than 10 percent of them. The sample of civil war joiners is a much smaller percentage of the whole, for there were close to 30,000 of this younger generation. Nevertheless, 227 is not an inconsiderable number of individuals, particularly since the generalizations derived from this sample can be tested against party census data amassed in the early 1920s.

Unfortunately, the information available on each individual in the data base is not as complete as one might wish. Much is known about the social origins and private lives of some Bolshevichki, but far less about their party careers after 1921. The careers of others can be precisely documented, but their prerevolutionary work is only vaguely outlined and the sources say nothing at all about their childhoods or families. As a result, the amount of information within the data base varies according to the item under consideration (e.g., marriage, education, party office-holding). This variability made it impossible to establish the sorts of statistical correlations, such as those produced by multiple regression analysis, that depend on the absolute comparability of all the items in a sample.

Just as problematical are the ways in which the historical record regarding the Bolshevichki has been affected by the Communist Party's controls over the writing of its history. Editors who published the Bolshevichki's memoirs and party historians who wrote biographies of them suppressed discussion of politically sensitive topics, such as the doubts Bolshevichki might have had about the wisdom of certain policies, repression they may have suffered at the hands of their own party, or repression they may have inflicted on others. The editors also omitted important information about these women's personal lives – their marriages, childbearing, relations with their relatives – because they judged such private matters to be historically insignificant. The Bolshevichki, as loyal party members, were fully acquainted with these standards, of course, and so they wrote to comply with them, practicing self-censorship before the editors even began to edit.

And yet the historical record they left behind does permit us to understand the Bolshevichki, even if it does not always answer all our questions satisfactorily. Newspapers published in the prerevolutionary years; obituaries, diaries, and personal letters written during the revolution and the civil war; periodicals and party documents from the Soviet period; autobiographical sketches composed in the 1920s, 1950s, 1960s, and 1970s – all these reveal a great many of the facts of these women's lives. They speak as well of the shared understandings and beliefs that prevailed among the Bolshevichki, and enable us therefore to get inside their minds, despite all the efforts to keep certain doors closed against our prying.

And one can learn even more about the Bolshevichki by comparing them to their male comrades. To this end, I created a data base on Bolshevik men from the files of *The Soviet Data Bank*, compiled by historians William Chase and J. Arch Getty (1986). This rich resource contains information on 28,000 communists, most of them men. There is very little in it about Bolshevichki, but computer-based analysis enabled me to separate the men from the women in Chase and Getty's files and thereby to construct a data base on male Bolsheviks. That done, I could analyze the demographic and career patterns of the men, and then compare them to my findings on women. One of the many interesting things that I discovered was that considerably more female than male Bolsheviks came from the middle and upper ranks of Russian society and were well educated. In turn, these differences between women and men help to expand and refine the picture of why young people became revolutionaries in Russia, and they also help to explain certain characteristics of the Bolshevichki's work before 1917. Comparing male to female Bolsheviks also makes it possible to assess the way in which gender affected the assignment of tasks and offices within the Communist Party from its early days through the revolution and into the Soviet period. (For a fuller discussion of the use of the two data bases, see the appendix, "Notes on the data bases," pp. 316–17 in this book.)

Equipped with the statistical information I had amassed, I then returned to the research with which this project began, that is, the biographies of Inessa Armand, Evgeniia Bosh, Konkordiia Samoilova, and Elena Stasova. Study of the two founding generations of communist women had now established to my satisfaction that Armand, Bosh, Samoilova, and Stasova were fairly representative of all the Bolshevichki in their social origins, their reasons for becoming revolutionaries, and their prerevolutionary and Soviet careers. I decided, therefore, to write a book that would set detailed examination of these four individual lives within a history of female Bolsheviks as a group. Paying particular attention to the experiences of a handful of women would humanize and personalize the more general discussion, as well as providing case studies to illuminate broader findings.

To make the selected group of prominent Bolshevichki yet more representative, I decided to add detailed studies of several other individuals to it. First came Rozaliia Zemliachka, the only woman to sit on the Council of People's Commissars under Stalin and an enthusiastic participant in the atrocities committed by the party during the civil war and then again in the 1930s. Zemliachka was an important political figure, if an unsavory one, and I decided that her brutality did not disqualify her from membership in my small pantheon. I also chose to bring in two women from the working class, Alexandra Artiukhina and Klavdiia Nikolaeva, both of them heads of the party women's department (the Zhenotdel) in the 1920s. Artiukhina and Nikolaeva were more typical of the party rank and file in their careers than were leaders such as Stasova and Armand. I considered it important also to have proletarian Bolshevichki among those given special attention, for working-class women constituted more than a third of the two founding generations of female communists.

The book that has emerged from all this pleasant research and tedious mathematical analysis chronicles the history of the first two generations of women in the Soviet Communist Party. It examines their lives from childhood to old age and assesses their motives, their experiences, and their contributions to their movement and their nation. My intention has been not only to fit the Bolshevichki into their times but also explain, whenever possible, the choices that they made. Central is that question so insistently posed by historians of the Communist Party: why did they become dictators? In the case of the Bolshevichki, one might be tempted to argue that in fact they did not, since most of them were excluded from power once the party of revolutionaries became a ruling regime. But the Bolshevichki were members of that regime, if only as lower-ranking functionaries – as red lieutenants, so to speak. And they were loyal lieutenants at that. They might have been expected to protest more than their male comrades against the rise of dictatorship. After all, they had far less to gain from it. Not only did it violate the democratic principles they had once professed, it violated as well their commitment to women's equality and marginalized them personally. And yet they appear to have accepted it. The fact that they did so reveals something of their character, their identity as a group.

It is also important to attempt to answer another question: why did they reject feminism? As the twentieth century ends, several core propositions of feminism have gained widespread acceptance in the European world – that patriarchy is a fundamental social evil, that women's liberation from it should be a prime imperative, and that women should seek this liberation through independent, women-led organizations. Each of these propositions the Bolshevichki contested. Indeed, they did more than simply criticize feminism; they condemned it as a bourgeois ideology that overrated the historical significance of gender inequality and ignored the obvious (to them) fact that all forms of social injustice sprang from the institution of private property. The Bolshevichki believed that women should not pursue their goals independently, but rather should join with men to promote a revolutionary upheaval that would lead to the only truly just society, that is, a socialist one. The Bolshevichki's insistence on participating in a broad movement and their refusal to grant priority to women's situation even when they themselves suffered from gender discrimination may strike today's observers as self-defeating, even masochistic. The participation of tens of thousands of women in an autocratic regime also troubles those who would like to believe that women are everywhere victims and never oppressors.

I have found it helpful in probing the consciousness of the Bolshevichki to import the concept of collective identity that has been developed in social-movement theory. The collective identity of a social movement consists of shared understandings about the larger society in which the group operates, and common definitions of the goals, tactics, and membership of the group. An aggregation of principles, attitudes, and interpretations of experiences, the collective identity changes over time and may vary slightly from subgroup to subgroup within the larger movement. Members create their own individual sense of self, their personal identities, by blending their beliefs about themselves with ideas taken from the collective identity. This process is an important part of the group's interaction, for that which is collective shapes that which is personal, and that which is personal, including the distinctive personalities of the leaders, shapes the collective.[15]

---

[15] For fuller discussions of the concept of collective identity, see Laraña, Johnston, and Gusfield, "Identities," in their *New Social Movements*, 12–18; and Bert Klandermans, "The Social Construction of Protest and Multiorganizational Fields," in Morris and Mueller, *Frontiers in Social Movement Theory*, 81.

The Bolshevichki adhered to the collective identity of the Russian Social-Democratic Party and its offshoot, the Bolshevik faction. They also took certain ideas from the general fund and adapted them to their situation as women in a predominantly male organization – that is, they constructed a subgroup identity. Many of the core ideas of this identity, ideas central to understanding the Bolshevichki, lie encapsulated in a word they often used, *tverdaia*, an adjective that literally means "hard," "firm," and "steadfast." A *tverdaia* revolutionary woman was tough, durable, and, if need be, merciless. She was also understood to be diligent, rational, and unsentimental. She was an equal member of an egalitarian movement; she had earned admission to the movement by being willing to sacrifice herself completely to its goals. Her primary loyalties were not to herself, her family, or other women. They were to her comrades, to the revolutionary movement, and to the cause of social transformation.

If a woman subscribed to the Bolsheviks' collective identity, she was welcomed into the party's great crusade. The liberation that young women felt on becoming Bolsheviks should not be underestimated; it was extraordinary in a society as traditional as Russia's, and in fact few other political organizations of the time anywhere were so open to female participation. But there was a price to be paid. Bolshevichki had to prove themselves worthy of inclusion by adapting to an ethos that was strongly masculinist. They were to be "hard," like men. They were to suppress their identifications with other women and not to think critically about the gender discrimination that occurred within the party. Feminist Bolshevichki such as Alexandra Kollontai and Inessa Armand found ways to pay attention to women's inferior situation, but even they did so with care, trying not to offend and endeavoring not to run afoul of the obligations of hardness. Women who were not so feminist in outlook simply shut their eyes to slights that might have caused them to call into question the sincerity of their male comrades' devotion to women's equality. As the party evolved from an egalitarian underground movement into a governing power, the pressures for conformity only increased. By the 1930s, being a communist meant suppressing one's own criticism of the party completely.

The essential dilemma of the Bolshevichki, therefore, was one often debated by feminists – how to oppose gender discrimination from a position of weakness within a patriarchal society. This dilemma has beset all the people working for women's betterment in the last 200 years. If women form independent movements, they can set their own priorities and develop their own tactics; but they then run the risk of being marginalized by power structures still dominated by men, as were the feminists in Britain and North America after they gained the vote. On the other hand, if women join predominantly male political organizations, they may gain power and influence, but they risk being coopted and having gender liberation subordinated to causes deemed more important by male leaders, as female socialists have discovered all over the world in the twentieth century. The whole dilemma is especially agonizing for women who want to work for other sorts of social reform as well as for women's equality, and who therefore must make Hobson's choices as to where to put their loyalties and with whom to affiliate.[16] The Bolshevichki did not think that they would ever have to deal with such difficulties, because they believed that revolutionary upheaval would destroy the sources of injustice and thereby make politics unnecessary. When instead their male comrades built a powerful new autocracy, the Bolshevichki had to choose between defending their earliest visions or adapting to the new realities.

As did most of their male comrades, they adapted. As did most of their male comrades, they complied, and not simply because they were coerced. The collective identity the Bolshevichki had built during decades of combat with the larger society bound them tightly to one another and to a core set of beliefs about the revolutionary process. As a result, women were just as likely as men to give their primary loyalty to their comrades and the party, and to accept the organization's rationale for building its power. They believed that the revolution was an ongoing, almost natural, process, complicated in Russia by the nation's backwardness. In time, the development of the economy and the social system, kept on course by a resolute, unified party, would bring their utopian Marxism to reality. Few of the Bolshevichki appear to have understood the connection between the party's autocracy (which many of them supported) and their own relegation to the sidelines of political life (which some of them protested). Most chose ultimately to remain faithful to allegiances and hopes forged in their youth.

This study will trace both the cultural and ideological differences that separated the Bolshevichki from the feminists of Europe, and the common experiences as political activists that rendered all of them species of the same genus – that is, women who wanted to build a world freed of invidious ideas about women. The study will also explore the Bolshevichki's participation in the great events of their nation's history, particularly the development of the Communist Party. It will analyze the

---

[16] Feminists throughout the twentieth century have struggled with this dilemma. For analysis of the problem and various solutions, see Vicky Randall, *Women and Politics: An International Perspective*, 2nd ed. (Chicago, 1987); Sheila Rowbotham, *The Past Is Before Us: Feminism in Action Since the 1960s* (London, 1989); and Louise A. Tilly and Patricia Gurin, eds., *Women, Politics, and Change* (New York, 1990).

connections between gender and power in the Soviet era. And it will attempt to tell the life stories of some of the most interesting, if also tragic, figures of the twentieth century.

In transliterating the Cyrillic alphabet into the English, I have used a modified Library of Congress system. Diacritical marks have been eliminated in the text, although not in the notes or the bibliography. Names widely known abroad under alternative spellings (Trotsky) or in Anglicized form (Nicholas II) have been rendered in their most familiar usage.

Until February 1918 Russia was on the Julian calendar rather than the Gregorian that prevailed throughout the rest of Europe. In the nineteenth century this meant that Russian dates were twelve days earlier (in the twentieth century, thirteen) than those in London and Paris. I have employed the Russian (Old Style) dates in referring to events that took place before February 1918, when the Bolsheviks adopted the Gregorian calendar.

I have also used Russian and Soviet geographical-administrative terms in the text and in tables. The empire was subdivided into (from largest to smallest) gubernii (singular, guberniia), uezdy (sing., uezd), and volosti (sing., volost). The Soviets changed guberniia to oblast and created republics and various other administrative subdivisions.

1   Becoming a revolutionary

Elena Stasova joined the Russian Social-Democratic Labor Party in 1898, after several members of the organization in St. Petersburg asked her to take on the work of an arrested comrade. Stasova agreed; it was a choice toward which she had been drifting for several years. And yet it was an unlikely one, for this tall, thin, blond 25-year-old was the daughter of one of the most illustrious families in Russia's capital. As she hurried down the city streets in her well-tailored, somewhat severe dresses, carrying a heavy leather briefcase, she looked like a schoolteacher or a college student, not a dangerous revolutionary.

Stasova had been born in St. Petersburg in 1873, the fifth of six children. Her grandfather, Vasilii Stasov, had served as court architect under the tsars Alexander I and Nicholas I. Her mother, Poliksena (née Kuznetsova) and her paternal aunt, Nadezhda Stasova, were noted feminists who raised money for charities and crusaded for expanding women's access to education. Her father, Dmitrii, was a founding member of the St. Petersburg Council of Barristers, and her uncle, Vladimir, was an influential art and music critic.

Elena grew up in comfort, surrounded by loving, cultivated relatives. She received her early education from tutors and from her parents, particularly her father, Dmitrii, whom she adored. Even in her old age Stasova still recalled trying hard to please him. "He prepared me for gymnasium [high school] in geography and I remember how diligently I prepared my lessons, since obviously it was impossible to go to the lesson [that I took from] him not knowing the assignment perfectly."[1] At sixteen she finished gymnasium and then studied medicine and history at the Bestuzhevskii courses, a college-level program for women, who were not permitted to attend Russia's universities.

Stasova grew into a young person who was determined to find socially useful work to do. She admired her mother and her aunt, but unlike them she did not want to be a lady philanthropist. Rather, she aspired to join

[1] RTsKhIDNI, f. 356, op. 1, d. 6, l. 8.

22

the tens of thousands of women all over the European world at the end of the nineteenth century who were eschewing traditional domesticity for full-time work in the professions newly opened to them – social work, medicine, and teaching. Stasova chose teaching, and in the early 1890s, at her aunt Nadezhda's suggestion, she became an instructor in the Sunday schools that provided elementary education to the factory workers of St. Petersburg. Here she came into sustained contact with the workers from the city's slums for the first time in her life and also met other teachers, many of whom were far more radical than she. Stasova was drawn particularly to the Marxists. By 1895 she was smuggling messages to jailed revolutionaries; when textile workers held huge strikes the next summer, she hid in her bedroom some of the pamphlets printed by the revolutionaries.

Yet Stasova also continued to live the life of an aristocratic young lady, spending her summers on the family's estate in Novgorod guberniia and traveling with her mother to spas in Germany. She became increasingly discontented with the triviality of her accomplishments, however, so when she was asked to take over the finances of the Social Democrats' operations in St. Petersburg in 1898, she agreed. Years later she wrote in her memoirs: "From this moment I considered myself a member of the party, and all my previous work was only doing good deeds.'"[2]

Somewhat different in her early experience was Rozaliia Zalkind – later known by her revolutionary alias, Zemliachka. Zemliachka came to the Social Democrats at about the same time as Stasova, but from a very different region of the Russian Empire. Zemliachka was born in Mogilev guberniia in Belorus in 1876, the daughter of a large, somewhat fragmented family of wealthy Jewish merchants. "Father had a big business in Kiev," she later remembered, "and lived there with his older brothers, students at Kiev University. Mother lived with us and taught us very democratic ways of thinking and living."[3] Rozaliia was the youngest child in this politically aware family, and she learned about revolutionaries early. She remembered hearing, as a five-year-old, her family discussing the assassination of Tsar Alexander II (1881). The Zalkinds sympathized with the revolutionaries who had done the deed and perhaps even had

[2] E. D. Stasova, *Vospominaniia* (Moscow, 1969), 28–29. On Stasova's early life, see ibid., 13–29. See also E. D. Stasova, ed., *Iz istorii nelegal'nykh bibliotek revoliutsionnykh organizatsii v tsarskoi Rossii* (Moscow, 1956), 17; V. V. Stasov, *Pis'ma k rodnym*, ed. E. D. Stasova, 3 vols. (Moscow, 1953–62), vol. I, 20, 23, 475 n. 2; vol. II, 450–52; vol. III, part 1, 177–79; G. A. Krovitskii, *Put' starogo bol'shevika. K shestidesiatiletiiu E. D. Stasovoi* (Moscow, 1933), 9; S. M. Levidova and E. G. Salita, *Elena Dmitrievna Stasova. Biograficheskii ocherk* (Leningrad, 1969), 8–48; and Pavel Podliashuk, *Bogatyrskaia simfoniia. Dokumental'naia povest' o E. D. Stasovoi* (Moscow, 1977), 4–12.

[3] RTsKhIDNI, f. 17, op. 4, d. 180, l. 24.

some connections with them. Later that year the police searched their house, looking for illegal pamphlets.

When she was six, Zemliachka moved to Kiev to live with her father and attend school. She proved to be an able student, first in elementary classes, then in gymnasium. When she was fourteen, one of her brothers began letting her read revolutionary literature. By now she considered herself to be a populist, that is, a socialist who argued that Russia was ripe for a peasant uprising that would overthrow the nobility and install a new regime based on the self-government of the village. When she was fifteen, in 1891, Rozaliia finished school; within a year she was arrested for the first time.

Zemliachka did not spend years deciding to become a revolutionary, as Stasova had, perhaps because her brothers and sisters led her into the movement at so young an age. But she did begin to develop serious doubts in her late teens about the populism her siblings had bequeathed to her. Living in Kiev, she came into contact almost daily with that city's artisans and factory workers, and these people, she realized, were far more likely to rise up against the government than were the more traditionally minded peasants. Zemliachka began to read Marxism, as many of her friends were doing, and by 1896 she, like Stasova, had become convinced that revolution in Russia would begin in the industrializing cities. Later that year this slim, dark-haired, gray-eyed young woman made her debut as a Marxist. She spoke to a clandestine meeting on "the workers' movement in western Europe." Shortly thereafter she was arrested and sent to prison, where she studied Marxism still more diligently. Zemliachka's career as a Social Democrat had begun.[4]

Konkordiia Gromova (later known by her married name, Samoilova) decided to become a revolutionary three years later, in 1901, while recovering at her parents' house in Irkutsk in Siberia from the effects of several months in prison. Samoilova was then twenty-five years old, a young woman of medium height, with a broad face graced by heavily lidded blue eyes and a kind, if somewhat severe, expression. She had been arrested in February 1901 at an illegal meeting.

Samoilova was a *kursistka*, a female college student. In the middle years of the 1890s she and her sister Kaleriia had worked long and hard to persuade their parents, particularly their mother, to finance their studying in the Bestuzhevskii courses in St. Petersburg, which Stasova had attended during the same decade. The family lived thousands of miles from the capital, in Irkutsk, where the girls' father was a priest who

---

[4] Ibid., ll. 24–25; *Slavnye bol'shevichki* (Moscow, 1958), 135.

ministered to the gold miners and merchants of Russia's frontier. Daughters of the clergy did not usually leave home to study in the capital, but Konkordiia and Kaleriia managed to persuade their parents to let them go, and in the summer of 1896 they made their way across Russia to St. Petersburg.

Samoilova, like Stasova and Zemliachka, was an able student (she had graduated with a gold medal from gymnasium in Irkutsk), so she had no difficulty with the courses given by the history and law faculty of the Bestuzhevskii program. She and Stasova do not seem to have known one another in the 1890s, probably because Stasova left the courses before Samoilova entered them. But Samoilova shared Stasova's interest in social issues. In Irkutsk she had learned about revolutionary thought from people exiled to Siberia for political offenses. In St. Petersburg she began reading about socialism, absorbing the newly popular works of Karl Marx, Friedrich Engels, and the Russian Marxist Grigorii Plekhanov, and she became friends with fellow *kursistki* who shared her discontent over the ills of Russia. Samoilova took part in her first demonstration in February 1897, when university students organized a protest over the death in prison of a Bestuzhevskii student named Mariia Vetrova. The march ended in a bloody riot in which a woman was trampled to death and hundreds of people were arrested.

Perhaps this vivid example of the power of the tsarist authorities intimidated Samoilova. Perhaps she was still dedicated to completing her studies. Whatever her motives, the young Siberian kept her distance from demonstrations for the next four years, as did many other students. Then, in 1901, unrest mounted when an economic depression increased the already considerable hardships of the urban poor. The police responded with arrests and threatened to conscript young men accused of political crimes. Samoilova once again became involved, this time to protest the imprisonment of university students in Kiev, but on this occasion she did not manage to escape the police. She was arrested for taking part in a demonstration.

After three months in prison, Samoilova was released because the police could not develop sufficient evidence to prosecute her. The authorities did recommend her expulsion from the Bestuzhevskii courses, however, on the grounds that she was "politically undesirable." The course directors concurred, and Samoilova went home to Irkutsk. There she stayed until early 1902, waiting for a passport that would permit her to travel abroad. It arrived in January, and in February she left Russia, bound for Paris, where she was determined to study Marxism in order to become a Social Democrat. It seems probable that the expulsion from the Bestuzhevskii courses and the stay in jail had decisively affected

Samoilova's outlook, persuading her to throw in her lot with the revolutionaries.[5]

Evgeniia Maish (she too would be known by her married name, Bosh) was only a few years younger than Stasova, Zemliachka, and Samoilova (she was born in 1879), but she did not join the Social-Democratic Party until 1906. Bosh helped revolutionaries for years, hiding illegal literature and attending illegal meetings, but she delayed throwing herself fully into the underground because she was married, with two young daughters and a loving husband. In 1906, when she finally did decide to become a Social Democrat, she left her husband, but took her children with her.

Bosh had had a far more tormented childhood than Stasova, Samoilova, or Zemliachka. Her father, Gottlieb Maish, was a mechanic from Luxembourg who had migrated to southern Ukraine with his brother, Theodore. There the two men had worked to maintain imported threshing machines and combines, and after some years each had managed to save enough money to buy an estate in Kherson guberniia, on which he settled to become a gentleman farmer. By then, Gottlieb had married a Moldavian woman, Mariia Krusser, with whom he soon had a large family. Evgeniia was one of the youngest of their children.

Gottlieb died while Evgeniia was still very young, and her mother then married her brother-in-law, Theodore. Relations between Evgeniia and her mother and uncle-turned-stepfather soon soured, and years of unhappiness ensued. Bosh and her mother fought so continuously that once the girl ran away, and once her brother Aleksei had to talk her out of committing suicide. Briefly she lived with another uncle in the provincial city of Voznesensk, but she fought with him as well and soon developed health problems (diagnosed as heart disease) that brought her back to her mother's house. The only warmth in Evgeniia's childhood came from the love of her older brother and sister, Aleksei and Nadezhda. They were Tolstoians, disciples of the writer Leo Tolstoy, who believed in living the simple life close to the peasantry. Aleksei worked a tiny farm, and Nadezhda taught in a village school.

Evgeniia Maish grew into a small, pretty young woman with dark hair and eyes. When she was seventeen, her parents exercised their prerogative according to Ukrainian custom and chose as a husband for her a

---

[5] For Samoilova's early life, see B. Breslav, *Konkordiia Nikolaevna Samoilova* (Moscow and Leningrad, 1926), 3–5; L. Katasheva, *Natasha: A Bolshevik Woman Organiser* (London, 193?), 5–6; G. Mishkevich, *Konkordiia Nikolaevna Samoilova* (Leningrad, 1947), 3–7; N. Rostov, "Samoubiistvo M. F. Vetrovoi i studencheskie besporiadki 1897 g.," *Katorga i ssylka*, no. 23 (1926): 50–66; *Slavnye bol'shevichki*, 245–49; *Leningradki. Vospominaniia, ocherki, dokumenty* ([Leningrad], 1968), 120–26; and *Zhenshchiny russkoi revoliutsii* (Moscow, 1968), 399–401.

nobleman from their neighborhood who was much older than she. The willful daughter rebelled, accepting instead the proposal of one of her brother's friends, Petr Bosh. His father owned a modest business that manufactured carriages and sledges in Voznesensk. Evgeniia married him over her parents' protests and moved back into the city.

The young wife soon had two daughters and spent her days on housework and children. She also dabbled in philanthropy, reading Russian literature and political pamphlets aloud to the workmen in her husband's shop. By 1900 Bosh had gotten to know several Social Democrats in the city and was helping to distribute their periodicals and broadsides. She was also contributing money to their cause. Beyond this, however, Bosh would not go, because she feared jeopardizing the hard-won happiness of her family life.

In 1904 her younger half-sister, Elena Rozmirovich, after announcing that she had joined the Social Democrats, left Voznesensk for Kiev, where she planned to devote herself to revolutionary agitation. Evgeniia remained where she was, reading Marxism, passing around illegal pamphlets, teaching peasants in the countryside during the summers, and rearing her daughters. In 1906 the police searched the Bosh home, looking for banned books. They found nothing, but after they left, she confessed to her husband the full extent of her contacts with the radicals. He was understanding and supportive.

Bosh grew increasingly dissatisfied with her domesticity, however. Elena, seven years her junior, had left her husband to take up the life of a revolutionary, while Evgeniia sat at home, fearful, unwilling to make the sacrifices of the truly committed. After the police raid in 1906, Bosh took her daughter Olga to a sanitarium in the Caucasus for medical treatment, and there she thought through her situation carefully. After a few weeks she returned to Voznesensk, waited until her husband was away on business, then wrote him a letter saying not to look for her, packed up both girls, and moved to Kiev. Soon she was accompanying Elena on local missions to hand out leaflets among railroad workers.[6]

Klavdiia Nikolaeva and Alexandra Sorokina came to revolutionary politics later still, in 1909 and 1910. (Sorokina would be known by her married name, Artiukhina.) Stasova, Zemliachka, Samoilova, and Bosh were born in the 1870s; Nikolaeva and Artiukhina were children of later decades – Artiukhina was born in 1889, Nikolaeva in 1893. Both of the younger women were Russians and members of the working class, drawn

---

[6] The foregoing summary of Bosh's early life is based on Evgenii Mar, *Nezakonechnoe pis'mo* (Moscow, 1970), 3–23; E. Preobrazhenskii, "Evgeniia Bogdanovna Bosh," *Proletarskaia revoliutsiia*, no. 2 (1925): 5–7; and T. F. Avramenko and M. N. Simoian, "Elena Fedorovna Rozmirovich," *Voprosy istorii KPSS*, no. 3 (1966): 99.

into party work through union activities. They also came from families headed by women.

Nikolaeva grew up without her father, for he had deserted his children when she was very young. Her mother earned a meager living in the St. Petersburg slums and, Nikolaeva, like many poor girls, contributed to the family's income from an early age. When she was eight, she became a babysitter to neighborhood children. An unusually determined and intelligent child, she taught herself how to read and attended an elementary school, where she learned a little geography and mathematics. In her early teens she secured a job at a printing company. This was quite an accomplishment, for printing was a skilled, well-paid trade that employed very few women. In 1908, at the age of fifteen, Nikolaeva became involved in the printers' union, for which activity she was very quickly arrested. In jail she took lessons in Marxism from her fellow inmates and read widely in the prison library. When she was released after a few months, she found work at another press.

In 1908 Nikolaeva also joined the Society for Mutual Aid to Women Workers, headed by Alexandra Kollontai. Kollontai, a general's daughter from St. Petersburg and also a childhood friend of Stasova, would later become one of the most famous of the Bolshevichki. In the first decade of the twentieth century, Kollontai was the only outspoken advocate for women's rights among Russian Social Democrats. In 1907 she had set up the Society for Mutual Aid to provide financial assistance and free education to poor women. She also made sure it dispensed surreptitious lessons in revolutionary Marxism. When Kollontai spotted Nikolaeva's unusual intelligence and fortitude, she took the girl under her wing, tutored her, and encouraged her to remain a union activist. She also convinced Nikolaeva that she would be welcome in the party. In 1909 the dark-haired young woman with the long, thin face became a Social Democrat.[7]

Alexandra Artiukhina took a similar path to the underground. She too came from a family of workers, in this case one living in the industrial town of Vyshnyi Volochek in Tver guberniia, north of Moscow. Her mother, like Nikolaeva's, headed her family; Artiukhina did not say in her memoirs why her father was absent during her childhood. In 1903, when Alexandra was fourteen, her mother was fired for taking part in a strike. Alexandra kept the family going by doing putting-out labor, finishing men's shirts for 4 kopeks each, while her mother looked for other jobs. Because the elder Sorokina had been blacklisted, however, no mill owner in Vyshnyi Volochek would hire her. The family migrated to St. Petersburg, where

---

[7] On Nikolaeva, see *Zhenshchiny russkoi revoliutsii*, 290–95; and K. Nikolaeva, "Slovo k molodym rabotnitsam," in *Zhenshchiny v revoliutsii* (Moscow, 1959), 118–19.

Alexandra's uncle, also a union member and a Socialist Revolutionary, was working. In Russia's capital both the mother and the daughter did find work. Soon the mother rejoined the textile workers' union, and in 1908 she inducted Alexandra into it as well.

Like Nikolaeva, Alexandra Artiukhina was drawn to the Social Democrats she met through her co-workers. For their part, male union leaders noticed that the intelligent young brown-haired woman with the high forehead, long nose, and close-set eyes had speaking ability. They encouraged her to run for union office. By 1910 Artiukhina was a member of the board of the textile workers' union and the union's representative on the Central Trade Union Bureau of the city of St. Petersburg. That same year, she also decided to join the Social-Democratic Party.[8]

Origins of the Bolshevichki

The early lives of these six Bolshevichki – Stasova, Zemliachka, Samoilova, Bosh, Nikolaeva, and Artiukhina – can be documented in detail because the women later became party leaders. In the particulars of their childhoods they seem very different from one another. Stasova grew up among the intelligentsia in St. Petersburg. Zemliachka lived in comfort in a liberal Jewish family in Belorus and Ukraine. Bosh too lived in Ukraine, but she suffered from the financial and social insecurity of newcomers into the provincial gentry. Samoilova was a priest's daughter from the rough-and-tumble frontier town of Irkutsk. Nikolaeva and Artiukhina struggled with the poverty of industrial workers in the Russian heartland. Stasova, Samoilova, and Zemliachka had happy, secure childhoods; Bosh was miserable. Nikolaeva and Artiukhina fended for themselves from an early age. Yet all became Bolsheviks. In their differences from one another these six are typical, for in truth, women from very different backgrounds became revolutionary Marxists in Russia during the late nineteenth and early twentieth centuries.

And yet there were common characteristics of their families and of the Russian circumstances that steered individuals as remote from one another as Stasova the noblewoman and Artiukhina the textile worker toward making the same dangerous choice, that is, to become a revolutionary. Thousands of young women made that choice in the period 1890–1910, with the consequence that Russia ended up with more female radicals than any other nation in Europe. Rough estimates put the

---

[8] On Artiukhina, see A. V. Artiukhina, "Polveka," in *Oktiabriem rozhdennye* (Moscow, 1967), 12–15; and *Bez nikh my ne pobedili by. Vospominaniia zhenshchin-uchastnits Oktiabr'skoi revoliutsii, grazhdanskoi voiny, i sotsialisticheskogo stroitel'stva* (Moscow, 1975), 236.

combined size of the two major revolutionary organizations, the Social-Democratic Party (SDs) and the Socialist Revolutionary Party (SRs), at 135,000 people in the peak membership year of 1907. If women were 10 percent of the members of both, as contemporaries believed, then there were around 8,000 female SRs in 1907 and 10,000 female Social Democrats. Perhaps as many as 2,000 of the SDs were Bolshevichki, that is, followers of Lenin and his theories of the way revolution should be made in Russia. The remaining 8,000 were Mensheviks, who advocated a more loosely organized party.[9]

In those demographic characteristics most easily quantified, the Bolshevichki were very like all the rest of these women. The majority of Russia's female revolutionaries (60 percent or more) were from the nobility and the middling ranks of society. Roughly one-third had working-class backgrounds; fewer than 10 percent were peasants. Fifty percent or more were ethnically Russian, with a strong minority of Jewish women (Jews were considered an ethnic group by the tsarist government) and a smattering of the other nationalities of the empire. There were fewer Jews among the Bolshevichki (probably no more than 15 percent of the total) than among the female Mensheviks (perhaps as many as 40 percent) or SRs (24 percent), but this is the most discernible difference between the three groups. All these young women joined the revolutionary movement in their late teens or early twenties, most commonly in years of great political ferment, such as 1905. The majority of the working-class recruits came into the party after 1905 and hence were somewhat younger as a group than those from more privileged backgrounds, who had joined earlier. The great majority of these women, even those from lower-class backgrounds, were well educated for their times.[10]

The Bolshevichki also had much in common with the men who were becoming Social Democrats and would soon be Bolsheviks. Most of the

---

[9] These estimates derive from the calculations of Beate Fieseler, "The Making of Russian Female Social Democrats, 1890–1917," *International Review of Social History* 34 (1989): 195–96; David Lane, *The Roots of Russian Communism* (Assen, Netherlands, 1969), 13; Maureen Perrie, "The Social Composition and Structure of the Socialist-Revolutionary Party Before 1917," *Soviet Studies* 24 (October 1972): 225, 235; and E. Smitten, "Zhenshchiny v RKP," *Kommunistka*, no. 4 (1924): 8–9.

[10] These comparisons are based on Fieseler, "The Making of Russian Female Social Democrats," and Perrie, "The Social Composition and Structure of the Socialist-Revolutionary Party Before 1917." I have confirmed their findings, drawn from biographical dictionaries of revolutionaries compiled in the late 1920s and early 1930s, by obtaining similar demographic data from: (1) arrest warrant lists published by the tsarist police, the Okhrana, for three years, 1904, 1907, and 1910 (Okhrana Archives, Hoover Institution on War, Revolution, and Peace, Stanford, Calif., Reels 300, 303, 306); (2) the biographical index in T. P. Bondarevskaia, *Peterburgskii komitet RSDRP v revoliutsii, 1905–1907 gg.* (Leningrad, 1975); and (3) a biographical encyclopedia of Polish members of the RSDRP, *Księga Polaków – Uczestników rewolucji październikowej, 1917–1920. Biografie* (Warsaw, 1967).

men were also Russians, came from the cities, and joined the revolutionary movement in early adulthood. (See tables 1, 2, and 3.) A greater percentage of male Bolsheviks were from the working class and the peasantry, however, evidently because lower-class men could rebel more easily than could lower-class women. The traditions of Russian society enjoined all women to stay out of the male business of politics, but this prohibition was enforced with particular severity within the working class and the peasantry. Women of the poorer classes also coped with a daily struggle to survive that left little time for exploring new ideas or analyzing existing ones. On more affluent women, the reins of economic need and custom lay more loosely, with the result that a greater percentage of female than male Bolsheviks hailed from the middle and upper ranks of the social hierarchy. These differences between the sexes prevailed among the Mensheviks and the Socialist Revolutionaries as well, a fact that provides further evidence of the constraining effects of patriarchal custom on women of the lower classes.

There were tens of thousands of female revolutionaries in Russia in the period 1900–14 because the nation was in political crisis and because the revolutionary movement there had long welcomed women into its ranks. For decades the Russian intelligentsia, from which the revolutionaries came, had taken a very liberated attitude toward what it called "the woman question." As early as the 1850s, when Alexander II encouraged discussion of the emancipation of the serfs, social critics had argued that the oppression of women should be considered one of Russia's great injustices. Women of the upper classes were granted only very limited admittance to education and employment. Most peasant girls received no formal schooling whatsoever. Women could not change their place of residence or travel abroad without the permission of a male guardian. Divorce was nearly impossible, and although women of all classes had property rights, these were significantly less than those possessed by their male relatives. Undergirding the legal restrictions was a patriarchal value system that granted men substantial power over the women within their families. Whether a girl was a peasant or an aristocrat, she was supposed to marry a man of her parents' choosing and live out her life as the dutiful wife of a benevolent, protective, authoritarian husband.[11]

Criticism of this state of affairs spread quickly among liberals and radicals in the 1860s. It was in this decade that the Russian feminist movement began, with Stasova's mother, Poliksena, and her aunt, Nadezhda, among its founders. Meanwhile public opinion sang the praises of liberated women, as did hugely popular literary works. Nikolai Chernyshevskii's *What Is to Be Done?*, a novel that inspired several

---

[11] On the law regarding women in nineteenth-century Russia, see William G. Wagner, *Marriage, Property, and Law in Late Imperial Russia* (Oxford, 1994).

Table 1 *Social origins of Old Bolsheviks*

Social origins	Women (%) (N = 318)	Men (%) (N = 254)
Nobility	9.4	4.3
Intelligentsia[a]	10.4	15.0
Sluzhashchie[b]	6.0	11.8
Meshchanstvo[c]	11.3	6.3
Workers	26.4	27.9
Peasantry	10.4	34.2
Clergy	1.6	0.4
Unknown	24.5[d]	—[e]
Total	100	99.9

Note: "Old Bolshevik" was a term used by the party itself to denote those people who had joined before 1917; "Old Bolshevichka" is the feminized form. The data on women in this table were derived from the data bank compiled for this book; the data on men come from William Chase and J. Arch Getty, *The Soviet Data Bank*, Version 1.0 (1986). These two data banks are the sources as well for all the tables and charts that follow, unless otherwise indicated. The social origins given here and in subsequent tables are those used by the Bolsheviks to identify themselves in party documents.
[a] Includes those who worked in the professions and the arts.
[b] Roughly, white-collar workers; includes low-ranking civil servants, middle management in the private sector, clerical workers.
[c] The merchantry; includes shop-keepers, small business owners, some artisans, miscellaneous other urban dwellers who did not fit into other categories.
[d] The origins of a large number of Bolshevichki were not identified, probably because many of those women came from the propertied classes. The true percentages of middle-rank and noble woman, therefore, were probably higher than indicated.
[e] No files in *The Soviet Data Bank* contain the category "unknown."

generations of young people, took as its central theme the transformation of a sheltered middle-class girl into a social reformer. A central character in Ivan Turgenev's famous novel *On the Eve* was a female revolutionary. Equally influential was the poet Nikolai Nekrasov, who praised the courage of Russian women while lamenting the hardships of their lives in poems that were widely read. Nadezhda Krupskaia, the daughter of a Russian army officer and a governess who grew up to be a Bolshevichka as well as Lenin's wife, testified in her later life that Nekrasov's poetry had opened her eyes to injustice in Russia. Meanwhile, the small revolutionary organizations of the 1870s included in their ranks substantial numbers of women, as many as one-third of their total members according to some estimates. By deploring the condition of women in Russia and by welcoming women into their organizations, Russia's political opposition made more and more space for women, with the result that, by the turn of the century, their nation was home to an unusually large number of female revolutionaries.[12]

Table 2 *Ethnicity of Old Bolsheviks*

Ethnicity	Women (%) (N = 318)	Men (%) (N = 144)
Russian	31.4	42.4
Ukrainian	1.9	4.9
Name sounds Russian or Ukrainian	21.7	—
Belorussian	—	0.7
Jewish	7.9	13.2
Latvian	4.4	11.1
Estonian0.3	2.1	
Lithuanian	—	2.1
Finnish	0.3	0.7
Cossack	0.3	2.8
Polish	0.9	4.9
Moldavian	—	1.4
Georgian	0.9	4.2
Armenian0.6	3.5	
Asian[a]	0.3	4.9
Non-Russian-Empire	0.9	1.4
Unknown	27.7	—
Total	99.5	100.3

[a]People from the area of Central Asia (Kazaks, Kirgiz, Tadzhiks, Turkmen, Uzbeks), Tatars, and a host of other, smaller ethnic groups, primarily from Siberia.

It must also be pointed out, however, that these radical women, 18,000 or so at their peak, were a tiny minority in a huge empire of 150 million people (80 million of them women).[13] Although discontent with the government was widespread, very few people, and far fewer women than men, chose to condemn themselves to a parlous life on the run from the police in pursuit of a popular upheaval that might never come. Those people who were willing to live that way were, by definition, very exceptional. And unfortunately it is not very easy to understand why they took up lives as revolutionaries, even when we study their own words on the subject, for they did not always speak with perfect freedom or candor.

[12] The estimate that the populist organizations of the 1870s had one-third female membership comes from Robert H. McNeal, "Women in the Russian Radical Movement," *Journal of Social History* 2 (Winter 1971–72): 144. For estimates on the order of 15 percent of female members among the populists, see Fieseler, "The Making of Russian Female Social Democrats," 196. For the intelligentsia's attitudes toward feminism, see Richard Stites, *The Women's Liberation Movement in Russia: Feminism, Nihilism, and Bolshevism, 1860–1930* (Princeton, 1978), 29–154. On Krupskaia's lifelong love of Nekrasov's poetry, see Robert H. McNeal, *Bride of the Revolution: Krupskaia and Lenin* (Ann Arbor, Mich., 1972), 16–17.   [13] *Zhenshchiny v SSSR* (Moscow, 1975), 9.

Table 3 *Age of future Bolsheviks upon joining the Russian Social-Democratic Labor Party*

Age	Women (%) (N = 318)	Men (%) (N = 574)
15–19	25.8	49.3
20–24	42.4	36.2
25–29	13.5	8.9
30–34	6.2	4.0
35–39	1.3	0.9
40+	1.6	0.7
Unknown	9.1	—
Total	99.9	100.0

The Bolshevichki recorded their reasons for joining the party in their memoirs. We have already considered the shortcomings of these sources, written as they were to conform to the party line of the moment and to the equally powerful and even more long-standing Bolshevik canon of self-presentation which prescribed that the individual portray herself as just another self-effacing member of the great revolutionary movement. Though woefully inadequate in many respects, the Bolshevichki's memoirs are perhaps most informative when recounting their subjects' early years, for doing so required discussing the women's families and personal feelings in some detail. Of course there was a general script for these accounts: a girl growing up encounters situations that sensitize her to Russia's evils, then learns about the revolutionary movement, realizes how right the revolutionaries are, and joins them. This scenario occurs in memoir after memoir, but not primarily because the Soviet censors demanded that it be there. Rather, it described what actually happened to these young women. In fact, what else could have happened? They did become revolutionaries, and unless one believes that revolutionaries are "possessed," as the novelist Dostoevskii suggested, they must have chosen to be revolutionaries because they came to believe that Russia needed massive change. Within the broad outlines of the scenario, however, there is, as we shall see, a good deal of variety in the ways the Bolshevichki described their various arrivals at their revolutionary calling. That variety is another indication of the basic truthfulness and therefore reliability of these hundreds of stories, taken as a whole.[14]

In their memoirs many future Bolshevichki reported that they learned

---

[14] For a list of the memoirs from which the following analysis is drawn, see the section entitled "Autobiographical and biographical sources on Bolshevichki" in the bibliography.

to be critical of their society from their families; this is the first major generalization that emerges from their accounts. (See table 4.) All the millions of girls living in Russia in the late nineteenth and early twentieth centuries were surrounded by systemic injustice that periodically spawned horrors such as the famine of 1891, which took the lives of tens of thousands of people, or the Bloody Sunday Massacre of 9 January 1905, in which rioting soldiers killed more than 500 peaceful demonstrators. Grinding poverty gripped the peasantry and the urban working class alike. The fading nobility was losing its economic power but held on tenaciously to its privileges. Medical care, education, social services in the growing cities – all were woefully inadequate. The government exacerbated these problems by refusing to grant the most elementary political reforms and harassing private undertakings, from charity projects to schools for the poor, so that people attempting to alleviate the misery of city or countryside frequently concluded that the government itself required drastic overhaul. This conclusion was all the easier to reach after 1894, when Nicholas II became emperor. Vapid, quixotic, reactionary, Nicholas was incapable of sustained commitment to any sort of reform. By the time his end came in 1918, this inept man had done more to promote revolution than any revolutionary. But a girl growing up while he sat on the throne could not see what lay behind his handsome face and splendid uniforms unless someone pointed it out to her. She had to be taught that Russia's status quo was not divinely ordained, as Nicholas believed and as the church and many parents declared, but instead was the sorry result of generations of greed, injustice, and governmental ineptitude.

The Bolshevichki learned precisely this lesson as children. They learned it from relatives who encouraged them to be critical of Russia's political arrangements and, who, in the case of the more privileged youngsters, inspired them with a deep sense of personal obligation to improve the lives of the poor. Stasova, for example, was reared with her grandfather's motto ringing in her ears: "A man [sic] is worthy of the name only when he is useful to himself and others." In 1894 her uncle Vladimir, the much admired art critic, felt obliged to reassure her that she too would find some way of making herself useful to Russia. "For everyone who wants to be a genuinely complete human being," Stasov wrote in a letter to his niece, "hours, days, and years will certainly come when one must display all one's soul and strength to help, physically and morally, many hundreds of thousands of people. One can and should wait for these hours and days; they certainly will come, and one must only be ready for them in advance."[15]

[15] Quoted in A. K. Lebedev and A. V. Solodovnikov, *Vladimir Vasil'evich Stasov. Zhizn' i tvorchestvo* (Moscow, 1976), 12; Stasov, *Pis'ma*, vol. II, 451.

Table 4 *Initiators of future Bolshevichki into the revolutionary movement*

	Social origins of joiner						
Initiator	Nobility (%)	Intelligentsia (%)	Sluzhashchie (%)	Meshchanstvo (%)	Workers (%)	Peasantry (%)	Clergy (%)
Parents	4.2 (1)	9.1 (2)	7.1 (1)	9.1 (2)	14.3 (7)	4.0 (1)	—
Siblings	33.3 (8)	27.3 (6)	21.4 (3)	36.4 (8)	18.4 (9)	24.0 (6)	25.0 (1)
Other relatives	—	—	—	—	—	4.0 (1)	—
Spouse	—	—	—	—	8.2 (4)	4.0 (1)	—
Fellow students	45.8 (11)	36.4 (8)	57.1 (8)	40.9 (9)	4.1 (2)	16.0 (4)	50.0 (2)
Fellow workers	4.2 (1)	9.1 (2)	—	4.5 (1)	38.8 (19)	16.0 (4)	—
Revolutionaries	12.5 (3)	18.2 (4)	14.3 (2)	9.1 (2)	16.3 (8)	32.0 (8)	25.0 (1)
Total	100.0 (24)	100.1 (22)	99.9 (14)	100.0 (22)	100.1 (49)	100.0 (25)	100.0 (4)

Note: Figures in parentheses are base *N*s for the adjacent percentages. Total *N* = 160.

Some families went beyond such philanthropic sentiments and actually introduced their daughters to revolutionary politics. Thirty-seven percent of the Bolshevichki about whom we have information report that they first heard radical ideas from relatives who were revolutionaries themselves. Rozaliia Zemliachka was only five years old when she saw her mother hiding illegal pamphlets printed by her brothers and sisters. Artiukhina's uncle was an SR. Many more families, politically liberal, were sympathetic toward revolutionaries. Stasova's father defended them in court. N. P. Chernosvitov, a lawyer and rich landowner, built his daughter Sofia a school where she could teach the local peasants, and sheltered the revolutionary students his son brought home in the summers.[16] Girls in such families were also likely to have unpleasant brushes with the police that fed their antipathy toward the regime. Stasova, Zemliachka, Alexandra Kollontai, and Mariia and Anna Ulianova (Lenin's sisters) saw members of their families harassed for their political opposition. The Ulianovs knew the grief of having their brother Alexander executed for conspiracy to assassinate the tsar. Sometimes all the children of such families became revolutionaries, as did the Ulianovs (Lenin, his two sisters, and his surviving brother, Dmitrii), the Zalkinds (Zemliachka's brothers), the Menzhinskiis (two sisters and a brother from the St. Petersburg nobility), the Novikov sisters (three textile workers from Tver guberniia), and the Volfs (two Jewish women and their brother from Warsaw).

A girl's family did not have to engage in radical politics in order for her to become critical of Russia's status quo; the ordinary experiences of daily life could also foster alienation. Most future Bolshevichki hailed from the penurious nobility and the growing business and professional elite. Nadezhda Krupskaia's father Konstantin Krupskii, although a member of the nobility, grew up an orphan in the care of the state, served a brief term in the army, and then undertook a series of jobs in the civil service, none of them lucrative. Her mother Elizaveta came from equally impoverished circumstances. Such people struggled to keep their foothold in the middle ranks of Russian society and coped routinely with the snubs of the powerful. Elizaveta Agrinskaia, for example, was the daughter of a civil-service employee of the city government of Penza, in central Russia. Her father died when she was very young, leaving her uneducated mother with four children to rear. They supported themselves by taking in sewing, and the mother managed to send her daughters to gymnasium, but life was difficult. "All of this was very hard for me to live through," Agrinskaia wrote much later, "and already as a child I felt class differences and

---

[16] *Slavnye bol'shevichki*, 275. Sofia Chernosvitova is better known by her married name, Smidovich. She headed the Zhenotdel, 1922–24.

involuntarily was drawn to hatred for the rich who were oppressing the poor."[17] Generations of middle-class Europeans had turned to radicalism while simmering with similar resentments against those born to wealth and privilege.

It is clear that many Bolshevichki had learned to perceive Russian society as unjust when they were children. It is also clear, however, that no single pattern of childhood hardship or family conflict produced revolutionaries. Happy, fortunate families – the Stasovs – as well as unhappy, fragmented ones – the Maishes – reared radical children, and the Bolshevichki were not, as a group, maladjusted young women from dysfunctional homes. In fact, many of them later remembered their childhoods as filled with love and their parents as very important, positive influences. Some Bolshevichki idealized their fathers, naming them as the central figures in their early lives. Stasova declared much later, "I write so much about my father because he had a huge influence on me and I owe him very, very much." Kollontai felt the same: "I cannot talk about my childhood without thinking about my father. If ever a man had an influence on my mind and development, it was my father."

Other women stressed the importance of their mothers in their lives. Zemliachka said she learned "democratic ways of thinking and living" from her mother. Evgeniia Adamovich, a noblewoman from Ukraine, wrote, "I passionately loved my mother. Her energy, diligence, attraction to the revolutionary-democratic ideals of the 1860s and 1870s had a decisive influence on the formation of my worldview."[18] There were Bolshevichki who, like Bosh, recorded conflict with their parents, particularly over their decisions to become revolutionaries. Others, like Nikolaeva, grew up relatively alone, after their nearest relatives died or deserted them. Loving families and neglectful ones produced young women who were critical of the authority that governed society and who also desired a much more independent life than was prescribed for women in Russia.

Whatever its source, there was a rebellious streak running through the characters of many of the future Bolshevichki, especially those from more privileged backgrounds. These women report that they grew into adolescents who rejected the control, however well meant, of parents or other relatives. Samoilova overcame her mother's objections to her entering the Bestuzhevskii courses. Evgeniia Levitskaia ran away from her parents when she was sixteen to find a freer life living with her physician brother in

---

[17] On Krupskaia, see McNeal, *Bride of the Revolution*, 5–14; on Agrinskaia, RTsKhIDNI, f. 124, op. 1, d. 14, l. 5.

[18] RTsKhIDNI, f. 356, op. 1, d. 6, l. 8; Kollontai, as quoted in Gustav Johansson, *Revolutionens ambassadör. Alexandra Kollontays liv och gärning, åren 1892–1917* (Stockholm, 1945), 52; RTsKhIDNI, f. 180, op. 4, d. 180, l. 24; A. V. Berdnikova, ed., *Zhenshchiny v revoliutsii* (Novosibirsk, 1968), 13.

Plate 1. Alexandra Kollontai as a child of five.

St. Petersburg. Kollontai adored her father, General Mikhail Domontovich, but she felt that her free-thinking, strong-willed mother, Alexandra Masalina, was too domineering. Years later she declared in her memoirs that her first rebellion as a teenager was against her mother's will.[19]

Lower-class Bolshevichki, of course, had more obvious material reasons for becoming revolutionaries, for they coped every day with poverty and endured the depredations of the powerful. When discussing their childhoods, they very frequently identify personal hardship as the spur that first awakened them to the injustices of Russia. Nikolaeva worked for wages from the age of eight; Artiukhina sewed shirts together while her mother searched for a job. Many Bolshevichki from the working class learned radical ideas from relatives, as did their more affluent future comrades, and then began to experience persecution by the authorities. Alexandra Artiukhina's mother was a union activist, her uncle was a Socialist Revolutionary, and the young Alexandra knew even greater hardship when her mother was blacklisted for working in the union. For Mera Sverdlova, a Jewish seamstress from Pskov, all these experiences flowed together: "The influence of my older sister, material need, and

[19] Evg. Levitskaia, "Pamiati starogo druga," *Proletarskaia revoliutsiia*, no. 8 (1922): 3–7; Barbara Evans Clements, *Bolshevik Feminist: The Life of Aleksandra Kollontai* (Bloomington, Ind., 1979), 12–15.

clashes with the police from my earliest years turned me against the tsarist regime," she remembered.[20]

Seeking an education

Working-class and more privileged girls came to be critical of their society for a variety of reasons, then, as they grew from childhood into adolescence. Some lived in sheltered homes where they aspired to impress beloved parents; others struggled to break free of parental control. Poor girls learned the difficult tasks of surviving at an early age. Rich and poor heard political criticism from their relatives, and a few watched in fear as the police ransacked their homes. These experiences did not make children into revolutionaries, but they did make them receptive to the revolutionary ideologies and activists they encountered when they became adolescents.

In their teen years the future Bolshevichki moved away from their family circles. Poorer girls joined the paid-labor force as factory or artisanal workers; more affluent ones went to secondary school, either gymnasium, which specialized in the humanities and sciences, or the vocational high schools commonly called *Realschule*. But all the Bolshevichki, even those who had to work for many hours a day, spent a good deal of their time while they were teenagers becoming better educated. Of the Bolshevichki in the data base compiled for this study, 75 percent attended secondary school, and 23 percent performed at least some work in university courses. Education was more accessible to the more privileged future Bolshevichki, of course, for Russia's propertied classes were routinely providing advanced schooling for their daughters by the last decades of the nineteenth century. More than 90 percent of the working-class girls also managed to complete primary school, however, and 28 percent of them attended secondary school. This level of education would be impressive for any group of women in turn-of-the-century Europe, but it is particularly striking as a feature of the Russian context, for the Russian Empire's female population experienced very low literacy rates. In 1897, only 46 percent of the girls and women living in the cities (where education was more available than in the countryside) could read and write. Among the female population of the entire nation, only 17 percent was literate.[21] (See table 5.)

[20] RTsKhIDNI, f. 124, op. 1, d. 1719, l. 5.

[21] The source of the statistics on general female literacy is *Zhenshchiny v SSSR*, 55. The *Soviet Data Bank* is unusable here, for it yields the ridiculously high figure of 76 percent of male Bolsheviks having university or advanced technical training. The statistic reflects the fact that the subdirectory housing data on education contains a disproportionate number of Old Bolshevik party leaders. Forty-two percent of the men listed in the biographical index in Bondarevskaia, *Peterburgskii komitet*, had higher education, a more believable figure but also probably inflated, for the Petersburg party committee was an elite group. More reasonable numbers come from a study of political exiles (mostly SRs and SDs) in Siberia in 1915 that shows only 9 percent of the individuals (males and females, SDs and

Table 5 *Social origins and education of Bolshevichki*

Social origins	Highest level of education attended				
	None (%)	Primary (%)	Secondary (%)	Higher (%)	Total (%)
Nobility	3.3 (1)	—	33.3 (10)	63.3 (19)	99.9 (30)
Intelligentsia	—	3.1 (1)	56.3 (18)	40.6 (13)	100.0 (32)
Sluzhashchie	5.9 (1)	5.9 (1)	35.3 (6)	52.9 (9)	100.0 (17)
Meshchanstvo	3.7 (1)	11.1 (3)	48.1 (13)	37.0 (10)	99.9 (27)
Workers	6.5 (3)	63.0 (29)	28.3 (13)	2.2 (1)	100.0 (46)
Peasantry	3.8 (1)	50.0 (13)	34.6 (9)	11.5 (3)	99.9 (26)
Clergy	—	—	60.0 (3)	40.0 (2)	100.0 (5)

Note: Figures in parentheses are base *N*s for the adjacent percentages. Total *N* = 183.

The Bolshevichki as a group were probably better educated than their male comrades in the Social-Democratic Party. These latter, in turn, were far better educated than the average men of the peasantry and industrial proletariat. That the great majority of male and female Social Democrats were well educated for their place and time testifies to the fact that schools and universities were the spawning grounds for revolutionaries in Russia in the late nineteenth and early twentieth centuries. In the classrooms, students learned the critical thinking that lay at the heart of the liberal arts and sciences from teachers and professors, many of whom were themselves politically critical. Outside the classrooms, radical ideas flourished in student reading circles and in clandestine meetings. Most future Bolshevichki, however, set off to school not with the intention of becoming revolutionaries, but with objectives a good deal vaguer and more legal than that. Many of them, remembering in their later years their reasons for seeking education, said that they had been trying to make sense of their rapidly changing world. Education offered them intellectual and spiritual liberation; it would enable them to escape the control of traditional customs and old faiths by giving them mastery over modern scientific principles and ideas. On a more mundane level, education promised lower-class young people mobility upward into the growing ranks of white-collar workers.

Education was also a way for young women to escape, or at least postpone, the conventional women's lives that lay ahead of them. Many Bolshevichki first rebelled against their parents by refusing to accept their families' plans for their futures. Olga Varentsova, the daughter of wealthy

SRs) had higher education (A. Tsvetkov-Prosveshchenskii, "Eniseiskaia ssylka v tsifrakh," *Katorga i ssylka*, no. 87 [1932]: 143–54). Maureen Perrie also arrived at 9 percent for male Socialist Revolutionaries (and 16 percent for females): Perrie, "The Social Composition and Structure of the Socialist-Revolutionary Party Before 1917," 239. Even 9 percent of members with higher education was substantial for Russia in the early twentieth century, however, so all these data sets sustain at least the generalization that male SDs and SRs were well educated for their time and place.

merchants in Ivanovo-Voznesensk, rejected her father's wish that she become a nun and instead obtained his reluctant permission to attend gymnasium. Ksenia Voinova pleaded for, but never could obtain, the approval of her father, an army officer, for her college plans. "He said that it would be better if he killed me with his own hands than see me a college student [*kursistka*]." Only after his death could she finally travel from her native Lublin to Moscow for higher education. Vera Velichkina, the daughter of a clerical family in Moscow, wrote of her need "to break out of the family circle"; she left home in 1891 over her mother's tearful protests to join Tolstoians doing famine relief.[22] Inessa Armand, a governess's daughter who grew up in a family of wealthy Moscow textile manufacturers, summed up her rejection of the destiny proscribed for her in a letter she wrote to her daughter, Inna, in 1915:

In *War and Peace*, there is one phrase that I first read when I was fifteen and that had an enormous influence on me. [Tolstoy] says there that Natasha became fully feminine [*samka*] when she got married. I remember this phrase seemed horribly offensive to me, it was like a whip to me, and it created in me a strong resolution never to become fully feminine, but to remain a person (there were so many fully feminine women around us).[23]

Inessa (when she became a prominent Bolshevichka she preferred to be called by her first name) defined herself at first in opposition to prevailing norms: she resolved not to turn into a typical matron but instead "to remain a person." Education provided an escape from the "fully feminine," a means to another, more individualized and independent identity. But many teenagers who undertook the search, Inessa among them, began with no very exact sense of what their new identity should be. Eva Broido, a Jewish girl from Lithuania who became a Menshevik, summed up in her memoirs the inchoate feelings that inspired future revolutionaries:

And yet – a preoccupation with the ideas of freedom, discontent with the stagnant provincial life, a vague desire for an ideal country peopled with perfect men and women, a passion for knowledge which would show the way to a better and more glorious future – yes, such moods and ideas were almost general among us. Young men and women alike strove to enter universities or technical schools, there to learn the "truth about life." This thirst for knowledge and learning, for self-improvement and a free unfolding of one's personality, however vague and aimless, was so typical of all of us that the then-current ludicrous term "a young girl with strivings" described the condition most aptly.[24]

After they completed their schooling, what were such young women to

---

[22] *Zhenshchiny russkoi revoliutsii*, 56–57; RTsKhIDNI, f. 124, op. 1, d. 389, l. 4; Levitskaia, "Pamiati starogo druga," 3; *Slavnye bol'shevichki*, 108.

[23] Quoted in Pavel Podliashuk, *Tovarishch Inessa*, 3rd ed. (Moscow, 1973), 18.

[24] Eva Broido, *Memoirs of a Revolutionary*, trans. and ed. Vera Broido (London, 1967), 9.

do? Ekaterina Kuskova, later a leader of moderate Social Democrats, recalled asking herself, "How to live? What to serve?"[25] The two questions were intimately connected in Kuskova's mind, because, for her, as for many activist women of her generation, escape from the domestic sphere called into question all the prevailing values defining womanhood. Kuskova qualified her rejection of those values by construing her search for another sort of life as a quest for a calling, one that would enable her to fulfill her deeply felt obligations "to serve." Such a construction of their rebellion was typical as well among Bolshevichki. To assert that they sought independence to develop themselves as individuals was as unacceptable to them as it was to Florence Nightingale or Jane Addams, independent women also noted for their declarations of devotion to social betterment. Some Bolshevichki, Kollontai for example, probably knew in their heart of hearts that they had also wanted an independent life for its own sake, but they would not admit such desires publicly. Stasova wrote later, in her typically indirect way, "Of course the results of all this internal work on myself and of events in external life, among which the history of the student movement played no small part, forced me to seek to apply my strengths to practical work."[26]

In Russia, as throughout the European world, the employments most accessible to young women from the propertied classes in the late nineteenth century were teaching and medicine. The majority of the Bolshevichki chose to train to be teachers. (See table 6.) Some of those from the middling orders undertook clerical work, which was just becoming a feminized occupation in the 1890s, because it paid better. The men from the nobility and the middle classes who later became Bolsheviks had more options, but many of them also studied education or medicine, probably because they possessed the same social conscience as the women and thought that those occupations offered the greatest possibilities for improving Russia. (See table 7.)

Becoming teachers did not fully satisfy the future Bolshevichki's search for new beliefs and ideas to replace the ones they were leaving behind, so while they were in school studying literature, history, science, and mathematics, they also became better acquainted with radical ideas. Those parents who did not harbor revolutionary sympathies themselves found their children's enlightenment dismaying. Glafira Okulova-Teodorovich later described the disappointment felt by her father, a

[25] E. Kuskova, "Davno minuvshee," *Novyi zhurnal* 48 (1957): 159–60, quoted in Barbara T. Norton, "The Making of a Female Marxist: E. D. Kuskova's Conversion to Russian Social Democracy," *International Review of Social History* 34 (1989): 235.

[26] E. D. Stasova, "Iz vospominanii o partiinoi rabote do revoliutsii 1917 g.," *Proletarskaia revoliutsiia*, no. 12 (1927): 187.

Table 6 *Prerevolutionary occupations of Bolshevichki*

Occupation	N (318)	Percentage of total N
Teacher	64	20.1
Seamstress, tailor	33	10.4
Textile- or garment-factory worker	32	10.1
Professional revolutionary	27	8.5
Student	15	4.7
Clerk	12	3.8
Feldsher[a]	12	3.8
Other factory worker	12	3.8
Librarian	5	1.6
Tobacco factory worker	5	1.6
Bookkeeper	4	1.3
Housewife	4	1.3
Physician	4	1.3
Dentist	3	0.9
Journalist	3	0.9
Printer	3	0.9
Actor	2	0.6
Confectionery worker	2	0.6
Domestic servant	2	0.6
Food-industry worker	2	0.6
Laundress	1	0.3
Metalworker	1	0.3
Midwife	1	0.3
Perfume-factory worker	1	0.3
Telephone operator	1	0.3
Unknown	67	21.1
Total	318	100.0

Note: The primary occupation of each woman was coded. Those women who had no occupation other than revolutionary were included in the category "professional revolutionary."
[a] A physician's assistant.

peasant who had made a fortune in Siberia and then invested some of it in his daughters' schooling: "He sent us to Moscow to study, dreaming of introducing his children to higher circles, and we came back home under police surveillance."[27] Thirty-seven percent of the Bolshevichki reported that fellow students had introduced them to revolutionary literature and organizations. If to this figure are added the influences on these young women of their siblings, many of whom had picked up forbidden ideas from their own schooling, it emerges that a total of 63 percent of the Bolshevichki from the nobility and the middle ranks of Russian society learned about radical politics in the students' world.

[27] *Zhenshchiny v revoliutsii*, 44.

Table 7 *Prerevolutionary occupations of Old Bolsheviks*

Field	Women (%) ($N = 318$)	Men (%) ($N = 235$)
Intelligentsia		
Education	24.8	5.1
Medicine	6.3	10.2
Other[a]	2.5	9.4
Other white-collar[b]	6.0	8.9
Revolutionary	8.5	0.8
Urban manual laborer	30.8	44.7
Military	—	18.7
Peasantry	—	2.1
Unknown	21.1	—
Total	100.0	99.9

[a] E.g., agronomist, attorney, engineer, journalist, librarian, student.
[b] E.g., actress, bookkeeper, civil servant, clerk, manager in a private company, salesperson, telephone operator.

Girls such as Artiukhina and Nikolaeva, who grew up in the slums, came to the revolutionaries rather differently, because they had to overcome far greater economic and cultural obstacles than did their more prosperous future comrades, even to obtain an education. Russia had a large number of female factory workers; in 1914 they made up one-third of the industrial labor force. And yet, within the increasingly politicized working class, the notion that politics was a male sphere on which women should not trespass remained stronger than it was among the propertied. Working women were expected to devote their time to surviving on miserably low wages and that is what most of them did. Those who married (the great majority) also bore the responsibility for housework and childcare. Enjoined to submit rather than to think critically about their situation, working-class women also lacked the leisure and the education to become politically informed. Instead, most of them, and most working-class men, spent their time struggling to keep body and soul together.[28]

Future Bolshevichki from the proletariat managed to resist the prevailing norms, just as more prosperous Bolshevichki did, and they too sought out education. Very few of them could afford to attend university courses or even complete high school, but almost all of them were literate by the time they were adolescents, and they also learned about revolutionary ideas in their formal and informal schooling. (See table 5.) The education of Artiukhina, the textile worker, was typical. A girlfriend from her home town who was also working in St. Petersburg persuaded her to go to night school and later introduced her to Marxism.[29] In night school and Sunday

[28] On factory workers, see Rose Glickman, *Russian Factory Women* (Berkeley, 1984).
[29] *Bez nikh my ne pobedili by*, 237.

Plate 2. Nadezhda Krupskaia about the time she graduated from
gymnasium in the late 1880s.

classes, in study circles that met after work, and in clandestine meetings in
the fields and forests, young female factory workers who would one day be
Bolshevichki read political tracts and heard lectures from students and
revolutionaries.

Working-class women also learned about radical politics in their
workplaces. The majority of future Bolshevichki who did manual labor
were employed in textile and garment factories, as were millions of women
elsewhere throughout the industrializing world. (See table 6.) Activism
was rising among these women all over Europe and North America in the
first decade of the twentieth century, and Russia was no exception. In the
great centers of Russia's textile industry – Moscow, Ivanovo-Voznesensk,
and St. Petersburg – the textile workers' union, in which many proletarian
Bolshevichki began their political careers, became particularly active after

1905. Revolutionary sentiment ran high among trade unionists, so entering their ranks, as Artiukhina did in 1908, brought future Bolshevichki into yet another of Russia's many schools of radical thought.[30]

Joining the party

Banned books and secret gatherings acquainted the Bolshevichki with radical ideas, but they did not make them revolutionaries. Of the tens of thousands of young people who developed leftist sympathies in the 1890s and 1900s, only a few decided to become deeply involved in the revolutionaries' illegal activities. The Bolshevichki were, of course, among them. They began attending meetings regularly, distributing illegal literature, and raising money for the movement. As they spent more time on these projects, they developed close relationships with people who were already revolutionaries or who were, like themselves, novices drawn to the underground. The most important such connection in Nikolaeva's life was her patron Kollontai; Bosh's was her sister Elena. Other future Bolshevichki talked over their political ideas with small groups of close friends from school or work. Matrena Razumova, a textile worker in Ivanovo-Voznesensk, began reading socialist pamphlets after a friend from the mill and her friend's radical brother introduced her to revolutionary thought. Over the protests of her frightened mother, who also worked in the mill, Razumova became a member of a circle of workers that gathered to discuss politics on their days off. When strikes swept through the city in 1904, she and several of her new friends joined the Social-Democratic Party together.[31]

Sociologists attest to the fact that affiliations of the sort Razumova established with the people in her circle are crucial to building revolutionary organizations, and indeed social movements of all types. Social movements – that is, large, often national organizations separate from established political parties that seek to achieve change through social mobilization – are formed by "rational actors embedded in networks," to use the phrase of Debra Friedman and Doug McAdam. They begin when small groups of people pool their ideas, as Razumova and her friends did, and begin to develop a sense of community and shared purpose. Revolutionaries typically come together in this way when in their late teens or early twenties, forming "dense interpersonal networks of young people." Moving within the network from cell to cell, a woman works her way toward her adult identity and vocation in close contact with others.

---

[30] On female textile workers, see Glickman, *Russian Factory Women*, esp. 197.
[31] Institut Marksizma-Leninizma pri TsK KPSS, Nauchno-metodicheskii kabinet, *Revoliutsionerki Rossii* (Moscow, 1983), 18.

Ideas and personal ties intermingle in a process at once psychosocial and intellectual. The greater the political risk attendant upon such activity, the tighter the bonds that develop between participants.[32]

This analysis derives from study of social movements in western Europe and North America in the late twentieth century, but it fits the Russian parties of earlier decades as well. Future Bolshevichki held study circles with trusted friends, met revolutionaries, participated in illegal activities, became close to people who were on the same exploratory journey, and took even greater risks with them, all the while continuing to develop their analysis of what was wrong with Russia and how it should be fixed. As their connections to their comrades strengthened through shared experiences, their ideas became more fully formed as well. Of course a young woman had to be receptive to radicalism in the first place or she would not have befriended people who shared her discontents. A variety of childhood experiences could nurture that receptivity, as we have seen, and so could personal goals driving these girls as they grew into women. Some, like Bosh, were escaping bourgeois confinement; some, like Artiukhina and Stasova, were following a course set for them by politically engaged parents; some, like Nikolaeva, were seeking a way out of poverty and powerlessness. From different places and for differing reasons, they found a common path into the revolutionary movement, and it lay through the small groups they joined in their early adulthood.

And yet Bolshevichki experienced no sudden blinding light of conversion the first time they talked late into the night about Russia's problems. Very few of them permitted themselves simply to be led into the revolutionary movement by people they admired. Instead most undertook a long process of initiation with their comrades, while going on with their ordinary lives. Those who held regular jobs, Nikolaeva and Artiukhina for example, went to them every day. Those who were students, like Samoilova, remained at school. Inessa Armand continued her charity work among prostitutes in Moscow; Bosh read to the men in her husband's employ. Stasova, Kollontai, their friends the Menzhinskii sisters, Praskovia Kudelli, and Nadezhda Krupskaia worked in schools for the poor in

---

[32] The first quoted phrase is italicized in the original and comes from Debra Friedman and Doug McAdam, "Collective Identity and Activism: Networks, Choices, and the Life of a Social Movement," in Aldon D. Morris and Carol McClurg Mueller, eds., *Frontiers in Social Movement Theory* (New Haven, Conn., 1992), 161. The second appears in Enrique Laraña, Hank Johnston, and Joseph R. Gusfield, "Introduction," in Laraña, Johnston, and Gusfield, eds., *New Social Movements* (Philadelphia, 1994), 14. See also Carol McClurg Mueller, "Building Social Movement Theory," in Morris and Mueller, *Frontiers in Social Movement Theory*, 12. The correlation between closeness of friendships and risk-taking has been argued by Doug McAdam in a study of civil-rights workers in the southern United States in the 1960s. See Doug McAdam, "Recruitment to High-Risk Activism: The Case of the Freedom Summer," *American Journal of Sociology* 82 (May 1986): 64–90.

St. Petersburg for several years. Secretly all these women carried messages, distributed pamphlets, and raised money for the Social Democrats, small tasks that tested their fortitude, earned the trust of the revolutionaries, and strengthened their ties to these people. They also read socialism and continued to talk with their friends. For every one such explorer who became a full-time revolutionary, there were dozens, if not hundreds, more who never went beyond this marginal state of involvement.

The process of becoming a revolutionary took years because it required a thoroughgoing transformation of a young woman's existence. She knew that once she committed herself fully to what the revolutionaries called "the cause" (*delo*), she would live a very unpleasant life on the fringes of legal society. Stasova, Kollontai, and Bosh reported doubting that they could stand up to the demands of such an existence. Ekaterina Shalaginova, a teacher in Perm, later confessed, "I was drawn to the Marxists but I didn't have the courage to ask them to give me any work."[33] For proletarian women the risks were even greater, because any brush with the police might leave them without a job and unable to secure another.

Many women also had to uproot their family lives before they became fully engaged in the revolutionary movement. Some had to break with their parents. Vera Karavaikova cut all ties with her family, successful Ivanovo-Voznesensk industrialists, when she moved into the underground. Others – Inessa Armand, Kollontai, and Bosh, for example – left husbands who were not revolutionaries. The data on the Bolshevichki's marriages are very fragmentary, but those available indicate that at least 46 percent of the women did marry before 1917, and at least 20 percent of those marriages ended in permanent separation, a very high rate of dissolution for a society in which divorce was illegal and socially stigmatized. There were also a few women who entered the party after they were widowed. Evdokiia Poliakova, a working-class housewife from Ivanovo-Voznesensk, learned in 1915 that her husband, a soldier, had been killed in World War I. "It was as if I had lost any purpose in life," she wrote. "Comrades whom I gotten to know earlier put a hard proposition to me, that there was a purpose in life and a very large one. Join the party and then there wouldn't be time to miss him."[34]

Future Bolshevichki also believed that they had to educate themselves in Marxism in order to become revolutionary Social Democrats. Klavdiia Kirsanova, a middle-class girl from Perm, later confessed, "I chose the SDs. Of course, I didn't know anything at all about this party, even their

---

[33] RTsKhIDNI, f. 124, op. 1, d. 2122, l. 15.

[34] *Oktiabriem mobilizovannye. Zhenshchiny-kommunistki v bor'be za pobedu sotsialisticheskoi revoliutsii* (Moscow, 1987), 176; RTsKhIDNI, f. 124, op. 1, d. 1548, l. 5.

Plate 3. The volunteer staff of a lending library that provided legal materials such as maps and illegal revolutionary pamphlets to Sunday-school and night-school teachers in St. Petersburg in the mid-1890s. On the far left is Alexandra Kollontai and next to her is Elena Stasova.

program, except that they were against the tsar and that Aleksei [one of her friends] was in this party and I even explained my choice very stupidly. 'I am in this party because it's for the workers, but it wants to free them slowly, without killing.'"[35] Many future Bolshevichki, as ignorant as Kirsanova, put off joining the party until they felt they sufficiently understood the movement's ideology. Nikolaeva studied Marxism in prison after her first arrest, as did Rozaliia Zemliachka. In fact, many Bolshevichki spent their jail time poring over socialist texts donated to prison libraries by former inmates. Others read Marx and Engels in their student or worker circles. Women already well into their adult lives – Bosh, Inessa, Kollontai, Samoilova, and Stasova, for example – devoted a year or more to studying socialism.

This study, usually carried on with friends and under the guidance of more knowledgeable socialists, convinced the future Bolshevichki that Marxism was superior to its most popular radical alternative, Russian

[35] RTsKhIDNI, f. 124, op. 1, d. 863, l. 3.

populism. The Marxist analysis of capitalism not only placed Russian developments within the context of the great international economic and political transformations of the age, it also promised that these changes would inevitably produce a revolutionary upheaval that would make way for a socialized, communalized society. Erudite and positivistic, Marxism's difficult abstractions gave it credibility among those who venerated the intellectual power of "modern" rationalism. Ekaterina Kuskova, a populist who became a Marxist in the early 1890s, summed up the appeal of "scientific socialism" this way:

All these Spencers, Lavrovs, and even Mikhailovskii did not give that conception of the *structure of society* and the position in it of the toilers that Marx did. Simply, clearly he cut the whole – society – into its component parts, defined the social significance of each of them, and besides did this so strikingly according to the example of English life that it was difficult to turn one's back on this iron logic.[36]

Marxism also appealed to young women because of its systematic critique of patriarchy. Indeed, August Bebel's *Woman Under Socialism* was the first of the major writings by the leading theoreticians that many Bolshevichki read. Bebel argued, in very accessible prose, that women's inequality was rooted in the institution of private property; men's control over the means of production made it possible for them to control women. Women should become fully equal members of society, but this would happen only when revolution destroyed private property itself and ushered in socialism. Under socialism, all the customs that prescribed women's subordination would be replaced by belief in the complete equality of the sexes. Women would work in any field they chose, housekeeping and childrearing would be handled by communal institutions, and children would grow up unaware that there were any important differences between boys and girls. This stirring utopian vision had enormous appeal to young women who were seeking, as the Bolshevichki were, to realize personal independence in the liberation of an entire society.[37]

In their memoirs, the Bolshevichki wrote that after they had mastered Marxism they were finally ready to become full-time party workers, for then they understood the world well enough to begin attempting to change it. Seen more psychologically, their apotheosis into educated

[36] E. Kuskova, "Davno minuvshee," *Novyi zhurnal* 50 (1957): 181–82, as quoted in Norton, "The Making of a Female Marxist," 244. Italics in original. "Spencer" refers to Herbert Spencer. Petr Lavrov (1823–1900) and Nikolai Mikhailovskii (1842–1904) were leading theoreticians of Russian populism.

[37] August Bebel, *Woman Under Socialism*, translated from the 33rd ed. by Daniel De Leon (New York, 1904).

socialists was the end of a long journey away from home. When they had learned the principles of Marxist socialism, when they had attenuated the ties that held them to their old lives and had created bonds to the people who would be their community in their new life, then they felt strong enough to cut themselves loose from the safety of conventional existence and become Social Democratic revolutionaries. That was their choice, to become Social Democrats. Whether to join the Mensheviks or the Bolsheviks came later, after they had become revolutionaries.[38]

Female and male Bolsheviks tended to make their decision when there was the greatest cause to believe that revolution was possible, that is, when political ferment was highest. (See figure 1.) Stepanida Lagutina, a worker from Moscow, expressed the feelings of many of her comrades when she wrote, "as a result of the events of 1905, I began to feel myself with the Bolsheviks."[39] The year 1905 was a particularly important time, for it began with strikes in St. Petersburg that culminated in troops killing hundreds of unarmed demonstrators in the infamous Bloody Sunday Massacre. There followed ten months of protests and uprisings that began to subside only after the tsar pledged in October to establish civil liberties, grant the right to organize unions, and permit an elected legislature. The majority of the Bolshevichki from more privileged backgrounds joined the party just before or during 1905, probably because this was the time when radicalism was most popular among Russia's propertied classes. From late 1906 until 1910, Russia was relatively calm, then workers and revolutionaries began to organize strikes again. In 1912 they were especially energized by outrage over another government assault on unarmed strikers, the Lena Goldfields Massacre. This was the point at which many working-class Bolshevichki came into the party, probably because working-class women as a whole were then more politically active than earlier.

Bolshevichki in general, like Stasova, Samoilova, Zemliachka, Bosh, Nikolaeva, and Artiukhina in particular, came from different places in

[38] Scholars have suggested that female Social Democrats were led more by their feelings than by their intellect in becoming revolutionaries (Fieseler, "The Making of Russian Female Social Democrats," 218–20; Stites, *The Women's Liberation Movement in Russia*, 276–77). Such generalizations are suspect because they seem to draw on gender stereotypes. Nor do they comport with the accounts of their decision given by most Bolshevichki, by the "economist" Social Democrat Ekaterina Kuskova, and by Mensheviks Eva Broido and Lidiia Dan. For representative discussions, see *Slavnye bol'shevichki*, 213–17; *Zhenshchiny russkoi revoliutsii*, 320–38; Norton, "The Making of a Female Marxist," 227–47; Broido, *Memoirs of a Revolutionary*, 5–16; and Leopold H. Haimson, ed., *The Making of Three Russian Revolutionaries* (Cambridge, 1987), 73–85. On religious conversion as a sudden spiritual awakening much different from the Bolshevichki's prolonged process of education, see David A. Snow and Richard Machalek, "The Sociology of Conversion," *Annual Review of Sociology* 10 (1984): 167–90.

[39] RTsKhIDNI, f. 124, op. 1, d. 1054, l. 6.

Plate 4. Elena Stasova, circa 1895.

Russia and became revolutionaries for different reasons. There are commonalities, however, in their origins, in their childhood experiences, and in their lives as adolescents. Many grew up in families sympathetic to political activism. By the time they were teenagers, they longed for more than conventional domesticity or a life of toil in the factory. Almost all of them were literate, many were highly educated, and most gravitated to revolutionary thought and the political underground in their late teens or early twenties. Close friends or relations who were Social Democrats played an important part in their maturation into revolutionaries. After serving an apprenticeship doing odd jobs for the organization, attending illegal meetings, and studying Marxism, they decided to dedicate themselves fully to illegal activities. Most took this step in years when the rising of social unrest seemed to bring revolution closer. As demonstrators filled the streets, the young women who would be Bolshevichki slipped away with their comrades into the parallel universe of the revolutionary movement.

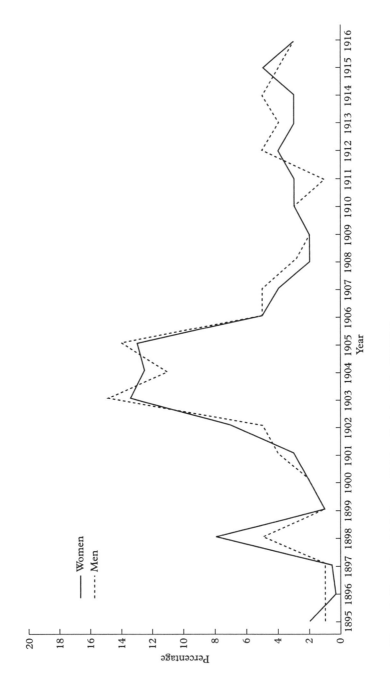

Figure 1. Years in which future Bolsheviks joined the RSDLP

2   The underground

At midday on 23 February 1913, Konkordiia Samoilova, the priest's daughter from Irkutsk, watched happily as a crowd gathered in St. Petersburg to commemorate the newly established socialist holiday, International Woman's Day. Samoilova had worked long and hard to persuade her party comrades to support the meeting. They had been skeptical because they thought the project sounded feminist; and besides, they argued, working-class women would not come. Only reluctantly had the St. Petersburg party committee finally given Samoilova permission to proceed, and so she felt vindicated on that cold winter morning when a crowd of people, many women workers among them, began presenting tickets for admission at the door to the Kalashnikov Stock Exchange. For the next several hours, the overflow audience filled a large hall within the temple of capitalism in Russia's leading city and listened attentively while speakers detailed the long hours, low pay, hazardous conditions, and sexual harassment that plagued the lives of Russia's female factory workers. As she watched, Samoilova realized that she had found the subject of her party career; she was going to concentrate on the female proletariat.[1]

In 1913 Konkordiia Samoilova was a seasoned Bolshevichka with more than a decade's experience in the hard world of the party's underground organization. Moving continually from assignment to assignment, she had lived in more dirty, dismal boarding houses than she could count, in cities scattered all across the Russian Empire. She had learned how to print leaflets on balky hectograph machines, how to drop pamphlets and newspapers at factory gates without being spotted by watchmen, how to persuade workers to meet with her secretly to study socialism. She had been attacked by women who accused her of being a prostitute because they had seen her with their husbands. The police had arrested her four times between 1902 and 1913 and had held her in prison for a year, but they had not been able to produce enough evidence to sentence her to

---

[1] *Zhenshchiny v revoliutsii* (Moscow, 1959), 96–98.

Siberian exile. In the course of her party work she had met and fallen in love with another Social Democrat, Arkadii Samoilov, a Jewish native of St. Petersburg, with whom she had lived for several years. By 1912, when Samoilova took an assignment as a founding editor of the newspaper *Pravda*, she was becoming one of the leading Bolshevichki, but she continued to see herself as simply another rank-and-filer. Most Bolshevichki lived as she did, toiling away in the half-light of the underground to keep the movement together and to spread its message.

The object of the Bolshevichki's devotion, the Russian Social-Democratic Labor Party, was at that time divided into several factions. Of these, the best known are the two famous groupings, the Mensheviks and the Bolsheviks, which developed after 1902 as a consequence of arguments over how to organize revolution in Russia. Bolshevichki – female Bolsheviks – followed Lenin in believing that the party must be tightly organized, disciplined, and secretive. The Mensheviks, among whom there were many women as well, aspired to a more open and democratic kind of party; their primary spokesperson, Iulii Martov, declared that only such an organization could develop the support among the masses of the underprivileged that would enable it to play a leading role during political upheavals. As important, however, as the "lateral" rift between the factions was the "vertical" separation between the party's leadership, which lived abroad to avoid arrest, and the majority of the SDs, who worked within Russia. The émigrés, led by G. V. Plekhanov, V. I. Zasulich, P. B. Akselrod, Iu. O. Martov, F. I. Dan, V. I. Lenin, and L. D. Trotsky, wrote theoretical treatises on how to make revolution and attempted to set policy for the movement. The mass of party members, males and females together, printed broadsides, smuggled in newspapers and books sent by the leaders, and ran circles of students and workers. They also labored to stay out of police custody, which required maintaining a far-flung network of conspirators who moved around Russia carrying forged identity papers in false-bottomed suitcases.

Most Bolshevichki did as Samoilova did, that is, they found the mission they had been seeking working within Russia. The world of the revolutionaries was a far more egalitarian place than the conventional society they had left, for the Social Democrats believed that women should work as men's equals in the party. The party also needed every able-bodied person it could recruit. Thus principle and necessity supported one another, with the result that there was very little gender-based division of labor among these revolutionaries. Bolshevichki organized printing presses, ran workers' circles, and learned how to make bombs and to fire guns. Women also served as leaders on party committees, and a few, among them Inessa Armand, Evgeniia Bosh, Alexandra Kollontai,

Nadezhda Krupskaia, Elena Stasova, and Rozaliia Zemliachka, also became active in the party's top leadership. Nowhere in law-abiding Russia could women find a life so emancipated from the constraints of their nation's patriarchal traditions.

The Bolshevichki also found in the underground new identities and new communities to replace those they had fled in their escape from convention. Russia's Social Democrats saw themselves as a band of comrades armed with a powerful understanding of their world, whose purpose it was to educate the workers and provide them with leadership in the coming revolution. The revolution would give birth to a socialist utopia that was politically decentralized, democratic, and harmonious. It would create an ideal community, ultimately global in expanse, from which class, gender, ethnic, and religious divisions would be banished, their sway having been replaced by a universalist humanism that would draw people together in perfect equality. Until the revolution came, the revolutionaries would prefigure the future by creating among themselves a liberated, unbigoted fellowship. It is true that the Social Democrats did not put as much stress on the revolutionaries' revolutionizing themselves as did other socialist groups, such as, for example, the anarchists. But just as sixteenth-century Calvinists had believed in predestination and sought to demonstrate their own election, so too did the Mensheviks and the Bolsheviks believe that they must conduct themselves better than the ordinary people in the society they inhabited. Consequently their idea of their movement, and hence the commitments and mores they accepted as conditions of its success, included the notion that they should create among themselves an egalitarian, supportive community, a tiny prototype of the brave new world.[2]

It was not always easy for them to maintain this essentially rosy view of the future. They were under constant police assault; the working class was usually reluctant to follow them to the barricades; and they themselves were often unsure how to encourage revolution in a nation as vast as Russia. Many SDs, including perhaps as many as 20 percent of the Bolshevichki, became discouraged and dropped out of the party, especially after the storm of 1905 had given way to an uneasy political calm. (See table 8.) A core membership held on because Russia's political situation remained so unacceptable that it sustained the SDs' sense of their own righteousness, as well as providing them with an audience among the

---

[2] For an interesting examination of the way such ideas functioned among a small group of Social Democrats, see Dave Pretty, "The Saints of the Revolution: Political Activists in 1890s Ivanovo-Voznesensk and the Path of Most Resistance," *Slavic Review* 54 (Summer 1995): 276–304. See, as well, Michael Walzer, *The Revolution of the Saints: A Study in the Origins of Radical Politics*, reprint of the original 1965 ed. (New York, 1974).

Table 8 *Prerevolutionary drop-out rate*

Years when people left the party permanently	Social Democrats leaving the party permanently					
	PereI[a]		PereII[b]		PK[c]	
	Men (%) (N=158)	Women (%) (N=58)	Men (%) (N=274)	Women (%) (N=62)	Men (%) (N=202)	Women (%) (N=33)
1905–11	18.3	12.1	20.4	17.8	7.4	12.1
1912–17	1.3	1.7	2.5	4.8		
Died before 1917	10.1	3.4	7.3	1.6	—	—
In party in 1917	41.8[d]	43.1[d]	62.0	51.6	76.2	63.6
Unknown	28.5	39.6	7.7	24.2	16.3	24.2
Total	100.0	99.9	99.9	100.0	99.9	99.9

Note: The data bases were not used for this table because they include only people who remained in the party. Data that included people who left the party were available from the biographical indices compiled by the editors of the volumes cited below.

[a] *Perepiska V. I. Lenina i redaktsii gazety "Iskra" s sotsial-demokraticheskimi organizatsiiami v Rossii, 1900–1903 gg.*, 3 vols. (Moscow, 1969), vol. III.

[b] *Perepiska V. I. Lenina i rukovodimykh im uchrezhdenii RSDRP s partiinymi organizatsiiami, 1905–1907gg.*, 3 vols. (Moscow, 1982–86), vol. III, part 2.

[c] Institut istorii partii Leningradskogo obkoma KPSS, Filial instituta Marksizma-Leninizma pri TsK KPSS, *Peterburgskii komitet RSDRP. Protokoly i materialy zasedanii, iiul' 1902–fevral' 1917* (Leningrad, 1986). This sample contains only Bolsheviks.

[d] These figures are so low because they include only Bolsheviks. The *Iskra* organization contained a large number of people who became Mensheviks; the editors of the indices from which this table was constructed did not list Mensheviks as "still in the party" in 1917.

disgruntled. The party also survived because its members kept faith with the cause and with one another, and kept believing in the idea that what they were doing was worth the hardship and risks it entailed. The movement thus managed to preserve its core personnel and collective identity.

The Bolshevichki and collective identity

To understand what sort of revolutionaries the Bolshevichki became and why they remained revolutionaries, it is essential to begin with an analysis of their beliefs and their commitments. The concept of collective identity, developed for the study of social movements, is useful here. A collective identity may be said to consist of three elements. One is a worldview that embraces a conception of the world as it really is and an alternative vision of what it might ideally become. Another element is a conceptualization of the movement itself that lays out the proper spheres of action for the movement and its goals and defines the proper character of members. And the third element in a collective identity is the movement's group memory, that is, shared interpretations of common experiences. Collective identities are more than ideologies, for they contain not just intellectual constructs, such as Marxism, but also powerful affective ties. Expressing self-definitions, personal loyalties, and the sense of community, they provide what might be called a corporate self-consciousness. Collective identities can be precisely defined if a group is small, short-lived, or very focused in its objectives. Large organizations are more likely to develop more general patterns of identification, under which a diversity of people can shelter. Such was the case with the Russian Social Democrats, who, as we have seen, attracted recruits from very different backgrounds. All of the party's recruits could accept its capacious "collective identity," while also affiliating with various subgroups. The Bolsheviks and Mensheviks were the largest and best defined of such subgroups, but there were others as well, some of which crossed the ideological lines drawn between the factions. People who specialized in work in the underground had a strong sense of themselves as distinct from the party leaders. Working-class Social Democrats were aware of themselves as different from party members who came from more privileged backgrounds. And Bolshevichki defined themselves as women within this predominantly male organization in ways that both set them apart from the males and at the same time asserted their fundamental sameness.[3]

The Bolshevichki fully believed and participated in the Social Democrats' general collective identity. They were revolutionaries who, subscribing to the Marxist interpretation of history, dedicated themselves to leading the working class toward a socialist future of equality and communal living. Yet they also established a more particular identity as female Bolsheviks. There were many elements in this identity, as we shall see; but the analysis of the whole can profitably begin with the examination of one core element, the Bolshevichki's sense of themselves as "hard" revolutionaries. *Tverdokamennaia*, "Hard-as-a-rock," was an alias sometimes used by Rozaliia Zemliachka. Stasova took "Absolute" as her underground name. Samoilova was nicknamed "*Surovaia Na-*

[3] On collective identities, see Verta Taylor and Nancy E. Whittier, "Collective Identity in Social Movement Communities," in Aldon D. Morris and Carol McClurg Mueller, eds., *Frontiers in Social Movement Theory* (New Haven, Conn., 1992), 104–29; Debra Friedman and Doug McAdam, "Collective Identity and Activism: Networks, Choices, and the Life of a Social Movement," ibid., 156–73. On the mentality of underground workers, see R. C. Elwood, *Russian Social Democracy in the Underground* (Assen, Netherlands, 1974), esp. 75–87.

tasha," severe Natasha; others who worked with her said she was *strogaia*, stern. Evgeniia Bosh was called "serious" by those who knew her. Inna Armand, Inessa Armand's daughter, remembered her mother as "restrained" and "reserved." Inessa wrote to Inna in the summer of 1915, "Life and life's many scrapes that I have had to get through have shown me that I am strong, have shown me that many times, and I know it."[4]

The Bolshevichki declared *tverdost*, hardness, to be their defining characteristic, and in so doing, laid claim to an entire set of revolutionary virtues. For hardness had many meanings and associations to contemporaries. A woman who was *tverdaia* was unsentimental, determined, efficient, and industrious. She was utterly dedicated to her work and ruthless toward opponents. She was coldly rational and unsentimental. Her emotions were always under control. Alexander Rosnovskii summed up the concept in describing Evgeniia Bosh, his co-worker in Kiev: "We always said that Evgeniia Bogdanovna Bosh was a 'typical Bolshevichka.' And it is true that all the best that was in the Bolshevik Party was concentrated in her – straightforwardness, selfless loyalty to the revolution, steadfast faith in the final victory of the proletariat, and that principled, hard-as-a-rock [*tverdokamennaia*] quality that did not allow her to make any ideological concessions."[5]

Tverdost was highly valued by male Bolsheviks as well. Indeed several generations of Russian revolutionaries had considered *tverdost* a virtue or, more properly, had construed it as a term embracing a collection of closely associated virtues. The most famous evocation of *tverdost* was in the fictional character of Rakhmetov, the revolutionary ascetic who wanders in at the end of Nikolai Chernyshevskii's famous novel *What is to Be Done?* (1863) to preach a regimen of self-abnegation in preparation for the coming armageddon. In the view of the revolutionaries of the 1860s and 1870s, *tverdost* was a repudiation of all the indecisiveness, the sentimentality, the moral flabbiness, and incompetence that were the abiding sins of the Russian intelligentsia and the liberal nobility. It was also a repudiation of national religious and folk traditions that prized emotional expressiveness.

When they came onto the revolutionary scene in the 1890s, the Social Democrats appropriated hardness as a quality that differentiated them from their principal rivals, the Socialist Revolutionaries. The SDs drew support for this contention from Karl Marx himself, who had condemned his socialist predecessors, Henri de Saint-Simon, Charles Fourier, and

---

[4] I. F. Armand, *Stat'i, rechi, pis'ma* (Moscow, 1975), 235–38, 12, 236.
[5] A. Rosnovskii, "Iz epokhi 'Zvezdy' i 'Pravdy' v Kieve," *Litopys revoliutsii*, no. 6 (1926): 130–31.

Plate 5. Evgeniia Bosh, 1908.

Robert Owen, as utopians, woolly-headed dreamers who had deluded themselves that they could build a new world by shepherding a few followers into carefully organized communes. Eschewing such quasi-religious enthusiasms, Marx had created what he imagined to be a rigorous analysis of social development based on that hardest of all hard-minded sciences, economics. Russian Social Democrats transferred Marx's critique of the utopians to the populist socialists of their own country. The well-meaning populists, the SDs argued, revealed their fatal softness and intellectual fuzziness when they proposed that the torpid, conservative peasants were the revolutionary class. The Marxists saw themselves as enemies of such sentimental illusions. They were the dispassionate instruments of changes which were emerging inevitably from the machine-like workings of political economy and the reality of a burgeoning, exploited proletariat.

To be hard was to think rationally, to examine facts and draw

Plate 6. Elena Rozmirovich, circa 1905.

conclusions in a disciplined, logical way. It was also to be realistic, strong-willed, and goal-oriented. When the Social Democrats turned from condemning the SRs to criticizing one another, they quite naturally employed the same argumentative weaponry. Lenin, the leader of the Bolsheviks, declared that he alone was hard-minded enough to apply Marx properly to Russia's realities and deduce the appropriate strategy for making revolution. Russia's economic and political development demonstrated to him that only a highly organized party of disciplined revolutionaries could lead the proletariat to victory. The Mensheviks shot back that only an organization open to the broadest possible participation could develop the roots in the working class that would enable it to play a mobilizing role when the great uprising came. Lenin was more the swashbuckling Jacobin than the rigorous Marxist, they declared, thereby attempting to score an intellectual point while conceding another – his hardness as a revolutionary. Thus hardness became a label particularly appropriated and valued by Lenin and by his followers, who proclaimed themselves more resolute, more daring, more *tverdye* than the Mensheviks.[6]

When, in turn, female Bolsheviks appropriated this generally Social-Democratic, particularly Bolshevik, virtue, hardness took on additional nuances, for those weaknesses of character of which *tverdost* was the antithesis were not only thought to be characteristically Russian, they were also considered universally feminine. By adopting hardness as their defining characteristic, the Bolshevichki asserted that they possessed qualities – rationality, self-control, subordination of the personal to the public and the general – that European society construed as natural to men, not women. In effect, the Bolshevichki declared that they too could size up the world coldly and rationally, and bear the burden of changing it. Inessa put this connection between *tverdost* and traditional notions of the feminine succinctly when she characterized other people's reactions to her: "When we met you, you seemed to us so gentle, fragile, and weak, but it turns out you are iron."[7]

The Bolshevichki were unusual among Russia's female revolutionaries in the emphasis they put on *tverdost*. There is too little information on female Mensheviks to make a definitive judgment, but *tverdost* does not appear to have ranked high in their values. As to the Socialist Revolutionaries, enough is known about them to say definitely that they did not prize hardness in women. Rather, they considered the crowning virtue of the revolutionary woman to be moral integrity, an integrity expressed in self-sacrifice and particularly in the suicidal self-sacrifice of an act of terrorism. This conception of the nature of the female radical was closer to that held by the populists of the 1870s than to the Bolshevichki's ideals, and closer as well to Russian religious traditions that sanctified women's self-sacrifice.[8] By contrast, the Bolshevichki agreed with their male comrades that assassinations were politically inefficacious and therefore

---

[6] On the earliest stages of this argument (1903–05), see Abraham Ascher, *Pavel Axelrod and the Development of Menshevism* (Cambridge, Mass., 1972), 168–269; Samuel H. Baron, *Plekhanov: The Father of Russian Marxism* (Stanford, Calif., 1963), 208–53; Israel Getzler, *Martov: A Political Biography of a Russian Social Democrat* (Cambridge, 1967), 45–89; and Robert Service, *Lenin: A Political Life*, vol. I, *The Strengths of Contradiction* (Bloomington, Ind., 1985), 85–121.

[7] Armand, *Stat'i*, 236. The distinction between the public, rational, and masculine, and the domestic, emotional, and feminine had been strongly drawn since the Enlightenment. See Joan B. Landes, *Women and the Public Sphere in the Age of the French Revolution* (Ithaca, N. Y., 1988).

[8] The SR ethic for female revolutionaries is expressed in Isaac Steinberg, *Spiridonova, Revolutionary Terrorist*, trans. and ed. Gwenda David and Eric Mosbacher, intro. Henry W. Nevinson, originally published 1935 (Freeport, N. Y., 1971); and in I. Kakhovskaia, "Iz vospominanii o zhenskom katorge," *Katorga i ssylka*, no. 22 (1926): 145–62; no. 23 (1926): 170–85. On the populists of the 1870s, see Barbara Alpern Engel, *Mothers and Daughters: Women of the Intelligentsia in Nineteenth-Century Russia* (Cambridge, 1983).

pointless. Furthermore, the Bolshevichki consciously resisted opportunities to transfigure themselves into female martyrs, after the populist tradition, primarily because they would not accept any definition of themselves that differentiated them from men.

For the Bolshevichki, like many independent women of their generation throughout Europe, understood at some level of consciousness that belonging to an organization of men required proving that they could be like men.[9] Adopting *tverdost* as their ideal asserted their ability to behave as male revolutionaries did, and thereby constituted one of their claims to acceptance within the movement. But it also opens them perhaps to the criticism that they subordinated their own welfare (some would even suggest their own nature) to their desire to be accepted. Feminists have argued that women in organizations of men usually must prove that they are capable of being what men admire in other men. If they are successful, they are declared "one of the boys" – faint praise that treats them as exceptions to the generally unfortunate female rule. The problem is that, by inadvertently indulging patriarchal prejudices, such women put themselves in a position from which they are unable either to change those prejudices or to alter the larger goals defined by the male leadership. To endorse the masculinist values prevailing within any movement, feminists have argued, is to concede gender issues in favor of what is often imagined to be the higher good for all.

Of course, the Bolshevichki would have rejected this analysis as misguided. They would have considered it nonsense to suggest that by accepting the values of Russian Social Democracy they reinforced the prejudice that the male was the standard against which women must be measured. Rather, they believed (as did many far less radical female social activists of their time) that they could overturn patriarchy by proving its premises false, by demonstrating that women too could be rational and tough. The Bolshevichki did not believe that *tverdost* was an attribute indissolubly linked to the masculine. Theirs was an age of science, when debates often saw "tender (but irrational) sentimentalists" arrayed against "tough (but hard-hearted) empiricists." The Bolshevichki, like all dutiful children of the Enlightenment, considered rationality, fortitude, and all the other virtues embraced by the concept of *tverdost* as universal ideals. Women, poor men, the people of despised minorities – indeed, all the disfranchised of the earth – had been told for centuries that they were intellectually incapable of reason and higher scientific understanding. By

---

[9] These attitudes were common among liberal and radical women throughout the European world in the early twentieth century. See, for example, the discussion of female physicians in Regina Markell Morantz, Cynthia Stodola Pomerleau, and Carole Hansen Fenichel, eds., *In Her Own Words: Oral Histories of Women Physicians* (Westport, Conn., 1982), 27. For a more general discussion of the attitudes of female professionals, see Nancy G. Cott, *The Grounding of Modern Feminism* (New Haven, Conn., 1987), 243–67.

demonstrating that women could be as rational as men and no more moved by emotional or other secondary considerations, the Bolshevichki believed they were moving toward a new world that would be free of invidious distinctions of class, ethnicity, and gender. They saw themselves as exemplars of scientific reason, not mindless imitators of a fraudulent, masculinist stereotype.

Women in the party leadership

The Bolshevichki further believed that they demonstrated the strength of their convictions by their successes as revolutionaries. Despite the deeply patriarchal society that surrounded them, they earned acceptance from their male comrades. Male and female SDs worked together, shared assignments, and relied on one another, at a time when throughout Europe women were barred from nearly all political activities. Indeed, some Bolshevichki, both within Russia and among the émigrés, were party leaders.

Before 1917, the basic unit of the party was the city committee. Some city committees were well-structured organizations controlling hundreds of revolutionaries, as in St. Petersburg or Moscow; others simply included the few Social Democrats in a town who were not in jail at the moment. Throughout the prerevolutionary period a series of national and émigré committees aspired to establish control over these widely scattered, very unstable city organizations, but generally they failed. National committee leaders, even if they had possessed more perfect communications networks, lacked the commanding stature of the émigré leaders. The émigrés lived abroad, scattered in small communities across France, Germany, Austria, and Switzerland. There they conducted Marxist analysis of Russian developments, formulated strategies and tactics, and maintained networks of supporters that extended into the city committees in Russia. They also published pamphlets and newspapers for distribution within Russia, the most famous being *Iskra* (*The Spark*, 1900–05). But the leaders, despite their standing as Russian Social Democracy's theoreticians, could not dominate the underground from abroad, given the enormous difficulties of communication and the fact that many underground workers regarded them as out of touch with Russian realities. Consequently, the prerevolutionary Social-Democratic Party remained a loosely linked network of city committees, the members of which honored the ideological leadership of the exiled luminaries, but distrusted any dictation from abroad.[10]

---

[10] The leaders of the émigrés were Plekhanov, Akselrod, Martov, Dan, Lenin, and Trotsky. See Allan K. Wildman, *The Making of a Workers' Revolution: Russian Social Democracy, 1891–1903* (Chicago, 1967); and Elwood, *Russian Social Democracy in the Underground*.

The evidence suggests that female Social Democrats were about as likely as males to hold party office, and that they constituted a significant presence on city committees. (See table 9.) Women were particularly common on the largest, most important committees, those in Moscow and St. Petersburg. For example, from the last months of 1904 to June 1907, the St. Petersburg committee had a total of 137 members, 27 of whom (20 percent) were women.[11] It might be argued that women's presence, so conspicuous in the party's leadership, was evidence of the genuine egalitarianism that prevailed within the Social-Democratic Party. Yet it probably also was a function of the fact that the party was so chronically short of people that it could ill afford to discriminate. Furthermore, many Bolshevichki had the education required to be effective committee members or secretaries. Among Bolshevichki, it was in fact the better educated who held party office. (See tables 10 and 11.)

The Bolsheviks may have had more female leaders than the Mensheviks. Of the twenty-seven women who served on the St. Petersburg committee from 1904 to 1907, for example, twenty-five were Bolshevichki, and two Menshevichki.[12] Comparable statistics are not available for other city committees, unfortunately. And it is also true that even determining who was a Menshevik and who was a Bolshevik is difficult, because the lines between the factions remained fluid, with many people moving back and forth over the years and others refusing to join either side. Sufficient evidence does exist, however, to suggest that the number of women of either faction who reached the ranks of the top leadership, whether among the theoreticians, on the Central Committee, or on other national or émigré committees, remained very small, amounting to no more than a dozen people in the entire prerevolutionary period.

The absence of women from the foremost positions attests to the fact that the Russian Social Democrats were more influenced by patriarchal ideas than they were willing to admit. Those influences show up as well in the assignment of jobs on the city committees. There the policy-making office of organizational secretary tended to go to a man, the administrative office of technical secretary to a woman. This was not a hard-and-fast distinction; women did serve as organizational secretaries, and since the great majority of SDs were men, most technical secretaries necessarily were men. But the division of labor appears often enough to suggest the existence of an assumption among Social Democrats that men should make the major decisions while women should do the support work of handing out assignments and handling money.

[11] The calculation of the percentages of women on the St. Petersburg committee was derived from the biographical index published in T. P. Bondarevskaia, *Peterburgskii komitet RSDRP v revoliutsii, 1905–1907 gg.* (Leningrad, 1975), 294–311.   [12] Ibid.

Table 9 *Party office-holding before 1917*

	Women (%) (N = 318)	Men (%) (N = 2124)
Local committee[a]		
Member	9.7	16.8
Secretary	11.3	5.5
Regional committee member	11.6	2.3
Emigré committee member	1.6	—
Party congress delegate	1.6	14.2
Central Committee member	0.9	0.8
Held no office	61.0	60.3
Unknown	2.2	—
Total	99.9	99.9

Note: The highest office held by each individual was coded.
[a] Raion or city committee.

Table 10 *Education, social origins, and prerevolutionary party office-holding by Bolshevichki*

	Bolshevichki holding party office		
Social origins	Primary education (%)	Secondary education (%)	Higher education (%)
Nobility	—	72.7 (11)	50.0 (18)
Intelligentsia	—	61.1 (18)	69.2 (13)
Sluzhashchie	—	33.3 (6)	22.2 (9)
Meshchanstvo	25.0 (4)	61.5 (13)	60.0 (10)
Workers	22.6 (31)	38.5 (13)	—
Peasantry	14.3 (14)	33.3 (9)	66.7 (3)

Note: The numbers in parentheses represent the total N in that category (i.e., women of that class and educational level), from which the percentages of such women holding party office were calculated.

Table 11 *Education and prerevolutionary party office-holding by Bolshevichki*

Education	Held office (%)	Held no office (%)
No formal	3.2 (3)	5.2 (7)
Primary	9.7 (9)	35.1 (47)
Secondary	50.5 (47)	32.8 (44)
Higher	36.6 (34)	26.9 (36)
Total	100.0 (93)	100.0 (134)

Note: Figures in parentheses are base Ns for the adjacent percentages.

So long as the Bolsheviks remained powerless and persecuted, they did not have to acknowledge that they harbored such unexamined beliefs. Comparing themselves to the larger society, they could take pride in how far they had advanced beyond its much more rigid gender segregation. While feminists in the democracies battled for the vote, Bolshevichki were leading party committees. Thousands of them proved their *tverdost* by surviving for years in the underground, even enduring long terms in prison and Siberian exile. In short, the Bolshevichki not only surmounted the difficulties of being revolutionaries in Russia; they made many significant contributions to the Social-Democratic Party.

Stasova and Zemliachka in the underground

The possibilities and the limitations of women's activity in the underground are well illustrated in the careers of Rozaliia Zemliachka and Elena Stasova. These two Bolshevichki headed the very important city committees in Moscow and St. Petersburg respectively.[13] Stasova and Zemliachka also acted as the specially designated agents of the émigré leadership, moving around Russia to rebuild organizations decimated by arrest and cultivating support for Lenin as they went.

Of the two women, Stasova was the more important, for she served as technical secretary of the St. Petersburg committee from 1901 to 1906. To hold any underground job for five years required considerable skill and luck, given the efficiency with which the police rounded up revolutionaries. Stasova survived so long because she had a genius for *tekhnika*, the Russian word meaning "technique" that embraced all the tasks connected with running an underground organization. *Tekhnika* included arranging meeting places, hiding revolutionaries on the run, collecting and disbursing money, keeping communications open with other party organizations within Russia and abroad, and distributing illegal literature. The St. Petersburg committee (and indeed all the larger party committees within Russia) was supposed to be led by three secretaries, one in charge of organization (setting policy and supervising all operations), one of propaganda (managing publications and propagandists), and one of *tekhnika*. Stasova was always a technical secretary.

This young lady from the cream of the intelligentsia who, as was noted earlier, chose for herself the nickname "Absolute" (after toying with "Categorical Imperative" and rejecting it as too much of a mouthful),

---

[13] The size of the St. Petersburg organization waxed and waned with the revolutionary tide, from a low of several hundred in early 1904 up to a high of 7,300 in early 1907. Any such figures about the underground party should always be viewed as rough approximations (ibid., 23, 292–93).

built a reputation as the quintessential *tverdaia* Bolshevichka. She was courageous; in fact, she got a thrill out of dodging the police and leading them down blind alleys. She was self-disciplined, even austere, with very high standards of dedication and decorum for herself and others. She easily intimidated people, even fractious revolutionaries. A. V. Shotman, who worked under her command in 1904, later confessed, "No offense meant, but I was rather afraid of her and prepared reports on work in my raion [neighborhood] very carefully, sooner underestimating the number of members in circles and the number of meetings held than there were in reality so that she wouldn't suspect that I had embellished the state of affairs in my raion."[14] Stasova had a prodigious memory, an important quality in an organization that avoided keeping written records for fear they might fall into police hands. She also had enormous energy, usually sleeping no more than five or six hours a night. And she was very well connected in St. Petersburg society, which made her an effective fund-raiser.

It is a sign of the profound political alienation pervasive in Russian society that Stasova could persuade upper-class people to contribute to a party of revolutionaries pledged to destroy the social order on which the well-being of those contributors depended. The most surreal of her money-raising ventures were the receptions she held with her parents' help. Well-dressed members of the capital's intellectual and social elite came to Poliksena and Dmitrii Stasov's huge apartment in downtown St. Petersburg to hear lectures by university professors, artists, and composers. On the surface these were simply gatherings of the intelligentsia; the topics of the lectures were always politically acceptable to the authorities and no discussions of revolutionaries or revolution ever darkened the placid atmosphere. But the guests were expected to drop donations on a tray in the foyer, and they could buy cognac or vodka, disguised as tea or water. (The Stasovs had no liquor license.) Elena Stasova usually stood close to the money, ready to snatch it up should the police arrive, for such solicitation of contributions was illegal. The Okhrana, the police agency charged with suppressing revolutionaries, in fact knew that the Stasovs were collecting money for the Social Democrats, but was loathe to move against them after 1900, because a raid in that year had netted the local Okhrana commander a reprimand from the high-ranking relative of one of the guests.[15]

[14] A. V. Shotman, *Zapiski starogo bol'shevika*, 3rd ed. (Leningrad, 1963), 93.
[15] The outraged guest was Sofia Panina, a well-known Petersburg philanthropist, her powerful relative a Prince Viazemskii, an official in the court system (E. D. Stasova, *Vospominaniia* [Moscow, 1969], 46). Sim Freiden quotes from a 1904 Okhrana report describing the purpose of the Stasovs' receptions in *Muzyka – revoliutsii*, 2nd ed. (Moscow, 1970), 365–66.

Stasova was also very good at maintaining communications between Social-Democratic organizations, both within Russia and abroad. She committed to memory the names (or aliases) of hundreds of people, their addresses, and the addresses of apartments where they could hide from the police. She built up caches of forged passports and other documents. She worked out codes for correspondence, mastered writing in invisible ink, helped people on the run with their disguises, and survived numerous mishaps and catastrophes – such as when she once mistakenly died a comrade's hair green! Practiced at spotting police surveillance, she knew how to transport loads of illegal pamphlets around the city in a briefcase. At a high point of her success in late 1902 and early 1903, the St. Petersburg Social-Democratic organization was producing and distributing at least one broadside every week, in runs of 10,000 copies, and bringing in 360 pounds of books and newspapers per shipment from abroad.[16]

Thus as secretary in charge of *tekhnika*, Stasova played a central role in maintaining the revolutionary organization of St. Petersburg. But the Social-Democratic underground did more than smuggle materials, people, and propaganda. It also struggled to chart its course through Russia's rocky landscape, and in the process fell into the arguments over strategy and tactics that produced the division between Bolsheviks and Mensheviks. Stasova was an early follower of Lenin, as were many of the Bolshevichki who later rose to prominence in the party. In 1901 she supported *Iskra*, the newspaper he was then editing with Georgii Plekhanov and Iulii Martov. *Iskra* rejected the argument of some Social Democrats that Russia could evolve gradually through parliamentary democracy to socialism; it declared instead that only revolution could succeed in overthrowing the established authorities. When Lenin began to contend with Martov in 1903 over how to bring on the revolution, Stasova agreed with him again. The organization open to all comers that the Mensheviks espoused struck her as tactically impractical because it would be easily infiltrated by police informants as well as diluted by people who had not really made up their minds to be revolutionaries. Neither sort could be counted on in a crisis. Stasova believed, as did Lenin, that the key to a successful revolution lay in establishing an organization of professional revolutionaries who had the training and the discipline to lead a politically inexperienced working class in the formidable task of overthrowing the tsarist government.

[16] S. M. Levidova and E. G. Salita, *Elena Dmitrievna Stasova. Biograficheskii ocherk* (Leningrad, 1969), 71–79, 153; Stasova, *Vospominaniia*, 34–41; N. E. Burenin, *Pamiatnye gody. Vospominaniia* (Leningrad, 1967), 9–65, 70–73; *Perepiska V. I. Lenina i redaktsii gazety "Iskra" s sotsial-demokraticheskimi organizatsiiami v Rossii, 1900–1903 gg.*, 3 vols. (Moscow, 1969), vol. III, 289; and Burenin, *Liudi bol'shevistskogo podpol'ia* (Moscow, 1958), 9–18.

Throughout the prerevolutionary period, Stasova was a staunch Bolshevik. For their part, Lenin and his wife Krupskaia considered her an important ally because of both her standing within the St. Petersburg organization and her abilities in *tekhnika*. From 1901 to 1906 Stasova acted as their advocate, working closely with agents they sent to the city and expressing often in correspondence her warm regard for them, her support for Lenin's ideas, and her ardent dislike of what was emerging as the Menshevik position.[17]

Stasova's influence on other Social Democrats is difficult to assess, but Bolsheviks who worked with her at the time later credited her with playing an important part in sustaining support for Lenin within the St. Petersburg organization. Her letters show her avidly arguing for Bolshevik positions from the *Iskra* days through 1907. She brought to this conflict in opinion a reputation for probity and relentlessness that must have impressed less decisive, less experienced revolutionaries. Rozaliia Zemliachka, an equally *tverdaia* Bolshevichka, wrote happily to Lenin in December 1904 that the dismal state of affairs in St. Petersburg had improved since her last letter, if only because "Absolute" had been released from prison.[18]

Yet for all her resoluteness and for all the regard other revolutionaries paid her, Stasova herself sought no independent leadership role within the St. Petersburg organization. She was usually willing to submit to the authority of those people Lenin sent from abroad to be organizational secretaries, and she was always willing to seek direction from Lenin himself. A letter she wrote him and Krupskaia on 23 June 1905 contains a typical request for guidance: "I beg you to set forth for me the plan for the current general organizational work that you consider correct. I would also like you to explain at length what you see as my personal responsibilities."[19] Stasova never attempted to be organizational secretary, even when she considered the people holding that office inept. On 24 June 1905, she wrote again to Lenin and Krupskaia, "De facto I have to give orders to people, for no one here is doing it and no one is giving orders. The general

---

[17] For representative letters, see *Perepiska V. I. Lenina i redaktsii gazety "Iskra"*, vol. II, 489–90, 504–05; vol. III, 20–21, 36–37, 69–71, 81–82, 165–67; "Perepiska V. I. Lenina i N. K. Krupskoi s Peterburgskoi organizatsiei," *Proletarskaia revoliutsiia*, no. 3 (1925): 23, 30–31.

[18] "Perepiska V. I. Lenina i N. K. Krupskoi s Peterburgskoi organizatsiei," *Proletarskaia revoliutsiia*, no. 3: 23. On Stasova's importance to Lenin, see A. Shotman, "Na vtorom s"ezde partii," *Proletarskaia revoliutsiia*, no. 1 (1927): 214, 215; Rozaliia Essen, quoted in G. A. Krovitskii, *Put' starogo bol'shevika. K shestidesiatiletiiu E. D. Stasovoi* (Moscow, 1933), 28; A. Il'in and V. Il'in, *Rozhdenie partii, 1883–1904* (Moscow, 1962), 111; and Levidova and Salita, *Stasova*, 59–87. References to her importance in the organization also occur in the correspondence. See Krovitskii, *Put' starogo bol'shevika*, 34–35, for a letter of 11 April 1905. See also Moscow, Institut Marksa–Engelsa–Lenina, *Partiia i revoliutsii 1905 goda. Dokumenty k istorii partii v 1905 godu* ([Moscow], 1934), 199–200.

[19] *Perepiska V. I. Lenina s rukovodimykh im uchrezhdenii RSDRP s partiinymi organizatsiiami, 1905–1907 gg.*, 3 vols. (Moscow, 1982–86), vol. II, part 2, 205.

situation is not very bright, and I expect little improvement, since there is no one . . . who is energetically running things, clearly formulating principles . . . and giving definite direction not only in the literary forms [broadsides] . . . but directly in the form of well-publicized pronouncements that could govern committees. I have talked about this . . . but my voice is not authoritative enough."[20]

Stasova was willing to take orders from abroad because she lacked confidence in her own intellectual abilities. She told a co-worker in the 1930s, "I am a speaking person, not a writing person." Later she described herself in her memoirs as "a technician and an organizer," not an ideologist and therefore not a policy-maker.[21] Since Social Democrats believed that ideology was the wellspring from which correct policies sprang, and since ideology and policy were typically made by the "theoreticians," that is, the leaders abroad who specialized in applying Marxist principles to Russian realities, Stasova looked for direction to them or to their emissaries. Her job was to keep the organization alive while they defined its direction. She would cling to this conception of her role until the end of her party career.

It seems odd that a woman who had grown up among highly educated people should be so lacking in confidence in her own intellectual abilities. Stasova's parents had given her an excellent education. Her father Dmitrii, the prominent attorney, tutored her himself, and her uncle Vladimir, the art and music critic, conducted a very affectionate, encouraging correspondence with her when she was a teenager. She had strong female role models: her mother and her aunt had both been feminists active for years in social causes; her principal tutor was Mariia Strakhova, a woman noted for radical views who had also tutored Kollontai. Stasova had acquitted herself capably under the guidance of all these people and had done well also at the Bestuzhevskii courses.

Ironically, her lack of confidence in her intellectual abilities may have arisen from the fact that she never cut her ties to the sheltering milieu in which she had grown up, and therefore never quite outgrew the definitions of her that prevailed within her family. Her very loving, very accomplished relatives had inadvertently taught her to doubt herself, for in the glittering circles they frequented she had always been assigned the role of the quiet, plain young woman who was to sit and admire the talents of the men who were the center of attention – her father, her uncle, artists such as Mussorgsky and Borodin. So Stasova modeled herself on her mother and aunt, and became an effective fund-raiser, organizer, and administrator. She could never shake herself loose from the notion, prevalent within the

---

[20] Moscow, Institut Marksa–Engelsa–Lenina, *Partiia i revoliutsii 1905 goda*, 193.
[21] Lidiia Bat', *Nezabyvaemye vstrechi* (Moscow, 1970), 21; Stasova, *Vospominaniia*, 33.

intelligentsia and within the Social-Democratic Party as well, that men generated the ideas and set the policy, while women took care of daily business. And indeed that is just what had always been done in the past. Stasova thus collaborated no less inadvertently than the people who loved her in limiting her scope of leadership.

Even Stasova, although she managed to avoid arrest longer than most revolutionaries, could not escape forever. In June 1904 the police picked her up for the first time. She then served eight months in prison. Dmitrii Stasov bailed his daughter out in December 1904 for the huge sum of 1,000 rubles; she went back to being technical secretary of the St. Petersburg committee. She held that post more or less continuously until the spring of 1907, but after 1904 she was hampered more than earlier by constant police surveillance.

Stasova also became entangled in a love affair that complicated her already difficult life. In 1905 she married a military doctor, Konstantin Krestnikov, who sympathized with her politics but was not himself a revolutionary. Krestnikov had been one of her contacts since at least 1902, receiving shipments of illegal publications, meeting her at railroad stations to hand over messages, even smuggling one of Lenin's pamphlets inside his M.D. dissertation. Stasova appears to have thought she could persuade this man whom she loved deeply to become a Bolshevik, but he refused and sought instead to convince her to leave the underground. When massive popular unrest swept Russia in 1905 and 1906, Stasova spent more time than ever in the underground, even leaving Russia for a time in the fall of 1905 to work with Krupskaia and Lenin abroad. The disagreement between her and her husband thus simmered throughout these turbulent years. Then, in 1907, Stasova finally agreed to quit her party work altogether in order to go to Tbilisi, Georgia, to nurse Krestnikov through an attack of tuberculosis.[22]

This trip to the Caucasus was a mission of mercy, but it was also a flight from St. Petersburg occasioned by a crisis in Stasova's belief in the revolutionary cause. She herself was ill with tuberculosis and needed a rest. She was also deeply depressed by the new political situation. The uprisings of 1905 had forced the tsar to grant limited civil liberties and authorize the establishment of a legislature, the Duma. As political unrest cooled in 1906 because of these concessions, the government regained control, then launched mass arrests of the revolutionaries. The radical left floundered in confusion and disarray, for the mass uprising on which it had fastened its hopes had come and gone, the workers were trudging off to their twelve-hour shifts in the factories again, the police were working

---

[22] Stasova, *Vospominaniia*, 39, 58, 61–63; Levidova and Salita, *Stasova*, 135, 172.

away more assiduously than ever, and many among the intelligentsia had become disillusioned with politics and withdrawn their support from revolutionary socialism. Thousands of Social Democrats, Stasova among them, dropped out of the underground altogether.

For a year or so Stasova devoted herself to her husband. "I live close to the person nearest and dearest to me," she wrote to a friend, Nikolai Burenin, in 1908. "I know that he needs me, that I bring a spark of light into his life." The couple could not resolve the differences between them, however, and by 1910 they had decided to separate permanently. Krestnikov left Tbilisi in the fall of that year. Shortly thereafter Stasova confided to Burenin, "There will always be a great grief in the depths of my soul that nothing will succeed in deadening." Decades later she was still mourning the loss of her husband; in 1959 she told Burenin, "Thirty-six years have gone by since Kostia died, and my soul always hurts when I simply remember him. And you know, the thoughts come independently of my will."[23]

As Stasova recovered from the collapse of her marriage, she began to interest herself in politics again. She did not go home to St. Petersburg, preferring instead to remain in Tbilisi, where she had secured a position teaching at a girls' gymnasium, but in 1911, when Bolshevik Suren Spandarian asked her to help out with some party work, she agreed. The year 1911 was one of rising worker unrest as well as a time when the Bolsheviks, recovering from the disarray that had followed the collapse of their revolutionary hopes in 1906, began to build a new party organization, one more independent of the Mensheviks. Her husband gone and prospects for the underground appearing to improve, Stasova came back. Her withdrawal from the movement and her subsequent return thus coincided almost perfectly with the ebb and flow of the revolutionary spirit common among Russia's Social Democrats after 1905.

This second stage of Stasova's underground career proved far shorter than the first, probably because the police had had her under surveillance all the time she had been in Tbilisi. In the summer of 1912, she was arrested. After ten months in prison, Stasova was tried and in 1913 she was given the very harsh sentence of permanent exile and loss of all the legal rights of the nobility. "Such a noble father has such a wicked daughter!," fumed one of the judges. "Give her deportation [for life]." Stasova knew that her family would help her to escape to western Europe, but she decided to serve her sentence instead. "What would I do abroad?," she asked decades later in her memoirs. "I am not a theoreti-

---

[23] Quoted in Levidova and Salita, *Stasova*, 172.

Plate 7. Rozaliia Zemliachka, circa 1905.

cian, not a literary person, and consequently after spending a short time abroad I would return to Russia and again fail and as a result [I would receive a sentence of] hard labor." Stasova went off to Irkutsk province in November 1913 with the fear that she would never again be allowed to live in European Russia.[24]

Rozaliia Zemliachka was as *tverdaia* a Bolshevichka as Stasova, but she

[24] The quotations are from Stasova, *Vospominaniia*, 113–14. On her party work in the Caucasus and her trial, see ibid., 59–61, 71; Levidova and Salita, *Stasova*, 102–03, 107, 135–38; and Pavel Podliashuk, *Bogatyrskaia simfoniia. Dokumental'naia povest' o E. D. Stasovoi* (Moscow, 1977), 68–70, 96. For more general coverage of her work after 1905, see "Perepiska V. I. Lenina i N. K. Krupskoi s Peterburgskoi organizatsiei," *Proletarskaia revoliutsiia*, no. 3: 22–23, 31–32, 35; Stasova, *Vospominaniia*, 75; *Perepiska V. I. Lenina s rukovodimykh im uchrezhdenii RSDRP*, vol. II, 9–11, 72–74, 205–06; Bondarevskaia, *Peterburgskii komitet*, 196–97; Moscow, Institut Marksa–Engelsa–Lenina, *Partiia i revoliutsii 1905 goda*, 192–93, 195–97, 199–200; and Stasova, "Iz vospominanii o partiinoi rabote do revoliutsii 1917 g.," *Proletarskaia revoliutsiia*, no. 12 (1927): 191–98.

suffered none of Stasova's doubts about her abilities as a policy-maker. Accordingly, she always insisted on being organizational, not technical, secretary. In 1902, after her husband, a revolutionary named Sh. Berlin, had died from tuberculosis, Zemliachka decided to become an Iskrist, that is, a person who worked to build support for Plekhanov's, Lenin's, and Martov's newspaper, with its calls for revolution. A friend of hers, the up-and-coming young Social Democrat Lev Bronstein (soon to be known as Trotsky), passed her name on to the St. Petersburg party committee, and soon I. I. Radchenko, a colleague of Stasova's, was reporting to Krupskaia that he had heard that Zemliachka was "a very valuable person, steady, devoted to the cause." He added: "Pero [Trotsky] has given her a very detailed recommendation." He had indeed, including his impression that Zemliachka was a forthright sort, though with a temper so prickly that she should not be assigned delicate tasks requiring diplomacy.

Krupskaia, married to Lenin since 1898, was now working as technical secretary to the *Iskra* organization, assigning people to jobs within and outside Russia, maintaining communications, and arranging the transport of the newspaper and other publications back to Russia. When she received the positive report on Zemliachka, she sent the new recruit orders to go to Odessa, where the local party leaders were dilatory and disorganized. Perhaps Krupskaia believed that a tactless but strong personality might win over local Social Democrats to *Iskra*. The city on the Black Sea was an important entry point for the newspaper, smuggled there by French sailors shipping out of Marseilles.[25]

Over the course of the next three years, Zemliachka became a leader in the underground. By March 1903 the Odessa party committee was firmly in the hands of the Iskrists and she had been elected their delegate to the upcoming Second Party Congress. She also served on the committee set up in Russia to coordinate elections to the congress and negotiate between the various party groups. In all these activities Zemliachka proved herself to be commanding, energetic, and hard-working. As indefatigable as Stasova, she was also just as resolutely pro-*Iskra* and then later pro-Lenin.[26]

In the summer of 1903 Zemliachka met Lenin for the first time at the Second Party Congress in London. She quickly declared her support for

[25] *Perepiska V. I. Lenina i redaktsii gazety "Iskri,"* vol. II, 394, 394. For others who concurred in this assessment of her, see ibid., 447.

[26] For correspondence about events in Odessa, see ibid., vol. II, 469, 531–32; vol. III, 14–15, 116–17, 139, 163, 218, 232–33, 284, 284–85; "Perepiska V. I. Lenina i N. K. Krupskoi s Peterburgskoi organizatsiei," *Proletarskaia revoliutsiia*, no. 3: 13. For letters in which Stasova asked for direction, see *Perepiska V. I. Lenina i redaktsii gazety "Iskri"*, vol. III, 139, 232–33.

his theories on how the party should be organized. Shortly thereafter she was appointed to the Central Committee, another sign of her rising star, but that elevation was short-lived. Lenin soon resigned from the committee rather than be consistently outvoted by his opponents in the majority, and Zemliachka followed suit. Returning to Russia, she traveled around the country drumming up support for another party congress at which the debate would be resumed (with, Lenin hoped, a clear victory for his positions).[27]

By early 1904 Zemliachka had settled in St. Petersburg. Stasova was then in prison in Moscow and the business of the St. Petersburg committee had ground to a halt without her; but Zemliachka did not take on *tekhnika*. In fact she avoided it, aspiring instead to the policy-making role of organizational secretary. In St. Petersburg in 1904, Bolshevik leadership required building alliances and mobilizing the underground workers sympathetic to Lenin. This work was not easy, for most SDs in the capital either sided with Iulii Martov and the elders of Russian Social Democracy, Plekhanov, Zasulich, and Akselrod, or pronounced a plague on all the émigrés' houses and labored away on their own local tasks. Zemliachka rushed around the city, ever more annoyed and frazzled, until at last in early January 1905 she wrote to Krupskaia that they must send someone to help her or else the work would surely kill her.[28]

Zemliachka served as a member of the St. Petersburg Committee off and on throughout 1905, working with Stasova after her return from Moscow and with the men (S. I. Gusev, A. A. Bogdanov, and others) who had arrived to lead the battle with the Mensheviks. Her assessment of the situation tallied with Stasova's, that is, she felt that the Bolsheviks, both the people dispatched by Lenin and Krupskaia and the locals from St. Petersburg, were wasting a good deal of time fighting with one another, were not developing support among the party rank and file, and thus were losing to the Mensheviks the struggle for influence among the workers. "Able to work, but not conscious and not solid" was the way she described the St. Petersburg committee in a letter on 24 July 1905. Stasova confided to Krupskaia and Lenin that Zemliachka herself was partly responsible for the sour mood among the Bolsheviks in the capital. "Zemliachka is sometimes less than tactful," she wrote in February

---

[27] R. S. Zemliachka, "Vospominanie o vtorom s"ezde i biuro komiteta bol'shinstva," RTsKhIDNI, f. 90, op. 1, d. 123, ll. 1–6; Institut Marksizma-Leninizma pri TsK KPSS, *Vtoroi s"ezd RSDRP, iiul'–avgust 1903 goda. Protokoly* (Moscow, 1959), 186, 187, 190, 279, 280, 387–89, 401, 402.

[28] For the correspondence between Zemliachka and Krupskaia during this period, see "Perepiska V. I. Lenina i N. K. Krupskoi s Peterburgskoi organizatsiei," *Proletarskaia revoliutsiia*, no. 3: 13–17, 21, 22–23, 34–35.

1905, "and because of this makes blunders that have to be smoothed over by others."[29]

Zemliachka felt none of Stasova's reluctance to lead; perhaps this accounts for the perception that she was tactless. At a meeting of Bolsheviks in London in May 1905 (which Lenin declared to be the Third Congress of the Russian Social-Democratic Labor Party in defiance of the fact that the Mensheviks were meeting separately in Geneva at the time), Zemliachka presented herself as a seasoned veteran of the underground. Her tone was usually polite but always assertive. Unlike Stasova, Zemliachka felt no inhibitions about playing a role in defining party policies. At the congress she called for strengthening operations in Russia by creating a unified national leadership closer to home than the émigrés' distant hiding places and by publishing a newspaper inside the country. She was not, however, a single-minded centralizer (as the Mensheviks alleged Bolsheviks to be), for she also called for more democratic behavior from local leaders. City committees, Zemliachka charged, were often cut off both from party people active in the neighborhoods and from the working class. To remedy this she proposed that more workers be included on the committees and that the committees take steps to consult more regularly with the rank and file.[30]

Most delegates to the congress agreed with Zemliachka's proposals. Indeed, how could any good Social Democrat disagree with calls for closer ties to the proletariat? P. A. Dzhaparidze, a delegate from Baku, did rise to defend the composition of his committee, to which Zemliachka tartly replied that she had been to Baku and had seen for herself that there were only one or two factory workers on that committee. The same was true in Tbilisi and elsewhere, she declared.[31]

Her ambitions seem to have been confined to leadership in the underground, however, for Zemliachka grew impatient at the length of the congress and urged everyone to stop talking and go back to Russia. When she returned to St. Petersburg she became organizational secretary of the city committee. She had to flee the capital in early autumn to avoid arrest, so she moved on to Moscow and another secretaryship. Once again she became a commanding figure. She continued to argue, as she had done all

---

[29] *Perepiska V. I. Lenina i rukovodimykh im uchrezhdenii RSDRP*, vol. III, part 2, 46; "Perepiska V. I. Lenina i N. K. Krupskoi s Peterburgskoi organizatsiei," *Proletarskaia revoliutsiia*, no. 3: 22. An example of Zemliachka's temper is recorded in the minutes of a St. Petersburg committee meeting in September 1905. Angry at a fairly mild rebuke, she walked out, leaving another member to deliver her report. See Institut istorii partii Leningradskogo obkoma KPSS, Filial instituta Marksizma-Leninizma pri TsK KPSS, *Peterburgskii komitet RSDRP. Protokoly i materialy zasedanii, iiul' 1902-fevral' 1917* (Leningrad, 1986), 178.

[30] Institut Marksizma-Leninizma pri TsK KPSS, *Tretii s"ezd RSDRP, aprel'–mai 1905 goda. Protokoly* (Moscow, 1959), 135–36, 714–15, 266–67, 294, 334, 336, 402.

[31] Ibid., 334.

summer, that any attempt at an armed uprising during that tumultuous year would fail to overthrow the tsar, but when just such an attempt took place in December, pitting the revolutionaries against the police and the army, Zemliachka fought on the barricades. The government crushed the rebels as Zemliachka had predicted, and she subsequently demanded angrily that the architects of the debacle be fired from the city committee.[32]

Zemliachka's leadership in Moscow came to an end when the police finally arrested her in the spring of 1906. She had remained free for a long time, possibly because she had moved around a great deal and used a variety of aliases, making it difficult for the authorities to identify her. Although she succeeded in fleeing Moscow before her trial, Zemliachka could no longer work as a secretary, for secretaries, with their network of contacts throughout the city organizations, were the party operatives most vulnerable to identification by the police and by the host of informants that the police cultivated within the revolutionary movement. Seeking anonymity, Zemliachka became a low-ranking operative in the St. Petersburg underground, but the police nonetheless found her in 1907, almost accidentally, when they burst into a meeting of the city committee to arrest everyone there. After a year and a half in prison in the capital, Zemliachka was released for health reasons (a recurrence of tuberculosis as well as heart disease).

When she came out of jail, Zemliachka was deep in the same sort of crisis of revolutionary faith that was plaguing Stasova at the same time, but she remained deeply in doubt even longer than did Absolute. After a period of recuperation in the Caucasus, Zemliachka left Russia altogether, and from late 1909 to 1914 she lived abroad, mostly in Switzerland. That alpine country was swarming with Russian revolutionaries, but Zemliachka chose to avoid them. Later she claimed that the factional politics of people so far from the realities of their homeland disgusted and depressed her, which was probably true. It was also true that she was profoundly depressed by the outcome of the 1905 uprisings and blamed her comrades, who, in her opinion, had bungled the great opportunities the revolutionary year had offered them. Zemliachka returned to Moscow in 1914, but she did not emerge again as a Bolshevik leader until the revolution of 1917.[33]

Stasova and Zemliachka are the pattern *tverdye* Bolshevichki. Both were resolute; both were willing and able to give orders; both believed in discipline and organization. Historians seeking the origins of the commu-

---

[32] Ibid., 214; Institut istorii partii Leningradskogo obkoma KPSS, *Peterburgskii komitet RSDRP*, 178.
[33] Institut istorii partii Leningradskogo obkoma KPSS, *Peterburgskii komitet RSDRP*, 329; *Slavnye bol'shevichki* (Moscow, 1958), 140–41; RTsKhIDNI, f. 17, op. 4, d. 180, l. 29.

nist autocracy could easily argue that these two women were, in all their spiritual essentials, the prototypical Bolshevik dictators, that their *tverdost* expressed a will to power and a ruthlessness in maintaining it. Their behavior could also be offered to support Menshevik charges that the Bolsheviks were always disputatious and fractious. But to sort out the many implications of these charges would be complicated. Stasova and Zemliachka became Bolshevichki not simply because they took easily to command, although they certainly did, but also because they agreed with Lenin's analysis of the way the party should operate in Russia. Social Democrats of both factions believed that the party existed to steer the powerful – but often misdirected and easily defeated – impulses of the dispossessed. Stasova and Zemliachka believed, as Lenin did, that those impulses should be directed unremittingly toward revolution, not permitted to dissipate when popular enthusiasm waned or the government granted reforms. An organization that was weak, divided, and full of unreliable people could not provide such single-minded direction, and in fact it was true that many Social Democrats had dithered while the crowds of 1905 had surged through the streets. They forgot assignments, they confided in informers, they lost their nerve, they simply refused to work hard. A. S. Shapovalov remarked in a typical report to Krupskaia from Odessa in 1905: "So, thanks to disorganization the committee remains without a kopek of money, without *tekhnika*, in a poor condition in which there are no decisive and active people." He had recently asked the committee treasurer for a financial report, at which point the treasurer had angrily replied that there was neither a report nor any money, and added that he was quitting as treasurer.[34] When Lenin argued that the party required more discipline and better organization, Stasova, Zemliachka, Shapovalov, and a host of other Social Democrats fed up with the disorder of the underground heartily agreed.

Yet they did not agree with all of his proposals. Neither Stasova nor Zemliachka favored as much organizational centralization as Lenin advocated, for that would have ceded too much power to leaders who were simply too far away. On principle they believed that the party should be democratically run and that its constituency, the proletariat, should be represented in its leadership. But they also believed that the organization had to be able to get its message out more effectively and to play a leading part once the hoped-for uprising came. Lenin understood how to achieve these ends, they believed, better than did the Mensheviks. Martov's proposals for a loosely structured party might be suitable for a parliamentary democracy such as Germany, but in Russia such a party would simply

---

[34] *Perepiska V. I. Lenina s rukovodimykh im uchrezhdenii RSDRP*, vol. III, part 1, 129.

encourage the movement to become yet more flaccid and permeable by the police.

Zemliachka and Stasova are vulnerable to the charge that they were political maneuverers, for they did seek to engineer the election of a Bolshevik majority on the St. Petersburg city committee in 1904 and 1905. They were opposed by equally partisan Mensheviks who managed to secure control of the committee for themselves. The reality of the underground was that the Bolsheviks, for all their critics' portrayals of them as ruthless schemers, performed in no more organized and deliberate fashion under fire than did the Mensheviks. Only during the revolution in 1917 did they cease simply to call for organization and decisiveness, and actually begin to become organized and decisive. Before then, they were primarily a collection of people within the larger party who believed that they were distinguished from other Social Democrats by their resoluteness, their collective *tverdost*. They paid allegiance to Lenin's insistence that the party should lead the workers, but most of them had very little idea how to translate that general principle into specific action. Collectively, they were not consistently more decisive or effective in a crisis than the Mensheviks. They made no innovations in party organization and came up with no new ways of mobilizing the workers. They were not even a well-defined group, for people moved back and forth between the factions, depending on local conditions, the particular personalities involved, and the issue under debate within the whole Social-Democratic Party. In the greatest of all tests before 1917, the Revolution of 1905, the Mensheviks of St. Petersburg led demonstrations and encouraged strikers more effectively than did the Bolsheviks, much to the chagrin of Stasova and Zemliachka. Lidiia Knipovich, a former populist and ardent Bolshevichka, found the same to be true in Odessa.[35] Throughout the underground years, then, Lenin's vanguard theory of the party, so often cited as the seed from which the dictatorship grew, remained little more than a theory, a rationale for an ideal type of revolutionary organization. When revolution came in 1917, Stasova, Zemliachka, and the other Bolshevichki would apply it then to a very different situation.

The revolutionary community

The majority of Bolshevichki were spear carriers, not leaders of the underground like Stasova and Zemliachka, but the work of all these women was very similar in character. Bolshevichki, whatever their rank in the organization, printed leaflets, attended party meetings, kept com-

---

[35] On Knipovich, see ibid., vol. III, part 1, 71–72, 80–81, 127–29, 203–07.

munications going with other revolutionaries, and propagandized workers and students. Committee members played a greater role in factional politics, policy-making, and job assignments; that was the primary distinction between leaders and followers, though it was not really a very large one. The SDs, priding themselves on being members of a movement of equals, looked askance at distinctions, ranks, and hierarchies. Decisions within party committees were supposed to be made democratically; instructions from the center were followed or ignored, according to the judgment of the people on the spot; and Mensheviks and Bolsheviks often decided whether to fight or cooperate with one another in response to the situation at hand and their own personal inclinations. What bound this shaky collection of wills and egos together was the collective identity, that sense of common purpose and shared understandings, and the communal activity connected with these.

Bolshevichki were particularly adept and influential in the maintenance of this sense of ongoing community activity. They devoted much time and attention, as did male Bolsheviks, to keeping together the networks of people with whom they worked and lived and they came to depend on them enormously for emotional, financial, and physical support. Russia's Social Democrats behaved as members of newly formed social movements typically do, that is, having left their former social groups, they built new communities in which they nourished the collective identity that bound them together. The inclination that many social activists feel to establish tight connections to one another became an essential method of self-defense for the SDs, as it does for any group that is under siege from the authorities. Where the likelihood of success is remote and the risks of belonging to a movement are considerable, those who continue to be members come to attach enormous importance to the group and particularly to their closest colleagues. Remaining within the circle of comrades can then become as important as the cause for which the group is fighting, and commitment to the cause becomes entangled with the bonds to one's comrades. So it was for many Bolshevichki. When Zemliachka and Stasova lost their faith in the cause, they cut their ties to their comrades as well and fled hundreds of miles away.[36]

In their memoirs, the Bolshevichki attested to the value they attached to the underground community by referring to it often as their "family." Generally it included whoever was working for the cause of revolution in a

---

[36] William A. Gamson has emphasized the importance of support networks to all social movements, but he also observes that the more "adversarial" the environment in which a movement operates, the greater the need for strong personal ties between the members. See Gamson, "The Social Psychology of Collective Action," in Morris and Mueller, *Frontiers in Social Movement Theory*, 53–76.

city, not only Bolsheviks, but Mensheviks, Socialist Revolutionaries, sympathetic fellow travelers – virtually anyone who might lend a hand or host a meeting. That broad community was in many ways unreliable, however, for it changed continually as people came and went, and as the police turned revolutionaries into informers. The Bolshevichki also needed more durable, trustworthy sources of support, and so they relied on still smaller collections of friends, family members, and lovers.

Strong friendships developed between Bolshevichki, both social equals and people of very different backgrounds. Krupskaia, Stasova, Zinaida Krzhizhanovskaia, Lidiia Knipovich, and Vera and Liudmila Menzhinskaia met while working as teachers in St. Petersburg. Alexandra Artiukhina and Klavdiia Nikolaeva first got to know one another when, as young workers, they were recruited into the party. Across the years these Bolshevichki shared work, prison, and exile, and exchanged advice and sympathy. The underground also made it possible for proletarian women to become the comrades of upper-class women. The friendships between such Bolshevichki as Nikolaeva and Kollontai, a printer and the daughter of a general, would have been virtually impossible elsewhere in Russian society. Often these were patronage relationships, in which older women educated younger ones in art, literature, revolutionary politics, even dress and deportment. Stasova had several younger protégés, as did Kollontai, Samoilova, and Praskovia Kudelli. Such friendships could cross party lines. Alexandra Artiukhina became close in prison to a Socialist Revolutionary named Natasha Kazantseva, who tutored her in the classics of Russian literature.[37]

Their natal families also provided essential support to the Bolshevichki. Parents and siblings had influenced the decision of many of these women to become revolutionaries in the first place, so it is hardly surprising to find that they helped them endure the vicissitudes of underground life. Some families provided emotional support and a place of refuge. Inessa, Kollontai, and Stasova all spent lengthy summer vacations on their relatives' estates. T. F. Ludvinskaia, a peasant from the Kiev region, was nursed back to health by her family after a stay in prison, while neighbors from the village dropped in to wish her well. Relatives also helped with illegal activities. Stasova's uncle and brothers regularly received shipments of literature and coded letters. Bosh's mother hid revolutionary leaflets from the police. And at least a few mothers kept house for their daughters in order to give them more time for their party work. Krupskaia's mother Elizaveta is the best known of these "revolutionary

---

[37] On Artiukhina, see *Bez nikh my ne pobedili by. Vospominaniia zhenshchin-uchastnits Oktiabr'skoi revoliutsii, grazhdanskoi voiny, i sotsialisticheskogo stroitel'stva* (Moscow, 1975), 238–39.

mothers," but there were others as well, including Bosh's. Few, however, went so far as a mother named Dilevskaia, who accompanied her two children Olga and Vera into Siberian exile.[38] Families also gave their revolutionary offspring financial help. Kollontai, Inessa, Bosh, Stasova, and many others received money regularly from their parents and other relatives. Menshevik Lidiia Dan later argued that these economic advantages helped explain the preponderance of middle-class and upper-class people among the revolutionaries.[39] Certainly the help was important, but it was also true that many of the Bolshevichki earned their own income, the upper-class women by teaching school or doing clerical and sales work, the proletarian ones by working in factories. Occasionally, some also received a small stipend from party funds. Given the miserable wages paid to women in tsarist Russia, however, and the penurious state of Social-Democratic finances, even employed women needed whatever financial help their families could give.

Of course, not all relatives accepted the Bolshevichki's activities with equanimity, and many who did did not do so all the time. There were mothers who begged their daughters to stop endangering themselves and the rest of the family. Elizaveta Kovalenko's mother came to see her textile-worker daughter in prison after her first arrest. The daughter later reported: "When I entered the office, my mother threw herself on me in tears and began to reproach me with the fact that nobody, she said, from our family had ever been in jail and thus I had disgraced them all." Emiliia Solin, also a factory worker in St. Petersburg, returned home from her first arrest to find that her brother had thrown all her clothes out onto the street. Her mother then greeted her on her knees with a tearful plea to quit the party. Solin refused, and soon moved out.[40] Other families split over their revolutionary relatives. Kollontai and Stasova were supported by their parents but denounced by sisters with more conservative political sentiments.

Even people sympathetic to the revolutionary movement became unhappy after the police closed in. Elena Stasova's parents were quite worried about their daughter when she was in Taganka prison in Moscow in 1904. Her father wrote to her that, if she loved her mother, she would not continue to cause her such anxiety. From prison Stasova wrote back an emotional declaration of what being a revolutionary meant to her:

[38] T. F. Liudvinskaia, *Nas Leninskaia partiia vela. Vospominaniia* (Moscow, 1976), 59–60; *Perepiska V. I. Lenina i redaktsii gazety "Iskra,"* vol. III, 721–22; Evgenii Mar, *Nezakonechnoe pis'mo* (Moscow, 1970), 31; K. T. Sverdlova, *Iakov Mikhailovich Sverdlov*, 4th ed. (Moscow, 1985), 149.

[39] Leopold H. Haimson, ed., *The Making of Three Russian Revolutionaries* (Cambridge, 1987), 144.

[40] *Zhenshchiny goroda Lenina* (Leningrad, 1963), 62; *Zhenshchiny v revoliutsii*, 99–101.

Remember, dear, that my life is in this, in this and only in this, that no other work can give me the strength to live, that without this work of mine I cannot live. This is the flesh of my flesh. This is not an expression, my own loved one; it is extremely difficult for me to make you and Mama suffer, but I cannot do otherwise. It would be better not to live then. Forgive me dear, good one, forgive me for writing you this with tears in my eyes. My whole heart aches when I think about you both, but I haven't the strength to do otherwise.[41]

Since they could not change it, the Stasovs had to accept their daughter's decision. Thereafter they continued to support her financially and to use their considerable influence to lighten the conditions of her subsequent imprisonments. For her part, Stasova lived with them when she was in St. Petersburg and nursed both of them through their last illnesses.[42]

Another source of support for revolutionary women was marriage. It was noted earlier that at least 46 percent of the Bolshevichki in the sample were married. The true percentage was probably greater, since Bolsheviks considered it immodest to discuss their personal lives publicly and hence rarely mentioned spouses or children in their writings. Consequently there is no information at all on the marital status of 52 percent of the women in the sample. Unfortunately, this reticence also complicates the task of characterizing the amorous relationships of the Bolshevichki in the prerevolutionary period. However, enough evidence exists to support the generalization that their sexual mores were, for their society and time, liberal, but not libertine. There were a few love affairs about which they gossiped, Lenin's liaison with Inessa being the most famous. Less well known but much better documented was Inessa's earlier relationship with her brother-in-law, Vladimir Armand. Her fifth child was born of this friendship, which the Armand family accepted with extraordinary good grace. Inessa remained on good terms with her husband Alexander for the rest of her life, and he reared his nephew Andrei as his own son.

The great majority of Bolshevichki were far more conventional, sustaining monogamous relationships with male revolutionaries for many years, despite frequent separations caused by their party work or by time in prison or exile. Lenin and Krupskaia are the most famous Bolshevik couple, but there were many others, Iakov Sverdlov and Klavdiia Novgorotseva, for example, and Zlata Lilina and Grigorii Zinoviev. Among the lesser-known couples were several important to this study – Evgeniia Bosh and Iurii Piatakov, Elena Rozmirovich and Nikolai

---

[41] Stasova, *Vospominaniia*, 71.
[42] V. V. Stasov, *Pis'ma k rodnym*, ed. E. D. Stasova, 3 vols. (Moscow, 1953–62), vol. III, part 2, 230, 231, 237–39, 244–45, 251–53; Levidova and Salita, *Stasova*, 200; Podliashuk, *Bogatyrskaia simfoniia*, 137.

Krylenko, Konkordiia Samoilova and Arkadii Samoilov. These people preferred not to have their unions solemnized by the Orthodox Church (there was no civil marriage in Russia), but some did so anyway, simply in order to make it easier for them to live together. Glafira Okulova, a teacher from Ukraine, married Ivan Teodorovich in the chapel of the prison where both were incarcerated; friends sent hors d'oeuvres for the reception. Samoilova and her husband Arkadii finally married legally in 1913, after seven years of cohabitation, so that she could be listed as his wife on his identity papers and thus establish legal residency in St. Petersburg.[43]

The Bolshevichki did depart from prevailing Russian values by believing that people should follow the promptings of their hearts in love affairs and pay minimal regard to social conventions. Many lived together without benefit of clergy. Many also married across class and religious lines. Particularly common were marriages between Christians and Jews. Samoilova, the daughter of a priest, married a Jew (he had to convert to Christianity in order to marry her). The Bolshevichki also practiced de facto divorce (legal divorce was virtually unobtainable in Russia). And, more generally, the Bolshevichki seem to have believed that a person's love life was her private concern, to be led as she chose. The one exception to this toleration was probably lesbianism, although homosexuality became so forbidden under the Soviet regime that it is impossible now to unearth the extent to which the revolutionaries before 1917 practiced it or tolerated it in others. Love affairs between women undoubtedly did exist, but the prevailing party culture condemned them before as well as after the revolution, forcing lesbian Bolshevichki, like most lesbians in Russian society, to cloak their true feelings in the garb of platonic friendship.

The Bolshevichki's notions about the way heterosexual couples should treat one another were also liberal, but not radical. In keeping with the long-standing ideals of Russian revolutionaries, they paid a good deal of attention to men's behavior, rejecting the Victorian ideal of the stern paterfamilias and adopting instead kinder, gentler notions that men should respect their wives, honor the women's commitments to their own work, and help them with domestic chores. This ethic of considerateness was a noteworthy departure from Russian patriarchalism, which accorded great power to husbands and subordinated most family relations to their preferences and comforts. It stopped short, however, of questioning the belief, widespread among even enlightened Europeans, that men should have the controlling hand in marriage. Although much of the Russian intelligentsia had been debating a more egalitarian

---

[43] *Zhenshchiny v revoliutsii*, 48–49; G. Shidlovskii, "Pamiati dvukh starykh pravdistov," *Katorga i ssylka*, no. 10 (1931): 175n., 177–78.

concept of marriage since the 1860s, the Social Democrats did not think it necessary even to discuss such matters, for they considered that power relations within marriage were a private and therefore relatively insignificant issue that would be resolved when the revolution had done away with power itself.[44]

Bolshevichki dealt with their romantic attachments much as professional women still do today. Some – Bosh, Kollontai, and Stasova, for example – made work their primary commitment. Kollontai was the most forthright in discussing her priorities. "Love-emotions are not the most essential thing in life for a woman," she wrote in her memoirs, "and if she has to choose between 'love and work' – let her never hesitate: it is work that gives the real satisfaction and makes life worth living."[45] Yet it would appear that most of the Bolshevichki in fact combined work with marriage (often, needless to say, to a fellow revolutionary). Samoilova, for example, pursued her own party assignments but tried whenever possible to be stationed near her husband, Arkadii. Still others, Alexandra Artiukhina for one, made it a priority to move with their husbands and find political work wherever that took them.

Naturally the family lives of the Bolshevichki also included children. There is no information available on the childbearing of 75 percent of the Bolshevichki in the data base, but of the remaining 25 percent, 22 percent had children. These fragmentary statistics suggest that perhaps as many as 80 percent of the Bolshevichki were mothers. Some coped with the tasks of caring for their offspring by leaving the underground altogether. Cecelia Bobrovskaia, a midwife from Belorus, wrote,

During the many years of illegal work I often came across women – wives of revolutionaries – who, because of their children, were obliged to play the unenviable role of mother and housewife even though they had all the attributes required to make them real party workers.[46]

However, the great majority of the Bolshevichki in the sample chose not to

[44] These generalizations are drawn from a general reading of the memoirs of the Bolshevichki as well as from the information available on the married lives of the following individuals: (1) Krupskaia – N. K. Krupskaia, *Reminiscences of Lenin*, trans. Bernard Isaacs (New York, 1970); Robert H. McNeal, *Bride of the Revolution: Krupskaia and Lenin* (Ann Arbor, Mich., 1972), esp. 67–87; (2) Inessa – her letters to her husband and to her lover in *Stat'i*, 179–211; R. C. Elwood, *Inessa Armand* (Cambridge, 1992), 33–35; (3) Kollontai – her discussions of marital relations, especially "Novaia zhenshchina," *Sovremennyi mir*, no. 9 (1913): 151–85; Barbara Evans Clements, *Bolshevik Feminist: The Life of Aleksandra Kollontai* (Bloomington, Ind., 1979), 14–22, 68–75; (4) Samoilova – the correspondence between her and her husband Arkadii (RTsKhIDNI, f. 148, op. 1, d. 3).
[45] RTsKhIDNI, f. 134, op. 1, d. 37, l. 272. There are many drafts of Kollontai's memoirs in her archive. The unfinished version cited here was written in English, apparently in hopes of finding an American publisher.
[46] Cecelia Bobrovskaia, *Twenty Years in Underground Russia* (New York, 1934), 150.

Plate 8. Sofia Smidovich, circa 1900.

take the duties of motherhood to such lengths that they gave up political work altogether. Some, Kollontai and Inessa for example, entrusted their children to their husbands, parents, or other relatives. Others, among them Sofia Smidovich, a future colleague of both Kollontai and Inessa, suspended party work from time to time to concentrate on their offspring, particularly when their husbands were under arrest or in exile. Most of the Bolshevichki, however, attended to childrearing even while staying active in the underground.

The result was that the children came into the underground too. They grew used to being roused from sleep by police breaking into their homes. They watched their mothers being arrested. "I was awake all night from the unusual noise and saw the police in the room searching it," Inna Armand remembered later. "They turned everything upside down, even the children's beds. Mother stood there completely calm; she smiled at me and made a sign that I shouldn't cry. Then they took her away."[47] Some children went with their mothers to prison or exile. Klavdiia Novgorod-tseva and Glafira Okulova-Teodorovich bore babies in prison hospitals, and Elena Rozmirovich and Sofia Smidovich took young children with them to jail. The youngsters seem to have acclimated, probably more readily than their parents. When Smidovich's father came to prison to take his granddaughter Tania off to live with him, the child refused to leave her mother and had to be lured out of the cell. Smidovich then slammed the door, and the little girl was carried screaming away. Elizaveta Drabkina, daughter of Feodosiia Drabkina and Sergei Gusev, remembered a childhood friend who had spent so many years in jail with his mother that he was afraid to walk through an open doorway without permission.[48]

The children also had to learn a discretion not natural to the young. Elizaveta Drabkina remembered herself as a particularly difficult pupil. There were many times when she listened in on conversations between her parents and their underground comrades, and then was sternly instructed not to repeat anything she had heard. Apparently she was a curious and talkative little girl, not easily silenced, so her mother Feodosiia Drabkina finally hit upon a fairly drastic disciplinary technique. Having caught her perhaps for the fifth or sixth time chattering about forbidden matters, Drabkina spread hot mustard on Elizaveta's tongue. Thereafter she could silence her daughter up by simply looking at her sternly and saying, "If you don't shut up, you're going to get the mustard." This threat seems to have worked, but Drabkina also had some difficulty impressing on her daughter the importance of honesty in ordinary human communications. Why should she tell the truth, the little girl wanted to know, when the grown-ups around her lied all the time to the neighbors and the police? "My poor mama," Elizaveta wrote later, "I caused her so much grief, care, bother, and trouble."[49] She might have added that she and many other children had been obliged to learn many things much faster than the ordinary youngsters of tsarist Russia.

Much later, after their party had become the ruling regime of a powerful Soviet Union, the Bolshevichki became heroes of the revolution. When their children wrote about them then, they naturally took great pride in their accomplishments and said very little about how they had felt when their mothers behaved so differently from more conventional women. Occasionally, however, a note of complaint does appear in the literary remains. Elizaveta Drabkina admitted feeling that her mother had less

[47] Armand, *Stat'i*, 10.
[48] *Zhenshchiny russkoi revoliutsii* (Moscow, 1968), 313, 51; Mar, *Nezakonechnoe pis'mo*, 48; *Slavnye bol'shevichki*, 276–77.
[49] *Leningradki. Vospominaniia, ocherki, dokumenty* ([Leningrad], 1968), 98.

Plate 9   Feodosiia Drabkina, circa 1900.

time for her than other children's mothers had for them. A. N. Emelianov remembered feeling distanced from his mother, Nadezhda Emelianova, because of her *tverdost*. She always "seemed stern," he wrote. "She would not drop an unnecessary word, she did not linger to have a chat at the gate with a neighbor." Inna Armand also described her mother as "stern" and "reserved," and also absent a great deal. "Inessa loved her children deeply," Inna wrote somewhat defensively, "and only constant persecution [by the police] forced her to live apart from them. But Inessa never forgot about the education of her children. She saw them, wrote them letters."[50]

It is also evident that many Bolshevichki, for their part, felt torn

---

[50] Ibid., 103–04; Armand, *Stat'i*, 11.

between their family obligations and their work. Some found the choice easier to make than others did. In an unpublished version of her memoirs written in her old age, Kollontai candidly described her feelings for her son Mikhail: "I started to love him after his first illness, when he was about a year old. But many other things interested me more than he did. And deep in my heart I always felt guilty toward him. When he got older, then I got closer to him. But he was never 'the center.' Work and love, they were more important." Inessa felt more divided loyalties than Kollontai. Sentenced to exile in 1908, she wrote to her husband, "I don't know how I'll live through two years without the children. It almost seems impossible to me." Sofia Smidovich stayed with her three girls most of the time, for she had to support them when their father was exiled, but she never felt that she had given them enough attention. She sadly described them to a friend as "unfondled and uneducated."[51]

The Bolshevichki in prison and exile

The lives of the Bolshevichki were compounded of work and family, public assignments and internal community chores, *tverdost* and coping. They were also full of arrests, imprisonments, exiles to remote corners of the Russian Empire, and, of course, the anxiety and daily fears occasioned by living a life on the edges of legal society. In the sample analyzed for this study, information is lacking on the arrests and the jail time, if any, of 28 percent of the women. Of the 72 percent whose history of imprisonment is available, 61 percent were jailed at least once, 38 percent twice or more. Every one of the Bolshevichki whose lives are well documented was arrested at least once, and most were arrested five, six, even seven times. The whole pattern of data on political arrests does not permit detailed comparison between the sexes, but it does clearly indicate that both women and men were arrested often, that the rate of arrest for both was highest in times of political unrest, and that once either a woman or a man had a police record, she or he was very likely to be picked up again. Bolshevichki as a group served less time in prison than their male comrades, a fact that suggests that they were detained less often or for shorter periods after each arrest. (See table 12.) The reasons for this disparity are not readily apparent, but the most likely explanation is that the authorities underestimated the extent of women's involvement in the party and therefore considered them less serious offenders than men.

The Bolshevichki were hunted down by the Okhrana, a police agency

[51] RTsKhIDNI, f. 134, op. 1, d. 48, l. 90; Armand, *Stat'i*, 194; *Slavnye bol'shevichki*, 280.

Plate 10. Inessa Armand with her children, 1909. From left to right, Inessa, Inna, Andrei, Fedor, Varvara, and Alexander.

within the Ministry of the Interior responsible for political offenders. The Okhrana owed its success to a widespread network of officers, both in Russia and abroad, and also to the assiduous cultivation of informers. Liza Volshtein, a seamstress from Odessa, remembered that "in 1907 . . . there were more provocateurs than workers in [our] organization." The most infamous of these police agents was Roman Malinovskii, a Bolshevik member of the Social Democrats' delegation to the Russian parliament, the Duma, from 1912 to 1914. Malinovskii turned in Stasova, Inessa, Samoilova, and Bosh's sister Elena Rozmirovich, among many others. There were thousands of less highly placed, less celebrated informers in Russia – workers in underground circles, party members or the acquaintances and relatives of party members – who reported regularly to the police, sometimes filing reports so detailed that they included minutes of committee meetings.[52]

Once arrested, Bolshevichki exchanged the insecurities of the underground for the miseries of the penal system. They were usually taken first

---

[52] Liza Vol'shtein, "Zapiski fabrichnoi rabotnitsy," *Proletarskaia revoliutsiia*, no. 9 (1922): 168. For examples of police reports on party meetings that have the quality of minutes, see Institut istorii partii Leningradskogo obkoma KPSS, *Peterburgskii komitet RSDRP*, 28 n. 2, 29 n. 2. On the Okhrana, see Elwood, *Russian Social Democracy in the Underground*, 52–53.

to a preliminary detention prison for booking, then transferred to a larger facility where they were held while the prosecutor's office developed the case. The government could prefer a number of charges against them – belonging to the Social-Democratic Party, participating in underground activities, or, most serious of all, engaging in terrorism, which included such crimes as the manufacture and possession of weapons, robbery, assault, and assassination. Non-violent offenses carried penalties that ranged from release on parole to release with limitations on freedom of movement (for example, being banned from the major cities) to exile in European Russia or Siberia. Terrorism or multiple offenses could bring a sentence of hard labor in prison or in a labor camp.

Most of the Bolshevichki were interrogated by Okhrana officers. This was not the brutal process that later developed during the Soviet period, under the Bolshevichki's own government. Women who have written about the prerevolutionary years have indicated that the investigating officers did not abuse them physically. Some, particularly noblewomen such as Stasova, were even treated courteously. The non-violent nature of the crimes that the Bolshevichki had committed may have mitigated the harshness of the investigation, for the same gentle treatment was not meted out to female SRs arrested after assassination attempts. Mariia Spiridonova, one of the leaders of the SR Party, was savagely beaten during questioning in 1906 after she had killed a general.[53]

The government usually completed the investigation of a case in a few months; thus for each arrest most prisoners, male and female, served a year or less in the central prisons of some major city. (See table 12.) It was not uncommon for a woman, particularly one with no prior convictions, to be released for lack of evidence. The practice may account in part for the fact that women in general appear to have served shorter terms than men. When the prosecutor's office determined that there was enough evidence to proceed to judgment, the sentence was handed down by administrative decree, or, after 1904, the accused might be granted a jury trial. Administrative sentencing remained the more common method throughout the first two decades of the twentieth century.[54] The investigators seem to have been held to a fairly high

[53] For Stasova's discussions of her interrogations, see *Vospominaniia*, 63–65. A. Roznovskii reprinted the Okhrana records from Bosh's arrest and interrogation in 1912 in "Iz epokhi 'Zvezdy' i 'Pravdy' v Kieve," 133–42. See also M. M. Essen, *Pervoi shturm* (Moscow, 1957), 108, for Essen's discussion of an interrogation she underwent (in which the officer mistook her for a gentile, and asked her why she wanted to consort with all the Jews in the revolutionary movement). Lidiia Dan described interrogations in 1904 as "unpleasant – there was no torture or anything like that" (Haimson, *The Making of Three Russian Revolutionaries*, 150). On Spiridonova's beating, see Margaret Maxwell, *Narodniki Women: Russian Women Who Sacrificed Themselves for the Dream of Freedom* (New York, 1990), 165–66.

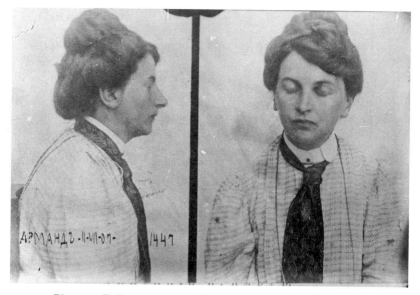

Plate 11. Police mug shot of Inessa Armand, date 2 July 1907. Inessa probably closed her eyes to make the photograph less useful to police.

standard of proof; there were few coerced confessions to non-existent crimes under the tsarist regime, and indeed there was no need for such a practice. The revolutionaries were usually guilty of the offenses charged.

Conditions in the prisons varied from place to place, from year to year, and according to the social rank of the inmate. In general, the regimen was harsh by the standards of contemporary western Europe or North America, lenient when compared to what it would become in the USSR in the 1930s. Prisoners were not required to do physical labor; they were simply confined to their cells except during brief exercise periods. They could communicate fairly freely with relatives and were permitted to hire attorneys (although the cost of legal counsel was prohibitive for poorer women). Those who could raise the money could also post bail and obtain release, pending trial. Some prison administrations, such as that at Taganka in Moscow, provided decent food, primarily soup, kasha (buckwheat porridge), and bread, and prisoners could buy butter, sugar, and tea from the commissary. In Moscow's Lefortovo in 1907, Inessa and her cellmates were even allowed to cook for themselves. The liberal wardens there and elsewhere also permitted regular exercise and communication between the inmates. Other prisons, such as the central

---

54 Levidova and Salita, *Stasova*, 116.

Table 12 *Length of prison terms*

	Women (%) ($N = 169$)	Men (%) ($N = 888$)
Less than 1 year	40.8	25.1
1 to 2 years	47.3	44.5
$2\frac{1}{2}$ to 3 years	5.9	10.7
$3\frac{1}{2}$ to 4 years	2.4	10.4
$4\frac{1}{2}$ years or more	3.5	9.3
Total	99.9	100.0

facility in Vilnius in Lithuania, were harsher, feeding the inmates rancid
cabbage soup and coarse black bread larded with straw. Solitary confinement was also widely used, both routinely (Taganka had only solitary
cells) and as punishment (the notorious *kartser*, usually a small, unheated,
windowless room where prisoners were fed on bread and water).[55]
   Even the most benign tsarist prison was a dark, dirty, verminous place,
dank with disease and despair, which took a serious toll on people's
physical and emotional health. Zemliachka, Stasova, and many other
Bolshevichki contracted tuberculosis while jailed. In November 1908,
Inessa detailed for her husband the effects of Lefortovo prison on the
women she had known there: one was beginning to recover from the strain
of the experience, two were still deeply depressed, and two had "gone out
of their minds." As she wrote, Inessa could hear the shrieks of the
eighteen-year-old girl in the cell next to her; "the sweet regime" of solitary
confinement had brought her to a state where she was hallucinating.[56]
   Those who survived prison best were those who were in good health
and had the will to resist depression. Such women banded together
wherever possible to recreate the revolutionary community. Dora Lazurkina, an eighteen-year-old student when she was arrested in 1902, at first
felt frightened "mured up in stone," but then she learned the code used
to tap messages on the walls. She soon found out who was in the nearby
cells and rejoiced that once again she was part of the revolutionary
"family."[57]
   The chief activity of this "family" was studying. Most prisons had

---

[55] Armand, *Stat'i*, 58. On the regime in Taganka, see Lidiia Dan's description in Haimson,
   The Making of Three Russian Revolutionaries, 146–48; G. A. Krovitskii, "Shest'desiat' let
   zhizni, tridtsat'piat let bol'shevistskoi bor'by," *Katorga i ssylka*, no. 9 (1933): 64; and
   Stasova, *Vospominanii*, 65. On the regime in Kiev's prisons, see Aniuta Belen'kaia, "O
   rabote Kievskoi organizatsii v 1905 g.," *Proletarskaia revoliutsiia*, no. 2 (1926): 263. On
   Vilnius, see Ida Zil'berblat, "Vilenskaia katorga, 1910–1914 gg.," *Katorga i ssylka*, no. 65
   (1930): 165.
[56] Armand, *Stat'i*, 192.   [57] *Zhenshchiny goroda Lenina*, 30.

rather good libraries, for inmates often left their books behind when they were released. The Bolshevichki made their cells into classrooms, reading for hours by themselves if they were in solitary or teaching one another if they lived in group cells. Inessa described her schedule in another letter to her family: "In the morning I read until two; around three we have dinner and tea, then French lessons . . . then we walk for an hour and a half, then supper, after supper two more French lessons (the last, in conspiracy)." As Inessa implied, the women did not confine themselves to politically safe subjects. While in prison, Mariia Mukhina-Zavadskaia, a student from Siberia, read Plekhanov's *On the Question of the Development of Monistic Views in History*, Bebel's *Woman Under Socialism*, Franz Mehring's *Legends of Lessing*, and Karl Kautsky's *Economic Studies of Karl Marx* and *The Agrarian Question*.[58]

The prisoners also kept their spirits up by rebelling against the prison authorities, most commonly by staging hunger strikes. Stasova led two such strikes, one in 1904 to protest the government's dilatoriness in preferring charges in several cases, another in 1906 to demand better treatment of ill prisoners. In 1914 Samoilova, Nikolaeva, and several other Bolshevichki began a hunger strike against the dreadful conditions in which they were being held and were force-fed in response; tsarist wardens had apparently decided to adopt the methods then being applied to feminists jailed in Britain. Samoilova's group ultimately obtained improved treatment from the authorities, as did Stasova's, probably because they managed to get their story out to the press. Other protesters were not so successful. The warden of Butyrka prison in Moscow broke a hunger strike by female prisoners in 1908 by refusing to meet their demands and telling them smugly that he was surprised that they, revolutionaries who were such ardent critics of the government, had not realized how bad prison conditions in Russia really were.[59]

A few female SDs and SRs managed to escape after being arrested. The largest jailbreak took place in 1901, when thirteen women overpowered their guards and fled the Novinskii Bulvar women's prison in Moscow.[60] Others ran away from prison by ones and twos throughout the prerevolutionary period. It was even more common for women released on bail to escape abroad. Inessa and Zemliachka, among many others, took this course, but it was a costly option available only to people with

[58] *Slavnye bol'shevichki*, 78; *Zhenshchiny goroda Lenina*, 45–46.
[59] Stasova, *Vospominaniia*, 68–69; Podliashuk, *Bogatyrskaia simfoniia*, 80; *Zhenshchiny v revoliutsii*, 24; *Bez nikh my ne pobedili by*, 243–44; and Z. Klapina, "Zhenshchiny katorzhanki v Butyrkakh," *Katorga i ssylka*, no. 4 (1922): 148–53.
[60] "Pobeg trinadtsatyi," *Katorga i ssylka*, no. 2 (1921): 14–33.

Plate 12. Police mug shot of Konkordiia Samoilova, circa 1910. Her maiden name, Gromova, is written across the picture.

financial resources. The majority of imprisoned Bolshevichki remained in jail until the government disposed of their cases. If they were repeat offenders, they could expect a sentence of exile in remote regions of European Russia or in Siberia.

Banishment to Siberia was one of the most notorious features of both the tsarist and Soviet prison systems, so much so that the very word Siberia summons up images of long lines of chained prisoners trekking across frozen landscapes. Under the tsars there was a network of hard-labor camps in the east, to which criminals and revolutionaries convicted of violent crimes were sent. The population of these camps was overwhelmingly male; only a handful of female revolutionaries, all SRs convicted of terrorism, was sentenced to hard labor in Siberia in the early twentieth century.[61] Women such as the Bolshevichki who were guilty of non-violent political offenses ended up in exile, required to live in remote towns or villages in European Russia or Siberia for terms of several years. (See table 13.)

Most of the Bolshevichki in the sample served their terms in Siberia. There they found that their greatest enemy was not the police, for surveillance was fairly lax; they were required only to report periodically to the authorities in the nearest city. The brutal climate did depress the

---

[61] For a fascinating collection of these women's memoirs, see M. M. Konstantinov, ed., *Na zhenskom katorge*, 2nd ed. (Moscow, 1932).

Table 13 *Exile*

Terms served in exile by Bolshevichki (%) (N = 318)	
None	24.2
One	30.2
Two	12.3
Three	5.3
Four	0.6
Five	0.3
Unknown	27.0
Total	99.9

Note: Such data are not available in *The Soviet Data Bank*.

Time served in exile

	Women (%) (N = 125)	Men (%) (N = 457)
1 year or less	16.0	40.3
1 to 2 years	16.0	24.5
3 to 4 years	28.8	21.4
5 years or more	39.2	13.8
Total	100.0	100.0

exiles, but still more demoralizing was their isolation from the revolution-ary community. Living in small villages, prohibited from working (and most revolutionaries were physically unable or unwilling to do agricultural labor in any case), many exiles descended into depression and alcoholism. Glafira Okulova-Teodorovich remembered: "We felt like little grains of sand that could be lost some day and no one would ever know about it." Inessa wrote to her husband in 1908:

People sicken spiritually, cease to be adjusted to the life they were formerly used to, and to which they will in time return. There's nothing here to be interested in, there are no real contacts with the population, there's not even simple physical work, or if there is, it's only temporary and occasional. The muscles forget how to work, the brain how to think intensively – and it's sad to see how comrades come here . . . cheerful, full of energy, and then waste away.[62]

Because the police could not keep close tabs on people spread across such a vast territory, it was possible to escape. In 1908 Inessa, hidden under a pile of furs on a sledge, left the tiny town in the far north to which she had been sent. Evgeniia Bosh obtained a false passport and took the

[62] *Zhenshchiny v revoliutsii*, 50; Armand, *Stat'i*, 200.

train out of Irkutsk in 1914. At least 24 percent of the women in the sample fled exile, either before or after arriving at their appointed place of residence. The data suggest that more male than female Bolsheviks escaped – 41 percent of the men listed in the files of *The Soviet Data Bank* did so – but it is difficult to know what to make of this difference, for the exiles themselves do not comment on it. If men were more likely to flee exile than women, they may have done so because they had received longer sentences than women. Men were also more able to escape than women, for women traveling alone in rural areas would quickly be noticed and reported, if not molested. Or perhaps women adjusted more easily to the conditions in exile and hence were more willing to stay.

More illuminating is the evidence available on the ways in which both women and men managed to survive exile with their physical and mental health intact. The prime method was similar to that which saw them through the underground or prison, that is, they recreated, as far as they were able, the revolutionary community and found work to do in it. In smaller cities with sizable numbers of exiles, the revolutionaries banded together into communes to pool expenses, take meals together, and study. Those spread farther apart wrote to one another. They also occupied their time tutoring local children. This teaching was against government regulations, but the people of Siberia had disregarded the rules for generations. Indeed Siberia, more than the exile sites within European Russia, hummed with a network of revolutionaries instructing one another and their pupils in all sorts of subjects, from basic grammar to the fine points of socialism. It was exiles in Irkutsk who had first introduced Samoilova, the priest's daughter, to revolutionary ideas.

Stasova proved as adept as any at the game of survival. Sent to the village of Rybnoe in eastern Siberia's Enisei guberniia in 1914, she gathered together with other exiles in the town to form a commune. Then she set about raising money by writing to her relatives and even sending appeals for contributions to *Novyi mir*, a Menshevik newspaper in New York City. She also persuaded the writer Maxim Gorky to ship her copies of socialist texts for her reading group. Stasova soon found tutoring work as well, teaching German to the local postmaster so that he could pass a civil service examination. The police did notice all the mail passing in and out of Rybnoe as well as the circle studying socialism, and in 1915 they transferred Stasova to Beia in Minusinsk krai, a town of 4,000 people, only one of whom was a fellow exile. Beia daunted even the redoubtable Absolute. "The solitude is beginning to depress me terribly," she wrote to a friend in the spring of 1915. Her father managed to convince his well-placed friends to arrange her temporary transfer to a bigger town for health reasons (Stasova was suffering from both tuberculosis and pleurisy). She then established contacts with the thriving exile community in Minusinsk, where Bolsheviks, Mensheviks, and SRs were conducting heated debates with one another and even publishing an underground newspaper. Back in touch with the revolutionaries' world, Stasova felt considerably better.[63]

The emergence of Bolshevik feminism

It is evident that in the years before 1917, Bolshevichki did much the same work in the underground as male Bolsheviks did. The tendency for women to serve as technical rather than organizational secretaries suggests the existence within the party of an assumption that women belonged in support roles, but the Social Democrats espoused at the same time a commitment to equal opportunity for women that enabled Bolshevichki such as Zemliachka and Bosh to rise to commanding positions. Because male and female Bolsheviks shared the work of the underground on such an equal basis, the collective contributions of the females to the party are virtually indistinguishable from those of the males.

The Bolshevichki's only independent pursuit before 1917 was "work among women," their phrase for efforts to cultivate the support of the female proletariat. Samoilova's Women's Day meeting in 1913 was one of the first of such projects, which brought together the people and delineated the ideas that were to produce the hugely important Soviet program of women's emancipation after the revolution. An enterprise organized exclusively by Bolshevichki with very little help from male party members, work among women was also one of the most significant contributions the Bolshevichki made to the party's development and to the subsequent history of the Soviet Union.

In the 1890s, the earliest period of the Social-Democratic Party in Russia, members had assumed that the women among them would concentrate on propagandizing female factory workers. The SDs believed then that working-class men would never submit to instruction from a woman and moreover would likely assume that any woman who approached them was a prostitute. Making contact with working-class

---

[63] Podliashuk, *Bogatyrskaia simfoniia*, 151; Stasova, *Vospominanii*, 114–27; Levidova and Salita, *Stasova*, 204–22; D. Puzanov, "Minusinskaia ssylka, 1910–1917 gg.," *Katorga i ssylka*, no. 39 (1928): 82–107; Iu. P. Gaven, "Revoliutsionnoe podpol'e v period imperialisticheskoi voiny v Eniseiskoi gubernii," *Katorga i ssylka*, no. 36 (1927): 112–29. For other discussions of coping techniques among the exiles, see N. I. Teterin, "Sukhaia gil'otina," *Katorga i ssylka*, no. 10 (1924): 178–95; L. Simanovich, "Ocherki iz zhizni v ssylki," *Katorga i ssylka*, no. 6 (1923): 240–46; and A. N. Cherkunov, "Zhizn' politicheskoi ssylki i tiur'my po perekhvachennym pis'mam," *Katorga i ssylka*, no. 26 (1926): 171–85.

women, however, proved extremely difficult for the SD propagandists. Miserably paid and usually unskilled, subject to abuse from bosses as well as their husbands, female factory workers were a very vulnerable minority in the new industrial labor force. They rightly feared the consequences of associating with revolutionaries. Housewives married to workers seem to have been even more resistant to radical appeals. Some of them not only refused to have anything to do with the revolutionaries themselves but attempted to keep their husbands away from them as well. Dora Lazurkina, a teacher who worked in the St. Petersburg underground, told Lenin in 1904, "The workers' wives greet us coldly; at times they declare openly that they don't like our visits. And this is understandable, for we draw their husbands into party work and the results are almost always prison or exile."[64]

Most Social Democrats, female and male, interpreted this hostility much less sympathetically than did Lazurkina. Rather than attempt to understand why poor women were so frightened of political activism, they wrote them off as hopelessly backward and adopted the position that efforts to propagandize them were a waste of precious resources. Cecelia Bobrovskaia, a midwife from Belorus, summed up the attitude prevailing in the party after 1900: "It never occurred to us to carry on work among them [women]; the job seemed such a thankless one. Besides, there was so much other work which we could barely cope with that agitation among the women was left for more favourable times." Social Democrats also argued that initiatives aimed at the female half of the working class would sow suspicion between the sexes, encourage feminist ideas, and thereby divide the revolutionary movement. Krupskaia remembered later how discouraged she had been by her comrades' resistance:

At one time [Liudmila] Stal and I had tried to do some work among the masses of emigrant women, such as milliners, dressmakers, etc. We organized a number of meetings, but underestimation of this work was a hindrance. At every meeting someone was bound to kick up a row and raise the question, "What's the idea of a women's meeting, anyway?" And so the thing petered out, although it might have done some good. Ilyich [Lenin] thought it a useful job.[65]

So who were female revolutionaries to propagandize, if workers of both sexes rebuffed their overtures? The first women in Russian Social

[64] *Zhenshchiny goroda Lenina*, 25. For other examples of women attacking Bolshevichki, see *Revoliutsionnaia deiatel' nost' Konkordii Nikolaevny Samoilovoi. Sbornik vospominanii* (Moscow. 1922), 23; G. Mishkevich, *Konkordiia Nikolaevna Samoilova* (Leningrad, 1947), 21; and Bobrovskaia, *Twenty Years in Underground Russia*, 108–09. On working with women in the 1890s, see Lidiia Dan in Haimson, *The Making of Three Russian Revolutionaries*, 80–82, 86.

[65] Bobrovskaia, *Twenty Years in Underground Russia*, 109; Krupskaia, *Reminiscences of Lenin*, 226.

Democracy were students who concentrated on spreading the word among fellow students. Then, in the early 1900s, some working-class men became more receptive, probably because they had been radicalized by several years of strikes and protests, and because they had gotten used to female teachers in Sunday schools and night schools. At this point many female SDs dropped their efforts to contact working-class women and turned instead to organizing reading groups composed mostly of men. For example, in 1900 Sofia Smidovich began her career in the underground by leading a circle of male workers in Moscow with Lenin's sister Anna Ulianova. Samoilova, Zemliachka, Bosh, Inessa, and most of the other prominent Bolshevichki educated men in such circles in the first years of the twentieth century. They did not turn their attention back to working-class women until 1905.[66]

In 1905, when demonstrations by people from all walks of life occurred on an unprecedented scale, working-class women also showed signs of political life. There were several well-publicized strikes by female workers, and women were elected to the soviets that served as strike committees in St. Petersburg and the textile center of Ivanovo-Voznesensk.[67] At the same time feminist groups, who advocated universal suffrage, equalization of women's legal rights, and improvements in working conditions for the poor, became very active, holding large demonstrations and well-attended meetings. Female Social Democrats condemned the feminists as bourgeois people interested only in improving the lot of the women of their own class, but they also realized that the feminists were building support throughout the intelligentsia and, to a lesser extent, among working-class women. Perhaps, some Social Democrats, including Kollontai, began to argue, the female proletariat could be reached after all. Perhaps the feminists would gain their support if the Social Democrats did not make any effort to do so.

After 1905 a few Bolshevichki, among them Samoilova and Inessa, set out to establish contacts with proletarian women through newly legalized unions and workers' clubs. They recruited female textile workers, who came to make up the preponderance of working-class Bolshevichki. They also attempted, with more limited success, to set up unions among workers

[66] *Slavnye bol'shevichki*, 275–76. For another reference to the importance of the evening-school courses as recruiting grounds, see Institut istorii partii, *V edinom stroiu* (Moscow, 1960), 25–34.

[67] F. Barkhina and V. Efimov, *Rabotnitsa v zabastovochnom dvizhenii* (Moscow, 1931), 54–57; Institut istorii partii pri TsK KP Belorussii, Filial instituta Marksizma-Leninizma pri TsK KPSS, *V bor'be i trude*, 3rd ed. (Minsk, 1985), 9–17; *Oktiabriem rozhdennye* (Moscow, 1967), 41–42; S. Serditova, *Bol'sheviki v bor'be za zhenskie proletarskie massy, 1903 g.–fevral' 1917 g.* (Moscow, 1959), 34–38, 43, 56–57. See also Vera Broido's pamphlet, *Zhenskaia dolia* (Geneva, 1905).

as yet unorganized – seamstresses, laundresses, shop clerks, and even domestic servants. Bolshevichki also became involved in women's clubs that offered cultural activities such as lectures, concerts, and museum tours. Kollontai, then still a Menshevik, established the first of these clubs in St. Petersburg, the Society for Mutual Aid to Women Workers, in 1907. It survived only a year, but its successors included the Sampsonievskii Society in St. Petersburg (where meetings of the board of directors were actually meetings of the local party committee) and the Third Women's Club in Moscow, a middle-class organization taken over by a board of Bolshevichki led by Zinaida Krzhizhanovskaia, a veteran Sunday-school teacher who was also a close friend of Stasova and Krupskaia.[68]

These activities, despite the fact that they were very small in scale, brought forth a rift between Bolshevichki over the question of "work among women," a rift that would persist past the revolution and into the Soviet period. Many Bolshevichki, perhaps the majority, continued after 1905 to consider proletarian women a backward lot and efforts to reach them a waste of time and energy. Such Bolshevichki probably also feared that working with women would damage their standing with male party members, who denigrated such activities. On the other hand, the Bolshevichki who rejected such fears, although they were few in number, came to have an importance within the party far beyond their numbers, for it was they who established the Soviet program of women's emancipation after the revolution. By 1912 they had been encouraged by their successes in unions and workers' clubs as well as by continuing signs of rising political consciousness among female factory workers. Out of their belief in the possibilities of propagandizing poor women came the most important development in work among women before 1917, the estab-lishment of the newspaper *Rabotnitsa* (*Woman Worker*).

Rabotnitsa was Samoilova's brain child. After the success of the Woman's Day meeting in February 1913, Samoilova had begun running a column in *Pravda* entitled "The Labor and Life of Women Workers," which contained articles on conditions in the factories. The enthusiastic response of the newspaper's female readers – dozens of them wrote Samoilova and came to see her at the *Pravda* offices – convinced her that an audience existed for a periodical devoted exclusively to working-class women. She contacted leading Bolshevichki abroad and soon acquired strong support from Inessa and from Liudmila Stal, a journalist from

---

[68] Bobrovskaia, *Twenty Years in Underground Russia*, 149–50; *Zhenshchiny v revoliutsii*, 61–65, 112–16; *Kaluzhskie bol'shevichki* (Kaluga, 1960), 89–90; *Leningradki*, 61–62; Institut istorii partii, *V edinom stroiu*, 29; Eva Broido, *Memoirs of a Revolutionary*, trans. and ed. Vera Broido (London, 1967), 133–35; E. D. Stasova, ed., *Iz istorii nelegal'nykh bibliotek revoliutsionnykh organizatsii v tsarskoi Rossii* (Moscow, 1956), 146–47; *Zhen-shchiny goroda Lenina*, 49–57.

Ukraine who was working closely with Krupskaia. Krupskaia, now the secretary-in-chief of the Bolshevik faction, proved somewhat more dubious, wondering whether they could raise the money to finance the venture and whether a separate magazine for women would encourage feminist ideas. In January 1914 Samoilova wrote to reassure her: "We are surely not feminists and we very much want the male estate [*soslovie*] to collaborate with us."[69] By then Lenin had approved the formation of an editorial board consisting of Krupskaia, Inessa, and Stal abroad, Samoilova, Anna Elizarova (Lenin's sister), and Elena Rozmirovich (Bosh's sister) in Russia. Some friction developed between Samoilova and the émigrés, whom she perceived to be making decisions without consulting her, but they all managed to cooperate well enough to prepare an inaugural issue of *Rabotnitsa* in time for Woman's Day 1914.[70]

On an evening in February 1914, Samoilova met with her editorial board, which had now grown to include Klavdiia Nikolaeva and Alexandra Artiukhina. They had just begun a final polishing of the copy for the first issue when the police arrived to arrest them all. Publishing the journal was not illegal, but being a Social Democrat still was. One member of the board, Anna Elizarova, managed to escape because she was late to the meeting, and she put out seven numbers of *Rabotnitsa* before the police banned the magazine altogether later in the year. After several months and a successful hunger strike in prison, Samoilova and the other editors were exiled to a village in Novgorod guberniia, from which most quickly escaped and returned to the underground.

Short-lived though *Rabotnitsa* proved to be, it laid the foundation for future developments in two ways. It brought together the women – Inessa, Krupskaia, Samoilova, Liudmila Stal, and Praskovia Kudelli – who would formulate and lead the Soviet program for women's emancipation. (Kollontai, soon to become a Bolshevik and already the Russian Social Democrats' most important writer on women's issues, was in contact with the editors and expressed warm support for the journal.)[71] *Rabotnitsa* also

---

[69] *Vsegda s vami. Sbornik posviashchennyi 50-letiiu zhurnala "Rabotnitsa"* (Moscow, 1964), 30–31. Although some sources (*Vsegda s vami*, 29, 48; Liudmila Stal', "Istoriia zhurnala 'Rabotnitsa,'" in *Zhenshchiny v revoliutsii*, 108–09) have claimed that *Rabotnitsa* was Lenin's idea, other, less hagiographic histories give the credit to Samoilova (*Leningradki*, 131–32). Krupskaia expressed her doubts in a letter to her sister-in-law Anna Elizarova, published in N. K. Krupskaia, *Pedagogicheskie sochineniia*, 11 vols. (Moscow, 1963), vol. XI, 156–57.

[70] On relations between Samoilova and the editors abroad, see Inessa's letters in Armand, *Stat'i*, 211–16. See also Pavel Podliashuk, *Tovarishch Inessa*, 3rd ed. (Moscow, 1973), 144. For Samoilova's account of the founding of the journal, see *Zhenshchiny v revoliutsii*, 104–05.

[71] *Rabotnitsa*, 16 March 1914, 6. See also her article "Zhenskii den'," *Pravda*, 17 February 1913, 1–2.

allowed these Bolshevichki to begin formulating their analysis of women's emancipation, an analysis that blended feminism and Marxism to create a set of propositions that can justly be labeled Bolshevik feminism. These propositions began with the premise that women were an increasingly important part of the labor force, but were more difficult to mobilize than men because they feared political activism, an attitude encouraged by the men around them. Hence *Rabotnitsa* and meetings aimed specifically at women, such as those on Woman's Day, were necessary to raise women's consciousness. Liudmila Stal captured the situation when she wrote: "The woman worker will not come to us, so we will go to her." The goal of this outreach was to draw women into the revolutionary movement, where they would participate as men's equals. "Since the Social-Democratic Party is the only party that demands women's equality and fights for it," wrote Zlata Lilina in the second issue of *Rabotnitsa*, "the female working masses should be in the ranks of this party and should strengthen the ranks of the fighters for the freedom and equality of all humanity by walking hand-in-hand with their comrades, male workers."[72]

The editors declared repeatedly that they were not encouraging women to believe, as feminists did, that men were the source of their oppression. Women suffered from an inequality visited on them by traditional customs and by the inhumanity of the modern factory system; they would overcome these difficulties only by banding together with men to destroy the status quo. Suspicions that the editors planned to set up a separate, feminist organization were groundless. Samoilova wrote reassuringly in *Pravda* in January 1914 that "the women workers' movement is very tightly connected to the general proletarian [movement], it is only a part of one whole. Therefore women workers' tasks can only be the same as those of the whole working class."[73] *Rabotnitsa* then went on to justify giving attention to proletarian women by documenting in article after article the difficulties of their lives, both those they endured in common with men, such as low wages and dangerous working conditions, and those that were

---

[72] Liudmila Stal', "K organizatsii zhenshchin-rabotnits," *Pravda*, 22 May 1913, 2; *Rabotnitsa*, 1 April 1914, 6. Lilina was a former medical student who had become a teacher; she was married to Grigorii Zinoviev.

[73] N. S—va, "K mezhdunarodnomu dniu zhenshchin rabotnits," *Pravda*, 29 January 1914, 2. See also "Vneshkol'noe obrazovanie i ekonomicheskoe polozhenie zhenshchin," *Pravda*, 9 January 1913, 2; 23 January 1913, 3; 14 February 1913, 3; "K mezhdunarod-nomu zhenskomu dniu," *Pravda*, 15 January 1913, 2; *Pravda*, 17 February 1913 (entire issue); the column "Trud i zhizn' rabotnits," *Pravda*, February–May 1913. See also *Rabotnitsa*, especially N. Sibiriakova [Samoilova], "Avgust Bebel i zhenskii vopros," 23 February 1914, 9–10; N. K. [Krupskaia], "Rabotnitsa, sem'ia, i prostitutsiia," 19 April 1914, 6–7; [Inessa Armand], "Izbiratel'naia prava zhenshchin," *Rabotnitsa*, 19 April 1914, 1–2. See also an article of Krupskaia's reprinted in *Vsegda s vami*, 30–33.

visited on them because of their gender, particularly sexual abuse, the burdens of caring for children, and lower pay than men even when the work they did was equally skilled.

The basic principles here were not original with Inessa or Krupskaia or Samoilova; they came directly from Marx and Engels, as well as from August Bebel, the German Social Democrat whose *Woman Under Socialism* was the most widely read statement of the Social-Democratic position on women's emancipation. Since 1908 Kollontai had made the same arguments in speeches, in articles, and in a book-length study, *The Social Bases of the Woman Question* (1908). Kollontai and the Bolshevichki who would soon be her close comrades believed, as did all revolutionary Marxists, that oppression sprang from the capitalist economy and that the only sure remedy would be a revolution in which the working class seized control of the levers of power. In their view, suffrage, then the goal of huge feminist movements in Britain and the United States, would not alter the fundamental injustices of society. Nor did the feminists wish it to, the Social Democrats argued, for feminists were middle-class women seeking reforms that would benefit themselves while preserving capitalism.

The *Rabotnitsa* editors added to this general Marxist interpretation a shrewd emphasis on the importance of women joining men in the revolutionary movement. Properly educated, the female members of the working class would "strengthen the ranks of the fighters," Lilina declared. Left in ignorance, on the other hand, they would weaken the fighters and more generally undermine support for the cause among men. This interesting argument constituted an important addition to fundamental Marxist premises, for Marx, Engels, and Bebel had neglected this undoubtedly significant dimension of sexual interaction and failed to grant women an active role in the revolutionary process. In their scenario, working men would overthrow the old order, construct the new one, and then bring women emancipation. Women would only need to sit at home and wait for the historical actors to fling the front door open.[74] The first prominent Social Democrat to contest this vision of passivity was Klara Zetkin, a leader of the German Social-Democratic Party, who in the 1890s advanced the proposition that mobilizing women would strengthen the movement and thereby accelerate the pace of change. Zetkin used this utilitarian argument to persuade her comrades to establish a party department specializing in propaganda among women. After conferring

---

[74] For an excellent analysis of Marx's conception of women's relationship to revolution, see Andrea Nye, *Feminist Theory and the Philosophies of Man* (New York, 1989), 37–64. On Klara Zetkin and the German Social-Democratic women's movement, see Jean H. Quataert, *Reluctant Feminists in German Social Democracy* (Princeton, 1979).

with Zetkin in Germany in 1906, Kollontai began to argue that the Russian SDs should establish their own "women's department," but her comrades, many Bolshevichki among them, responded that such a venture was at best a waste of time, at worst a divisive distraction. The idea of a woman's department languished until after 1917, but the Bolshevichki who established *Rabotnitsa* did adopt Zetkin's basic rationale for reaching out to women.

The *Rabotnitsa* editors can fairly be labeled feminist Marxists because of the priority they gave to women's liberation. These Bolshevichki did not consider patriarchal customs and women's secondary position in the labor force merely unfortunate consequences of the property system, to be remedied at some indefinite point in the future; they considered them central concerns, primary injustices that should figure prominently in the list of capitalism's bad deeds. They did not want proletarian women to suffer and be still until the revolution came. Rather, despite the doubts and disapproval this raised among more conventional Social Democrats, they dedicated themselves to drawing women into the revolutionary movement.

Yet it should hardly need to be emphasized that these Bolshevichki did have very fundamental differences with the feminists then active throughout the European world. Feminists were not usually political revolutionaries. Their ambition was to build a broadly based movement, led by women, to achieve reforms for women. It was not true, as the Bolshevichki charged, that feminists were only interested in improving the status of the propertied. Feminists all around Europe were concerned about the situation of working women. In fact, Russian feminists' efforts to reach out to the poor had alarmed some of the Bolshevichki. Nor were all feminists simply reformers basically content with the structure of capitalist democracy, as the Bolshevichki charged. Feminism by the early twentieth century had grown to be a large movement containing a broad spectrum of opinion. Radical feminists were advancing a variety of proposals for fundamental change, many focused on equalizing the relations between women and men in family life and on granting women control over their own sexuality. The left wing of feminism was then (as it is now) strongly influenced by socialist ideas. Sylvia Pankhurst, Lily Braun, and Charlotte Perkins Gilman, to name only three of the best-known activists, were socialists with very strong feminist affiliations. And all suffered from divided loyalties, for as feminists they believed that supporting woman-centered, woman-led organizations working within established political systems was the best way to achieve their ends, but as socialists they wanted to participate alongside men in the general movement for the improvement of all humanity. Many of them had decided only after considerable debate and soul-searching to make change for women their central objective.[75] Most socialists, including all the Bolshevichki, disagreed with this decision. They declared that the emancipation of women was but one of a host of necessary social changes that must be achieved through revolution. Patriarchy rested on a foundation of class power. Rally the downtrodden, women and men, to destroy that power, and patriarchy would fall. Women pursuing their own agenda, however worthy it might be, would only hinder the development of the solidarity necessary for revolutionary transformation. Samoilova was absolutely sincere when she wrote approvingly: "The women workers' movement is very tightly connected to the general proletarian [movement], it is only a part of one whole."[76] In her view, class struggle would bring gender equality.

All the Bolshevichki were eager believers in socialism's compelling vision of a unified proletariat led to victory by a unified political party. Unity was a core value for them, and as such it found its way into their conception of themselves, into their collective identity. They expressed it in their understanding of the organization they were building in the present (a movement of comrades drawn from all the peoples of Russia) and the world they were seeking in the future (a place of communal sharing). It was a unity based on equality, the equality of those women and men who had rejected hierarchical society and who now, through effort in the party, devoted themselves to making a just world. This vision of universal harmony was deeply prized by socialists everywhere, but it had particular appeal to Russian SDs, who lived in a crumbling, multi-ethnic empire, where national, religious, and gender differences often led to hatred and injustice.

The Bolshevichki cherished the prospect of the dispossessed making common cause with one another. They took comfort from an analysis that saw all evils, including those plaguing women, as connected in a single corrupting system that could be destroyed in one great upheaval. They also felt deep loyalty to the ideal of solidarity because this ideal promised them acceptance in the men's party they had joined. For all these reasons they considered any independent women's movement fundamentally wrong-headed. The editors of *Rabotnitsa* were to spend the rest of their

---

[75] For a fascinating collection of the writings of French feminists of this era, which includes a section analyzing the situation of the working class, see Jennifer Waelti-Walters and Steven C. Hause, eds., *Feminisms of the Belle Epoque* (Lincoln, Neb., 1994). See also Mary Armfield Hill, *Charlotte Perkins Gilman: The Making of a Radical Feminist* (Philadelphia, 1980); Alfred G. Meyer, *The Feminism and Socialism of Lily Braun* (Bloomington, Ind., 1985); and Patricia W. Romero, *E. Sylvia Pankhurst: Portrait of a Radical* (New Haven, Conn., 1986).

[76] S—va [Samoilova], "K mezhdunarodnomu dniu zhenshchin rabotnits," 2.

careers seeking to emancipate women, but they would never alter their opinion that women could only find liberation in tandem with men.

Women of the émigré leadership

There is one last topic in the history of the Bolshevichki in the prerevolutionary years that requires consideration, and that is these women's presence among the party's émigré leadership. Of the hundreds of Bolshevichki who lived abroad at some point before 1917 and took part in émigré politics, four – Inessa Armand, Evgeniia Bosh, Alexandra Kollontai, and Nadezhda Krupskaia – were prominent figures whose careers deserve attention.

None of these women achieved the rank of the premier male theoreticians – Plekhanov, Akselrod, Martov, Dan, Trotsky, Lenin – or even of such lesser lights as Anatolii Lunacharskii and A. A. Bogdanov. Indeed, Rosa Luxemburg, the German Social Democrat of Polish-Jewish extraction, was the only esteemed female theoretician in all of European Social Democracy. Kollontai claimed a role in interpreting Marxism, but she wrote on women's emancipation, a subject of lesser importance in the view of the leadership. Perhaps there were no women among the party's theoreticians because many Bolshevichki had the same doubts about their intellectual abilities as Stasova. Perhaps they felt a pervasive, if unspoken, assumption that the party's deepest thinkers about politics, economics, and history were properly men. It is also true, however, that only a handful of men did Marxist interpretation. The great majority of Russia's émigré Social Democrats who lived in western and central Europe filled their days with exactly the same sorts of activities without regard to distinctions of gender. They attended meetings, helped in communications with Russia, worked with local socialists, and scrounged to support themselves. In this world, Inessa, Bosh, Kollontai, and Krupskaia played important parts that prepared them for positions of leadership after 1917.[77]

Of the four, Kollontai was the least engaged in the politics of the Bolsheviks. A Menshevik throughout most of the prerevolutionary period, Kollontai came over to the Bolsheviks in 1915 because she believed that Lenin was the Russian Social Democrat most resolutely opposing World War I. She then worked as one of his agents in Scandinavia and made two trips to the United States to raise money and publicize his views. She also wrote a pamphlet, *Who Needs the War?*, which was translated into several languages and distributed among the troops bogged down in the trenches

---

[77] On Kollontai, see Clements, *Bolshevik Feminist*, and Beatrice Farnsworth, *Alexandra Kollontai: Socialism, Feminism, and the Bolshevik Revolution* (Stanford, 1980). On Krupskaia, see McNeal, *Bride of the Revolution*. On Inessa, see Elwood, *Inessa Armand*.

of World War I. Because Kollontai arrived late in Bolshevik ranks and because she was living far from the center of their political life most of the time, she did not play a major role in the faction's émigré organizations. Kollontai's primary, and considerable, accomplishment before 1917 was her participation in the formulation of a feminist variant of Marxism.[78]

By contrast, no one was more important to the Bolsheviks than Krupskaia; her work as Lenin's administrative assistant enabled him to remain the leader of the faction. Krupskaia was an extraordinarily diligent, competent woman, who could write 300 letters a week (most in code), keep track of the addresses and aliases of people almost constantly on the run within Russia, and maintain financial accounts. She was also an administrator able to assess the strengths and weaknesses of potential supporters and to cajole allies into working effectively. She did all this while living in foreign locales where she was never happy, and while coping with worries about money, her own health (she suffered from hyperthyroidism), and her moody husband's demands.[79]

Krupskaia had interests of her own, mainly in education, but she put them aside during the underground years to work for Lenin. If she ever had differences with him over strategy or tactics, she kept them private and confined her voluminous correspondence to the nuts-and-bolts questions that were in her domain. Service to her husband was also service to the cause of liberating Russia, but Krupskaia did not think of herself primarily as a woman doing her wifely duty. Rather, she saw herself as a revolutionary who was married to the man best qualified by the penetrating power of his intellect and the purity of his resolve to play a leading role in finding the way to the revolution. Few other Bolshevichki arranged their careers in the underground as successfully as Krupskaia, and none made a greater contribution to the creation and maintenance of the Bolshevik faction.

Inessa Armand became known after 1910 as the other important woman in Lenin's inner circle. In 1909 she escaped from a sentence of exile to the remote north of Russia in order to go to Switzerland to nurse her ill lover, Vladimir Armand. Two weeks after she arrived, he died of tuberculosis. Inessa decided to remain in western Europe, for if she returned to Russia she was likely to be sent back to exile. She enrolled at the University of Brussels, and in the summer of 1910 she passed her baccalaureate examinations in history and political economy "with distinction." Thereafter she moved to Paris, where she quickly became a close friend and staunch supporter of Lenin and Krupskaia.[80]

[78] On Kollontai during the war years, see Clements, *Bolshevik Feminist*, 82–102.
[79] McNeal, *Bride of the Revolution*, 101–03, 158–60.
[80] Elwood, *Inessa Armand*, 55–80.

Inessa had much to recommend her to the leaders of Bolshevism. She was a seasoned party worker, having been in the Moscow underground since 1904 and having been arrested three times and having served more than six months in prison, in addition to the time in exile. She was a firm supporter of Lenin's doctrines on party organization. Unlike Stasova and Zemliachka, Inessa had not become discouraged after the political ferment of 1905–06 died down. She explained her resolve to Vladimir Armand in a letter in 1908:

The fact is that in the first place I came this route later than others. Marxism wasn't an enthusiasm of youth for me but the completion of a long evolution from right to left. In the last steps of this evolution, you did a lot for me. Thanks to you I learned and understood better and sooner, because you yourself were so correct [verno] and deep . . . Finally and last not least [sic, in English], this last, reactionary year [1907] I spent among the proletariat, while others were spending it in an entirely different atmosphere. So not I, but the situation, made me firmer.[81]

Inessa had the personal qualities Lenin and Krupskaia respected. She was reserved, thoughtful, hard-working, reliable, intelligent, and culti-vated. She was, as well, a sympathetic friend. Inessa missed the large, loving Armand family, particularly her five children who lived most of the year with their father, so she attached great importance to the revolution-ary community. She enjoyed cooking for people who turned up to visit her in her tiny rented rooms in Paris, or Krakow, or wherever she might be, and when she could manage it she rented a piano, on which she played Chopin and Beethoven expertly. Krupskaia later wrote, "Things seemed cozier and more cheerful when Inessa was there."[82]

Very quickly she became a close associate of Lenin and Krupskaia. In the summer of 1911 she lectured on the history of the socialist movement at the summer school for émigrés and Russian workers that Lenin organized in the Paris suburb of Longjumeau. A year later Lenin asked her to return to Russia to work as his representative on *Pravda*. The police tracked her down after only a few months, probably on information from Roman Malinovskii, the Bolsheviks' Duma delegate. A year later, after having been bailed out of prison by her husband Alexander, Inessa was back in western Europe, where she remained until 1917.[83]

Once again Inessa went to work as Lenin's agent. In July 1914 she represented him at a meeting of the International Socialist Bureau in

[81] Armand, *Stat'i*, 210.
[82] N. K. Krupskaia, ed., *Pamiati Inessy Armand* (Moscow, 1926), 36; Krupskaia, *Remini-scences of Lenin*, 131.
[83] Podliashuk, *Tovarishch Inessa*, 101–21, 126–27; Krupskaia, *Pamiaty Inessy Armand*, 12, 95–96; A. P. Iakushina, "Iz istorii deiatel'nosti komiteta zagranichnoi organizatsii RSDRP, 1911–1914 gg.," *Voprosy istorii KPSS*, no. 4 (1966): 72–80; K. Ostroukhova, *Shestaia (Prazhskaia) vserossiiskaia konferentsiia RSDRP* (Moscow, 1957), 33, 79.

Brussels. When World War I began, she turned her attention to building alliances among anti-war socialists in western Europe. This project involved the usual émigré activities – writing letters, translating Lenin's articles into French, promoting publication and distribution of his pamphlets. In all of this Inessa bowed to Lenin's authority and the force of his arguments. Like Stasova and perhaps Krupskaia, Inessa doubted that she could hold her own in the intense political debate wherein socialists proved their mettle.[84] Such a lack of self-confidence made it easier for all these women to work with Lenin, and indeed women may have been better able than men to cope with his exceedingly demanding and controlling personality. Of the handful of men around him, only Grigorii Zinoviev submitted so consistently to Lenin's dictation as did Krupskaia and Inessa.

Of course there is another explanation for Inessa's deference to Lenin, and that is that she and he were lovers. A rumor to this effect began during World War I, then persisted throughout the 1920s, embellished along the way by people such as Kollontai, who delighted in such stories (the more so since her own love affairs were much tittered at). The gossips offered only circumstantial evidence: the close proximity in which Inessa and Lenin lived from time to time, the anguish Lenin displayed at Inessa's funeral in 1920, the fact that the editors of his collected works in the 1920s declined to publish his letters to her in their entirety.[85] But there is now at least one piece of solid evidence that supports the rumors, a letter from Inessa to Lenin that the late historian Dmitrii Volkogonov discovered in the Communist Party archives. In December 1913 Inessa wrote to Lenin from Paris, to which she had just returned after having spent several months with him and Krupskaia in Krakow. In it she discussed her love for him and his decision that she move back to France:

Looking around this place I know so well, I realize as never before what a huge place you occupied in my life here in Paris, that almost all my activity here in Paris was connected by a thousand threads to thoughts of you. I wasn't completely in love with you then, but I loved you then, very much. I could manage now without kisses if I could only see you; to talk to you sometimes would be a joy, and it could

---

[84] For correspondence on the meeting in Brussels, see V. I. Lenin, *Polnoe sobranie sochinenii*, 5th ed., 56 vols. (Moscow, 1958–66), vol. XLVIII, 301, 305, 307 (hereafter cited as *PSS*). For examples of her taking a straight Leninist line on the war, see Olga Ravich, "Mezhdunarodnaia zhenskaia sotsialisticheskaia konferentsiia, 1915 g.," *Proletarskaia revoliutsiia*, no. 10 (1925): 165–77; Armand, *Stat'i*, 30–31, 224–25, 227–28, 239–46. She did question Lenin's advocacy of support for colonial wars in 1916 (Lenin, *PSS*, vol. XLIX, 328–45). On her lack of self-confidence, see Podliashuk, *Tovarishch Inessa*, 89.

[85] For the gossip, see Marcel Body, "Alexandra Kollontai," *Preuves*, no. 14 (April 1952): 12–24; Victor Serge and Natalia Sedova Trotsky, *The Life and Death of Leon Trotsky*, trans. Arnold J. Pomerans (New York, 1975), 86; Bertram Wolfe, "Lenin and Inessa Armand," *Slavic Review* 22 (March 1963): 96–114.

not cause anyone pain. Why was I deprived of this? You [*ty*, the familiar form of the pronoun] ask if I am angry that you "carried out" this parting. No, I think you didn't do it for your own sake.[86]

Inessa then defended herself, lamely, by declaring that she had always gotten along very well with Krupskaia and that Krupskaia had told her, during their work at the summer school in Longjumeau in 1911, how much she cared for her. Inessa then allowed herself another declaration, one as revealing of Lenin's nature as of hers: "I so love not only to listen to you, but to look at you when you talk. In the first place, your face becomes so animated and, secondly, it's easy to look then because you don't notice." She then turned to reporting on the work she had done since returning to Paris. Only in closing the letter did she again become intimate. "I kiss you affectionately. Your Inessa."[87]

None of the Bolsheviks who gossiped about Lenin and Inessa ever had any difficulty explaining why he was attracted to her. She was accomplished, sympathetic, and beautiful. She also followed his lead, a behavior Lenin must have found endearing, particularly in such an appealing woman. Gossips did not ask what she saw in him, but now it would appear that Inessa herself supplied the answer. She was drawn to his intellect and will, the same qualities that men found compelling in him. Bereft of Vladimir Armand, the lover whom she considered her guide in revolutionary politics, cut off from her children and her home, Inessa probably found it quite easy to fall in love with the leader of the cause that had brought her into exile, particularly when it became clear that he admired her in return.

Their mutual feeling persisted through the decade, into the revolution, and the civil war. They lived near one another from time to time, but were more often separated, with Inessa based in Paris and Lenin and Krupskaia in Switzerland. Those of their letters that were published after editing by Soviet censors reveal them angry with one another from time to time. Lenin considered it intolerable that Inessa should ever disagree with him. She learned that he could be peremptory, demanding, and patronizing. Nevertheless they remained close friends. Lenin was deeply solicitous of Inessa's well-being during the civil war years, so much so that people who knew him well concluded then, if they had not done so before, that he loved her.[88]

For her part, Krupskaia remained Inessa's friend and they worked

---

[86] Dmitrii Volkogonov, *Lenin. Politicheskii portret*, 2 vols. (Moscow, 1994), vol. II, 303.
[87] Ibid., vol. II, 304.
[88] For examples of Lenin hectoring Inessa when she disagreed with him, see Lenin, *PSS*, vol. XLIX, 54–57, 279–81, 344–48. For examples of her irritation with him, see ibid., vol. XLVIII, 314, 324; vol. XLIX, 54–57, 327.

closely together on various projects for years. After Inessa's death in 1920, Krupskaia extended her protection and help to the five Armand children. Dmitrii Volkogonov may be right when he declares that this was one of those remarkable *ménages à trois* that the Russian intelligentsia had long idealized, in which each member practiced an extraordinary tolerance for the feelings of the others.[89] Or perhaps Lenin remained true to his determination to break off his physical relationship with Inessa and thereby earned his wife's forgiveness. Or perhaps Krupskaia was Russia's Eleanor Roosevelt, keeping up appearances in order to remain a force in the party her husband led.

Evgeniia Bosh was yet another women prominent among the émigrés, but her relationship with Lenin was very different from those of other Bolshevichki. Inessa, Krupskaia, Stasova, Zemliachka, and even the long time Menshevik Kollontai accepted Lenin's leadership and his tutelage. Bosh did not. She treated him as an equal, and when he tried to impose his will on her, she not only resisted, as Inessa sometimes did, she fought back. Although she considered herself a Bolshevik, Bosh shared the belief of most underground workers that the émigrés were unnecessarily quarrelsome and doctrinaire. She also thought she knew a good deal more than Lenin about the realities of work inside Russia, and consequently about how revolution should be made. Unlike Inessa and Stasova, Bosh was never reticent in expressing her opinions. Unlike Zemliachka, she sought a place in émigré politics.

When Bosh arrived in Switzerland in February 1915, she came with a well-established reputation as an experienced leader who had played a prominent part in the underground in Kiev. She had lived there from 1906 onward, working with her sister Elena Rozmirovich. Several years after she had moved to the city, her mother's second husband (Elena's father) had died, and Mariia Maish had moved to Kiev to keep house for her two revolutionary daughters. Bosh and her mother seem to have achieved some sort of reconciliation at last, although Bosh remained scarred by their earlier conflict as well as by her health problems. She was always, by comparison with the far more cheerful and outgoing Elena, somewhat dour, reserved, and distrustful.

The two sisters worked together until Rozmirovich was arrested in 1910 and sentenced to a term in exile. Leaving her daughter with Bosh, she escaped to western Europe. Bosh remained in Kiev, doing what little she could in a decimated party organization. Alexander Rosnovskii, a member of the Kiev committee, later described the mood: "The party dwindled

---

[89] Volkogonov, *Lenin*, vol. II, 296. Carter Elwood, in his recent biography of Inessa, did not find gossip about an affair between her and Lenin persuasive. He was not given access to the archives where the letters were kept, however (Elwood, *Inessa Armand*, 173–89).

away before our eyes. New factions, groups, tendencies arose every day. There weren't any people, there wasn't any faith, there wasn't any desire to work. The Okhrana was working at top speed: searches, arrests, exiles every day. The poison of provocation [informers] decomposed every beginning in embryo. No one trusted the closest comrade."[90]

In 1910 Bosh met Iurii Piatakov, a law student eleven years her junior who had just been expelled from the university in St. Petersburg for revolutionary activities. The son of the director of a sugar refinery in the Ukraine, Piatakov considered Kiev his home town; hence he went back there in late 1910 or early 1911 and sought out contacts among the Social Democrats. Piatakov's intelligence impressed those he found, and the few still intent on organizing an underground movement welcomed him to their small circle.[91] Bosh was one of these; their relationship quickly deepened into a love affair.

Bosh and Piatakov managed to assemble a functioning committee in Kiev in the fall of 1911. They followed the familiar division of labor – she became technical secretary and he organizational secretary – but there is no evidence that Bosh deferred to Piatakov. Rather, they shared leadership of the committee. Both gravitated to the Bolsheviks because Lenin advocated building a strong underground movement, but they disagreed with him when he called for a permanent break with the Mensheviks. Instead, they tried to reconstruct a unified Social-Democratic organization in Kiev. David Shvarts, a printer and member of the Kiev committee, later described their reasons for refusing to fight with the Mensheviks: "We thought then that all the factional struggles and the huge number of groups were exclusively the result of 'the emigration,' of being cut off from Russian organizations and not being acquainted with the conditions and needs of local work."[92]

By early 1912 the six-member Kiev committee had created an organization of three raion (neighborhood) committees and twelve or thirteen workers' circles. Bosh was also developing a reputation as a hard

[90] Rosnovskii, "Iz epokhi 'Zvezdy' i 'Pravdy' v Kieve," 102. On Rozmirovich, see T. F. Avramenko and M. N. Simoian, "Elena Fedorovna Rozmirovich," *Voprosy istorii KPSS*, no. 3 (1966): 98–102.
[91] See Piatakov's autobiographical sketch in Georges Haupt and Jean-Jacques Marie, *Makers of the Russian Revolution*, trans. C. I. P. Ferdinand (Ithaca, N. Y., 1974), 182–88.
[92] Shvarts [D. M. Shvartsman], "Kievskaia partorganizatsiia v 1911–1912 gg.," *Litopys revoliutsii*, no. 4 (1928): 150. For Bosh's and Piatakov's activities, see also M. Maiorov, "K perepiske N. K. Krupskoi so Shvartsmanom," *Litopys revoliutsii*, no. 4 (1928): 153–57; E. Preobrazhenskii, "Evgeniia Bogdanovna Bosh," *Proletarskaia revoliutsiia*, no. 2 (1925): 8; Rosnovskii, "Iz epokhi 'Zvezdy' i 'Pravdy' v Kieve," 101–42; Shvarts, "Kievskaia partorganizatsiia v 1911–1912 gg."; Shvarts [D. M. Shvartsman], "Iz revoliutsionnogo proshlogo," *Voprosy istorii KPSS*, no. 1 (1967): 115–20. On party attitudes toward underground activities after 1905, see Elwood, *Russian Social Democracy in the Underground*, 173–74, 179.

Bolshevichka, described by her co-workers in terms similar to those applied to Stasova and Zemliachka. Alexander Rosnovskii later wrote, "When Evgeniia Bosh appeared at our meetings, involuntarily somehow the conversations took on a business-like character and the workers, especially the youth, addressed themselves to business seriously. Comrade Bosh was not a lover of long conversations, arguments, and discussions. But every word of hers was imbued with true belief and deep revolutionary spirit, and therefore it was hard to raise an objection in debate."[93]

Having become a leader in the underground, Bosh was destined for prison. David Shvarts estimated that it usually took the Okhrana in Kiev seven to eight months to track down revolutionaries; in the case of this group they were right on schedule. Police agents were following Bosh from December 1911 on, but only in April 1912 did they feel that they had enough evidence to arrest her and ten of her comrades. Piatakov and the rest of the committee were picked up in June. After eighteen months in prison, they were all sentenced to lengthy exiles in Siberia. Bosh and Piatakov set off for Irkutsk in April 1914, but they had no intention of staying there. In the fall they fled east, traveling on false passports and money sent to them by their families. The two circumnavigated the globe, crossing the Pacific, the United States, and the Atlantic before arriving in Switzerland in February 1915. Almost immediately they became embroiled in the émigrés' disputes.[94]

There were two connected issues then confronting Russian Social Democrats: how to analyze the current political situation, and how to organize an effective opposition to World War I. The war had deeply divided European socialists, for many of those in the combatant nations, swept up by nationalist feeling, were supporting their countries' war efforts, leaving the remaining few who opposed the war uncertain of how to proceed. The leading spokespeople for the anti-war socialists, Robert Grimm from Switzerland, Henrietta Roland-Holst of the Netherlands, and Oddino Morgari from Italy, favored bringing socialists from the combatant and non-combatant countries together. To that end they sought to take a pacifist stand opposing all war. Lenin disagreed. Outraged by carnage on the battlefields, he demanded that socialists denounce the war as a product of imperialist rivalries and urge the troops turn their guns on their leaders. This call for "war on war" struck other Social Democrats as unnecessarily inflammatory and divisive. German

[93] Rosnovskii, "Iz epokhi 'Zvezdy' i 'Pravdy' v Kieve," 130.
[94] Shvarts, "Iz revoliutsionnogo proshlogo," 119; Mar, *Nezakonechnoe pis'mo*, 37–59; Haupt and Marie, *Makers of the Russian Revolution*, 183; E. Bosh, "Vospominaniia uchastnikov Bernskoi konferentsii," *Proletarskaia revoliutsiia*, no. 5 (1925): 179.

and French socialists, whatever their opinions on the unjustifiability of the conflict, would only be alienated by Lenin's appeal for civil war. The head Bolshevik was also alienating potential allies with his analysis of the relationship between nationalism and imperialism. For decades, socialists had denounced nationalism as a bogus ideology whipped up by the ruling class in order to divide and weaken the proletariat. But as early as 1912, Lenin had begun to reconsider the power of national loyalties. He made no defense of the chauvinism that led to war, but he did suggest that future political arrangements in eastern Europe should probably take the principle of national self-determination into account. He also argued that nationalist movements then rising far away in the colonies of the imperial powers might have revolutionary potential, for they could undermine imperialism itself. They might warrant, therefore, the socialists' support. Rosa Luxemburg, who was now fervently denouncing the war, and Nikolai Bukharin, a rising star among Bolshevik leaders, did not agree. They responded that nationalism, wherever it reared its ugly head, would thwart the development of proletarian internationalism. This position was more consistent with orthodox Marxism than Lenin's, but it was also less sensitive to the political forces at work in the early twentieth century.[95]

Newly arrived in Switzerland, Bosh and Piatakov sided with Bukharin and Luxemburg. In November 1915, when Bukharin submitted an article stating his position to the Bolshevik journal *Sotsial Demokrat,* they co-signed it to indicate their support.[96] One reason why Bosh and Piatakov felt that nationalism was everywhere and always a retrograde force was because they came from Ukraine, a region where the working class was split ethnically between Ukrainians, Jews, Russians, and Poles. In the experience of Bosh and Piatakov, national feeling generated hostility, even vicious animosity, between people who should have been working together. They believed, therefore, that the advocacy of national self-determination in their homeland would legitimate prejudice and lead to the oppression of minorities. Having worked in Kiev to build coalitions among socialists, Bosh and Piatakov also thought Lenin's "war on war" proclamations were impolitic.

In a matter of weeks it became clear that the "Japanese" – Lenin's sardonic nickname for Piatakov and Bosh, taken from the fact that they had crossed Japan as they headed toward Europe – had very fundamental disagreements with the leader of their faction. Their refusal to endorse his

[95] On Lenin, see Robert Service, *Lenin: A Political Life,* vol. II, *Worlds in Collision* (Bloomington, Ind., 1991), 42–47, 88–89, 108–18. On Luxemburg's views, see J. P. Nettl, *Rosa Luxemburg,* 2 vols. (Oxford, 1966), vol. II, 520–36, 627–43. On Bukharin, see Stephen F. Cohen, *Bukharin and the Bolshevik Revolution* (New York, 1973), 22–43.
[96] The article was entitled "On the Slogan of the Right of the Nations to Self-Determination" (Lenin, *PSS,* vol. XLIX, 194).

ideas had serious repercussions, for the couple had brought along money, probably from Piatakov's wealthy parents, with which they intended to fund a journal for anti-war socialists. Of course they expected Lenin to be an important contributor, but when he asked for complete editorial control of the publication, they refused, fearing that he would promote only his own ideas and exclude those with which he disagreed.[97]

According to the historian Robert Service, Lenin was "in a state of constant and even near-hysterical irascibility" in 1915; he reacted to Bosh's and Piatakov's refusal to grant him the power he wanted with insults and vituperation.[98] He also came to conceive a deep dislike for both of them, but more particularly for the strong-willed, outspoken Bosh. By mid-summer 1915 he was blaming all the arguments then dividing the émigré Bolsheviks on the "Japanese." Early the next year he narrowed his focus to Bosh. "Evg. Bosh ran everything in Russia," he wrote to Alexander Shliapnikov in March 1916. "There she could be useful; here *there's nothing for her to do*, she will *concoct* something. You know this émigré calamity, 'concocting' things for people sitting abroad? A terrible calamity." Later in 1916 he confided to Shliapnikov that it was Bosh – she who "called herself a Bolshevik" but had not a brain in her head – who had encouraged Bukharin to oppose him. And as for Piatakov, he was "a complete piglet" with whom it was impossible to do business. Piatakov and Bosh responded to Lenin's foul mood by going off to Stockholm to work with Bukharin. *Kommunist*, the journal they funded, published only two issues.[99]

Bosh was one of the few women Lenin could not intimidate. Unlike Stasova, Inessa, or Krupskaia, she was not overwhelmed by his intellectual gifts or his standing in the party. Throughout their acquaintanceship and in the memoirs she wrote about him after his death, Bosh treated Lenin with respect, but not awe, and never submission.[100] In the confrontations of 1915 and 1916 she remained the same sort of Bolshevik she had been in Kiev, that is, she rejected any proposals that she saw as conflicting with Marxist internationalism, while at the same time seeking to build the broadest possible coalition of revolutionaries. It is possible

[97] For a report that Bosh and Piatakov were providing the money for the journal, see S. P. Mel'gunov and M. A. Tsiavlovskii, *Bol'sheviki. Dokumenty po istorii bol'shevizma s 1903 po 1916 god byvshego Moskovskogo Okhrannogo otdeleniia*, 2nd ed. (Moscow, 1918), 159–61.
[98] Service, *Lenin*, vol. II, 98. A more sympathetic recent interpretation of Lenin's motivation is R. Craig Nation's *War on War: Lenin, the Zimmerwald Left, and the Origins of Communist Internationalism* (Durham, N. C., 1989).
[99] Lenin, *PSS*, vol. XLIX, 196, 248, 331–32. Italics in the original. Lenin's correspondence on this matter is contained ibid., 109–348. See also Service, *Lenin*, vol. II, 108–13.
[100] Bosh, "Vospominaniia uchastnikov Bernskoi konferentsii"; Bosh, "Vstrechi i besedy s Vladimirom Il'ichem," *Proletarskaia revoliutsiia*, no. 3 (1924): 155–73.

that Lenin fastened on her as the architect of his troubles because he did not want to take the responsibility for provoking the rifts himself by insisting on dominating the discussion. Nor did he want to believe that Piatakov and Bukharin, men whose intellectual abilities he admired and whose support he craved, could disagree with him for valid reasons. It was an easier course to blame the disputes on a machinating woman. He was wrong, of course. Piatakov and Bukharin prided themselves on their own abilities to interpret Marxism and resisted being manipulated by anyone, including Lenin. Bosh had simply stated her point of view very plainly in conversations among them; that was her custom throughout her life. She always demanded the right to make her own judgments, and Lenin never really trusted her.

Stasova, Zemliachka, Samoilova, Kollontai, Krupskaia, Inessa, and Bosh were leaders of the Russian Social-Democratic Party. They possessed many of the qualities of the male leaders, indeed of leaders in any political organization. They were ambitious and assertive. They were intelligent and well educated. They preferred work in the underground to Marxist theorizing, as did the great majority of male leaders. They were willing to put their family lives on hold while they worked as revolutionaries. They were hardy, physically and emotionally. Even Bosh, with a history of heart disease, endured the harrowing underground existence for years without breaking. Inessa, Stasova, and probably Krupskaia doubted their intellectual abilities and therefore followed Lenin's lead. Bosh, Zemliachka, and Kollontai claimed more independent voices. But each of these women had a strong sense of personal, self-made identity and an equally strong commitment to the collective identity of the movement. Bosh, Inessa, Kollontai, Krupskaia, Stasova, and Zemliachka were *tverdye*, in the many meanings of that term. They would continue to be leaders in the revolution soon to come.

The underground was the formative experience of the generation of Bolshevichki that was to lead the party through revolution and civil war. Life in the underground demanded great self-sacrifice, in return for the promises of a better future for all and the satisfaction of taking part in a righteous movement. Those Bolshevichki who survived this life with their commitment intact had assimilated themselves closely to the revolutionaries' collective identity and forged strong ties to their comrades. They had also carved out places for women at nearly every level of the organization. Then, twenty years after the oldest of them had first embarked on their crusade, the revolution they sought finally came.

3   The revolution

By February 1917 outrage over worsening economic conditions and despair at continuing losses in the endless war extended from the top to the bottom of Russian society. In December 1916, cousins of the tsar murdered his favorite, Grigorii Rasputin, the disreputable Siberian faithhealer who had come to symbolize the moral bankruptcy of the government. During the early weeks of 1917, as strikes rumbled through the capital's grimy factory districts, liberal Duma delegates talked in tones of rising desperation about forcing the blockheaded monarch to share power. At the same time, poor women stood in long lines on the frozen streets, waiting to buy bread. Frustrated, angry, and cold, they shouted their complaints to one another as they trudged home. Occasionally someone picked up rocks off the street and threw them at shop windows. A prescient tsarist police official reported to his superiors in late January that these women, "mothers of families, who are exhausted by the endless standing in line at the stores," were "a store of combustible material." "One spark," he predicted, "will be enough for a conflagration to blaze up."[1]

That conflagration began on 23 February (8 March by the Western calendar), International Women's Day. Four years after Samoilova's peaceful meeting at the stock exchange, working-class women streamed out of their workplaces and homes, shouting for bread and an end to the war. They marched through the industrial neighborhoods of the city, and as they passed factories and tenements they called on the people inside to join them. The swelling crowds then headed toward Nevskii Prospekt, the broad boulevard that ran through the heart of Petrograd. Police blocked the bridges that led to the city center, so the women slid down embankments along the river and walked across the ice. Crowds of tens of thousands ebbed and flowed through the downtown all morning and afternoon. When the springlike warmth of the day faded with sunset, the

---

[1] Quoted in Z. Igumnova, *Zhenshchiny Moskvy v gody grazhdanskoi voiny* (Moscow, 1958), 11.

demonstrators went home, but the next morning even more people gathered to protest the government's incompetence and the hardships of the war. Over several days of disturbances, troops sent out to control the marchers mutinied. Liberal and socialist leaders began to organize a new government. Even the military high command turned against the emperor. On 3 March 1917 Nicholas II abdicated the throne at the request of his generals. The Romanov dynasty was dead and the Russian Revolution had begun, sparked by a Woman's Day march.

Elena Stasova heard the noise of the demonstrations from a prison cell. She had been back in Petrograd since the autumn of 1916, there on a furlough from exile that her father had arranged so that she could recuperate once again from tuberculosis. Stasova had spent the fall and winter with her parents, away from illegal activities. "I'm living completely properly here," she wrote to Krupskaia in November.[2] The Okhrana was watching her day and night, and she did not want to betray anyone else to them or give them an excuse to send her back to Minusinsk.

The day after the Woman's Day demonstrations, 24 February, Stasova went with her father to a meeting of Petrograd attorneys hastily called to discuss the rising tide of protest. There she heard a rousing speech by Alexander Kerensky, soon to be the minister of justice in the Provisional Government. Later that night, the police came banging on the Stasovs' door. They searched Elena's room and found nothing incriminating, but arrested her anyway. They intended to make sure that as many known revolutionaries as they could find would sit out the uprising in jail.

Stasova thus spent the early days of the February Revolution locked up in a women's prison. She could hear shots echoing from the nearby streets, but news of what they signified did not penetrate the stone walls. For two days she speculated on events with her cellmates, also revolutionaries picked up in the police sweep. Then, on 27 February, the streets fell silent. After some hours, footsteps rang along the prison's stone floors, the door opened, and several guards, all men, ordered the women to come with them. Stasova's cellmates gathered around her, waiting for her, the prison veteran, to decide what to do. Stasova hesitated; the solemn men standing in the hall gave no sign of their intentions. Perhaps they were Black Hundreds, the anti-Semitic thugs who had preyed on revolutionaries in the past, with the government's blessings. Perhaps they would lead the women to some darker corner of the prison and assault them. And yet, Stasova thought, it was pointless to stay in the cell. Maybe if they came out, they could manage to escape. She told the others to get their things. Then they all followed the taciturn guards down the corridor. The men

[2] E. D. Stasova, *Vospominaniia* (Moscow, 1969), 130.

opened the first door they came to and stepped aside. Stasova feared that an ambush awaited them on the other side, but she saw no point in turning back. She remembered feeling like a mother hen leading her chicks as she went through the door, down another empty hallway, and through yet another door. The guards did not follow. Now the women were standing in a courtyard, across which they could see another group of men. For a moment they hesitated in fear. The men turned, caught sight of them, threw up their hands in a happy salute, and began shouting, "Hurrah, freedom!" They were, it turned out, a harmless lot, the prison fire brigade. Only now did Stasova and her charges realize that they were being released. Within twenty-four hours she had located the Bolshevik city committee and resumed her old place as its secretary.[3]

Other Bolshevichki came back to political life in less dramatic ways. Those who were abroad hurried to arrange passage home. Bosh and Kollontai returned from Scandinavia in March, Inessa and Krupskaia from Switzerland in April. By April, Samoilova was also back from Moscow, where she had been in hiding, and Bosh's sister, Elena Rozmirovich, had made her way from exile in Siberia. The Petrograd veterans, Kollontai, Stasova, Krupskaia, Samoilova, and Rozmirovich, stayed on to work in the capital city. Inessa soon went home to Moscow, where Zemliachka was just coming out of retirement. Bosh set off for Kiev.

All the Bolsheviks, male and female, emerged from the underground euphoric, but also confused and dazed by the chaotic liberation going on around them. Alexandra Rodionova, a tram conductor in Petrograd, later remembered the moment: "It seemed so recently that I had walked with the demonstrators around the city. I yelled 'Down with the tsar!' and it seemed to me that I had lost touch with solid ground and flew in giddy uncertainty. Yes, I had participated in many strikes and demonstrations. But this had happened secretly; I had never taken a clear political position. And suddenly, all at once, the unknown future became real." Giddiness also beset T. F. Liudvinskaia, a seamstress living in Paris, when she heard of the revolution. "We Bolsheviks felt as though we had grown wings," she wrote many years later. "We ran to meetings, got together, argued, quarreled, and made up, argued again tirelessly."[4] The arguments arose out of their attempts to understand what the events in Petrograd meant and how they should deal with them. Revolutionaries who had contemplated revolution as a distant possibility now had to cope with the reality.

[3] Ibid., 132.
[4] *Zhenshchiny goroda Lenina* (Leningrad, 1963), 89; T. F. Liudvinskaia, *Nas Leninskaia partiia vela. Vospominaniia* (Moscow, 1976), 102.

Bolshevichki respond to the revolution

There was much to delight the Bolshevichki in the events of the spring and summer of 1917. As the old regime collapsed, it took with it the structure of authority throughout Russia, creating enormous social instability that was frightening but at the same time exhilarating.

Never had the working class in the cities been more energetic. Demonstrations were a daily event, and, just as significant from the Bolshevik point of view, the representation of the poor by socialist parties was institutionalized in soviets, popular, elected assemblies that sprang up in all the major cities. Trade unions became assertive in their negotiations with suddenly weakened industrial managements. Women's organizations found their voice as well: the feminists spoke out (to the irritation of the Bolshevichki), but so too did female trade unionists and the wives of soldiers. By mid-summer the Russian military, still at war with Germany and Austria, had begun to disintegrate and the peasants in the countryside were seizing control of the nobility's land.

People with political ambitions experienced some difficulty in orienting themselves amid this sea of change. The liberal Constitutional-Democratic Party, the radical SRs and SDs, and a host of other alliances and organizations agreed on the necessity of building a representative, republican government. But they agreed on little else. Each party brought to the revolution its prior experience and beliefs, but, however well developed these were, they could provide only general guidance in the fundamentally changed situation. To respond to Russia's new realities effectively, political actors had to read the shifting popular mood, calculate their options carefully, and act decisively. The Bolsheviks, particularly Lenin and Trotsky, proved the ablest of all the contenders in this dangerous game. By September they had amassed considerable support in the cities, particularly St. Petersburg and Moscow. In October they overthrew the stumbling Provisional Government and seized power in the name of the soviets.

The Bolsheviks arrived at this course of action under Lenin's persistent prodding. In March, most of them had come out of the underground under the assumption that the Provisional Government would be led by liberals, who would cooperate with socialist parties based in the soviets. Their expectations in this regard had been governed by the notion, widespread among Social Democrats of both factions, that Russia must pass through a capitalist stage of development, during which it would be ruled by a liberal parliamentary government. Lenin had rejected this proposition long before 1917 and had adopted instead Trotsky's conception of "permanent revolution," according to which Russia could move

Plate 13. A demonstration of soldiers' wives in Petrograd in 1917,
probably March. The banner in th foreground rewads "For a Raise in the
Allotment for the Families of Soldiers, Defenders of Freedom and the
People's Peace." The banner in the background reads "Feed the
Children of the Defenders of the Motherland." Demonstrations such as
this provided support for the Bolshevik feminists' arguments that
working-class women could be reached by party propaganda.

directly from monarchy to rule by the left without any intervening phase of
bourgeois supremacy. Once the revolution actually began, Lenin rejected
as well any power-sharing arrangement with moderate politicians and
became suspicious too of coalitions with Mensheviks and SRs. Boldly he
called instead for an immediate transfer of power to the soviets, for an
equally immediate withdrawal of Russia from the war, and for a confrontational posture toward all political rivals.

The prominent Bolshevichki followed Lenin enthusiastically. Kollontai
and Bosh carried his earliest calls to arms back to Russia in March, before
he himself returned. He made peace with Bosh in a series of letters in
January and February, in which he never mentioned their earlier disagreements. She then presented his case to the party organization in Petrograd
in late March, before heading off to Ukraine to preach his message in
Kiev. Kollontai, with whom he had always been on good terms, became
Lenin's most ardent and visible supporter in April 1917, when many

Bolsheviks were convinced that he was vastly overestimating what they could accomplish. In Moscow, Inessa was an equally convinced disciple, as were Sofia Smidovich and Zemliachka. Stasova seems to have wavered a bit, perhaps because she felt more kindly disposed toward the Mensheviks, but soon she was persuaded as well.[5]

The attitudes of less well-known Bolshevichki are harder to assess, for they are not as fully documented. The majority of Bolsheviks, male and female, appear to have come around to supporting Lenin by May. The crucial issue then became developing the tactics that would win support among the workers and soldiers, and gain elective seats in the soviets. The party sent speakers to all the many public meetings, arranged delegations to march at demonstrations, and published newspapers, flyers, and pamphlets. It put forward slates of candidates for election to the soviets and to the municipal dumas, assemblies that had been part of city government under the old regime. Bolsheviks also devoted a good deal of time to building their own organization, recruiting new members, and expanding and regularizing the party's administrative structure.[6]

Bolshevichki as agitators

The Bolshevichki were engaged in all the activities that prepared the way for their party's seizure of power in October. (See table 14.) They made speeches, wrote newspaper articles, served as soviet and duma delegates, did clerical work, ran committees, and, in the fall, as the party began to plan its coup, built bombs and trained with the pro-Bolshevik militia units, the Red Guards. As they had in the past, Bolshevichki did what was needed, with little regard being given to their gender. Men were more likely to work with the army and navy than were women, but many Bolshevichki also went into the barracks to speak to the troops. The revolution actually intensified the party's long-standing practice of engaging women in all its activities, because it sustained the crisis atmosphere that had nurtured egalitarianism

---

[5] On Kollontai, see Barbara Evans Clements, *Bolshevik Feminist: The Life of Aleksandra Kollontai* (Bloomington, Ind., 1979), 103–09. On Bosh, see "Protokoly i rezoliutsii Biuro TsK RSDRP(b), mart 1917 g.," *Voprosy istorii KPSS*, no. 3 (1962): 145–47, 149–51. On Inessa, see R. C. Elwood, *Inessa Armand* (Cambridge, 1992), 206–08. Speeches in April by Inessa and Smidovich are recorded in "Protokoly pervoi (Moskovskoi) oblastnoi konferentsii tsentral'nogo-promyshlennogo raiona RSDRP(b) proiskhodivshei v g. Moskve (2–4 maia) 19–21 aprelia 1917 g.," *Proletarskaia revoliutsiia*, no. 10 (1929): 137–42, 148. On Zemliachka, see *Oktiabr' v Moskve* (Moscow, 1967), 66; and RTsKhIDNI, f. 17, op. 4, d. 180, l. 29. On Stasova, see her *Vospominaniia*, 134–35; and N. N. Sukhanov, *The Russian Revolution*, ed., abridged, and trans. Joel Carmichael (New York, 1955), 405.

[6] On the Bolsheviks in Petrograd in the spring and early summer, see Alexander Rabinowitch, *Prelude to Revolution: The Petrograd Bolsheviks and the July 1917 Uprising* (Bloomington, Ind., 1968).

Table 14 *Fields of activity of Bolsheviks, February–October 1917*

	Women's activities (%) (N = 159)	Men's activities (%) (N = 685)
Journalism	6.3	9.3
Government[a]	31.4	33.7
Military	8.8	16.9
Party	50.9	33.3
Trade unions	2.5	6.7
Total99.9	99.9	99.9

Note: This table records all types of work by women, including more than one activity per individual in some cases. The column for men records only one activity per individual.
[a] Soviets at all levels, and city dumas.

throughout the underground years, and it strengthened the commitment most Bolsheviks professed to women's equality. The revolutionary year 1917 was so filled with general ideas of freedom that in fact it quickly became a special point of official pride with the Bolsheviks that they had so many women working in their organization.

The most invigorating projects for the Bolshevichki were those that took them out among the poor to do what the party came to call "agitation," that is, spreading the party's message. For years these women had struggled to find a sufficient audience, often discovering not only that the police thwarted their efforts but that the workers themselves were unreceptive. With the fall of Nicholas II the situation changed quickly. Now the party had the funds to publish not just one newspaper but several, aimed at different audiences, and printing presses were free to print whatever the party could afford to publish. Still more encouraging was the fact that the Bolshevichki found lots of people willing, even happy, to listen to them. They responded by writing newspaper pieces, pamphlets, and leaflets, cultivating personal contacts with sympathizers in their neighborhoods, training workers and soldiers to spread the party's message among their mates, and speaking at public meetings.

Public speaking was the one of these activities of which the Bolshevichki possessed the least experience, but it became a major means of communicating with the public in 1917. Dozens, if not hundreds, of Bolshevichki mounted rickety platforms on shop floors or street-corners to issue to milling crowds the party's call to arms. This was not an entirely unprecedented activity for women in Russia. Female radicals had addressed the demonstrations of 1905 and the revolutionaries' secret gatherings throughout the underground years, but the best-known women orators in Russia before 1917 were the feminists, philanthropists, and other social activists who spoke at conferences and other sorts of meetings permitted by the government. These women had been careful to stay within the limits imposed on them by the police. The Bolshevichki were under no such constraints after the fall of the tsar, so they could model themselves on such socialist firebrands as Emma Goldman and Sylvia Pankhurst. Shouting to be heard in an era before microphones, they condemned the Provisional Government and preached revolution to crowds that numbered in the tens of thousands.

Alexandra Kollontai was widely considered to be the party's most accomplished female orator in 1917. Very pretty and always well dressed, Kollontai looked like the noblewoman she was, but when her voice, accented with the tones of the privileged, began to sail out over the crowds, her message was all confrontation. "Where is the people's money going?," Kollontai demanded to know in a speech in the spring of 1917,

> To the schools, the hospitals, to housing, to maternity and childcare benefits? Nothing of the sort is happening. The people's money is going to finance bloody skirmishes. The bankers, the factory owners, the landlord-moneybags are responsible for this war. They all belong to one gang of thieves. And the people die! Stand under the red banner of the Bolshevik Party! Swell the ranks of the Bolsheviks, fearless fighters for soviet power, for the workers' and peasants' power, for peace, for freedom, for land![7]

Not all the Bolshevichki who took the podium in 1917 were as eloquent as Kollontai, but many of them seem to have received warm receptions from their audiences. There can be little doubt that the revolution weakened popular resistance to the idea of women speaking in public. Of course there were instances when the Bolshevichki were shouted down, but even the military was willing to listen attentively to female orators with whom they agreed. Kollontai spoke frequently to audiences of soldiers and sailors, as did Liudmila Stal and Elena Rozmirovich. Rozmirovich's sister, Evgeniia Bosh, was so successful in rousing the troops to support her that she even managed to lead a regiment of infantry into battle against the Provisional Government in the fall of 1917.

Bosh circulated among the men of the southwestern front in Ukraine throughout the summer and fall of 1917; historian Allan Wildman has described her as "the flaming evangel" of the Bolshevik organization there.[8] Bosh's public persona was very different from Kollontai's, suggest-

---

[7] Quoted in A. M. Itkina, *Revoliutsioner, tribun, diplomat. Stranitsy zhizni Aleksandry Mikhailovny Kollontai*, 2nd ed. (Moscow, 1970), 143–44. Excerpts of recordings of Kollontai's speeches can be heard in the documentary film *A Wave of Passion*, prod. Kevin M. Mulhern, Kevin M. Mulhern Productions, 1994, videocassette.

[8] Allan K. Wildman, *The End of the Russian Imperial Army*, 2 vols. (Princeton, 1980–87), vol. II, 360.

Plate 14. Alexandra Kollontai speaking from notes at the First
All-Russion Women Workers Congress, November 1918.

ing that in 1917 there was no one model of the ardent female revolutionary, and no one means to success with crowds. Kollontai, who rejected the
notion common among Russian revolutionaries that women should pay
little attention to their physical appearance, cultivated her looks. She also
wrote about heterosexual relationships and had a series of love affairs. Her
reputation as a sexual rebel, her beauty, the ardor of her delivery, and the
uncompromising tenor of her speeches intrigued her audiences and made
her a celebrity, something she enjoyed immensely. Bosh, although equally
pretty, was sober, dour, even puritanical. She wore simple, dark blouses
and skirts, and severe hairstyles. She, like Kollontai, persuaded with
impassioned words and calls to confrontation, but she also overawed the
crowds with her intellect and impressed them with her powerful will.
There was nothing alluring about Evgeniia Bosh on the speakers'
platform, but her school-teacher seriousness appears to have been as
effective in winning the support of the soldiers as Kollontai's glamor.[9]

Bosh, in her history of the revolution in Ukraine (written in 1924),
described with muted pride one of her more successful appearances. It

[9] There is rare footage of Kollontai speaking at meetings in *A Wave of Passion*.

occurred early in October of 1917, after the Keksgolm Regiment of the Second Guards Corps came to the town of Zhmerinka in central Ukraine, on leave from front-line duty. Also known as "The Wild Division," these men were reputed to be little more than a collection of bandits, but Bosh took their unsavory reputation as a sign that they might be favorably disposed toward her anti-war, anti-Provisional Government message. She therefore persuaded their officers to let her speak to the regiment. When she and two bodyguards entered the courtyard of their barracks on the outskirts of Zhmerinka, Bosh had no idea what sort of reception she would receive. These men were armed, she had reason to believe that some of them had been drinking heavily, and no one could tell her exactly where their political sympathies lay or how they would receive a woman speaker.

"The complete quiet of the audience there, more than a thousand strong, the tense attention of those present, the noticeable excitement and fussing of the organizers – all this created the impression of a calm before a storm," Bosh wrote later. For two hours she dissected before them the evils of the Provisional Government and explained the necessity of replacing it with a soviet government representing poor people. The men listened to her quietly and attentively. Then they began to ask her questions. When Bosh finally told the soldiers, some four hours later, that she had to leave, the company's musical band rushed off to find its instruments, and the Wild Division escorted her to her car with hurrahs and music. One month later, on 8 November, the Chief of Staff of Southwestern Front, N. N. Stogov, gruffly testified to Bosh's effectiveness in a report filed with his superiors: "In the majority of units of the [Second Guards] regiment, the unhindered comings and goings of agitators, such as the Jewess [*sic*] Bosh ... has contaminated all the units of the regiment."[10]

It is difficult to determine how many Bolshevichki became public speakers in 1917, for the sources often record that a woman was a party agitator without going into greater detail as to her precise activities. "Agitation" was a catch-all term that embraced all the many ways of building support in the working class and the military through public speaking, producing and distributing leaflets and newspapers, and sending emissaries to talk with the leaders of trade unions and soldiers' and sailors' committees. Most Bolshevichki were involved in agitation in 1917, so it is likely that many of them did some speaking, if only to small gatherings in a neighborhood or workplace.

Bolshevichki also worked to establish the party's political presence in popular organizations, particularly the soviets and the trade unions, and especially those unions with strong female membership. For example,

---

[10] E. B. Bosh, *God bor'by* (Moscow, 1925), 29; L. S. Gaponenko, ed., *Oktiabr'skaia revoliutsiia i armiia. Sbornik dokumentov* (Moscow, 1973), 103.

Ekaterina Shalaginova, Anna Sakharova, and Iadviga Netupskaia, factory workers in Petrograd, organized a laundresses' union in their neighborhood in the spring of 1917. At the same time, Kollontai was coordinating the creation of a city-wide laundresses' union. Bolshevichki in Petrograd, Moscow, and several provincial cities competed energetically with feminist organizations to gain support among the *soldatki*, the soldiers' wives who had organized themselves to press for higher military allotments. Liudmila Stal spent most of the year at Kronstadt, the naval base in the Gulf of Finland, winning over the sailors there and paying attention as well to their wives. Other Bolshevichki attempted to recruit female factory workers already in unions, particularly those employed in textile mills and in military-related manufacturing.[11]

Bolshevichki made these efforts because they realized that there were many more women in the factories than there had been in the past, and that among these tens of thousands, hundreds at least were receptive to the party's ideas. The female percentage of the industrial labor force had grown enormously during the war, from 26 percent in 1914 to 43 percent in 1917.[12] The revolution had then opened channels of communication to women which had formerly been blocked by the old regime, and had made political participation the order of the day. Furthermore, the faltering economy was feeding the discontent of the working class throughout 1917. Women angry over miserable working conditions, falling wages, and food shortages, and emboldened by the general spirit of liberation, were indeed, as the Okhrana official had written, "a store of combustible material." Although most of them probably continued to believe that politics was, in the common phrase, "not a woman's business" (*ne zhenskoe delo*), a substantial minority, especially in Petrograd, was becoming involved in demonstrations, meetings, and unions. Bolshevichki did not rush off en masse to seek out the female proletariat; most of them divided their time between a variety of agitational activities aimed at men as well as women. But more Bolshevichki than in the past, in Petrograd, Moscow, and such provincial cities as Saratov, did become engaged at least part-time in "work among women" during the revolutionary year.[13]

[11] *Leningradki. Vospominaniia, ocherki, dokumenty* ([Leningrad], 1968), 65; Institut istorii partii pri TsK KP Belorussii, Filial instituta Marksizma-Leninizma pri TsK KPSS, *Pod krasnym znamenem oktiabria* (Minsk, 1987), 191–94; N. D. Karpetskaia, *Rabotnitsy i velikii oktiabr'* (Leningrad, 1974), 27–61; *Oktiabrem mobilizovannye. Zhenshchiny-kommunistki v bor' be za pobedu sotsialisticheskoi revoliutsii* (Moscow, 1987), 56–57, 76–77; *Zhenshchiny goroda Lenina*, 77–86.
[12] Barbara Evans Clements, *Daughters of Revolution: A History of Women in the USSR* (Arlington Heights, Ill., 1994), 29.
[13] On the efforts in Moscow, see Elwood, *Inessa Armand*, 211–13. On Saratov, see Donald J. Raleigh, *Revolution on the Volga: 1917 in Saratov* (Ithaca, N. Y., 1986), 133.

The revival of work among women

Before the leaders of the party's earlier efforts among women – Inessa, Samoilova, Krupskaia, and Stal – returned to Petrograd, a Bolshevichka previously unknown to them had already begun setting up an organization to reach out to the female proletariat. She was Vera Slutskaia, a dentist from a merchant family in Minsk who had joined the Social Democrats in 1902. Slutskaia came to Petrograd in March 1917 from the Caucasus and went to work as secretary of the party committee in the working-class neighborhood of Vasileostrovskii raion. Quickly she emerged as a good speaker. Just as quickly she realized that there were poor women in her neighborhood who could be persuaded to support the Bolsheviks. Soon Slutskaia had obtained authorization from the raion party committee to organize a subcommittee specializing in work with women. She then went to the city committee with a proposal for work among women that called for publication of pamphlets and leaflets addressed to the female proletariat, the revival of *Rabotnitsa*, and the creation of a city-wide "bureau" to coordinate activities. The usual opposition arose to what committee member Olga Livshits criticized as "a special women's organization of the party," but after several meetings and some debate, Slutskaia secured authorization and funding for everything she had requested. When Samoilova, Inessa, Krupskaia, and Kollontai arrived in the city, Slutskaia already had a small organization ready to work with them.[14]

The new *Rabotnitsa* (the police had closed the prior one after the war began in August 1914) became the centerpiece of work among women in 1917, the leading voice of the Bolshevichki's agitation aimed at the female proletariat, and the forum in which they worked out an analysis of the place of women's issues in the revolution. Edited by Samoilova, Klavdiia Nikolaeva, and Praskovia Kudelli (the last was a teacher and alumna of the Bestuzhevskii courses), *Rabotnitsa* was a lively, engaging, tabloid-sized magazine containing poetry, fiction, news stories on conditions in the factories, articles on the history of the revolutionary movement, and editorials on political events. Samoilova, Nikolaeva, and Kudelli, in addition to editing, wrote many of its articles and managed its publication and distribution. They enlisted Stal, Kollontai, Zlata Lilina, and a few male journalists as contributors and specially commissioned female workers to file reports on political developments in their factories. The magazine soon found a large readership in Petrograd, with occasional

---

[14] *Slavnye bol'shevichki* (Moscow, 1958), 265–67; *Zhenshchiny goroda Lenina*, 90, 93–94; "Protokoly pervogo legal'nogo Petersburgskogo komiteta bol'shevikov i ispol'nitel'noi komissii za period s 15 marta po 7 aprelia (c 2 po 25 marta) 1917 g.," *Proletarskaia revoliutsiia*, no. 3 (1927): 318, 350–51, 355, 360–61, 382.

copies making their way to the other major cities of the empire and even to places as far away as Barnaul in Siberia.

As they had done in 1914, the editors of *Rabotnitsa* declared their socialist bona fides often. An unsigned editorial in the first issue justified the existence of a newspaper for women by arguing that other periodicals did not cover issues of particular concern to them, such as maternity insurance and child care. Such issues would only be addressed politically, the article asserted, when women joined men in the struggle for socialism. In later articles the editors declared that they did not blame men for women's problems, as feminists did. Instead they emphasized that they considered the old regime to be the enemy, and explained that their purpose was to draw women into a common effort with their working-class brothers to construct a better world for all people.[15]

Despite such diplomatic disavowals, the *Rabotnitsa* of 1917 was actually more feminist than its predecessor, in the sense that it accorded women's emancipation an even higher priority within the revolutionary process. Its editors and contributors denounced the burdens heaped on women by patriarchal traditions and capitalism. They declared women's rights to political and legal equality, to improved wages and working conditions, to a greater voice in the union movement, and to protective labor regulations. They argued that women had now proven their entitlement to those rights. "If a woman is capable of climbing the scaffold and fighting on the barricades," Samoilova wrote, "then she is capable of being an equal in the workers' family and in workers' organizations." Samoilova and other contributors, emphasizing the point that the Bolshevichki had stressed earlier, repeatedly argued that the revolution would not be won without women's participation. "The time has passed when the success of the workers' cause will be decided only by organizing men," an unsigned editorial in the first issue proclaimed. And they called on women to become politically active so as to guarantee their liberation. "Many female comrades say that everything will be done without us," wrote Prokhorova, a *Rabotnitsa* staffer, in a May issue, "but comrades, what is done without us will be dangerous to us!"[16]

The 1917 *Rabotnitsa* was also more critical of the sexist behavior of men, its disclaimers to the contrary notwithstanding. This criticism usually came from female factory workers themselves and was aimed at their male comrades. Correspondents attacked trade-union leaders for discriminating against female workers, called for female representation on

---

[15] "Rabotnitsa, 1914–1917 goda," *Rabotnitsa*, 10 May 1917, 1–2.
[16] N. Sibiriakova [Samoilova], "Rabotnitsy i professional'nye soiuzy," *Rabotnitsa*, 30 May 1917, 6–7.

factory committees and union boards, and asked male workers to put women's demands on their political agenda. Male factory workers "are all for equal rights in words," wrote M. Boretskaia, who identified herself as a *rabotnitsa* in a June issue, "but when it comes to deeds it turns out that a chicken is not a bird and a *baba* is not a human being."[17] Other contributors supported the principle of equal pay for equal work and criticized proposals floated in various unions to lay off married women. *Rabotnitsa* also published letters and articles publicizing the sexual harassment of women in the workplace. And there was even an occasional suggestion, seemingly aimed more at Lenin and his associates than at female readers, that the Bolshevik Party should increase its efforts to reach out to working-class women.[18]

Rabotnitsa carried these central ideas of Bolshevik feminism to tens of thousands of party members. Samoilova and Kudelli hoped that the newspaper would do more than cultivate the support of working-class women; they hoped its propaganda would also help to allay the fears of male Bolsheviks that female activism would be detrimental to the party's interests. That had been an important goal of the 1914 version as well. But the *Rabotnitsa* of 1917 was not nearly so supplicatory as its predecessor. It contained the usual denunciations of the feminists, particularly in articles by Kudelli, and pledges that its editors were not seeking to divide the revolutionary movement. But far more common in its pages than reassuring words to the skeptical were assertions of women's rights and denunciations of their continuing inequality. The developments of 1917 were inspiring Samoilova, Kudelli, and Nikolaeva to demand that women's liberation become a high revolutionary priority, and perhaps were awakening them as well to the possibility it would not be unless women themselves made it so.[19]

---

[17] *Rabotnitsa*, 28 June 1917, 5. *Baba* was a mildly pejorative term for "woman." "A chicken is not a bird and a *baba* is not a human being" is one of the most frequently quoted examples of Russian folk misogyny. It is noteworthy for being wrong in both its propositions.

[18] All of the following references are to *Rabotnitsa*, 1917. On layoffs, see 13 August, 11–14. On sexual harassment, see 20 May, 7; 30 May, 11; and 28 June, 13–14. On equal pay for equal work, see 10 May, 12; 14 June, 3, 6–8; 19 July, 8; and 18 October, 12. On the attitudes of trade unionists toward women workers, see 30 May, 1, 6; 19 July, 8; and 1 September, 9–10. On the party paying more attention to women, see 13 August, 1.

[19] On Samoilova's motivation, see Clements, *Bolshevik Feminist*, 111–12; Sibiriakova [Samoilova], "Rabotnitsy i professional'nye soiuzy." For Kudelli's articles against the feminists, see P. F. K., "Ob organizatsiiakh burzhuaznykh zhenshchin," *Rabotnitsa*, 30 May 1917, 10–11; P. F. K., "O respublikanskom soiuze zhenskikh organizatskiiakh pri soiuz ravnopravikh," *Rabotnitsa*, 14 June 1917, 9–10.

Plate 15. Konkordiia Samoilova, circa 1918.

Bolshevichki in revolutionary leadership

If power is, as writer Carolyn Heilbrun has observed, "the ability to take one's place in whatever discourse is essential to action and the right to have one's part matter," then many Bolshevichki had power in 1917.[20] They participated in the revolutionary discourse in the pages of *Rabotnitsa* as well as on street-corners and in barracks all over Russia. Bolshevichki also spoke up within the narrower confines of party committees. In fact, in the sample analyzed for this study, more women held party office in the seven months between February and October 1917 than had ever been the case earlier, during the entire period of the underground. Of the Bolshevichki in the sample, 36 percent had served on city or émigré

[20] Carolyn G. Heilbrun, *Writing a Woman's Life* (New York, 1988), 16.

committees before 1917; 57 percent occupied comparable positions in 1917.

The party proved more hospitable to women than other political institutions of the new Russian democracy. A comparison of all political posts held by Bolsheviks in 1917 reveals that males were more likely to serve as soviet or municipal duma delegates, women as party officials. (See table 15.) These differences probably reflect the party's relative enlightenment; it was easier for a woman to become a member of a Bolshevik committee than to be elected to a city soviet's executive committee. Yet it was also true that women's opportunities were, in general, greater in the major cities than in lesser ones, as had been the case before 1917: 60 percent of the women in the sample who held party office in 1917 did so either in Moscow or Petrograd. In less cosmopolitan locations, more Bolshevichki stayed in the rank and file. (See table 16.)

The process of choosing party officials remained as unsystematized in 1917 as it had been in the underground. Some were elected by the local organization as a whole, some by the committee members themselves, and some were appointed by higher-ranking Bolsheviks. The criteria employed in judging candidates appear to have been equally unstandardized, so it is difficult to determine why some Bolshevichki became party officials while others did not. Of course personal merit and desire to serve were important qualifications. Seniority was not; many of the Bolshevichki who held party office in 1917 had only recently joined the Social Democrats and had not held party office in the past. A primary qualification seems to have been the long-standing one of education. Of the Bolshevichki in the sample who had attended secondary school, 62 percent held party office in 1917, as compared with 32.5 percent of those with less schooling.[21] (See table 17.)

The revolution seems also to have brought some class bias to the process of selecting party officials, for women of noble birth were slightly less likely to hold office than were middle-class women. Yet this bias worked in the other direction too. Women from the peasantry and the working class were decidedly less likely to serve than were their more privileged comrades, a difference that probably resulted in part from their lack of education. It is also probable that working-class and peasant women were impeded by the difficulties that beset all poor women – the necessity of earning an income, family responsibilities, and pressure from the men in their lives. Given the notions about the backwardness of working-class women that prevailed among Bolsheviks themselves, one

---

[21] For a general discussion of the selection process, see Robert Service, *The Bolshevik Party in Revolution: A Study in Organisational Change, 1917–1923* (New York, 1979), 49–51.

Table 15 *Offices held by Bolsheviks, February–October 1917*

Office	Women (%) (*N* = 182)	Men (%) (*N* = 458)
Duma		
Delegate (raion, city)	4.9	4.1
Executive committee	2.8	0.2
Factory committee member	0.5	2.0
Party		
Local party committee member (raion, city, uezd)	37.3	20.7
Military-revolutionary committee member	4.9	10.9
Provincial party committee member	6.0	6.3
Central Committee member	1.6	3.5
Soviets		
Local soviet delegate (raion, city, guberniia)	30.7	30.3
Local soviet executive committee member	6.5	15.1
Soviet congress delegate	2.2	3.3
Trade unions		
City trade union board member	1.6	2.6
Guberniia trade union council member	0.5	0.6
All-Russian trade union council member	0.5	0.4
Total	100.0	100.0

Note: Only one office held per individual was coded.

Table 16 *Levels of party office-holding, February–October 1917*

Level of party office	Women (%)	Men (%)
Raion, uezd	41.9 (36)	9.4 (13)
City	36.0 (31)	59.4 (82)
Guberniia	17.4 (15)	21.0 (29)
Central Committee	4.7 (4)	10.1 (14)
Total	100.0 (86)	99.9 (138)

Note: Figures in parentheses are base *N*s for the adjacent percentages.

cannot rule out the possibility of discrimination against them within the party. (See table 18.)

Most Bolshevichki who held office in 1917 did the same sort of work that women had done in the underground, that is, they were party secretaries handling the 1917 equivalent of *tekhnika* in neighborhood committees. They kept records, collected dues, made job assignments, wrote pamphlets and newspaper stories, and organized meetings and

Table 17 *Patterns in Bolshevichki's party office-holding, February–October 1917*

Of the Bolshevichki who held party office between 1898 and 1917: 27.6% (40) did so both before 1917 and in 1917; 33.8% (49) did so in 1917 but not before; 38.6% (56) did so before 1917 but not in 1917. *Of the Bolshevichki holding office both before and during 1917:* 30.0% (12) held a higher-ranking office in 1917 than that held earlier; 60.0% (24) held an office in 1917 equivalent to that held earlier; 10.0% (4) held an office in 1917 lower than that held earlier.

Note: The total $N = 145$ (all women who held a party office at any time between 1898 and November 1917), which constitutes 45.6 percent of all female Old Bolshevichki in the sample.

Table 18 *Social origins and party office-holding by Bolshevichki, February–October 1917*

Social origins	Held party office (%)	Held no party office (%)	Total (%)
Nobility	40.0 (12)	60.0 (18)	100.0 (30)
Intelligentsia	29.0 (9)	71.0 (22)	100.0 (31)
Sluzhashchie	42.1 (8)	57.9 (11)	100.0 (19)
Meshchanstvo	62.9 (22)	37.1 (13)	100.0 (35)
Workers	31.2 (24)	68.8 (53)	100.0 (77)
Peasants	12.1 (4)	87.9 (29)	100.0 (33)

Note: Figures in parentheses are base Ns for the adjacent percentages. Total $N = 225$.

demonstrations. The earlier tacit understanding that it was the men's role to set policy and the women's to handle administration continued right through the revolution. Nor did that great upheaval, which led to enormous growth in the size of the party, lead to upward mobility for Bolshevichki. Most of those women who held office both before and during 1917 occupied positions at the same, lower level of the hierarchy (although they rarely did exactly the same jobs). (See table 17.) Thus the upper reaches of the party remained more or less exclusively male preserves. As in the past, the higher the party committee, the lower the number of women to be found on it.

And yet, the relationship between the Bolshevichki and power was not so simple as these generalizations suggest. There was space within which an enterprising woman could maneuver during the revolution. Raion and city committees remained democratic because of the party's egalitarian traditions and the institutional informality that inevitably accompanied such rapidly changing times. This openness made it possible for Bolshevichki to "take [their] place in [the] discourse," to use Heilbrun's phrase, and make their voices heard. Women could also still rise to the very top of the party. Bosh, Stasova, and Zemliachka became leaders of national stature in 1917, and Kollontai earned appointment as commissar in the first Bolshevik government.[22]

It would also be mistaken to assume that the Bolshevichki measured their standing within the party by criteria such as rank and upward mobility. They would have denounced such calculations as disreputable. The Bolshevichki were, after all, revolutionaries. In 1917 their intentions were not to aggrandize themselves as individuals, or to build their own regime so as to hand power and privilege around among themselves. They were going to lead Russia to a new plateau of historical society from which power and privilege would be banished. Being a Bolshevik was not yet a career planned with personal advancement in mind; it was a calling, at least in the view of the Bolshevichki. One's position in the party was simply the place from which one made a contribution. In an article in *Rabotnitsa* in June 1917, an anonymous female recruit voiced the devotion to the cause so central to the Bolshevichki's sense of vocation: "With all my soul I want to participate in this life, in this struggle," she wrote, "with all my strength to help it go forward." Such notions of a great popular enterprise to which the individual committed herself as an act of faith and devotion were as old as revolutionary movements themselves, but they had particular appeal to women, for they drew on traditional notions of the feminine duty to serve.[23]

The Bolshevichki had other reasons to think that the grass-roots organizing in which most of them were engaged was as important as the debates of the Central Committee. As Marxists they believed that the great moving mass of the people would carve out Russia's future. Historians today agree, and argue that the Bolsheviks managed to seize power not only because Lenin and Trotsky were audacious, but also because the party had a firm base of support in Petrograd, Moscow, and other major cities by the fall of 1917.[24] That support grew from the success of the rank and file in getting the party's message out, as well as from the radicalizing of public opinion as the revolutionary process continued. If power means taking part in the discourses that matter, then the Bolshevichki who were agitators in 1917 had power, for they believed,

[22] On the democratic nature of the party in 1917, see ibid., 50–53; Rabinowitch, *Prelude to Revolution*; Alexander Rabinowitch, *The Bolsheviks Come to Power: The Revolution of 1917 in Petrograd* (New York, 1978). Donald J. Raleigh has analyzed similar characteristics outside Petrograd. See his *Revolution on the Volga*, 128–36.

[23] *Rabotnitsa*, 14 June 1917, 7. See also 10 May, 3–4; 20 May, 7–8; and 14 June, 15–16.

[24] See Rabinowitch, *The Bolsheviks Come to Power*, 83–93; Service, *The Bolshevik Party in Revolution*, 43–45.

with good reason, that the discourses that counted in that revolutionary year were taking place in the streets; and that is where they were, in the streets, handing out leaflets, talking to factory workers, marching in demonstrations, swaying crowds.

There is another element of the Bolshevichki's attitudes toward power that is more difficult to probe, but that is as important as their revolutionary consciousness in shaping their behavior. Their conception of the party as serving a cause, and their contempt for the usual business of politics, were attitudes shared with many male Bolsheviks, but the Bolshevichki could embrace these attitudes with special fervor because they, as women, were more distanced from politics than were male Bolsheviks. Throughout Europe, politics – the discourses that mattered and the distributions of power, status, and wealth that they validated – had long been a male-dominated endeavor to which women gained access only through their male kin. The political marginalization of women was particularly great in the early twentieth century, for the rise of capitalism and parliamentary government had decreased the importance of kinship and had concentrated power instead in public organizations, chiefly government departments and political parties, to which women were denied access. Strangers to the multifarious negotiations and the web of personal obligations that sustained such institutions, even politically active women such as the Bolshevichki tended to regard all politics as alien territory.[25]

Krupskaia and Inessa avoided it altogether. Each was entitled by virtue of her loyal work as Lenin's assistant to claim a role in the top leadership in 1917, but neither chose to do so, preferring instead grass-roots organizing. Krupskaia settled in a neighborhood in Petrograd where she was able, for the first time in decades, to work in her first love, education. As a member of a municipal duma, a neighborhood-level assembly that was part of the city government of St. Petersburg, she labored to keep the schools open. Inessa, for her part, spent the year in Moscow, her home town, as a low-ranking committee member, involving herself also in agitation. She reemerged as a major figure only after the Bolshevik seizure of power. It is instructive by way of contrast to note that Grigorii Zinoviev, the male Bolshevik who had stood closest to Lenin during the prerevolutionary period of the emigration, simply stepped off the train from Switzerland directly into positions on the Petrograd committee as well as the Central Committee.[26]

[25] On the development of political parties and the consequences for women in the United States in the late nineteenth and early twentieth centuries, see Suzanne Lebsock, "Women and American Politics, 1880–1920," in Louise A. Tilly and Patricia Gurin, eds., *Women, Politics, and Change* (New York, 1990), 55–58.

[26] On Krupskaia in 1917, see Robert H. McNeal, *Bride of the Revolution: Krupskaia and Lenin* (Ann Arbor, Mich., 1972), 168–82. On Inessa, see Elwood, *Inessa Armand*, 205–14.

Neither Krupskaia nor Inessa ever explained her withdrawal from the center of party life in 1917. Stasova wrote later that both women had been nominated for positions as Central Committee secretaries in April 1917, but neither was elected. Robert H. McNeal, Krupskaia's biographer, argues that Krupskaia thought she had been displaced by Stasova, but this seems unlikely. There was ample work and responsibility for all three women, and Krupskaia and Stasova had always been on cordial terms. Krupskaia and Inessa probably wanted to get back in touch with Russia after years as émigrés. Whatever their motives, they sought out political anonymity while male Bolsheviks who had occupied important positions as émigrés continued as the party's top leaders.

Kollontai, for all her prominence in that year of the revolutionary agitator, also remained outside the ranks of the top leadership, even after she was elected to the Central Committee in August 1917 on the strength of her popularity with the crowds. She attended the meetings of the Central Committee in September and October, and participated in its debates over whether to seize power, but there is no evidence that she sought to enter the inner circle, the Politburo. Nor did she establish strong ties to any of the men at the top. Instead, Kollontai focused her attention on becoming preeminent among the Bolshevik feminists and cultivated her relationships with Samoilova, Nikolaeva, and Kudelli, rather than Lenin, Trotsky, or Stalin. She also continued to devote herself to efforts to reach out to working-class women. By identifying herself so completely with "work with women," Kollontai consigned herself to a marginal place in the party leadership.[27]

Stasova, on the other hand, occupied an important position in the leadership. In April she was elected technical secretary of the Central Committee, where she served under Iakov Sverdlov, the organizational secretary. Sverdlov formulated policy regarding party structure and financing and made major personnel assignments; Stasova and a staff of three or four women, including Sverdlov's wife Klavdiia Novgorodtseva, maintained correspondence with provincial party organizations, assigned workers to various jobs, kept financial records, and distributed some of the party's money.[28]

Stasova was returning to the sort of work she had left when she went to

---

[27] On Kollontai in 1917, see Clements, *Bolshevik Feminist*, 103–21. On her increasing standing among Bolshevichki working with women, see *Rabotnitsa*, especially the coverage of organizational meetings for a woman's conference held in October (18 October, 14–15).

[28] V. V. Anikeev, *Deiatel'nost' TsK RSDRP(b)–RKP(b) v 1917–1918 godakh* (Moscow, 1974), 60, 63–64, 72, 83–84, 116, 123, 125, 135; Akademiia nauk SSSR, Institut istorii, *Velikaia oktiabr'skaia sotsialisticheskaia revoliutsiia. Khronika sobytii, 12 sentiabria–5 oktiabria 1917 goda* (Moscow, 1961), 217, 232.

the Caucasus in 1907, but she took it up in much changed circumstances. The party was now legal, it was huge and growing, and she was serving in its national leadership. But Stasova did not seize the opportunities the revolution had created to redefine herself. Rather, she chose to do what she had always done – administration. While Kollontai took to the podium and Krupskaia and Inessa worked among the poor, Stasova stayed in an office, content to hand out assignments and to write memos. She made few public appearances and published no articles. She considered *tekhnika* "most important work,"[29] as indeed it was, but her unwillingness to explore other activities, to mingle with the crowds or to raise her voice to welcome the revolution, seems curious, if not timid, nonetheless.

Nor did Stasova rethink her old idea that she should defer to others in policy-making. As technical secretary she was a voting member of the Central Committee, entitled to speak up in the group's deliberations. She attended the meetings regularly, but, according to the committee's published minutes, rarely said anything. Rather, she acted as a secretary in the clerical sense of that term, listening intently and taking notes, but not participating in discussions. The revolution appears to have changed nothing in her definition of her revolutionary role. She continued to be what she had been in the underground – a good soldier who executed the decisions of others.[30]

Krupskaia, Inessa, Kollontai, and Stasova do not appear to have been told by the men on the Central Committee in 1917, many of whom were their close comrades, that they were not welcome in the top counsels of the party. Instead, they appear to have chosen of their own accord not to assert themselves in those counsels. This is not to say that their choices, and the similar ones made by so many other Bolshevichki in the revolutionary year, were not affected by assumptions about the division of labor between women and men that had been established in the underground among Bolsheviks. Clearly they were. Women at the center of the party and in its rank and file went where they felt capable and accepted, that is, into agitation and administration. But the Bolshevichki were not simply conforming to the collective expectations about them as women. Speaking to demonstrations or running a neighborhood committee also

[29] Stasova, *Vospominaniia*, 130.
[30] For protocols of Central Committee meetings, see "Protokoly pervogo legal'nogo Peterburgskogo komiteta . . . za period s 15 marta po 7 aprelia"; Akademiia nauk SSSR, Institut istorii, *Revoliutsionnoe dvizhenie v Rossii v aprele 1917 g. Aprelskii krizis* (Moscow, 1958), 15–16, 17–24, 30–35, 107, 508; "Protokoly i rezoliutsii Biuro TsK RSDRP(b), mart 1917 g."; "Protokoly Tsentral'nogo komiteta RSDRP(b), avgust–sentiabr' 1917 g.," *Proletarskaia revoliutsiia*, no. 8 (1927): 322–51; "Protokoly Tsentral'nogo komiteta RSDRP(b), noiabr' 1917 g.," *Proletarskaia revoliutsiia*, no. 11 (1927): 202–14; "Protokoly TsK RSDRP(b) perioda Brestskikh peregovorov (fevral' 1918 g.)," *Proletarskaia revoliutsiia*, no. 2 (1928): 132–69.

enabled them to live out their vision of the revolution as a great forward movement of the masses, guided by enlightened revolutionaries closely connected to the people. The personal preferences of the Bolshevichki, like the personal preferences of all human beings, were shaped by the assumptions, experiences, and ideals of the group of which they were members, that is, by the party's collective identity.

That other options did exist, that individual women possessed of more conventionally masculine political ambitions, could seize political power if they so chose, is indicated by the careers of Zemliachka and Bosh. Both became important leaders in 1917, Zemliachka in Moscow, Bosh in Ukraine. Their achievements, particularly Bosh's, reveal the possibilities that the revolution had opened up for a few Bolshevichki to move into the male sphere of policy-making and party politics.

Zemliachka and Bosh as leaders

In February 1917 Zemliachka become secretary of the Moscow city committee. Unlike Stasova, she was again an organizational secretary, a "secretary-organizer," as she put it in an autobiographical sketch written in 1918.[31] She plunged immediately into the debates of the leadership as an enthusiastic supporter of Lenin's confrontational politics. In April she praised his insistence that the Bolsheviks should refuse to cooperate with other political parties. By mid-summer she was calling on the Moscow party committee to gather weapons and organize a militia in preparation for a seizure of power. Zemliachka had shrunk from the prospect of violent action in 1905 because she had then believed, correctly, that the revolutionaries were too weak to win. The situation in 1917 was, in her view, altogether different; the Bolsheviks now had substantial support in the military as well as among factory workers. Zemliachka was not frightened by the rout the party suffered in mid-summer, when Kerensky, then prime minister, attempted to puncture the party's rising popularity by accusing it of being in the pay of the German government. Despite setbacks in July, Zemliachka continued to believe that the Bolsheviks could seize power if they marshaled their forces. These positions put her in the minority on the Moscow city committee; its majority was composed of cautious people, anxious to work within the structures of Russia's fledgling democracy because they were afraid to provoke the forces arrayed against them.

Unable to persuade their colleagues, Zemliachka and the men on the Moscow committee who shared her views (she was the only female

---

[31] RTsKhIDNI, f. 17, op. 4, d. 180, l. 29.

member) then attempted a move that was classically Leninist. They constituted themselves as a separate, regional organization and tried to assert their predominance over the city committee. The result of this infighting was weak Bolshevik leadership in Moscow throughout the summer of 1917. The two committees came back together only in October, when their comrades in Petrograd began the decisive revolutionary coup. Then, after days of bloody fighting in which the Moscow Bolsheviks defeated troops loyal to the Provisional Government, Zemliachka emerged with her reputation as a resolute, *tverdaia* Bolshevichka refurbished by success. She continued to work as secretary of the Moscow committee until the fall of 1918, when she volunteered for service at the front in the civil war.[32]

Bosh made her mark as a staunch Bolshevik as well, but in Ukraine, a region where the party was far weaker than in Moscow. The cities of Ukraine were home to people of various nationalities, primarily Russians, Jews, Poles, and Ukrainians. The Bolsheviks enjoyed support among Russian workers in the large factories and mines in the east of the region, particularly in Kharkov. They were far weaker in Kiev, where the artisans who made up the bulk of the proletariat backed the Mensheviks, the Ukrainian Social Democrats, and the Jewish Bund. By early summer, Kiev was also the seat of the Rada, an elected assembly composed of liberals and socialists who aspired to make themselves the government of an autonomous Ukraine. To Bosh, the lamentable lesson of all this ethnic division was obvious. In fact, it was just as she had predicted: nationalism was dividing the workers and empowering the bourgeoisie.

The Bolsheviks of Kiev understood full well that they were one of the weakest of the many political parties in the city, but they drew varying strategic conclusions from this undeniable fact. The majority argued that they should cooperate with fellow socialists and with the Rada. This tactic required adaptation of official Bolshevik policy, particularly of Lenin's prescriptions of hostility to other political parties. Kiev's Bolsheviks therefore argued that they could work with the liberals and moderate socialists in the Rada to promote opposition to the Provisional Government in Petrograd. At the same time, they would also strive to control the soviets and represent the workers.[33]

Bosh led a small minority in denouncing this conciliatory posture as wrong-headed. The Bolsheviks in Ukraine were weak, she argued,

---

[32] Ibid.; Institut istorii partii MGK i MK KPSS, Filial Instituta Marksizma-Leninizma pri TsK KPSS, *1917. Letopis geroicheskikh dnei* (Moscow, 1973), 490; *Oktiabr' v Moskve*, 54, 66, 79, 299–300, 309.

[33] A sympathetic view of the thinking of the majority of Kiev's Bolsheviks is presented in S. Shreiber, "K protokolam pervogo vseukrainskogo soveshchaniia bol'shevikov," *Litopys revoliutsii*, no. 5 (1926): 55–62.

because they were afraid to take resolute positions that would rally the workers to them.[34] Cooperating with the Rada amounted to collaboration with a strong, dangerous enemy. It also amounted to endorsing Ukrainian nationalism, a course which constituted a betrayal of Marxist internationalism and which played into the hands of the Bolsheviks' enemies.

Bosh was in the minority among Kiev Bolsheviks, but she refused to change her mind. By July she had fallen out with Iurii Piatakov, her partner for years, and with most of the other members of the city party committee. Making common cause with the few who agreed with her, among them Leonid Piatakov, Iurii's younger brother, Bosh did as Zemliachka had done in Moscow and established a separate party organization, the Kiev regional committee. She then attempted to pull together under its aegis Bolshevik organizations from the other cities of western Ukraine. She had little success, for Bolsheviks elsewhere were as interested as the Kievans in setting up coalitions with rival socialist parties and cooperating with nationalist elements. Bosh's regional bureau turned out to be little more than herself and several colleagues, alone in an office in Kiev, writing letters that were rarely answered.

Increasingly alienated from her former comrades, Bosh spent more and more time visiting military bases. For her, this was fertile territory. Many of the troops stationed on the southwestern front were ethnic Russians, immune to the calls for Ukrainian independence; and substantial numbers of them were also radical politically. The front being largely quiet, the thousands of men had little to do in the summer and early fall of 1917 except hold meetings to discuss politics. There, Bosh continued to build up her reputation as a great agitator. By October she began to parlay her popularity into political power.[35]

Shortly after Bosh's well-received appearance in October before the Wild Division (described pp. 128–29), a mutiny erupted in the garrison town of Vinnitsa, 120 miles southwest of Kiev, less than twenty miles from Zhmerinka, the Wild Division's base. On 20 October a commissar sent by the Provisional Government to restore order among the 30,000 soldiers carousing in Vinnitsa announced that he was going to transfer trouble-makers back to the front.[36] Three days later, some of those troublemakers refused to pull out when ordered and began rampaging through the town instead. Bosh, who was working nearby with a handful of other Bolshevik agitators, rushed to Vinnitsa to declare her support for the rebels. The

---

[34] This idea emerges very strongly in Bosh's history of 1917 and 1918, *God bor'by*, as well as in E. Bosh, "Oktiabr'skie dni v Kievskoi oblasti," *Proletarskaia revoliutsiia*, no. 11 (1923): 52–67.

[35] On the southwestern front in summer and fall 1917, see Wildman, *The End of the Russian Imperial Army*, vol. II, 350–78.

[36] N. N. Mints, *Istoriia velikogo Oktiabria*, 3 vols. (Moscow, 1967–73), vol. III, 539.

commanders of the southwestern front then called in reinforcements from Kiev. Bosh responded by heading off to Zhmerinka to persuade the Wild Division to bring its guns to Vinnitsa.

"The fog was drizzling a cold rain," she wrote later, "but the square was tightly packed with gray overcoats. Good-hearted comments could be heard: 'We'll listen, we'll listen to what the *baba*'s going to say to us.'" Bosh, railing against the high command, warned them that the generals were once again sending their brothers off to be cannon fodder. "We'll show the officer scum who's got the power," the angry soldiers responded.[37] The next day she rode back to Vinnitsa at the head of an artillery company. After a week of fighting that spilled through the streets, killing many civilians, the rebel troops won control of the town.[38]

The Zhmerinka incident did not ignite any more general mutiny at the front, and indeed, Bosh did not intend that it should. Until the Bolsheviks overthrew the Provisional Government in late October, her main goal was to undermine military order by fanning the discontent that was rife among the troops. The aspirations and intentions of the soldiers who cheered Bosh were equally vague, and she deliberately did not try to clarify them. A side effect of her popularity with the Wild Division, however, was to enhance her standing in the ranks of Kiev Bolsheviks; and when they began to debate how to proceed after the party seized power in Petrograd, Bosh enjoyed still greater prominence within their councils.

Zemliachka and Bosh took strong positions in 1917 in opposition to the opinion of the majority of their comrades. They made common cause with like-minded colleagues and accumulated considerable authority even among those Bolsheviks who disagreed with them. Both became powerful, respected, even feared leaders. In short, they sought and won political power. Of course they had been leaders in the underground, too, and their successes both before and after 1917 may serve as proof that women could indeed claim a voice in the highest of party councils. Yet it is also evident that very few did so. The only other woman of comparable stature in 1917 was Varvara Iakovleva in Moscow, secretary of the regional party committee, a small operation that generally took a back seat to the Moscow city committee.[39] The great majority of Bolshevichki remained rank-and-file workers because the prevailing party culture and their own

[37] Bosh, *God bor'by*, 71; Bosh, "Oktiabr'skie dni v Kievskoi oblasti," 63.

[38] For Bosh's account of these events, see Bosh, "Oktiabr'skie dni v Kievskoi oblasti." See also V. Leikina, "Oktiabr' po Rossii. Chast' 2ia: Ukraina," *Proletarskaia revoliutsiia*, no. 12 (1926): 238–54; and Mints, *Istoriia velikogo Oktiabria*, vol. III, 540–44.

[39] For Iakovleva's accounts of her work, see V. Iakovleva, "Partiinaia rabota v Moskovskoi oblasti v period fevral'–oktiabr' 1917 g.," *Proletarskaia revoliutsiia*, no. 3 (1923): 196–204; Iakovleva, "Podgotovka oktiabr'skogo vosstaniia v Moskovskoi oblasti," *Proletarskaia revoliutsiia*, no. 10 (1922): 302–06.

variant of the collective identity made that the acceptable choice for them. Many were party secretaries at the local level, positions not inconsequential in 1917, but remote from the party's top leadership. Those who reached the heights of the party did so because they were women of exceptional ambition and will.

Zemliachka and Bosh did join the rest of the prominent Bolshevichki – Inessa, Kollontai, Krupskaia, Rozmirovich, Samoilova, Stal, and Stasova – in supporting Lenin's strategies and scorning collaboration with other parties, even socialist ones. Whether these attitudes were common among less well-known Bolshevichki is not easy to say, due to the paucity of evidence on the subject. Nor is it clear why the more prominent were so uncompromising in their politics. It is tempting, however, to posit a connection between the reluctance of most of them to reach for a leadership role in the party and their distaste for political compromise. Both attitudes could stem from the same alienation from politics. Uneasy amid the negotiations, the competition for influence, and the self-assertion that were essential to party politics at the highest levels, the Bolshevichki avoided the smoke-filled rooms where the men of the Central Committee fought bitterly with one another. Varvara Iakovleva described how Sofia Smidovich happily turned over to her the job of technical secretary of the Moscow committee in March 1917. "Comrade Smidovich, giving me the secretarial responsibilities, disappeared into the ranks [*peredely*] of the Moscow organization."[40] Closer to the surging crowds, Smidovich could paint the world in black and white, and hear in the cheers a promise that her utopian dreams were coming true.

The Bolshevichki saw no contradiction between embracing the crowd and supporting their party's quest for power. They had convinced themselves that the Bolsheviks had the popular mandate, or would soon have it, because the party understood best how to lead Russia to liberation. In the fall of 1917, with voters electing Bolsheviks to soviets all over Russia and soldiers cheering them from Zhmerinka to Petrograd, the Bolshevichki could believe that they had finally become what they had so long aspired to be – a unified party surging forward at the front of a great, onrushing workers' movement. Such a view was partly an illusion, because Russia was in fact more divided in October 1917 than it had ever been; revolutionaries seem to require illusions and in this the Bolsheviks were no different from any others.

Thus when Lenin took the podium at a national soviet congress on 25

---

[40] Iakovleva, "Partiinaia rabota v Moskovskoi oblasti v period fevral'–oktiabr' 1917 g.," 197. For an interesting discussion of American women's sense of alienation from the operations of political parties, see Lebsock, "Women and American Politics, 1880–1920," 35–62.

October to declare the Provisional Government overthrown, Kollontai, Krupskaia, Samoilova, Slutskaia, and Stasova stood in the great crowd and exulted. Lenin announced that they would immediately seek peace with Germany, that the soviets were now Russia's government, and that the land henceforth belonged to the people. As the delegates stood to sing the socialist anthem "The Internationale," American journalist John Reed noticed that Kollontai had tears in her eyes. Leaving the hall after the meeting, Samoilova ran into Slutskaia. "Isn't it true, Vera," Samoilova beamed, "that even if all of us have to die, it will have been worth it just to live through this evening?" "Yes, of course," Slutskaia agreed immediately. This encounter stuck in Samoilova's memory because a few weeks later Slutskaia was killed in a skirmish with troops loyal to the Provisional Government.[41]

Women as leaders in the new order

The euphoria of October passed as quickly as Slutskaia's life, for the significance of what they had done soon bore in on the Bolsheviks. Russia was in a shambles, its economy and its social order collapsing, its politicians at one another's throats. The Bolsheviks had no clearly formulated plan of government and no experience in governing – not that experience would have helped much in such chaotic conditions. In December, acting on the generally accepted socialist propositions that the economy should be nationalized and social welfare programs established, they declared public control over banking and communications. Kollontai, the commissar of social welfare, drafted maternity insurance in January while Shliapnikov, the commissar of labor, drew up regulations on working conditions. Meanwhile Lenin, Trotsky, and the other party leaders were dealing with issues of power that had not been dreamt of in Marx's philosophy. Trotsky attempted to make peace with Germany while Felix Dzerzhinski, a Polish nobleman, assumed command of an Extraordinary Commission (soon known by its acronym, Cheka) designed to quell opposition to Bolshevik rule. In short order the Bolsheviks began jailing their opposition. In January they dismissed the Constituent Assembly, elected in November to write a constitution for Russia, but suspect in Bolshevik eyes because the majority of the delegates were SRs.

Those people who expected the Bolsheviks to falter just as the Provisional Government had done were quickly disappointed. Not only did the party demonstrate an ability to use force to maintain itself, it continued to court public opinion, now with a barrage of publications and

[41] Samoilova, "Pamiati tovarishch Very (Bronislavy Klement'evny Slutskoi)," *Rabotnitsa*, 8 December 1917, 5. On Kollontai, see Clements, *Bolshevik Feminist*, 120–21.

speeches delivering a new message for the new situation. From November onward, the Bolsheviks proclaimed a vision of the world they intended to build, a world in which civil and legal equality would be established, publicly funded education and medical services would be available to all, and in which the peasants would control the land and the workers the factories. Never again, the Bolshevichki declared in their speeches, would landlords charge exorbitant rents to peasants, or bosses pay miserable wages to factory workers. Never again would women stand in line for hours for bread. The party knew how to end the manifold injustices of the old order and bring about a fair new society. It only required that the great masses of the people support it.

The great masses were the peasants, who had elected SRs to the Constituent Assembly. Winning their support was going to be a formidable undertaking. More reliable was the industrial proletariat, the popular base of support for the Bolsheviks; but even among the factory workers there were many who waited through the winter of 1917–18 to see if the party could make good on any of its many promises. To cultivate the working class, the majority of the Bolshevichki continued after October to do the same jobs they had done earlier in the year. They worked in local party organizations, wrote newspaper articles and pamphlets, and spoke at neighborhood meetings. Their message had shifted from attacks on the Provisional Government to promises of the better world to come, but the essentially missionary nature of much of their work remained.

In the party's new government, there were a few important women. One of the best known, because of her reputation as an agitator and feminist as well as her willingness to talk to the foreign press, was Kollontai. As commissar of social welfare, Kollontai was one of the first women in history to hold cabinet rank in a European government. Lenin offered her the position because of her popularity and because of her standing as the Russian Social Democrats' most prolific author on the woman question. Kollontai had published an extensive study of the state of maternity and infant care in Europe in 1916, so she was also the logical choice to head up a department with responsibilities in the field of public health. As commissar she issued important decrees on the public funding of maternity and infant care, and she also acted as an advisor to those rewriting the marriage law and drafting labor regulations to protect the health of female workers. Kollontai thus became an architect of Soviet socialized medicine as well as a contributor to legal and labor reform.[42]

Kollontai, with her appointment as commissar of social welfare, also fulfilled her ambition to become a leader on women's issues within the

---

[42] On Kollontai as commissar, see Clements, *Bolshevik Feminist*, 122–48.

party. She had long been recognized as a major writer on women's concerns, but the scent of feminism had always clung to her, and for a while she also had to live with mistrust engendered by the fact that she had been a Menshevik for most of the prerevolutionary period. Indeed, she had only become a close collaborator with leading Bolshevichki, particularly Krupskaia and Inessa, in 1915; and even then she was only in contact with them by mail. In 1917 she set out to close the remaining political and intellectual distance by cultivating good relations with all the Bolshevichki involved in projects among women, and particularly with Samoilova, who held the important editorship at *Rabotnitsa*. Meanwhile, her two likely competitors for leadership on women's issues, Inessa and Krupskaia, went off into other projects. Samoilova exercised great authority in the small circle of Bolshevik feminists, but she was content to confine herself to editing and giving the occasional speech to groups of working women. Consequently, Kollontai met no resistance when she stepped forward after October 1917 to present herself as the party's leading spokesperson on women's issues. In that role she became a prominent member of the Bolsheviks' first government.

In Ukraine, Bosh pioneered in quite another direction. Kollontai was the articulate public voice of the Bolshevik feminists and the commissar who set out to translate the party's commitment to women's emancipation into concrete social policy. Bosh pursued a quest to bring Ukraine under Bolshevik rule, in the process making herself into a military commander of mythic proportions. Victor Serge, Bolshevik and historian, later described her as one of "the most capable military leaders to emerge at this early stage" of the civil war.[43]

Bosh came to be a commander by continuing on her course of confrontation with political enemies. In November, after the fall of the Provisional Government, the Rada in Kiev quickly moved to assert itself as the government of an independent Ukraine, and proved, as Bosh had predicted, a much more formidable adversary for the Kiev Bolsheviks than the Provisional Government had been. In early November, Rada leaders declared their support for democratic institutions and land reform, at about the same time demanding the right to negotiate separately with Germany and Austria for peace. They also fortified themselves militarily by disarming pro-Bolshevik army units, concentrating ethnically Ukrainian troops under their command, and encouraging the anti-Bolshevik Cossack general A. M. Kaledin, who was operating in eastern Ukraine. All these initiatives put them on a collision course with the Bolshevik government in Petrograd.

[43] Victor Serge and Natalia Sedova Trotsky, *The Life and Death of Leon Trotsky*, trans. Arnold J. Pomerans (New York, 1975), 85.

And of course the same initiatives complicated immensely the situation of the Kiev Bolsheviks. Throughout November, Bosh's comrades debated what to do. Should they still work with the Rada? Could they pull off an arrangement whereby the Rada would rule Ukraine as a whole while the soviets, led by the Bolsheviks, would govern the cities? Could they gain control of the soviets? Bosh declared a plague on all these proposals and offered instead to bring the Wild Division to town to blow up the Rada. She was very serious in this proposal; and by making it she simply played into the hands of Rada leaders, who claimed (not without justice) that the Bolsheviks were Russian nationalists intent on turning Ukraine over to a continuance of rule from Petrograd.

In early December, relations between the Rada and the Kiev Bolsheviks deteriorated into complete rupture. Bosh, now known as the most irreconcilable Bolshevik of all, began to receive death threats. Frightened, she headed off to Kharkov with a dozen or so of her colleagues. There they declared a rival Ukrainian government that they christened "The People's Secretariat." Backed by the Bolsheviks' government in Petrograd and by a few regiments of friendly troops, they then attempted by force to wrest control of Kiev from the Rada. They succeeded in January 1918. Bosh soon became minister of internal affairs in the Bolsheviks' People's Secretariat, still stationed in Kharkov.[44]

Unlike Stasova, Bosh had no difficulty making policy. On the contrary, she had to be restrained from issuing orders without the approval of other members of the government. She was also willing, perhaps even eager, to assert her prerogatives. When Vladimir Antonov-Ovseenko, commander of Bolshevik troops in the region, began appointing civilian officials, Bosh fired off angry complaints to Lenin. Lenin responded by ordering Antonov-Ovseenko to confine himself to military matters and leave local administration to the People's Secretariat.[45]

After a few weeks in Kharkov, the Secretariat moved to Kiev. The city was in a shambles, low on supplies and full of undisciplined soldiers

[44] The foregoing account of events in the fall of 1917 is drawn from Bosh, *God bor'by*, 30–51; Jurij Borys, *The Russian Communist Party and the Sovietization of Ukraine* (Stockholm, 1960), 102–37, 164–78; Institut istorii partii pri TsK Kompartii Ukrainy, *Bol'sheviki vo glave trudiashchikhsia v period bor'by za ustanovlenie sovetskoi vlasti na Ukraine, oktiabr' 1917 g.–fevral' 1918 g.* (Kiev, 1982), 267, 295–96, 379–80, 431–33; "K otchetu o I vseukrainskom s"ezd sovetov RS i KD," *Litopys revoliutsii*, no. 1 (1928): 257–66; "Vseukrainskii s"ezd sovetov," *Litopys revoliutsii*, no. 1 (1928): 267–92.

[45] Institut istorii partii pri TsK Kompartii Ukrainy, *Bol'sheviki vo glave trudiashchikhsia*, 798; Borys, *The Russian Communist Party and the Sovietization of Ukraine*, 182. Bosh and Antonov-Ovseenko were still fighting with one another four years later in critiques of one another's memoirs of the war years. See Bosh, "Pis'mo k redaktsiiu," *Proletarskaia revoliutsiia*, no. 11 (1924): 269–70; Bosh, "Neskol'ko zamechanii o knige V. A. Antonov-Ovseenko ('Zapiski o grazhdanskoi voine')," *Proletarskaia revoliutsiia*, no. 12 (1924): 318–23.

brandishing guns. Bosh wanted to concentrate on setting up the Interior Ministry, but instead she spent most of her time dealing with the hordes of needy people who descended on her office. "The leaders of an orphanage brought in a group of emaciated children, who began to sob loudly at the word 'bread,'" Bosh remembered later, her impatience still evident:

Paralyzed, legless, and armless invalids came creeping in, backing up their demands with hysterical screams and wild threats. From early in the morning the reception room of the former governor's house was dammed up with these delegates and nothing could free it. One wave broke on another, the demands came one after another, and a sea of tears, hysteria, and threats made productive work extremely difficult.[46]

While Bosh struggled with the crowds in her waiting room, Rada forces, bolstered by units of the German army, were forming outside Kiev.[47] So isolated within their Kievan enclave were the revolutionary ministers of the People's Secretariat that they did not know their enemies were within striking distance until the day before shells began raining down on the city.[48] When, on 26 February, they heard the rumble of artillery in the distance, most of the secretaries jumped onto a train out of town. Unaware that they had left, Bosh remained at her office, "receiving her endless delegations," as she later described it, "and demonstrating the power, or, actually, the absence of power in the city."[49] When she did learn that most of her colleagues were gone, she declared that she would stay. On 1 March, other members of the People's Secretariat remaining in Kiev lured her and several equally recalcitrant comrades to a meeting in a railway car at 3 a.m. While they argued about what to do next, the train jerked to life and Bosh found herself locked into her compartment and on the way to Poltava.

Bosh's refusal to face the inevitable was only beginning as she rattled the doors of that escaping train. Two days later, on 3 March 1918, Lenin's government signed the Treaty of Brest-Litovsk making peace with Germany and then beat its own hasty retreat, from Petrograd to Moscow. Bosh was outraged. The treaty ceded a huge amount of territory, including western Ukraine, to Germany. As did many Bolsheviks, Bosh thought this humiliating surrender had resulted from a craven collapse of will before a German High Command that embodied the great evils of contemporary European society – militarism, monarchism, nationalism,

---

[46] Bosh, *God bor'by*, 146–47.
[47] On 9 February 1918, Germany signed a peace treaty with the Rada that permitted its forces to occupy western Ukraine. In February and March the German commanders worked with the Rada. In April they brought to power the more pliable Cossack general Pavlo Skoropadsky. German occupation of Ukraine ended in the fall of 1918.
[48] M. Maiorov, "Na putiakh k I s"ezdu KP(b)U," *Litopys revoliutsii*, no. 4 (1928): 8–9.
[49] Bosh, *God bor'by*, 162.

and capitalism. The iron logic of Lenin's argument – the revolutionaries could not fight on because the Russian army had disintegrated – did not persuade her. Bosh was delighted, therefore, when Iurii Piatakov arrived in Poltava, having resigned from Lenin's government because he was as outraged as she. The two made common cause again, and on 5 March Bosh quit her post in the People's Secretariat. Then she and Piatakov, joined by her daughter Mariia, signed up for service in Antonov-Ovseenko's army.

The three embarked on a hopeless, hapless mission. Antonov-Ovseenko was charged with putting down anti-Bolshevik forces in territory still under Russian rule in eastern Ukraine. Bosh, Piatakov, and a rag-tag bunch of volunteers were supposed to guard his western flank against the Germans. Since the Russian government they all represented was officially at peace with Germany, the Kievans should have stood down in orderly fashion, but instead they set out to halt the spread of the German occupation. To this end they pulled together a few units from troops that were drifting away from the southwestern front in the wake of the treaty. Demoralized and vastly outnumbered, the men of these units were also critically low on equipment and food, and they were surrounded by a peasant population that was, as Bosh put it with some understatement, "not hospitable."[50] They were capable of only the most token resistance; usually they broke and ran at the first news that the Germans were nearby. Bosh and Piatakov spent a month trying to keep these men together while retreating along the railroad lines that led from Kiev to the east. Although they soon realized the hopelessness of the undertaking, they could not bear to surrender Ukraine to Germany without putting up some sort of fight.

Bosh was technically in charge of propaganda, but she actually performed a plethora of tasks. She negotiated with local people for food and other supplies, and wrote articles for a unit newspaper. She also made decisions on troop movements, issued commands to junior officers, and communicated with headquarters. Comrades later paid tribute to her intelligence and courage. She herself was glum when she recalled the work she did:

At that time the party worker in the command staff answered for everything, and they came to him [sic] for decisions in all questions, from deciding military movements to distributing jars of jam or pairs of footcloths. So it wasn't surprising that twenty-four hours a day weren't enough for these comrades. They didn't sleep for two to five days – they slept a bit at work, standing up.[51]

[50] E. Bosh, *Natsional'noe pravitel'stvo i Sovetskoi vlast v Ukraine* (Moscow, 1918), quoted in Borys, *The Russian Communist Party and the Sovietization of Ukraine*, 186.
[51] Bosh, *God bor'by*, 195. Italics in the original.

Bosh never admitted to feeling any reservations about her role as a woman commanding men at war. Instead, in a series of articles and in a book-length history of these events (written in the early 1920s), she portrayed herself as a "hard" Bolshevik, accepted by the men because of the righteousness of her ideas and her reputation for indomitability. Following standard party notions that prescribed a show of personal modesty in such histories, Bosh referred to herself in the third person, sometimes even adopting the masculine pronoun, as in the description of the "party worker" quoted above. But that very identification of herself as masculine, in a language as heavily gendered as Russian, suggests that she believed herself to be the equal of the men with whom she worked. Equally suggestive is the fact that Bosh did not openly discuss the problems she encountered as a woman commanding men. Other Bolshevichki, writing of their experiences at the front in later decades, testified to a whole gamut of harassment they were forced to endure. Bosh never mentioned such difficulties. She simply presented herself as a strong, tough leader whose orders were obeyed.

Bosh did recount several episodes which addressed, albeit obliquely, the way she established her authority. One such encounter took place in the town of Konotop. Bosh arrived there to discover that a captain named Sharov, enlisted in her army, had set himself up as a local warlord and had arrested all the Bolsheviks he could find, as well as the delegates to a provincial soviet congress then in session. Furious, she marched into Sharov's headquarters. "I pushed aside the adjutant, who had become somewhat embarrassed on learning that this was Bosh in front of him (I don't know how to explain the fact that all the wretched hangers-on were afraid of me) and went in without being announced." Sharov was too drunk to be conciliatory, but "I spent another hour in conversation with this type, showing him the unacceptability of his actions, the drunkenness all around, the lack of activity and standing around at the station, etc., etc., and although I believed strongly that this was a total waste of time, there wasn't any other solution – he had the broadest possible powers from the commander-in-chief [Antonov-Ovseenko]." Sharov agreed to release the soviet delegates and within a day or so had run off, taking most of his men with him. Bosh was left to explain to the townsfolk that they should not blame the Bolsheviks for his excesses. "I didn't want to explain," she later remembered. "I wanted to shoot this scoundrel immediately."[52]

The Sharov episode was similar to several others recounted in Bosh's histories. In each, she enters a dangerous situation, faces down a disreputable commander, and reestablishes a faltering Bolshevik com-

[52] Ibid., 199–201.

mand. By pointing out that her opponents are armed, hostile, and usually drunk, Bosh makes it clear that there is risk in her confrontation, but she never admits to feeling any personal fear. Instead, she portrays herself as attacking the threat on her own and establishing control by asserting her rank and demonstrating her *tverdost* ("This was Bosh in front of him"). The triumphs she recalls are short-lived; they end with the soldiers, still disgruntled and drunk, slinking away, rather than fighting for the Bolsheviks. But they show Bosh cowing local renegades into ceasing their depredations in her immediate vicinity.

No self-doubt, no timidity, no reluctance to take command in the most masculine of worlds appear in Bosh's retelling of the events less than ten years later. She presents herself as a courageous, authoritative leader, the equal (if not the superior) of the men with whom she works. Colleagues who wrote about her in the 1920s seem to confirm her presentation of herself. They praised her for courage, ideological purity, and determination, lauding, in the words of one tribute, "the huge role and gigantic service of Evgeniia Bogdanovna to the party and the revolution." Her admirers and even her critics, those who blamed her for contributing to the fractiousness that beset the Ukrainian Bolsheviks in 1917 and 1918, remarked on Bosh's ability to lead men in chaotic conditions that left others floundering in indecision.[53]

There are many signs that Bosh's experience as military leader was essentially similar to that of thousands of other Bolshevichki who served in the Red Army during the civil war. They too helped to energize demoralized men, hotly contended with inept, corrupt officers, worked for days without sleep, and endured the hardships of life at the front and the terror of combat. Their ability to bear the burdens of military life refuted the old assumption that women were too weak, emotionally and physically, to be soldiers. Bosh was one of the first Bolshevichki to prove herself, and her exploits became well known. Thus her example not only illustrates the experiences of many Bolshevichki subsequently at war, but paved the way for them and provided them with an inspiring example.

The achievements of her little army were considerably less noteworthy than her own. For three weeks in March 1918, they retreated down the railway lines south and east of Kiev, putting up only token resistance to the oncoming Germans. When the enemy's forces had spread across most of

---

[53] The quote is from the preface to Bosh's *God bor'by*, signed by "A Group of Old Comrades," 4. Bosh recounted four other confrontations with rebellious troops in *God bor'by*, 201, 206–07, 208, 215. For colleagues' tributes to her, see the introduction ibid., 1–6; E. Preobrazhenskii, "Evgeniia Bogdanovna Bosh," *Proletarskaia revoliutsiia*, no. 2 (1925): 11–13; and Victor Serge, *Year One of the Russian Revolution*, trans. Peter Sedgwick (New York, 1972), 181. For criticism, see Shreiber, "K protokolam pervogo vseukrainskogo soveshchaniia bol'shevikov"; Maiorov, "Na putiakh k I s"ezdu KP(b)U," 7–24.

western and central Ukraine, Bosh, Piatakov, and their troops had to take to their feet, fleeing east toward Kharkov, which was still in Bolshevik hands. "In a cold rain, wallowing in the mud of dirt roads, without transport, without a cookstove, without provisions, we trudged along day and dark night, not knowing what was going on around us and what was waiting for us ahead," she remembered.[54] She worked to hold the men together and to find food and boots for them, while they all struggled to get to the protection of Antonov-Ovseenko's lines. In early April they reached the Red forces.

Away from the battle, Bosh's strength gave out. She collapsed, exhausted in body and spirit. "It's impossible even now," she wrote in 1924, "to imagine the torture of unlimited despair." She blamed the Bolsheviks' defeat on their own failures as political leaders. She refused to accept the necessity of the Treaty of Brest-Litovsk. She railed against Antonov-Ovseenko and his staff for not giving her men adequate support. She was contemptuous of those Bolsheviks who had sat out the confrontation with the Germans and were still arguing among themselves. In short, she was alienated from just about everyone else in the Ukrainian branch of the party. Co-worker D. Frid later described her in April 1918 as unable to "endure the excessively nerve-wracking disturbance of the confrontational struggle in which she had taken an active and fierce part."[55] Bosh's solution was to have nothing more to do with her erstwhile comrades. For the next several months she stayed in Taganrog in eastern Ukraine, recuperating in the care of her daughter, Mariia.[56] After she recovered her health, she volunteered for assignments in Russia. The woman who had proved herself able to do anything but compromise had withdrawn from the politics of the homeland she had fought so hard to defend.

Bolshevichki in the spring of 1918

Bosh was not alone in her disillusionment. The surrender to Germany – which was, as Lenin argued, both necessary and inevitable – had alienated many Bolsheviks. As Bosh trekked toward Kharkov, Kollontai was quitting her post as commissar of social welfare because she was so angry about what she called "the peace treaty with Austro-German imperialism." In her letter of resignation, Kollontai also charged that current plans to enlist sympathetic officers from the tsarist army in the army being formed by the Bolsheviks would "give support to the bourgeois counter-

---

[54] Bosh, *God bor'by*, 212.
[55] D. Frid, "Taganroz'ka Narada," *Litopys revoliutsii*, no. 4 (1928): 42.
[56] Preobrazhenskii, "Bosh," 13.

revolution."[57] She, Bosh, and Inessa Armand also viewed with alarm the fact that their government still employed many of the people who had been bureaucrats under the tsar. Furthermore, Lenin was beginning to talk about the necessity of signing up professionals – engineers, doctors, teachers, factory managers – to work in the new regime. Lenin, so recently the apostle of uncompromising struggle with liberals, astonished Kollontai and Inessa by arguing that workers could not run industry without guidance from more experienced, better-educated people.[58]

A standing army full of tsarist generals, ministries full of tsarist bureaucrats, the factories and schools staffed by bourgeois engineers and teachers – what next? Such compromises with the reality of governing Russia alienated revolutionary purists such as Kollontai, Inessa, and Bosh. The dread thought was beginning to dawn on them that their party was becoming an agency willing to capitulate to, even cooperate with, its enemies in order to retain its grip on power. Disgusted, Bosh withdrew from her comrades, Kollontai did the same by resigning as commissar, and Kollontai and Inessa affiliated themselves with the Left Opposition, a group led by Bukharin that was publicly criticizing the decisions of the Politburo majority.

Stasova shared their doubts, but, as was her wont, she would not condemn the leadership openly. In her reluctance to speak up she was far more typical of Bolshevichki disillusioned in the spring of 1918 than were Kollontai and Bosh. Like them, however, she also disliked the Treaty of Brest-Litovsk. "I could not explain to myself where the truth was," she wrote in her memoirs decades later, "and only the unshakable confidence of Vladimir Ilich [Lenin], his explanations that we could not convince the soldiers (the peasant masses) to go to war now, that peace of any kind was the key to our peasant masses and that without it we would lose more than we would gain from making peace, his categorical statement that otherwise he would leave the government and the CC [Central Committee], made me make up my mind and vote with him." Stasova also opposed enlisting tsarist officers in the Red Army. She did not support the Left Communists because she did not think their leaders as able as Lenin and Trotsky. But she was highly critical of the sort of people who were now joining the party, calling them "trash" in a letter to Novgorodtseva. She also worried about the general misery in Petrograd caused by continuing food shortages. Even people who had been Bolshevik supporters were beginning, in the spring of 1918, to blame the party for not alleviating their problems. Crime was also on the rise. In April, Stasova herself was mugged by a soldier and a sailor who

[57] RTsKhIDNI, f. 17, op. 4, d. 180, l. 1.
[58] On Inessa's response to the treaty, see Elwood, *Inessa Armand*, 214–16.

demanded her money at gun-point. She escaped unhurt, but she was badly frightened.[59]

Stasova sought refuge from her doubts by burying herself in familiar work and by refusing to leave Petrograd when the rest of the Central Committee, including its secretarial staff, moved to Moscow in early March. She stayed behind to become secretary of the Petrograd bureau of the Central Committee as well as of the committee of the Petrograd region. To Novgorodtseva's and Sverdlov's repeated requests that she come to the new capital, she replied that there was much useful work to be done where she was. She also said she had to stay in Petrograd to look after her aged parents (Dmitrii Stasov was now ninety and Poliksena Stasova seventy-nine). "My old folks are both poorly and I always return home fearful," she wrote to Novgorodtseva.[60]

When Dmitrii Stasov died in early May 1918, Stasova plunged into depression. She had always been very close to her parents, living with them when she was in St. Petersburg, remaining in touch throughout her years in exile. She had been particularly close to her father, and he had returned her love with deep affection and support. After his death, Stasova felt utterly alone, alienated from the party that was changing in ways that repelled her, distanced from comrades who did not share her doubts. A few days after the funeral, she wrote to Novgorodtseva, "I have already buried him, and I have taken up regular work, but my head and spirit still have not returned to normal. I feel that my last personal connection in life has been broken and therefore the future is in great disarray."[61] No one in the party had ever cared about her, she observed glumly, the way her family had.

Sverdlov understood Stasova's feelings of isolation and wrote back to reassure her: "I only want you to know that you're not just connected to all the comrades by shared views, by friendly intellectual work. I'm talking about myself. I have very warm, friendly feelings for you, completely independent of our party connections. And I am not the only one to esteem you as a dear, sympathetic friend-comrade. All your personal ties have not been broken. Even without blood relationships there are the deep relationships between friends. I kiss you heartily. Your Iakov."[62] His kindness did not persuade her to move to Moscow; she kept her distance from the party's leaders and remained in Petrograd to nurse her sorrows.

[59] S. M. Levidova and E. G. Salita, *Elena Dmitrievna Stasova. Biograficheskii ocherk* (Leningrad, 1969), 266; *Zhenshchiny russkoi revoliutsii* (Moscow, 1968), 66; "Iz perepiski E. D. Stasovoi i K. T. Novgorodtsevoi (Sverdlovoi), mart–dekabr' 1918 g.," *Voprosy istorii*, no. 10 (1956): 86–87; Stasova, *Vospominaniia*, 159–60.

[60] E. D. Stasova, *Stranitsy zhizni i bor'by*, 1st ed. (Moscow, 1957), 130.

[61] Ibid., 136.

[62] Levidova and Salita, *Stasova*, 270.

How many Bolshevichki shared the unhappiness of Bosh, Inessa, Kollontai, and Stasova in the spring of 1918 is impossible to tell at this remove. Probably many came trudging home after long days at work, as Kollontai did, and thought longingly of the old days, when they had been "ordinary party agitator[s] traveling around the world and dreaming of revolution."[63] Overall party membership dropped considerably in the early months of 1918, in part because of the widespread disillusionment that Bosh and Kollontai voiced so openly. The figures that document this decline are too fragmentary to permit any gender analysis, however. Only three of the prominent Bolshevichki, Kollontai, Inessa, and Varvara Iakovleva, joined the Left Opposition.[64]

The Bolshevichki who entertained doubts were correct in their percep-tions that their movement was changing. By the spring of 1918 its transformation from a loosely organized faction into a highly structured, centralized party exercising power was well underway. At the top, the Politburo, a standing subcommittee of the Central Committee that had only been in existence since the fall of 1917, set policy and issued directives. Below, committees proliferated in the neighborhoods and at the regional level. Meanwhile, ambitious Bolsheviks from top to bottom were beginning to vie for position and privilege. They built alliances with old comrades from the underground and they sought the support of new recruits. They also exerted what control they could over the people in the regions they governed, behaving peremptorily, demanding deference, and ordering their critics jailed. It was individuals who eagerly used the party's increasing power to establish their own authority and feather their own nests that Stasova had in mind when she condemned the "trash" among the Bolsheviks in the spring of 1918.[65]

Kollontai, Bosh, Inessa, and Stasova had accepted the righteousness of grasping and holding power by undemocratic means. They had raised no protest when opposition newspapers were closed or rival politicians were harassed. Indeed, Bosh and Kollontai themselves had ordered people arrested. Inessa had endorsed the dismissal of the democratically elected Constituent Assembly in December 1917, more than a month before it convened. "We should destroy constitutional illusions," she had pro-claimed to a meeting of Moscow Bolsheviks.[66] Ironically, she and Kollontai and Bosh then began to experience alarm just in proportion to

[63] A. M. Kollontai, "Iz vospominanii," *Oktiabr'*, no. 9 (1945), 88.
[64] For an analysis of the decline in party membership, see Service, *The Bolshevik Party in Revolution*, 70. On the Left Communists, see Ronald I. Kowalski, *The Bolshevik Party in Conflict: The Left Communist Opposition of 1918* (London, 1991).
[65] On the party in the spring of 1918, see Service, *The Bolshevik Party in Revolution*, 65–83.
[66] "Protokoly tret'ei Moskovskoi oblastnoi konferentsii RSDRP(b) 1917 goda," *Prolet-arskaia revoliutsiia*, no. 10 (1930): 124.

the party's growing accumulation of power, for it undermined not only the egalitarian values they cherished, but also the illusion that they inhabited a special enclave of the reborn, walled off from the vices of the old world. Other Bolshevichki, Zemliachka for example, had far fewer qualms in the spring of 1918, for they concentrated their attention not on the changes within their own movement but on the continuing struggle to survive. In their view, the party was locked in a mortal combat with vicious enemies. Establishing a more centralized, efficient organization, ready and willing to use all the force at its disposal, was the necessary means to the end of assuring the success of the revolution. Like many politicians in many other ages, Bolshevichki such as Zemliachka were already beginning to have difficulty in the spring of 1918 distinguishing between the good of the cause and the good of their group. Wedded to the party by their collective identity, they appear to have been as likely as men to accept the rationale for becoming dictators.[67]

This finding is not as surprising as it may appear at first glance. Women, disfranchised in patriarchal systems, might be expected to be more persistent advocates of democratic values than men. But studies of election results and polling data from many nations during the twentieth century have demonstrated that ethnicity, class, religion, education, and age have proved more decisive than gender in shaping political attitudes. One result of this is the fact that women have been far more likely to agree politically with the men who are their peers than to disagree with them; the gender gap in politics predicted by feminists (and their critics) for more than a century has yet to appear to any substantial degree.[68] Further, it must be remembered that the Bolshevichki shared their party's powerful sense of collective identity. The Bolsheviks had quite consciously attempted to control one another's ideas for years, a practice that only grew more intense after they seized power. The Bolshevichki, women eager to prove their acceptability, had always bowed to the pressure to conform. It is probable, therefore, that they, like the majority of male Bolsheviks, accepted the prevailing party rationale that the methods they were employing in the spring of 1918 and the changes that were developing in their own ranks were necessary, temporary adaptations.

The greatest differences between male and female Bolsheviks in the earliest days of the Soviet regime lay in their relation to the political changes ongoing within their party. Male Bolsheviks held virtually all the high-ranking and mid-range party offices, and when they came to

---

[67] For Zemliachka's attitudes in 1918, see RTsKhIDNI, f. 90, op. 1, d. 66, ll. 1–40.

[68] Louise A. Tilly and Patricia Gurin, "Introduction" in their *Women, Politics, and Change*, 24–25; and also Nancy Cott, "Across the Great Divide: Women in Politics Before and After 1920," ibid., 170–71.

construct the personal connections through which governmental power flowed from level to level, they fell back, without realizing they were doing so, on one of the most fundamental practices of patriarchy. They formed alliances with other men. Bolshevichki, most of whom had not inserted themselves into the politics of the men in the past, remained remote from this developing hierarchy of the powerful.

Men who had pledged themselves to end all gender discrimination might have been expected to behave differently, but then such men might also have been expected to build a democratic government. Both the Bolsheviks' dictatorial tendencies and their inclination to marginalize women had existed within their collective identity in the underground; they had appeared then in the bitter polemics against other socialists and in male control over policy-making. But, generally speaking, these autocratic and patriarchal appetites had been of minor consequence before 1917, because the party was a small underground movement with very little power to distribute and because the revolutionary ethos prescribed countervailing egalitarian values. When Russia's very imperfect, very incomplete revolution brought few of the Bolsheviks' utopian predictions to fruition, they exercised the option history did give them: they seized power and determined to use all the means at their disposal to hold onto it. They then continued to endorse women's equality while resorting to the age-old practice of governing through networks of men. Nor was this a response peculiar to Bolsheviks: republicans in Spain in the 1930s as well as the Students for a Democratic Society in the United States in the 1960s behaved similarly. Furthermore, all these radicals operated in conditions of extreme emergency, indeed, in the case of the Bolsheviks and the Spanish republicans, of life-and-death struggle. The surrounding danger only strengthened the age-old tendency of men to rely on and ally with other men.[69]

For their part, the Bolshevichki reacted to the new political realities much as did female radicals in predominantly male organizations elsewhere. Most treated the party's political arena as alien territory, which

[69] On such behavior among the Students for a Democratic Society in the United States in the 1960s, see Sara Evans, *Personal Politics: The Roots of Women's Liberation in the Civil Rights Movement and the New Left* (New York, 1980). For the same behavior by trade unionists in the United States, see Ruth Milkman, "Gender and Trade Unionism in Historical Perspective," in Tilly and Gurin, *Women, Politics, and Change*, 87–107, esp. 92–93. Milkman has found that emergency intensified the bonds between men and the sense of women as outsiders in trade unions in the nineteenth and twentieth centuries. On the exclusion of women altogether from the high politics of a communist movement, see Christine Gilmartin, "Gender, Politics, and Patriarchy in China: The Experiences of Early Women Communists, 1920–1927," in Sonia Kruks, Rayna Rapp, and Marilyn B. Young, eds., *Promissory Notes: Women in the Transition to Socialism* (New York, 1989), 82–105.

they entered warily, if at all, and from which they quickly retreated. Probably those who conceded to men the right to lead could make their peace more readily with the party's growing power than those who did not. Bolshevichki who remained more wedded to egalitarian ideals – Inessa, Kollontai, Stasova, and Bosh most prominently among them – condemned the corruptions creeping into the party. Carolyn Heilbrun has written: "However unhappy the concept of power and control may make idealistic women, they delude themselves if they believe that the world and the condition of the oppressed can be changed without acknowledging it."[70] Such "delusions" had long been the deeply cherished expectations of many Bolshevichki, who had thought revolution would abolish power altogether.

Tough historical realities would soon fortify the realists among the Bolshevichki and overwhelm the doubters. The civil war that had been sputtering in scattered skirmishes across the country since October broke out with full fury when, in the summer of 1918, Czech troops on their way to the war in France took over sections of the Trans-Siberian railway and a large army under the command of Admiral A. V. Kolchak declared itself in control of Siberia. The prospect of armies led by tsarist generals driving on Moscow called forth from most Bolsheviks, female and male, a determination to defend the revolution by preserving their fledgling government, whatever the costs in blood and integrity. All the *tverdost* the Bolshevichki had learned in the underground would now be poured into the winning of a brutal and brutalizing war, during which most of them would lose what remained of their democratic scruples.

[70] Heilbrun, *Writing a Woman's Life*, 16.

4 The civil war

The civil war that surged across the collapsed Russian Empire between 1918 and 1921 was a brutal, brutalizing struggle that the Bolsheviks won only with great difficulty. Bolshevichki were engaged in every aspect of the conflict. Stasova served as secretary of the Central Committee; Bosh and Zemliachka were officers in the army; Rozmirovich became a judge; Krupskaia led the Commissariat of Education; Kollontai, Inessa, and Samoilova set up a department for work among women within the party. Other Bolshevichki fought at the front or labored in military supply, in factories, and in government. With the rest of the nation they also endured great hardship, for the war brought the already weakened economy to a state of collapse. And yet, even while famine, disease, combat, and premature death were making life a daily horror, the Bolshevichki were also crafting programs designed to lay the foundations for a socialist society. Moving into leadership positions in government and the military, they were establishing roles for women in the new regime. (See table 19.) And they were recruiting thousands of young women into the party. For the Bolshevichki the civil war was a time when despair alternated with hope, destruction with creation, doubt with resolve, coercion and force with persuasion and compassion.

The new generation

The civil war saw a new generation of people join the party, among whom were thousands of women. It is difficult to determine how many women there actually were because figures on party membership in these years are not very reliable. A survey in early 1922 reported that the party then had 30,547 female members, of whom 29,172 had joined since the February Revolution. Altogether, the Bolshevichki constituted 8 percent of the party membership at that time.[1]

---

[1] These estimates are drawn from E. Smitten, "Zhenshchiny v RKP," *Kommunistka*, no. 4 (1924): 9; T. H. Rigby, *Communist Party Membership in the USSR, 1917–1967* (Princeton, 1968), 361.

Table 19 *Fields of employment of Bolshevichki during the civil war*

Field	Old Bolshevichki (%) ($N=229$)	Civil war joiners (%) ($N=205$)
Economy	4.8 (11)	2.4 (5)
Education	25.8 (59)	11.7 (24)
Journalism, publishing	11.8 (27)	6.3 (13)
Medicine	5.7 (13)	7.8 (16)
Military	24.9 (57)	29.3 (60)
Miscellaneous government[a]	33.6 (77)	11.7 (24)
Party	42.8 (98)	39.5 (81)
Police, courts	6.6 (15)	5.4 (11)
Social welfare	10.5 (24)	3.9 (8)
Trade unions	8.3 (19)	6.8 (14)
Underground	14.8 (34)	23.9 (49)
With women	10.5 (24)	33.7 (69)

Note: All types of work performed were recorded, including more than one assignment per individual. The percentages represent, therefore, the number of Bolshevichki in the total N performing that type of work.
[a] Work for government agencies not included under the other categories in the table.

Plate 16. First All-Russian Women Workers' Congress, November, 1918, in Moscow. In front, from right to left, unidentified woman, Klavdiia Nikolaeva, Konkordiia Samoilova, Alexandra Kollontai, Inessa Armand, and (probably) Alexandra Artiukhina. The banner reads "Long live the 1st All Russian Congress of Women Workers, from the Moscow Gates Raion Committee of the City of Petrograd."

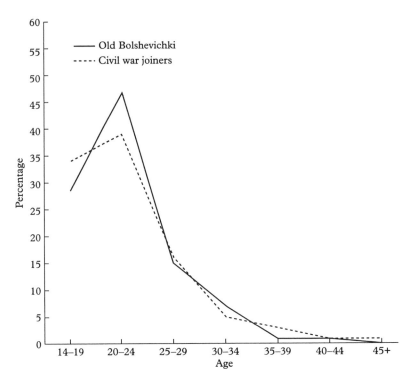

Figure 2. Age of Bolshevichki on joining the party

Collectively, the new Bolshevichki were younger than the women who had been in the party before the revolution, but they shared certain characteristics with their predecessors. The majority of them came from the middling ranks of Russian society. Most were Russians or Ukrainians, with Jews still figuring as a sizable minority. They were well educated, 31 percent possessing at least a secondary education and 8 percent with at least some university education. They were as young as the women of the older generation had been when they joined the party, the median age for both groups on joining being twenty. (See figure 2 and tables 20, 21, 22, 23, and 24.)

The primary difference between two groups was that more of the younger women were from the working class, while fewer were from the nobility. Thirty-seven percent of the civil war generation in the data base came from the proletariat, as compared to 26 percent of the Old Bolshevichki.[2] This increase in the numbers of proletarians among

2 An "Old Bolshevik" was a person who had joined the party before 1917. I use the feminized form, "Old Bolshevichka," to refer to the prerevolutionary generation of women.

Table 20 *Social origins of Bolshevichki*

	Old Bolsheviks		Civil war joiners	
Social origins	Women (%) (*N*=318)	Men(%) (*N*=254)	Women (%) (*N*=227)	Men (%) (*N*=100)
Nobility	9.4	4.3	3.5	3.0
Intelligentsia	10.4	15.0	4.8	16.0
Sluzhashchie	6.0	11.8	3.5	9.0
Meshchanstvo	11.3	6.3	1.3	7.0
Workers	26.4	27.9	36.6	33.0
Peasantry	10.4	34.2	9.2	32.0
Clergy	1.6	0.4	—	—
Unknown	24.5	—	41.0	—
Total	100.0	99.9	99.9	100.0

Note: Sources often specify class origin, particularly if that origin is lower class. It is highly likely, therefore, that when the sources are reticent about origins, as they are in a significant percentage of women, this is because the women were not from the peasantry or proletariat. Statistics from a survey of party members conducted in 1922 support this contention. They report that 38 percent of Bolshevichki joining during the civil war were from the working class, 5 percent were from the peasantry, and 57.5 percent were from other social groups, that is, the middling levels and the nobility (E. Smitten, "Zhenshchiny v RKP," *Kommunistka*, no. 4 [1924]: 8–10).

Bolshevichki testifies to the fact that the revolution had weakened the political and social constraints on such women, especially young, single women relatively unencumbered by family obligations. Some responsibility for the change was due also to the older Bolshevichki, who had worked diligently to attract proletarian women to the party. By contrast, the percentage of recruits from the nobility now only was half that of the prerevolutionary generation. The numbers of noblewomen attracted to the party had been falling since 1905, when sympathy for the revolutionaries had begun to cool among the propertied. The revolution and the Bolsheviks' coming to power appear to have increased the antipathy between party and noblewomen still more. Peasant women, who remained remote from the party's outreach efforts as well as from the cities where revolutionary ideas were most accessible, contributed no greater percentage of party members during the civil war than they had done before 1917.

The working-class women of the civil war generation had much in common with such veteran proletarian Bolshevichki as Klavdiia Nikolaeva and Alexandra Artiukhina. They too had suffered from poverty, had managed to obtain at least a primary education, and had imbibed radical ideas from their families. For example, D. Fedorova, a printer from Petrograd who joined the party in 1919 or 1920, had grown

166   The civil war

Table 21 *Ethnicity of Bolshevichki*

Ethnicity	Old Bolshevichki (%) (N = 318)	Civil war joiners (%) (N = 227)	1922 party census[a] (N = 24,495)
Russian	31.4	32.6	66.3
Ukrainian	1.9	1.8	3.5
Name sounds Russian or Ukrainian	21.7	32.2	—
Belorussian	—	0.9	0.6
Jewish	7.9	7.0	16.0
Latvian	4.4	2.2	6.0
Estonian	0.3	—	0.9
Lithuanian	—	—	0.4
Finnish	0.3	0.9	0.6
German	—	—	0.7
Cossack	0.3	—	0.03
Polish	0.9	—	2.2
Moldavian	—	0.4	0.1
Georgian	0.9	—	0.6
Armenian	0.6	0.4	0.7
Asian[b]	0.3	—	1.0
Non-Russian Empire	0.9	0.4	—
Unknown	27.7	21.1	—
Total	99.5	99.9	99.63

[a] This census reflects the ethnicity of the civil war joiners, for they made up the overwhelming majority of Communist Party members in 1922 (Tsentral'nyi komitet VKP(b), Statisticheskii otdel, *Sotsial'nyi i natsional'nyi sostav VKP(b)* [Moscow, 1928], 139).
[b] People from the area Central Asia (Kazaks, Kirgiz, Tadzhiks, Turkmen, Uzbeks), Tatars, and a host of other, smaller ethnic groups, primarily from Siberia.

up in the countryside, where she learned, as she put it in 1920, that "the poorer a person was, the more contempt there was from those around him, the less they took him into account." She admired her father, who refused "to bow his head to the rich," and felt pity and contempt for her submissive, religious mother. Fedorova was an able student in the village school, but the priest there did not encourage her intellectual aspirations. Rather, he taught her, as did her mother, that she should accept the established order of things and pray for God's blessings. Fedorova cherished greater ambitions, so when she finished her primary education, she set off for Petrograd. As had Nikolaeva before her, she was able to secure a job as a printer; this was highly skilled work to which few women gained admittance. The revolution then opened up to her the possibility of changing the world that had treated her so unfairly. "So I became a

Table 22 *Education of Bolshevichki*

Education	Old Bolshevichki (%)	Civil war joiners (%)
None	2.2 (7)	0.4 (1)
Primary	15.1 (48)	5.7 (13)
Secondary	28.9 (92)	23.3 (53)
Higher	22.6 (72)	8.4 (19)
Unknown	31.1 (99)	62.1 (141)
Total	99.9 (318)	99.9 (227)

Note: Figures in parentheses are base Ns for the adjacent percentages.

Table 23 *Social origins and education of Bolshevichki*

	Old Bolshevichki		Civil war joiners	
Education	Upper[a] (%) (N = 106)	Lower[b] (%) (N = 77)	Upper[a] (%) (N = 26)	Lower[b] (%) (N = 32)
None	2.8	5.2	—	3.1
Primary	4.7	54.5	—	37.5
Secondary	44.3	32.5	50.0	46.9
Higher	48.1	7.8	50.0	12.5
Total	99.9	100.0	100.0	100.0

[a] "Upper" designates nobility, intelligentsia, *sluzhashchie*, and *meshchanstvo*.
[b] "Lower" designates clergy, workers, and peasantry.

communist," she declared, "only because I had gained this right through suffering, being poor myself, and observing the poverty of others."[3]

Fedorova's story is similar to those of many proletarian Bolshevichki of both generations. Working-class women often portrayed their early lives as filled with deprivation that they were taught to accept as divinely ordained. They variously described the learning experience that brought them to the recognition that their personal unhappiness was the result of social injustice. For example, in 1919 a Petrograd worker named Chernysheva recounted her struggle to make sense of her situation after her soldier husband was killed in World War I. Chernysheva had been obliged to take a factory job, leaving her baby alone at home while she worked to keep them both alive. In her misery she wondered why God was punishing her. "Perhaps I had had too little faith? Had I prayed too little? Perhaps I didn't love my fatherland?" After months of agonizing,

[3] "Stran rabotnits," *Petrogradskaia pravda*, 12 December 1920, 4.

Table 24 *Occupations of Bolshevichki before joining the party*

Occupations	Old Bolshevichki (%)	Civil war joiners(%)
Teacher	20.1 (64)	15.0 (34)
Seamstress, tailor, weaver	10.4 (33)	6.2 (14)
Textile, garment factory worker	10.1 (32)	8.8 (20)
Professional revolutionary	8.5 (27)	—
Student	4.7 (15)	11.9 (27)
Clerk	3.8 (12)	—
Feldsher[a]	3.8 (12)	1.8 (4)
Other factory worker	3.8 (12)	7.0 (16)
Librarian	1.6 (5)	—
Tobacco factory worker	1.6 (5)	0.4 (1)
Bookkeeper	1.3 (4)	0.9 (2)
Housewife	1.3 (4)	1.8 (4)
Physician	1.3 (4)	—
Dentist	0.9 (3)	—
Journalist	0.9 (3)	0.4 (1)
Printer	0.9 (3)	1.3 (3)
Actor	0.6 (2)	—
Confectionery worker	0.6 (2)	0.9 (2)
Food-industry worker	0.6 (2)	0.4 (1)
Domestic servant	0.6 (2)	0.9 (2)
Laundress	0.3 (1)	0.4 (1)
Metalworker	0.3 (1)	0.4 (1)
Midwife	0.3 (1)	—
Perfume factory worker	0.3 (1)	0.4 (1)
Telephone/telegraph operator	0.3 (1)	0.4 (1)
Agricultural laborer	—	1.3 (3)
Tram conductor	—	0.9 (2)
None	—	2.2 (5)
Unknown	21.1 (67)	36.1 (82)
Total	100.0 (318)	99.8 (227)

Note: Figures in parentheses are base *N*s for the adjacent percentages.
[a] A physician's assistant.

Chernysheva's self-doubt turned to anger. "Didn't I give the tsar my husband? And what did I get in return? I worked in a factory . . . I worked for all those who didn't work . . . My child was at home, in a dirty . . . basement, my husband was far away, in a damp grave." When she concluded that the government and the capitalists had brought about the misfortunes in her life, "I decided to join the party that didn't limit itself to the overthrow of the tsar but went farther. And I found such a party; it was the Bolsheviks."[4]

---

[4] "Iz zhizni rabotnits," *Petrogradskaia pravda*, 21 December 1919, 3.

These accounts, written soon after the time these women became Bolshevichki, have the ring of truth. Hardship alone did not make female communists; had it done so, there would have been many more. A woman of the younger generation, whatever her social origins, had to learn to read her society as unjust, as older Bolshevichki had done before 1917. And the new Bolshevichki reported much the same pattern of influences awakening them to that realization as did their senior colleagues, despite the very different circumstances in which the two groups came of age. (See table 25.) The younger women declared that relatives and friends had played central roles in their becoming political radicals. A few even learned revolutionary ideas from their children. Elena Stasevich, a housewife in Belorus, left her husband to join the party after her fourteen-year-old son volunteered for the Red Army. Other women became politically aware in that time-honored institution, the study circle. "We read books, we didn't like idle talk, and in spite of our being eighteen and nineteen years old, we were 'very serious girls,'" wrote A. Andzhievskaia, an aide at a sanitarium in the Caucasus in 1918.

Almost one-quarter of the new recruits credited party operatives with drawing them into the movement. Khristina Suvorova, a housewife in the far northern town of Veliki Ustug, met weekly with other *soldatki* (soldiers' wives) and the local party secretary:

We talked about freedom and the equality of women, about warm sinks for rinsing clothes; we dreamed about running water in the apartment. In those days women rinsed clothes in the river winter and summer, under the seven winds. The gubkom [guberniia committee] workers treated us with sincere attention, respectfully listened to us, delicately pointed out our errors, little by little taught us wisdom and reason. We felt like we were one happy family.[5]

That familiar word, "family," attests to the fact that the same general processes of initiation into the party were operating among the younger generation as had operated among the older. Still personal connections to people who were already political activists were central to a woman's decision to become a party member, as they had been in the prerevolutionary period, as they are in the genesis of most social movements. Still deep feelings of emotional commitment to a new group welled up to replace the ties to her old life that the new Bolshevichka had severed when she decided to become a political activist.

The great difference between the politicization of the Old Bolshevichki and the new sprang from the hugely changed world in which they all now lived. The revolution delegitimated traditional ideas and made political participation the order of the day. The civil war then plunged the nation

---

[5] *Docheri zemli Vladimirskoi* (Iaroslavl', 1982), 17–20; *Zhenshchina v grazhdanskoi voine. Epizody bor'by na severnom kavkaze v 1917–1920 gg.* (Moscow, 1937), 106; A. Pomelova, *Slovo o zhenshchinakh severa* (n.p., 1968), 38.

Table 25 *Initiators of Bolshevichki into the party*

Initiators	Old Bolshevichki (%) ($N=176$)	Civil war joiners (%) ($N=71$)
Parents	8.0 (14)	19.7 (14)
Siblings	24.4 (43)	22.5 (16)
Other relatives	0.6 (1)	2.8 (2)
Spouse	4.0 (7)	4.2 (3)
Fellow students	29.5 (52)	12.7 (9)
Fellow workers	15.9 (28)	14.1 (10)
Party workers	17.6 (31)	23.9 (17)
Total	100.0 (176)	99.9 (71)

Note: Figures in parentheses are base Ns for the adjacent percentages.

into a struggle in which the battle lines were clearly drawn between the Bolsheviks, the champions of revolutionary change, and the Whites, an uneasy alliance of monarchists, liberals, and socialists whose goals and social program were very unclear. In this dangerous world, the younger Bolshevichki did not have the luxury afforded the older generation of spending years making up their minds to join the party. On the other hand, they never were required to face persecution from a powerful tsarist establishment. The women of the younger generation were courted by the party and urged to join its great crusade to build a just society on the ruins of the old one that had made their lives miserable. In such a radically changed environment, the process of choosing to be a Bolshevichka became telescoped into a much shorter period. Rather than studying Marxism in a lengthy process of preparation, the new generation embraced Bolshevism with an emotional urgency that resembled the experience of sudden religious conversion. The revolution had shaken the familiar society to its core, they later remembered; the party's ideas then helped them make sense of what was happening. "Everything became clear and intelligible to me," declared L. Ded, an apprentice in Petrograd who confessed that she had paid very little attention to politics until the summer of 1917. The party offered more than understanding, however; it also called on women to join the great cause of liberation. Evdokiia Poliakova, a worker from Kaluga, wrote, "In the Bolsheviks I saw people who had entered a decisive struggle with despotism and injustice, a struggle with a bright future for working people. I wanted to be with them and I was justly proud that they had taken me into their great stern family."[6]

[6] "Stranichka zhenshchin-rabotnits," *Pravda*, 9 October 1919, 4; *Kaluzhskie bol'shevichki* (Kaluga, 1960), 141.

Poliakova learned to see the party as a "great stern family" from her seniors; her terms – "stern," "family" – are their terms because the younger generation was taught the collective identity that the older had established. But the collective identity the young imbibed was not and never had been a static collection of ideas, feelings, and practices. It had changed in the past, its prerevolutionary elasticity most apparent perhaps when stretched by tensions between the Mensheviks and the Bolsheviks. During the civil war it continued to change as the party adapted to the realities of being in power. The war became a central shaping influence in this adaptation, for it militarized the collective identity of the Bolsheviks so as to accentuate "stern" values of endurance, determination, and ruthlessness. These notions had been there all along, cherished by the Old Bolshevichki, as we have seen, and fashioned by them into a badge of achievement and claim for acceptance. But during the civil war, *tverdost* was joined to conceptions of hierarchy and discipline that had been far less highly valued before 1917. The new Bolshevichki learned not just hardness, although that was still highly prized, but also obedience to their superiors and submission to the will of the "great, stern family." Their variant of the collective identity contained commensurably less of the egalitarianism that had been a hallmark of the party's prerevolutionary collective identity.

The war was a particularly formative experience for the younger generation because its members were just entering into their careers as communists, and also because many of them actually participated in the conflict. Most of the new Bolshevichki began their party lives by going to meetings of workers' clubs or the Komsomol (the Communist Youth League, founded in 1918) and doing volunteer work – distributing newspapers and pamphlets, collecting donations for the war effort, nursing wounded soldiers at hospitals, and cleaning the litter and snow from city streets on their days off. After some months in such activities, during which they also listened to speeches, read newspapers, and attended political-education courses, the young women felt qualified to apply for party membership. During their apprenticeship, whether before or after they joined the party, tens of thousands of them set off for service at the front.

Bolshevichki in the military

The Russian civil war was a terrible initiation rite, more grueling physically and emotionally for many of its participants than the underground had been. A series of brutal campaigns fought by rag-tag armies, it raged at its most intense from the summer of 1918 into the fall of 1920.

The front swung back and forth, primarily across Siberia, southern Russia, and Ukraine, and everywhere the rampaging troops went they confiscated crops, destroyed roads, bridges, and railroads, and wreaked havoc on one another and on the civilian population. Food supplies in the cities, already low because of the preceding years of war and revolution, shrank still further, forcing millions of people to flee to the countryside to seek help from their relatives. The refugees found that the peasants were hungry too, because of all the unrest and because of low rainfall in the grain-growing regions along the Volga. The result was malnutrition that made the population vulnerable to epidemics. The greatest killer in the Russian civil war, as in so many such conflicts, was not combat but the infectious diseases, especially typhus, cholera, and influenza, that swept through military and civilian ranks alike. Estimates place the total number of dead in the Russian Empire from the consequences of war, 1914 to 1921, at 16 million.[7]

By the fall of 1920, 66,000 women were serving in the Red Army, making up 2 percent of that force. Among all these thousands, roughly 25 percent were Bolshevichki, mostly new recruits. Of the younger Bolshevichki in the sample, 48 percent worked at the front, as compared to 19 percent of the older. The authorities sent young women to war for the same reasons that governments send young men, because the young are physically better able to stand the rigors of military life and because they are malleable. Most of the women went to work as clerks or nurses.[8] (See table 26.)

Tsiva Frumkina was typical of the new Bolshevichki who saw front-line service. A seventeen-year-old student in the city of Kaluga in 1918, she volunteered to go when everyone else in her Komsomol group, including her brother and sister, did so. After completing training in basic first aid as well as the fundamentals of Marxism and the current party line, Frumkina climbed on a train and headed south. She remembered later that she ate better on military rations – 500 grams of bread a day as well as hot soup

---

[7] Barbara Evans Clements, *Daughters of Revolution: A History of Women in the USSR* (Arlington Heights, Ill., 1994), 45.
[8] The estimate of the percentage of Bolshevichki among the women in military service is calculated from figures on the number of Bolshevichki in the civil war generation of party joiners, the total number of women who served in the Red Army, and the percentages of Bolshevichki in the data base who were in the military. Alexandra Artiukhina reported in 1927 that 60 percent of the women in the Red Army during the civil war did "administrative-economic work," and 40 percent were in the medical service. In the eighteen months from January 1919 to June 1920, 50,000 women were trained for military nursing (Z. Igumnova, *Zhenshchiny Moskvy v gody grazhdanskoi voiny* [Moscow, 1958], 64; *Kaluzhskie bol'shevichki*, 152, 65; P. M. Chirkov, *Reshenie zhenskogo voprosa v SSSR, 1917–1937 gg.* [Moscow, 1978], 155, 156; *Pravda stavshaia legendoi* [Moscow, 1964], 249–52).

Table 26 *Military assignments of Bolshevichki during the civil war*

Assignment	Old Bolshevichki (%)	Civil war joiners(%)
Clerk	14.0 (8)	3.3 (2)
Combat soldier	—	15.0 (9)
Nurse	17.5 (10)	33.3 (20)
Political officer	26.3 (15)	28.3 (17)
Political worker	19.3 (11)	18.3 (11)
Assignment not specified	22.8 (13)	1.7 (1)
Total	99.9 (57)	99.9 (60)

Note: All types of assignments held by all Bolshevichki were coded. Figures in parentheses are base Ns for the adjacent percentages.

and kasha – than she had back home. She also marveled at the fact that there was a regular supply of firewood to heat the hut she lived in. But medical equipment and supplies were hard to come by. Many hospitals were filthy, for soap was scarce. And disease, particularly typhus contracted from the lice that infested soldiers and medical personnel alike, took a terrible toll. There was also tension with veteran military doctors and nurses, many of whom regarded the newcomers as poorly trained, ignorant spies for the party, and it is indeed true that Bolshevichki did, from time to time, report uncooperative doctors to the military authorities. At best each side got over its antagonism toward the other and cooperated to help the legions of wounded men.[9]

In bringing women to the front to work as nurses or clerks, the Bolsheviks were following precedents set by the Entente powers during World War I. The British, French, and Russian governments had all employed women in the medical services. In 1917 the British high command expanded the female presence in the military still further when it established women's auxiliary corps in the army and navy, primarily to do clerical work.[10] As befitted a revolutionary government, the Bolsheviks also broke new ground for female participation in a war by training women to be spies, couriers, and political officers.

There had been female spies in other wars, but the Bolsheviks used far

[9] On Frumkina, see *Kaluzhskie bol'shevichki*, 157. A. G. Nikiforova, a seamstress from Riga, admitted to having a doctor arrested. See ibid., 105–06. For other references to conflict with the regular doctors and nurses, see Institut Marksizma-Leninizma pri TsK KPSS, Nauchno-metodicheskii kabinet, *Revoliutsionerki Rossii* (Moscow, 1983), 211; *Zhenshchina v grazhdanskoi voine*, 175. Instructions for the curriculum of "political-literacy" courses for nurses are included in VKP(b), TsK, Otdel po rabote sredi zhenshchin, *Sbornik instruktsii otdela TsK RKP(b) po rabote sredi zhenshchin* (Moscow, 1920), 35–43.

[10] On British developments, see Jenny Gould, "Women's Military Services in First World War Britain," in Margaret Randolph Higgonet and Jane Jenson, eds., *Behind the Lines: Gender and the Two World Wars* (New Haven, Conn., 1987), 114–25.

more of them far more systematically than had other governments. Eight percent of the Old Bolshevichki in the sample and 14 percent of the new recruits worked behind White lines, reporting troop movements, maintaining party organizations, publishing broadsides and newspapers, managing communications and safe houses, and storing weapons. Elena Sokolovskaia, a graduate of the Bestuzhevskii courses and a party member since 1915, led the party organization in Odessa from early 1918 until the Red Army seized that city in 1919. Sokolovskaia was so skilled at disappearing to avoid arrest that several times her own people thought she was dead, and once they even printed her obituary.[11] This work was much like that which the Old Bolshevichki had done before the fall of the tsar, but now party members were doing it in far more dangerous conditions. Capture would certainly mean rough treatment by White soldiers; it might even lead to execution. Particularly at risk were those Bolshevichki who fought in partisan units or in uprisings staged in White-held areas to support Red Army offensives.

The Whites considered the Bolsheviks' willingness to send women to war depraved and contemptible, but their indignation over this outrage against propriety did not stop them from imprisoning and sometimes torturing the women they captured. They appear to have assumed, rightly, that Bolshevichki were not usually commanders, and therefore they spared them more frequently from execution than they did captured men. But female partisans sniping at their troops did provoke them. A colonel named Tomashevskii of Admiral Alexander Kolchak's Siberian army issued the following proclamation in April 1919:

I am personally convinced that in the revolt of the Bolshevik band at the city of Kustana and the surrounding area, women, not just men, in fact took part, venturing to fire shots from corners, windows, roofs, and garrets. Until now these criminals have stayed on the sidelines and have not received just punishment. I consider it completely acceptable and very honorable to shoot and hang such criminals, and therefore I give advance warning that the birch rod will be used by me exclusively, right up to flogging to death. I am more than confident that this domestic remedy will have the proper influence on this imbecile element, who by the rights of their destiny belong with the pots and the kitchen, not in politics, which is absolutely alien to their understanding.[12]

Tomashevskii must have been even more outraged when he learned that women were routinely lecturing Red Army soldiers on politics. It was in employing women in the newly created position of "political worker"

---

[11] I. I. Mints and A. P. Nenarokov, eds., *Zhenshchiny – revoliutsionery i uchenye* (Moscow, 1982), 137–53. For the obituary, see E. Korotkii, "Pamiati Soni Sokolovskoi," *Petrogradskaia pravda*, 19 April 1919, 1.
[12] Quoted in *Leningradki. Vospominaniia, ocherki, dokumenty* ([Leningrad], 1968), 175.

that the Bolsheviks challenged most directly the accepted norms on
female participation in warfare. Ordered in a hierarchy of ranks roughly
parallel to those of the regular army, political workers were charged with
maintaining the commitment of the soldiers to the cause – that is, they
were propagandists. "The political departments strive for every Red
soldier to understand what he is fighting for, what he is dying for, and who
his enemy is," declared an army broadside in 1920. The goal, in short, was
to preach to Red troops the virtues of Redness (and the evils of the
Whites). Available evidence does not state exactly how many of the
political workers in the Red Army were women, but it is clear that they
were a small minority, probably no more than 10 to 15 percent. Among
the Bolshevichki in the data base, 26 percent of those who saw military
service became political workers, 19 percent rising to officer rank. Their
primary activities consisted of editing unit newspapers, distributing
printed materials, organizing lectures, and conducting literacy classes. In
any other European army women doing such work would have been an
extraordinary innovation, but the Bolsheviks had long been accustomed
to women teaching men politics. They simply transferred their underground practice to the new situation.[13]

The relationship between women and men in an army at war was
bound to be problematical. Little in the experience of even the most
hardened Bolshevichka prepared her to cope with the hostility of soldiers
to whom she had come, not temporarily as an agitator like the female
orators of 1917, but as a permanent supervisor. Red troops made the
same complaints about women at the front that subsequent generations
of soldiers in other wars and countries were to raise. They charged that
women could not carry their share of the load and therefore burdened the
men with the necessity of taking care of them. They claimed that women
disrupted the male camaraderie on which unit cohesion was built.
Perhaps they even feared the shaming that took place when women stood
firm under conditions that broke the courage of men. They also resented
having to listen to lectures from young women no older than themselves,
particularly when they perceived that those young women came from
more privileged backgrounds than their own.[14] To drive the women
away, the men used tactics that soldiers have used all over Europe in the
twentieth century: they told the women they did not belong there, they
refused to work with them, and they resorted to verbal and physical
abuse.

---

[13] *Pravda stavshaia legendoi*, 53. The best history of political departments in the Red Army
during the civil war is in Mark von Hagen, *Soldiers in the Proletarian Dictatorship* (Ithaca,
N. Y., 1990), 21–126.
[14] Mark von Hagen makes this point, ibid., 105.

Bolshevichki responded in a variety of ways to such harassment. The older ones – Bosh and Zemliachka being prime examples – simply summoned up the authority of their office and intimidated the men into taking orders from them. Younger women, who did not have the rank, standing, or *tverdost* of veteran Bolshevichki, were more vulnerable. Zinaida Patrikeeva, a tobacco-factory worker from Nikolaevsk, spent her first few days in a cavalry regiment riding the worst horse in the unit. "Bouncing along on my filly, I simply could not keep up with my comrades. I really wanted to cry. But I didn't cry. I only thought: wait, the time will come, I'll show you." She reports being saved from her humiliation by the commander, who ordered the men to cooperate with her. Elizaveta Drabkina also testified to the importance, particularly to young, low-ranking women, of winning the support of influential men. "It was always frightening to a girl [*devushka*] to enter a new military unit," she remembered years later. "I was lucky; wherever I ended up, I was sure to find an elderly soldier who took me under his tutelage." There are also signs that Bolshevichki banded together to defend themselves.[15]

A much rarer but even greater affront to male sensibilities occurred when women served as combat soldiers. Elsa Glazer, a twenty-year-old peasant from Latvia in 1918 when she volunteered for the front, became a machine gunner who was soon promoted to non-commissioned officer. Anna Novikova, the daughter of a railroad worker from Tambov guberniia, seventeen years old in 1919, also became the commander of a machine-gun platoon.[16] Some 15 percent of the younger Bolshevichki in the sample held combat assignments at some point during the civil war.

Overall, only a tiny handful of women served as combat troops in the Red Army. The military high command made no effort to enlist women for combat units and consequently most of those who did become machine gunners, sappers, cavalrywomen, or infantry soldiers managed to do so because a group of people, women and men together, had signed up together. For example, the 220th Infantry Regiment of the Chapaev Division had many female members because it had been recruited in the great textile center of Ivanovo-Voznesensk, where there were thousands of female factory workers. Stories did circulate about women who had disguised themselves in order to enlist and who were only uncovered, so to speak, after some grievous injury; but such subterfuges were not commonplace. Rather, such stories gained currency because people on both sides

---

[15] *Pravda stavshaia legendoi*, 111–12; *Bez nikh my ne pobedili by. Vospominaniia zhenshchin-uchastnits Oktiabr'skoi revoliutsii, grazhdanskoi voiny, i sotsialisticheskogo stroitel'stva* (Moscow, 1975), 143.   [16] M. Palant, *Kursant Ania* (Moscow, 1985), 122, 9–29.

in the civil war were unsettled by the fact that women were actively participating in it.[17]

Although they had long been willing to employ women in jobs conventionally reserved for men, even the Bolsheviks had some difficulty adjusting their minds to the idea of females in the military, that *sanctum sanctorum* of masculinity. The upshot was a division in the party's opinion between those who argued that women should be involved as equals in all public enterprises, even war, and those who believed that women were at the front as auxiliaries in an essentially male undertaking. That split then resulted in a debate in the party press over the role of women in the army. And it led to a rather mixed set of messages that the party put out to the nation in its efforts to explain women's roles in the struggle and to encourage still more women to participate.

Since the days of the French Revolution there had been feminists who declared that women should have full citizenship rights and responsibilities, including the obligation to perform military service on equal terms with men. During the Russian civil war some Bolsheviks, most prominently Kollontai and Inessa, picked up that argument. If women were equal, they declared, there was no job they should not take, and most particularly they should fight to defend the revolution that was emancipating them. By so doing, they would lay yet another stone in the foundation of a new, free world. "The fewer the purely female or purely male responsibilities in human society," wrote I. Vardin in *Pravda* in 1919, "the fewer will be the bases to talk about inequality between the sexes." But this argument did not persuade the party majority. Most Bolsheviks, male and female, took a far less radical view of women's participation in the war: they construed it as a temporary necessity, not something that called into question the belief that men were more naturally suited to soldiering than women.[18]

This latter belief has certainly been the dominant one in the European world in the twentieth century. Even though women's contributions have

---

[17] References to women pretending to be men appear in E. Bochkareva and S. Liubimova, *Svetlyi put'* (Moscow, 1967), 69; *Zhenshchina v grazhdanskoi voine*, 100–01; *Zhenshchiny russkoi revoliutsii* (Moscow, 1968), 232. For the biography of a woman who did not disguise herself, but managed to secure a combat assignment, see Palant, *Kursant Ania.*

[18] I. Vardin, "Vooruzhennaia rabotnitsa," *Pravda*, 27 May 1919, 4. On Kollontai's and Inessa's views, see A. M. Kollontai, *Rabotnitsy, krest'ianki, i krasnyi front* (Moscow, 1920), 27–30; Blonina [Inessa Armand], "Rabota sredi zhenshchin proletariata na mestakh," VKP(b), TsK, Otdel po rabote sredi zhenshchin, *Kommunisticheskaia partiia i organizatsiia rabotnits* (Moscow, 1919), 17. For the more characteristic party line on women's relationship to the war, see the columns for women workers in *Pravda* and *Petrogradskaia pravda*, 1918–20; N. I. Bukharin, *Rabotnitsa, k tebe nashe slovo!* (Moscow, 1919); Z. I. Lilina, *Nuzhna li rabotnitsam i krest'iankam sovetskaia vlast'?* (Petrograd, 1921); and G. Zinoviev, *Rabotnitsa, krest'ianka, i sovetskaia vlast'* (Petrograd, 1919).

become ever more essential to success in war, propagandists have taken great pains to reassure their various publics that the new roles are only temporary, that women are only flying airplanes or building ships to support their fighting men, and that they will do so only as long as their country needs them. The world may be in chaos, says such propaganda, but what is male and what is female have not changed. These reassurances are backed up by visual images and written text that emphasize women's femininity and submission to men, even while praising their contribution to the war effort. "I'm proud . . . my husband *wants* me to do my part," declares one American poster issued in World War II. Rosie the Riveter, the quintessential US symbol of the female volunteer, was usually portrayed in coveralls, headscarf, bright red lipstick, and nail polish. Even her name was a non-threatening diminutive.[19]

Twenty-five years before Rosie, Bolshevik newspapers sent similar messages. Articles in the press during the civil war urged women to work hard in the factories, volunteer at military hospitals, or go to the front as a way of helping their male relatives. By so doing they would, in the words of a 1919 appeal in *Petrogradskaia pravda*, prove themselves "the worthy wives and sisters of the heroic Red Army soldier." Journalists and party propagandists (women among them), arguing that women could make a meaningful contribution in a support role, also tended, as did their American counterparts years later, to belittle women while praising them. For example, L. A. Teppolen, a female sapper, detailed in an article in 1919 how she and several other women had proved themselves to the men in their unit. And then she concluded: "So comrades, don't think that each of us [women] taken separately is nothing. Yes, separately we aren't important, but taken all together, we helped our male comrades."[20]

Of course, Bolshevik propagandists were not so conventional in their gender ideas as were American ones. Committed to revolutionary change, they saw winning the civil war as a necessary step in women's emancipation. They argued that only after women helped to repulse the enemies of the revolution would they be able to construct a society in which they

[19] On propaganda's treatment of women in the United States during World War II, see Maureen Honey, *Creating Rosie the Riveter: Class, Gender, and Propaganda During World War II* (Amherst, Mass., 1984). On imagery of women in twentieth-century wars, see Sharon Macdonald, Pat Holden, and Shirley Ardener, eds., *Images of Women in Peace and War: Cross-Cultural and Historical Perspectives* (Madison, Wis., 1988), esp. 1–22. The poster cited is reproduced in G. H. Gregory, ed., *Posters of World War II* (New York, 1993), 97. Italics in the original.

[20] *Petrogradskaia pravda*, 18 May 1919, 4; "Sredi rabotnits," *Petrogradskaia pravda*, 30 November 1919, 4. For another example of the appeal to women to support men, see "Ko vsem rabochim i rabotnitsam tekstil'noi promyshlennosti," *Petrogradskaia pravda*, 19 April 1919, 1.

would be freed from patriarchy. They also sometimes praised the heroism of individual women in terms very close to those applied to men. An article in *Pravda* in 1920 hailed the "boldness, decisiveness, resourcefulness, [and] devotion to the revolutionary cause" of female officers. The article told the story of T. Ianson, a Moscow Bolshevichka and political officer. Confronted with recalcitrant railway workers who refused to provide water for the troop train on which she was traveling, Ianson raised her rifle and pointed it at the head of the crew chief. She told him that if he did not begin filling the train's water tanks, she would put a bullet in his forehead and then deliver the same treatment to his co-workers. The men complied immediately.[21]

Tverdye Bolshevichki such as Ianson received a lot of coverage in the press. They were praised for their self-sacrifice and courage, and for their understanding of and devotion to the cause. By hailing the emergence of such women as efficacious, authoritative, rifle-wielding officers, the party's messengers affirmed what women in uniform could accomplish. They also drew their audience's attention to the power of the revolutionary changes the Bolsheviks were leading. A woman, armed by the party and enabled to impose her will on unruly workers, testified to the extraordinary process of liberation underway. She also gave women a glimpse of the sort of personal transformation which they too could achieve if they joined the cause.[22]

People less committed to fundamental change in gender norms constructed interpretations of female officers carrying guns that were quite different. Outside the fold of official propaganda, a smear campaign raged against the emancipated Bolshevichka. Stories, rumors, and even cartoons and caricatures circulating at the front and the rear portrayed the women of the Red Army as masculinized and demonic. These representations acknowledged that the women were liberated, but they were far from accepting the proposition that freeing them from the control of conventional definitions of femininity had made them into paragons of revolutionary virtue. Rather, they had become Amazons; they had slipped free of society's controls and let their native wildness loose. They dressed like men; they cut their hair short, like men's; they smoked; they were, perhaps, lesbians; at the least, they were sexually promiscuous. Qualities appropriate to a male soldier – resoluteness, toughness, willingness to use force – as well as rough dress and habits such as smoking and drinking became signs of monstrosity when appropriated by a woman.

[21] *Pravda*, 18 January 1920, 3.
[22] For examples of positive images of women in the press, see *Pravda*, 18 January 1920, 20–23; and "Pamiati krasnykh sester," *Kommunistka*, no. 8–9 (1921): 38–41.

People opposed to the Bolsheviks were particularly likely to spread such stories, but even supporters of the Red Army were prey to doubts about women at war. Among the Bolsheviks' enemies, tales of furies at the front expressed their conviction that the Bolsheviks had armed society's "imbecile element" and were intent upon destroying civilization itself. They could imagine no more evocative symbol of the overturning of established authority than a woman with a rifle, backed up by male soldiers who would do her bidding. The lethal Bolshevichka was even more fearsome than that most famous revolutionary harridan, Dickens's malevolent Madame Defarge, for the Bolshevichka did far more than incite mobs while knitting. Possessed by ideological zeal (her commitment to the cause was another sign of her rejection of the feminine), she dressed like a man and rode at the head of armies.[23]

In reality, the Red Army was securely under male command. Only a few women achieved high rank within it. The Director of Agitation and Enlightenment of the PUR, the political department of the army, was Valentina Suzdaltseva, a 22-year-old who had joined the party in 1917. Larisa Reisner, a student from Lublin who joined in 1918, served as secretary of the Communist Party organization of the Volga fleet and headed an intelligence department. She later wrote a much acclaimed book, *Front*, about her civil war experiences. Glafira Okulova-Teodorovich, the Siberian who had married much earlier in prison, was chief political officer of the Political Department of the Eastern Front in 1918, of the Eighth Army in 1919.[24] But perhaps the best known and most infamous of all the female commanders were Evgeniia Bosh and Rozaliia Zemliachka. There was just enough of the Amazon in each of them to fuel the rumors trained against them, but the reality of their experience was considerably less romantic than the folklore. Far from running wild and free, both were tightly enmeshed in a hierarchy run by men.

Zemliachka and Bosh at war

Bosh and Zemliachka seemed tailor-made for the rigors of civil war. Both had cultivated their toughness since underground days, both eagerly sought military assignments, and both adapted readily to the exercise of

---

[23] For such negative images, see V. Volodin, "Natsionalizatsiia zhenshchin," *Petrogradskaia pravda*, 3 December 1919, 1; Nina N. Selivanova, *Russia's Women* (New York, 1923), 199, 201. For a discussion of Amazons, see Ilse Kirk, "Images of Amazons: Marriage and Matriarchy," in Macdonald, Holden, and Ardener, *Images of Women in Peace and War*, 27–37.

[24] *Bez nikh my ne pobedili by*, 61–62; *Pravda stavshaia legendoi*, 43–56. PUR was the acronym for the Political Administration of the Revolutionary Military Council of the Workers'–Peasants' Red Army.

Plate 17. Rozaliia Zemliachka, probably during the civil war.

power and the use of force. But, of the two, Zemliachka made a greater success of her war work because she got along well with her peers and superiors. Bosh, ever the loner, still refused to learn the art of being a team player. As a result she made few friends and had few defenders when she got into trouble, while Zemliachka won supporters as well as military laurels.

Zemliachka made her first foray into the army in August 1918, when she was still working in the Moscow party organization. She and several other Bolsheviks were sent on a mission to Orsha, a Belorussian town some 100 kilometers southwest of Smolensk that was home to a large contingent of supposedly pro-Bolshevik troops. The men there had received orders for front-line duty, but four regiments had refused to ship out and were on the verge of full mutiny. Zemliachka and her colleagues were assigned the task of reviving the troops' commitment to the Red cause. Her first step on arriving at Orsha was to interview the commander, who threw up his hands and declared himself at a loss. Zemliachka concluded that he was a kulak (a wealthy peasant) with monarchist sympathies. Perhaps he was, or perhaps he simply shared the reluctance of the troops to go to war. When Zemliachka demanded that he call a meeting of the regiments, he complied, proving himself as unable to oppose her as to control his men. She then gave a rousing speech that was well received, and she and her colleagues followed up that success with days of persuasion directed at individual units. In two weeks, according to an account Zemliachka wrote in the 1920s, the men had boarded trains for the front.[25]

Zemliachka lingered in Orsha a bit longer to participate in a local soviet congress and raise more volunteers for the Red Army; then she returned to Moscow. Throughout the fall of 1918 she divided her time between party business in the capital and short trips to problem areas. "Our group was called a group of agitators," she wrote in the 1920s, "but in fact, with the exception of two or three, no one had ever spoken at a big meeting, no one had given a long speech. They were only workers from the Moscow factories, but this was enough to do great work in establishing order and discipline at the front and organizing great work in the zone behind the front." In other words, she and her colleagues held agitational meetings of soldiers, visited local political authorities to stiffen their resolve, and requisitioned food to send back to feed Moscow. Zemliachka did not always depend on her oratorical powers to overcome local resistance. When, on one occasion, she and her colleagues encountered a group of deserters, "partly by persuasion but mostly by force (we were armed), we returned them all to the front."[26]

In November or December of 1918 Zemliachka requested a full-time military assignment and received an appointment as chief political officer of the Eighth Army, then operating in Ukraine. She took to the job quickly, for her resolute, confident personality was perfectly suited to military command. Hardworking and efficient, Zemliachka was also, according to her subordinates, "able to make the most important decisions without vacillating."[27] Like Bosh before her, she communicated well with the troops and knew how to establish her authority quickly. She was also a demanding commander who issued instructions on everything from speech-writing to personal hygiene. Zemliachka's passion for order and discipline were not newfound; she had been such a Bolshevik from her earliest days in the party. More unexpected was the fact that she was able to overcome her tendency to fractiousness and stay out of the political

[25] R. S. Zemliachka, "Zhizn' na fronte" (handwritten manuscript), RTsKhIDNI, f. 90, op. 1, d. 66, ll. 4–14.
[26] Quoted in *Pravda stavshaia legendoi*, 10. On Zemliachka's work as an agitator in the fall of 1918, see also Zemliachka, "Zhizn' na fronte," RTsKhIDNI, f. 90, op. 1, d. 66, ll. 1–40.
[27] RSDRP, TsK, *Perepiska sekretariata TsK RKP(b) s mestnymi partiinymi organizatsiiami, aprel'–mai 1919 g.* (Moscow, 1972), 543.

infighting that bedeviled the Red Army command. Very quickly, Zemliachka became an officer who took and gave orders well.

Her only major misstep came early in her military career. In April 1919 Zemliachka was relieved of her position in the Eighth Army on the grounds that morale had plummeted on her watch. She responded with an acerbic report blaming the situation on woefully poor supplies (the troops had no boots) and inadequate support from the high command. Her co-workers backed her by sending letters to Moscow attesting to her good work, as did her immediate superior, S. S. Krzhizhanovskii, the chief political officer of the southern front. Perhaps their testimony rescued her reputation, for Zemliachka was reassigned later in 1919 to the equally important post of chief political officer of the Thirteenth Army.[28]

Her arrival in that army's headquarters in Ukraine was something less than auspicious. Coming into town in the middle of the night, Zemliachka sought out the office of the political department. She found a dusty schoolroom filled with people sleeping on the floor and guarded by a soldier drowsing behind a desk. He was jolted awake by her arrival, but he did not speak immediately, so astonished was he by her appearance. Zemliachka had taken to wearing men's clothes, probably because they were the only military issue available, but possibly also to enhance her authority. The soldier stared up at her overcoat, jodhpurs, high boots, holstered revolver, and officer's cap, and tried to figure out whether this angry person with the close-cropped hair and wire-rimmed spectacles was a man or a woman. Zemliachka loudly informed him that she was his new commander; then she ordered him to clear out the soldiers sprawled all over the room. This was the political office of the Thirteenth Army, not a flophouse, she shouted. The intimidated soldier complied; the sleepers were roused and shooed out the door. Only after the crowd had left did Zemliachka calm down enough to ask the guard who the sleepers were and where they had gone. He replied that they were her staff and that he had no idea where they had gone. They were sleeping in the schoolhouse because there was no housing for them in the town. Zemliachka found the group grumbling in the courtyard outside, mumbled an apology, and invited them back in. Next day she ordered them to clean up the mess in which they had been living and get to work.[29]

Obviously Zemliachka adapted readily, perhaps a bit too readily, to the responsibilities of command. She took part in combat and she ordered executions of captured Whites. Unlike other Bolshevichki, she expressed no qualms about using force on disobedient Red Army troops. In a report filed in the spring of 1919, she described with satisfaction the outcome of a

[28] RTsKhIDNI, f. 90, op. 1, d. 67, ll. 1–9; RSDRP, *Perepiska sekretariata . . . aprel'–mai 1919 g.*, 542–43, 555.   [29] *Pravda stavshaia legendoi*, 18–20.

confrontation with rebellious soldiers: "Within three hours the gang [leaders of a group refusing to fight] was disarmed by the masses, a few plotters escaped, the rest were shot. This shows how politically mature the troops are."[30]

Zemliachka's military career ended in a brutal campaign in the Crimea in the fall of 1920. She was assigned to a three-person team with Hungarian revolutionary B—la Kun and Sergei Gusev (the father of Elizaveta Drabkina). Their orders were to cleanse the Crimea of White sympathizers, an assignment they interpreted as an authorization to conduct mass executions. By January 1921 when the operation was over, Zemliachka returned to Moscow with her reputation for *tverdost* secure. White survivors later reported a bloodbath across the peninsula, and horror stories about Zemliachka fueled the fears of Bolshevik Amazons.[31]

The rumors do not appear to have harmed Zemliachka's reputation with the party leadership. She was now a distinguished veteran, not just of the underground, but of the Bolsheviks' most important life-and-death struggle. A woman, she had proved herself to be tough and reliable. She had also demonstrated that she would carry out orders unflinchingly, unlike many Old Bolsheviks who still cherished the underground's egalitarianism and therefore tended to be disputatious and independent-minded. Zemliachka's achievements were recognized in 1922 when she received the Order of the Red Banner, Soviet Russia's highest military decoration.

Bosh had a more checkered wartime career because she remained more democratic in her instincts than Zemliachka and was more insistent on making her own independent judgments. When she requested an assignment to the front in July 1918, she was ordered to report to Moscow, perhaps so that Lenin and Sverdlov, the party secretary, could interview her to determine whether she had calmed down enough to be trustworthy. She visited her daughter Mariia, who had just landed a job working for Klavdiia Novgorodtseva in the Secretariat, and attended several meetings of the Ukrainian communists gathered in Moscow that summer; but she made no effort to return to the leadership of the Ukrainian branch of the party, despite the fact that Piatakov had done so.

---

[30] RTsKhIDNI, f. 90, op. 1, d. 67, l. 9. For a Bolshevichka's laments over executing Red troops, see Larisa Reisner, "Sviiazhsk (avgust–sentiabr' 1918 g.)," *Proletarskaia revoliutsiia*, no. 6–7 (1923): 177–89.

[31] Historians have debated whether Kun, Gusev, and Zemliachka were ordered home in disgrace. William Chamberlin (*The Russian Revolution, 1918–1921*, 2 vols. [Princeton, 1987], vol. II, 74) and Robert Conquest (*The Great Terror* [New York, 1968], 80) say that they were. A biographer of Béla Kun disagrees, arguing that the source of this report is gossip from the White side (György Borsönyi, *The Life of Béla Kun*, trans. Mario D. Fenyo [New York, 1993], 241–43).

Rather, she waited for an assignment from Lenin. It arrived in early August.

Bosh was sent to Penza, a major grain-growing region some 400 miles southwest of Moscow. Penza was an important source of food for the hungry cities, as well as the place where the Bolsheviks had set up a press for printing banknotes. All this was now threatened by Czech troops active in the area and by SRs who had declared war on the government. Bosh was sent as a "special plenipotentiary," that is, a party official armed with extraordinary powers and charged with resolving short-term crises, particularly those that resulted from inadequate performance by local party leaders. Her job in Penza was to rally the party committee there to face down their enemies and collect grain for shipment to Moscow.[32]

In a few weeks she succeeded. Fears of peasant uprisings and SR death squads had intimidated the local communists, but they did not deter Bosh. On the contrary, this kind of situation – fighting real enemies as well as slackers in her own party, with the top leadership behind her – energized all her combativeness. "The leading Penza comrades were against decisive measures in the battle with the kulaks, but they did not object to the directive they had received [from Moscow]," Bosh wrote in 1924. "[Instead] they created every obstacle and difficulty they could to carrying it out. Thus I had to answer Vladimir Ilich [Lenin] succinctly, 'It will be done.'" Bolstered by more than fifty Bolsheviks sent from Petrograd and a company of Latvian infantry, Bosh set herself up as head of the guberniia party committee and ordered the arrest of SRs as well as of men identified to her as peasant leaders. She also organized the transport of grain out of the province, actually the more formidable undertaking, for she had more guns than railroad cars at her disposal. Lenin kept a close watch on her from Moscow, telegraphing instructions frequently. On 8 August he admonished, "I don't want to think that you are showing delay or weakness in suppressing or in confiscating all of the property and especially the bread from the rebellious kulaks." The next day he instructed her to conduct "mass terror against the kulaks, priests, and White Guards." He need not have worried. There is no evidence that Bosh conducted "mass terror," but after several weeks she had rounded up some grain and breathed new life into the party organization.[33]

[32] E. Bosh, "Vstrechi i besedy s Vladimirom Il'ichem," *Proletarskaia revoliutsiia*, no. 3 (1924): 164–67.

[33] Ibid., 169, 166–70; V. I. Lenin, *Polnoe sobranie sochinenii*, 5th ed., 56 vols. (Moscow, 1958–66), vol. L, 148, 143 (hereafter *PSS*); Evgenii Mar, *Nezakonechnoe pis'mo* (Moscow, 1970), 86–88; V. V. Anikeev, *Deiatel'nost' TsK RSDRP(b)–RKP(b) v 1917–1918 godakh* (Moscow, 1974), 369, 386; RSDRP, TsK, *Perepiska sekretariata TsK RKP(b) s mestnymi partiinymi organizatsiiami, avgust–oktiabr' 1918 g.* (Moscow, 1969), 122.

Bosh enjoyed far less success at her next assignment because it required compromise rather than confrontation and because it tested her loyalties as the job in Penza had not. In the fall of 1918 she decided to return to Ukraine, perhaps hoping that the imminent departure of occupying German troops would make possible the victory that had escaped her six months before. Again she was named a Bolshevik special plenipotentiary, this time charged with organizing the political department of the Military Revolutionary Committee of the Caucasian front, headquartered in Astrakhan. Military revolutionary committees, composed of a region's party leaders and the officers of the armies operating nearby, were supposed to promote cooperation between civilian and military authorities. Instead they often became the sites of heated arguments over the distribution of power and responsibilities among those authorities. Bosh came to Astrakhan without clear instructions on how to set up the political department. Very soon she was embroiled in fights with Red Army commanders of the Caucasian front. She also clashed with local representatives of the Cheka, political police who were going around the city arresting people they judged to be enemies of the revolution and in the process trampling on the toes of civilian and military authorities alike.

Like Zemliachka, Bosh had few qualms about using force. She did not shrink from ordering executions of prisoners and mutinous soldiers. Bosh did not fit so readily into the chain of command, however, because she resisted the increasing centralization of the Bolshevik regime rather than promoting it, as Zemliachka had. She thus made common cause with the chair of the Astrakhan Military Revolutionary Committee, Alexander Shliapnikov, a former metalworker who distrusted the military as much as she did. The two together then attempted to elevate the power of the guberniia Communist Party organization over the region's army commanders and balked at obeying orders from Moscow. By December 1918, outraged members of the Military Revolutionary Committee were sending angry telegrams to Sverdlov, singling Bosh out as the main reason why the disputes could not be resolved. Sverdlov and Lenin took the side of the army; they had already faced the fact, as Bosh would not, that in order to win the war they must make local party committees obey the orders of the Red Army commanders, even if doing so undermined the long-time independence of such committees. Bosh was ordered to stand down in mid-December.

She refused. Instead, she cultivated her support in the local party organization and, to the loud hurrahs of the delegates to a city party conference, ordered the arrest of a despised Cheka official, K. Ia. Grasin. Sverdlov again and again telegraphed her to come back to Moscow. Bosh ignored him. Finally on 8 January Lenin sent her the most dire threat he could muster: "It has already been demanded repeatedly that you immediately leave there. Sverdlov sent you many telegrams. If you don't leave immediately, you will be expelled from the party . . . Refusal to obey this order will be judged under martial law."[34] Bosh finally submitted, and she and Shliapnikov were reassigned.

Bosh had showed herself to be a supporter of the Military Opposition, a group of communists, including her old friend Iurii Piatakov, who considered the emerging hierarchy of the military and the party in late 1918 and early 1919 to be yet another step down from the government imagined in their revolutionary idealism. Bosh was in touch with Piatakov as well as with other members of this new opposition, but in the months that followed her removal from Astrakhan, she backed away from any further confrontation with the party leaders. In March 1919 she attended the Eighth Party Congress in Moscow as a delegate from the Astrakhan guberniia party organization, but she did not speak in the ardent debates there over the military. Perhaps she was trying to win her way back into Lenin's good graces. It seems more likely, however, that she was simply withdrawing again from politics after another bout with it had left her feeling wounded and isolated.[35]

Later in 1919 Bosh did receive new assignments. They constituted demotions from the Astrakhan appointment and were far more tightly circumscribed and clearly defined. Reined in, she acquitted herself well, even obediently. First she was sent to Gomel in Belorus to put down a peasant uprising and rebuild the local party organization. Then she was appointed to the Soviet for the Defense of Belorus, charged with conscripting soldiers and cultivating support among the local population. In May 1919 Lenin backed her up with telegrams to the commanders in the region to issue her staff and weapons. For her part Bosh filed calm, businesslike reports of accomplishments and difficulties.[36]

[34] Ia. M. Sverdlov, *Izbrannye proizvedeniia*, 3 vols. (Moscow, 1960), vol. III, 105–10. On Bosh's adventure in Astrakhan, see also E. Preobrazhenskii, "Evgeniia Bogdanovna Bosh," *Proletarskaia revoliutsiia*, no. 2 (1925): 13; RSDRP, TsK, *Perepiska sekretariata TsK RKP(b) s mestnymi partiinymi organizatsiiami, ianvar'–mart 1919 g.* (Moscow, 1971), 15–16; Lenin, *PSS*, vol. L, 465–66. On her ordering executions, see Mar, *Nezakonechnoe pis'mo*, 88–89.

[35] Preobrazhenskii, "Bosh," 13; VKP(b), *Vos'moi s"ezd RKP(b), mart 1919 goda. Protokoly* (Moscow, 1959), 561, 85. On the disputes between the military and local party leadership in 1918, see Robert Service, *The Bolshevik Party in Revolution: A Study in Organisational Change, 1917–1923* (New York, 1979), 94–101. On the Military Opposition, see von Hagen, *Soldiers in the Proletarian Dictatorship*, 56–60.

[36] RSDRP, *Perepiska Sekretariata . . . aprel'–mai 1919 g.*, 279–80; Lenin, *PSS*, vol. L, 330–31; RSDRP, TsK, *Perepiska sekretariata TsK RKP(b) s mestnymi partiinymi organizatsiiami, iiun'–iiul' 1919 g.* (Moscow, 1974), 553; Preobrazhenskii, "Bosh," 13; Institut istorii AN USSR, *Grazhdanskaia voina na Ukraine, 1918–1920 gg.*, 3 vols. (Kiev, 1967), vol. II, 312–13, 333–34.

In July 1919 Bosh fell ill with a recurrence of heart disease as well as tuberculosis. When she had recovered she volunteered for more work in Ukraine and was again sent to the front to organize agitation among the peasantry. In November, sick again, she returned to Moscow. When a brief war erupted between Soviet Russia and Poland in 1920, she requested assignment to that front as well, but she was refused on the grounds that she was still too ill. There may have been political or personal motives behind the orders that she take medical leave, but it is also clear that Bosh was in fact quite weak. For the rest of 1920 and into 1921 she held several minor administrative jobs in Moscow between bouts of illness. Never again would she occupy a leadership position in the party or the military.[37]

Perhaps Bosh had been the main culprit in the feuding in Astrakhan. She was contentious, and, like many contentious people, she was often isolated. It may also have been the case that the Bolsheviks were less willing to tolerate self-assertion from women than from men. Many probably agreed with the soldiers who thought that women did not belong in the army. Many probably also subscribed to the ancient idea that women exacerbated discord among men. Undoubtedly they expected those Bolshevichki who were at the front to prove themselves good comrades, not troublemakers. Zemliachka fit readily into the command structure and made strong alliances with co-workers. She prospered. Bosh insisted on her own view of things, asserted her prerogatives, and fought with her comrades. No rumors of bloodbaths clouded her reputation as they did Zemliachka's, and yet Zemliachka returned to Moscow to receive military decorations, while Bosh came back to semi-retirement and semi-disgrace.

The participation of all the thousands of women in the civil war affected later developments in the Soviet system. It supported the contention of the Bolshevik feminists that women could make a valuable contribution in spheres far outside the traditional, domestic one, thereby buttressing their claims for programs and policies that would promote women's participation in the labor force after peace had come. Working with female political officers probably served to weaken the traditionalism of tens of thousands of new party members and begin their exposure to emancipatory Marxist conceptions of women. The civil war experience also became a precedent for World War II, when one million women served in the Soviet armed forces, making up 8 percent of the total enlistment and holding a huge variety of jobs from fighter pilot and truck driver to marine nurse.[38]

As we have seen, the party's calls for women to participate in the civil

[37] Mar, *Nezakonechnoe pis'mo*, 91; Preobrazhenskii, "Bosh," 13–14.
[38] Clements, *Daughters of Revolution*, 82.

war were ambiguous. On the one hand, feminist Bolsheviks argued that women would win their freedom if they supported the war effort, not only because they would make more certain the preservation of the revolution but also because their accomplishments would help break down gender stereotypes. At the same time, more conventional propaganda appeals reinforced those stereotypes by calling on women to help their men. This duality in the Bolshevik message reflected long-standing limitations in the party's commitment to women's emancipation. Many Bolsheviks had seen women as support troops in their ranks before the revolution. Those who had done so could readily transfer this perception to the civil war and construe female participation in it as assistance to the male standard bearers. Yet such people also could believe that women's "helping out" at the front had the additional benefit of advancing the liberation of women themselves. There was, however, a contradiction between these beliefs. People who held them, whether they recognized it or not, were simultaneously endorsing and rejecting the central idea of patriarchy – that women should occupy a position subordinate to men.

The Bolsheviks demonstrated the contradictions embedded in their conceptualization of women's emancipation even more powerfully, and with more serious consequences, in their politics during the civil war period. Although they appointed Bolshevichki to commands in the army, they did not encourage or expand their participation in the party leadership. In fact, even while the party's newspapers were lauding the exploits of female machine gunners, the Bolshevichki were steadily losing ground to male Bolsheviks in the party hierarchy. Their political marginalization, a process that began in earnest during the first months after the October coup, accelerated throughout the civil war as the party responded to the crisis by becoming ever more autocratic, hierarchical, and gendered in its divisions of labor and power.

Women in party work

Both the percentages of Bolshevichki holding party office and the level at which they served declined from 1917 to 1921. (See table 27.) There had always been very few women at the top of the party; this did not change significantly during the civil war. The percentage of women in guberniia committees, a new and increasingly important level of the hierarchy, rose from 1917 levels with the rapid proliferation in the number of these committees. But on the city and raion committees, Bolshevichki made up a falling percentage of members from 1918 to 1921. Furthermore, the number of women in the sample who held no party office at all during these years increased slightly.

Table 27 *Levels of party office-holding by Old Bolshevichki, November 1917–December 1921*

Level of party office held	1917 (%)	1918–1921 (%)
Raion, uezd	11.3 (36)	7.2 (23)
City	9.7 (31)	6.0 (19)
Guberniia	4.7 (15)	6.9 (22)
National	1.3 (4)	2.8 (9)
Zhenotdel (all levels)	—	2.5 (8)
Held no office	68.2 (217)	69.5 (221)
Unknown	4.7 (15)	5.0 (16)
Total	99.9 (318)	99.9 (318)

Note: The highest office held by each woman was coded. The figures in parentheses are base Ns for the adjacent percentages.

Comparing the Bolshevichki who were party officials during the civil war to those who were not reveals no demographic differences that account for the office-holders' success. (See table 28.) Social origins were not a factor. Despite the greater numbers of proletarian Bolshevichki in the party after 1917, only women of peasant origins, a tiny percentage of the whole, increased their office-holding to any significant extent between 1917 and 1921. Perhaps surprisingly, women with long histories of service were no more likely to hold party office during the civil war than those who had less seniority. (This lack of upward mobility by the longtime party members had been a feature of women's experience in 1917 as well, as we have seen.) Of the forty-four women in the sample who held office from the prerevolutionary era through the civil war, sixteen moved up into higher-ranking appointments after 1917, seventeen stayed at the same level, and eleven moved down. The most significant change from earlier patterns occurred in the relation of education to office-holding, for better-educated women lost more ground than did the less educated. All these data suggest that where party rank and promotion were concerned, neither social class, experience, nor education could overcome the fundamental disadvantage of being female.

At first glance, the loss of party rank suffered by the Bolshevichki during the civil war is perplexing. Conditions of emergency and the ideological commitment to women's equality had long been the two great facilitators of women's participation in the party. The emergency had never been greater than during the civil war, and the commitment then to women's emancipation seemed no less determined than earlier, but the civil war also saw the party change in ways that did not promote women's advancement. It became an ever more powerful organization with

Table 28 *Social origins, education, and party office-holding by Old Bolshevichki during the civil war*

	Percentage of each social group holding party office	
Social origins	1917 ($N=226$)	1918–1921 ($N=210$)
Nobility	40.0 (12)	31.0 (9)
Intelligentsia	29.0 (9)	41.2 (7)
Sluzhashchie	42.1 (8)	41.2 (7)
Meshchanstvo	62.9 (22)	36.1 (13)
Workers 30.8 (24)	32.0 (25)	
Peasantry 12.1 (4)	27.3 (9)	

Note: The figures in parentheses are the base Ns for the adjacent percentages.

	Percentage of those at each educational level holding party office	
Education	1917 (%) ($N=223$)	1918–1921 (%) ($N=203$)
Primary	29.2 (14)	25.5 (12)
Secondary	39.8 (35)	29.5 (26)
Higher	55.7 (44)	36.8 (25)

Note: The numbers in parentheses are the base Ns for the adjacent percentages. Figures for office-holding by civil war joiners were too fragmentary to be meaningful.

increasingly tangible rewards to bestow on its favored leaders. Alliances among the ambitious and networks of clientage and patronage grew commensurably. In the competition for advancement, military service became an important credential, a development that benefited men more than women, for the obvious reason that men were the great majority of combatants in the war.

War also strengthened the masculinist cast of Bolshevik political culture. Even before the revolution, the Bolsheviks' collective identity was more in tune with traditionally male heroic ideals than were those of other socialists of the Russian Empire. We have seen that the quasi-religious cult of martyrdom that appealed to the Socialist Revolutionaries and some anarchists had never been popular among the Bolsheviks, whose leaders, male and female, prided themselves on being tough-minded pragmatists. The civil war encouraged them to cherish still more the warrior virtues of endurance, resoluteness, and obedience to authority. Bolshevichki such as Zemliachka and Bosh adapted quickly to this milieu, dressing like men, marching with men, and ordering men shot. Such individual transformations could not dethrone the dominant interpretation already discussed here – that women were present at the fray to give men support. Women were outsiders, witnesses at a crucible experience that made men into

Bolsheviks and into comrades. The war thus fed the Bolsheviks' predilection to believe that the party's primary bonds were those that bound man to man.[39]

The long-standing differences of opinion among Bolsheviks on the "woman question" increased during the war. The best-educated members of the leadership subscribed to Marxism's goals of substantially expanding women's civil, political, and economic rights. The less well educated, who often were also the more recently recruited, knew far less about Marxism and had not imbibed the Russian intelligentsia's liberalism on gender issues. Lenin criticized the attitudes of these newer Bolsheviks in an interview with Klara Zetkin in the summer of 1920. "Scratch the Communist and a philistine appears," he declared. "To be sure, you have to scratch the sensitive spots – such as their mentality regarding women. Could there be any more palpable proof than the common sight of a man calmly watching a woman wear herself out with trivial, monotonous, strength- and time-consuming work, such as her housework?" Lenin went on, in an often-quoted passage, to criticize such men for demanding of their wives "the ancient rights of her husband, her lord and master." They should purge their minds of this "slave-owner's point of view," take on their share of the housework, and encourage their wives to concentrate on useful occupations in the public sector. Lenin also told Zetkin that he believed that both men and women should participate in "work among women," for if woman were not drawn out of her domestic isolation she would vegetate, "her spirit shrinking, her mind growing dull, her heartbeat growing faint, and her will growing slack." Without her participation, the revolution would languish as well.[40]

There was considerable distance between Lenin, a man who described marriage as slavery and had been known to sew on his own buttons, and the rank-and-file Red Army soldier newly come from the village where husbands still routinely beat their wives. Lenin and his comrades at the top of the Bolshevik Party did in fact believe in a whole-hearted attack on

---

[39] The scholarship on war and gender is growing. For two works that discuss the topic of martial values and masculinity, see Arthur Brittan, *Masculinity and Power* (New York, 1989), esp. 74–75; and Macdonald, Holden, and Ardener, *Images of Women in Peace and War*. On Bolshevik presentations of women as supporters of men at war, see the sources cited in note 18. On the influence of the civil-war experience on the party culture of the 1920s, see Sheila Fitzpatrick, "The Legacy of the Civil War," in Diane P. Koenker, William G. Rosenberg, and Ronald Grigor Suny, eds., *Party, State, and Society in the Russian Civil War* (Bloomington, Ind., 1989), 391–95; and Mark von Hagen, "Soldiers in the Proletarian Dictatorship, from Defending the Revolution to Building Socialism," in Sheila Fitzpatrick, Alexander Rabinowitch, and Richard Stites, eds., *Russia in the Era of NEP* (Bloomington, Ind., 1991), 156–73.

[40] V. I. Lenin, *The Emancipation of Women: From the Writings of V. I. Lenin* (New York, 1966), 114–15.

patriarchy, in a revision of roles within the family, and in the involvement of women in the public world. One need only compare them to other leaders of their time, Woodrow Wilson or David Lloyd George for example, to understand how truly radical their criticism of patriarchy was. But there were always limits in their understanding and in their behavior, as we have seen. Even those Bolsheviks who held the most liberal attitudes toward women paid little attention to supporting their female comrades' political fortunes, and in fact appear to have been just as likely as any hard-bitten Red Army commander to treat Bolshevichki as outsiders, to be disregarded or even jettisoned when the occasion warranted. Bosh may have experienced this treatment in 1918 and 1919. Elena Stasova definitely did in 1920, when she lost the highest office any woman ever held in Russia's Communist Party as a consequence of a deal her old comrade Lenin made behind her back.

Stasova, the party secretary

Stasova spent the summer and fall of 1918 in Petrograd. Her primary responsibility was setting up the Northern Oblast Bureau, a newly formed department charged with supervision of party committees in a huge area that extended from Arkhangelsk in the north to Novgorod in the west. Stasova sent out instructions to communists working in provincial cities in the area, answered their letters to her, and met with emissaries come to Petrograd to confer. From April to October, according to a report Stasova filed in the fall, her office interviewed 2,178 people and wrote 2,798 pieces of correspondence. She handled this work with a staff that grew to nine women by the fall.[41]

The doubts Stasova had had about changes in the party did not diminish in the summer and fall of 1918. She complained about incompetent, corrupt people, poor organization, bureaucracy in the soviets, bad communications with Moscow, overwork, and understaffing. She was critical of Zinoviev, head of the Petrograd party committee.[42] She also deplored the excesses of Bolshevik rule in her home town. Stasova was particularly troubled by the mass arrests carried out by the Cheka in the fall of 1918, in the aftermath of several SR attacks on Bolshevik leaders, one of which left Lenin gravely wounded.

[41] RSDRP, TsK, *Perepiska sekretariata s mestnymi partiinymi organizatsiiami, noiabr'–dekabr' 1918 g.* (Moscow, 1970), 126–30.
[42] E. D. Stasova, "Iakov Mikhailovich Sverdlov," in *Rasskazy o Sverdlove. Sbornik vospominanii* (Moscow, 1962), 121; K. T. Sverdlova, *Iakov Mikhailovich Sverdlov*, 1st ed. (Moscow, 1957), 549–53. On Stasova's attitude toward Zinoviev, see E. D. Stasova, *Vospominaniia* (Moscow, 1969), 161; RSDRP, *Perepiska sekretariata . . . avgust–oktiabr' 1918 g.*, 302–03.

In October, Stasova herself was assigned to the Cheka. She rationalized working with the organization by vowing to correct some of its mistakes. On 25 October she wrote to Novgorodtseva,

Now I am occupied there [at the Cheka] primarily in unloading the prison, for they are arresting harmless people in the raions who don't have the slightest involvement, like hostages. At the same time they are filling up the prisons. Something dreadful in sanitary conditions has been created and it thickens the atmosphere into an absolute hell. I want to leave the Cheka but there are so many undesirable tendencies there that I think for the time being I'll pull this load.[43]

Stasova's mercifulness in the Cheka is confirmed by one of those she cleared. Viktor Shklovskii, a literary critic and tsarist army veteran, came to her in January 1919, charged with being an SR terrorist. "She let me go without insisting on my arrest," he wrote in 1922, after having emigrated from Soviet Russia, "and she advised me not to come back to her office, but to telephone her. I walked out with sweat running down my back. I called her a day later and she told me my case was closed. All in a very satisfied voice."[44]

Stasova opposed the Cheka's terror not only because she thought it would blacken the party's reputation, but because she thought it was morally reprehensible. She was not alone among Bolshevichki in her scruples. Earlier in 1918 Kollontai had agonized over the fact that the Bolsheviks, who had suffered so much at the hands of tsarist jailers, were turning into jailers themselves. Bosh ordered a hated Cheka official arrested in December 1918. How widespread such feelings were among the Bolshevichki is impossible to tell, but it is easy to understand why Stasova felt as she did. Intellectuals such as Shklovskii were the people with whom she had spent most of her life. In 1918 she was still friends with many of the artists and writers she had known since childhood. She was also sharing her food rations and extending her protection to her brothers and to other relatives, none of them Bolsheviks. These deep personal connections made it difficult for her to rationalize mass arrests of the intelligentsia or of rival socialists.

In March 1919 Stasova received the most important promotion of her career, to secretary of the Central Committee, replacing Sverdlov, who had died of influenza. By now her mother had also died, and the call to head the party Secretariat overcame the doubts and feelings of resentment that had kept her from transferring to Moscow a year before. Within weeks she had moved into an office in the Kremlin to take on the same sort of "technical" matters she had handled for the northern bureau and, before

[43] RSDRP, *Perepiska Sekretariata . . . avgust–oktiabr' 1918 g.*, 380.
[44] Viktor Shklovsky, *A Sentimental Journey*, trans. Richard Sheldon (Ithaca, N. Y., 1970), 174. Shklovsky wrote the first draft of this memoir in 1922.

that, for the St. Petersburg committee. She composed and mailed out "circular letters" that issued instructions and announced Politburo and Central Committee decisions. She answered inquiries from local party organizations. She assigned people to work in the provinces. She was even in charge of the ciphers used to communicate with agents working behind White lines. Stasova also attempted to organize the Secretariat into departments with clearly demarcated functions, but this project went slowly because she herself was absorbed in the daily tasks of communicating with the provinces, and because she received little support from the Politburo or the Central Committee. Lacking resources and instructions on how to proceed, she spent most of her time in correspondence, simply coping with the mail.[45]

Stasova brought to the job of Central Committee secretary all her formidable energy and her eagerness to supervise people. "A Secretary really has to be nosing around like a dog everywhere," she wrote to Novgorodtseva; "[she must] think of everything, push everyone, keep things going, and not sleep."[46] Ensconced in offices filled with her burgeoning staff, Stasova was a formidable figure. She still looked like the schoolteacher she had once been, for she usually wore a shirtwaist blouse and plain wool skirt, a watch on a chain around her neck and a pince-nez perched on her thin nose, her graying blond hair wound into a tight bun. Many a rough Bolshevik soldier or worker newly arrived from the provinces found this tall, aristocratic woman intimidating. A cartoon that appeared in the Kremlin one day portrayed her in blouse and jodhpurs, socks, and spurs, under the caption, "Secretary of the Militarized Party."[47]

This anonymous cartoonist, Viktor Shklovskii, whom she had rescued, and everyone else who met her realized that Stasova had no trouble giving orders. She had become a skilled manager who could inspire hard work and dedication in her subordinates. Still, however, she was loathe to make

[45] These generalizations about Stasova's work in the Secretariat are drawn primarily from the published correspondence, that is, RSDRP, *Perepiska sekretariata . . . aprel'–mai 1919 g.*; and RSDRP, *Perepiska sekretariata . . . iiun'–iiul' 1919 g.* In these two volumes, 126 letters bear Stasova's signature. For representative examples, see RSDRP, *Perepiska sekretariata . . . aprel'–mai 1919 g.*, 146–47, 278–79; and RSDRP, *Perepiska sekretariata . . . iiun'–iiul' 1919 g.*, 35, 56–57. See also the orders Lenin sent her in Lenin, *PSS*, vol. LI, 34, 83–84, 91, 173; vol. LIV, 421. Stasova's attendance at Central Committee meetings is documented in Jan M. Meijer, ed., *The Trotsky Papers, 1917–1922*, 2 vols. (The Hague, 1964), vol. I, 296–302; the Trotsky Archive, Houghton Library, Harvard University, Cambridge, Mass., T 159–63, 165, 166, 195, 225, 235, 260, 329, 330.

[46] Pavel Podliashuk, *Bogatyrskaia simfoniia. Dokumental'naia povest' o E. D. Stasovoi* (Moscow, 1977), 198.

[47] Stasova, *Vospominaniia*, 175–76. For impressions of Stasova during this period, see A. I. Mikoian, "K vospominaniiam E. D. Stasovoi," in Stasova, *Vospominaniia*, 7; Podliashuk, *Bogatyrskaia simfoniia*, 189; Polina Vinogradskaia, *Pamiatnye vstrechi*, 2nd ed. (Moscow, 1972), 43; and *Pravda*, 28 December 1919, 3.

policy or play politics. Trotsky later described her as "the technical secretary" of the Central Committee, and that was probably what she considered herself to be.[48] Unfortunately for her, she had moved too high in the organization to remain so detached from politics.

In 1919, controversy swirled around the Secretariat and its sister department, the Organizational Bureau (known by its acronym, Orgburo). The party leadership was anxious to establish a centralized command structure so as to get on with winning the war and running the country. Many Bolsheviks lower down in the hierarchy agreed that local party committees must obey orders from Moscow, but they pointed out that success depended on Moscow's doing its job as efficiently as it expected them to do theirs.[49] The Secretariat and the Orgburo were overworked, understaffed, and led by people experienced only in running a tiny underground movement. They regularly failed to send clear instructions or even to keep in touch with provincial party officials. They also struggled to define their respective responsibilities, stepping on each others' toes in the process. Critics of the whole concept of centralization, such as Bosh and Shliapnikov, argued that the resulting confusion showed that centralization would not work. In response to the complaints of their supporters and opponents, the party leaders fumbled about for ways to improve the operation of the center.

All this turmoil Stasova tried to avoid. When she did take a public position on the issues of party structure, she sided with those arguing for the rights of local party organizations. In her daily routine she tried to defend the Secretariat from attack by doing her work as well as limited resources would permit. This strategy left her coping from day to day, rather than thinking systematically about restructuring the department. Nor did she come forward with plans for reorganization.[50]

NPTXHowever hard she worked, Stasova could not make the ill-defined, overburdened, and very important Secretariat immune from criticism. By the end of 1919, lower-ranking communists and some leaders in Moscow were complaining loudly that the department was still

---

[48] Leon Trotsky, *Stalin, an Appraisal of the Man and His Influence*, trans. and ed. Charles Malamuth (New York, 1967), 316.

[49] This is the analysis of Service, *The Bolshevik Party in Revolution*, 76–78, 103–06.

[50] Stasova opposed the creation of guberniia party committees that would be superior to city committees at a party conference in December 1919. She argued that guberniia committees would have a largely peasant membership and would thus weaken the role of the proletariat as "our leading element." This was a position similar to that Bosh had taken, when she argued that the local party committee in Astrakhan should not be subordinated to the military revolutionary committee of the region. Stasova was in the minority at the conference, the majority of which voted for the strengthening of guberniia committees. For her comments, see KPSS, *Vos'maia konferentsiia RKP(b), dekabr' 1919 goda. Protokoly* (Moscow, 1961), 151.

Plate 18. Elena Stasova with Vladimir Lenin. Probably 1919 or
early 1920

too small. They also griped that Stasova had too much authority. Months
later, in September 1920, I. M. Vareikis, a Latvian communist who
deplored the rising power of the center, summed up the general criticism
by grousing that "the whole party apparatus was in Comrade Stasova's
pocket."[51] Mail was not answered soon enough, instructions got garbled
in transmission. If the party was going to be centralized, communists
complained, it must get its house in order.

These legitimate grievances, undoubtedly justified, demanded some
response from Moscow. In January and February of 1920 the Politburo
bruited about a reorganization of the center that would expand the
Secretariat and clarify its relationship to the Orgburo. At some point
during these discussions, the male leaders made an arrangement to which

---

[51] KPSS, *Deviataia konferentsiia RKP(b), sentiabr' 1920 goda. Protokoly* (Moscow, 1972),
103.

Stasova was not privy. They chose three men to run the Secretariat, Central Committee members N. N. Krestinskii, E. A. Preobrazhenskii, and N. N. Serebriakov. The arrangement was a move up for Krestinskii, who had chafed during the year as the Politburo continually encroached on terrain supposedly under the jurisdiction of the Orgburo, on which he sat. For Stasova it was a stunning rebuke. Not only would she no longer lead the Secretariat; she was not even to be nominated for re-election to the Central Committee.

Like the good party soldier she was, Stasova kept her public silence about this humiliation. In fact she kept it for decades. Then, in a carefully worded memoir published in the 1960s, she implied that when she was first informed about the reorganization, shortly before the Ninth Party Congress convened in March 1920, she had been led to understand that she would be reassigned to another important position. Only when the nominations for the Central Committee were made at the congress did she realize that she was the only member who had not been put forward for another term. The assembled delegates ratified the new arrangements and demoted her from the party leadership. Afterwards, in a very unpleasant interview with Krestinskii, Stasova requested assignment to the Orgburo, but he refused on the grounds that she was too inexperienced. He suggested instead that she apply at the Zhenotdel, the party's women's department. "This work did not appeal to me and I refused," Stasova wrote dryly in her memoirs. She left it to her readers to draw the obvious conclusion that both she and Krestinskii considered it an insult to send her off to work with women.[52]

Stasova might have saved herself if she had acted less like a technical secretary and more like a policy-maker and politician. She herself implied as much in her memoirs when she explained that she had refused to assume more "political responsibilities" because "I didn't feel myself strong enough theoretically."[53] This lame excuse, one she often used, did not go to the heart of her difficulties. She was not dumped because of her theoretical incompetence and Krestinskii was not chosen because of his skill at Marxist exegesis. Stasova was fired because she was not a member of the counsels of power, because she had continued to define herself as a technical secretary, and because that is the way the men had continued to define her. Had she asserted herself more in policy-making she might have strengthened her hand. Perhaps she should also have become more involved in the politics of the Central Committee and Politburo. Stasova should have understood, as Zemliachka did, that powerful people need strong ties to other powerful people, so that they can muster support when pressures mount.

[52] Stasova, *Vospominaniia*, 176.   [53] Ibid., 164.

It may be that Stasova would have survived the reorganization if she had been more politically involved, but the primary reasons for her firing were probably not her own failures. She had coped as well as possible with an impossibly difficult job, the best evidence for her competence in administration being the fact that Krestinskii, Preobrazhenskii, and Serebriakov managed no better than she had. When the time came to send a dramatic message to the party, though, she was expendable. Replacing one woman with three men was intended to demonstrate to the clamorous local party workers that the leaders were indeed serious about improving the Secretariat. "We are paying attention," read the subtext of the shake-up; "we are putting men in charge."

What Stasova might have salvaged, had she been more adroit at cultivating allies, was a demotion to a lesser rank in the central leadership. Instead, she received insults from Krestinskii, whom she believed to be the main architect of her disgrace. Rather than cool her heels waiting for him to find something for her to do, she returned to Petrograd. After a few weeks an old friend, the Georgian Sergo Ordzhonikidze, called her to Tbilisi, to work with him in that city where she had gone to recuperate so many years before. When Stasova boarded a train for the Caucasus in mid-summer 1920, her long career as a Bolshevik leader was over.

Stasova's fate exemplified that of the women in the party during the civil war. Everywhere, in the localities and at the center, they lost standing within the organization to men. Because they constituted a large group of women and held differing perspectives on their participation in the party, they reacted in different ways to their political marginalization. Some, Stasova and Kollontai for example, perceived that women were being shoved aside and resented it. Others, borne along by the militarization of the collective identity, probably accepted the idea that men should lead the party at war. Bolshevichki had never been encouraged to think critically about their situation as women within this male-dominated organization, and the life-and-death struggle in which they were engaged only strengthened the pressures for solidarity and conformity.

Unfortunately their private thoughts on this subject, if they recorded them, have not often survived. But their behavior speaks for them. Most Bolshevichki, the feminist and the not-so-feminist, the underground veterans and the recent recruits, did as Stasova did, did as they had done in 1917 – that is, they shied away from the alliances and disputes of the men. Bosh and Kollontai were more willing than most to take part in political debates, but they also kept their distance from party politics. Bosh never returned to the Ukrainian communists after her disillusionment with them in the spring of 1918. She supported the Military Opposition but would not defend it at the Ninth Party Congress. Kollontai was an outspoken member of the Left Opposition in 1918 and of the Workers' Opposition in 1921, but she was not an important member of either group's leadership. Most Bolshevichki avoided even such temporary participation in the political struggles of the civil war. This behavior, so consistent with their activities in 1917, suggests again that they saw politics as an alien male game, where they were unwelcome.

Bolshevichki's attitudes toward the rising authoritarianism of the party also remained much as they had been in the past. Some of them opposed the development of the dictatorship. Kollontai became a champion of party democratization. Bosh supported the independence of local party organizations. Stasova privately criticized the persecutions perpetrated by the Cheka and worked to mitigate their excesses. But many male Bolsheviks also took such positions, and it does not appear that women were more likely than men to defend the party's democratic traditions or to protest its trampling on its enemies. If they did protest, they did not do so openly. Very few Bolshevichki participated in the factions that called for democratization during the civil war. Most seem to have avoided that form of political activity as well.

Bolshevichki in government work

After all, there was much more than party politics to occupy the minds of Bolshevichki during the civil war. There was survival, their own and that of their party, and there was the revolutionary vision, the "cause" that had inspired them to become Bolsheviks in the first place. The war, as we have seen, changed the collective identity in significant ways, strengthening its authoritarianism and weakening its egalitarianism, but it did not touch the great enabling myth that lay at the heart of Bolshevism, the "cause" of leading a workers' revolution that would usher in a socialist utopia. Indeed, if anything, the war increased the inspirational power of the cause by appearing to bring its achievement within reach. The Bolsheviks now were out of the underground and onto the battlefield; their armies were attacking the forces of reaction while their government laid the foundations for a new society behind the front lines. Bolshevichki could rationalize the pernicious changes in their own movement as temporary adjustments to the demands of this climactic, world-historical struggle. They could also point to many developments that showed the way to the new world, developments in which they were taking an active, leading part.

Thirty-five percent of the older generation and 20 percent of the younger worked in the government departments of the new regime during the war years; close to 10 percent more of each group split their time between party and government assignments. (See table 19.) Many entered fields for which they had received training before 1917. Vera Lebedeva, an M.D. with an interest in pediatrics, became head of the Department for the Protection of Maternity and Infancy of the Commissariat of Health. Krupskaia became a leading official of the Commissariat of Enlightenment (the education ministry known by its acronym, Narkompros), and she soon signed up as assistants Zinaida Krzhizhanovskaia and Liudmila and Vera Menzhinskaia, women with whom she had taught in St. Petersburg in the early 1890s.

The majority of Bolshevichki in government during the civil war worked in education, medicine, social services, journalism, the arts, and clerical work – specialties that professional women of their generation were entering across Europe. But Bolshevichki also moved into fields still closed to women elsewhere, such as economic management and the court system. Late in 1917 Elena Rozmirovich, Bosh's sister, became a member of the investigatory commission of the revolutionary tribunal in Petrograd, a position that combined the functions of police officer and judge. In December 1919 she was promoted to chair the commission. Varvara Iakovleva, the Moscow communist, became a high-ranking official in the Petrograd Cheka in 1919. Iraida Ulianova, a spinner in the city of Kolomna before 1917, served on the presidium of the city soviet's executive committee in 1918 and was commissar of the city economy. Other Bolshevichki were soviet delegates, judges, and trade-union officials. Thirty-two percent of the older generation and 26 percent of the younger held office in a variety of departments. Many women were in Narkompros, but even larger numbers became officials in the soviets, particularly at the city and provincial level.[54] (See tables 29 and 30.)

Party propagandists pointed to the presence of women in government as evidence that women were being emancipated by the revolution. Many Bolshevichki agreed, for suddenly they had acquired personal opportunities far beyond anything they had imagined possible before. Teachers once at the bottom of the pedagogical ladder were invited to participate in overhauling the education of an entire nation. Physicians were charged to create new health-care systems. Textile workers became trade union leaders, tram conductors became judges. Sofia Efremova, the daughter of a forester in Smolensk guberniia, had been a seamstress and nanny

---

[54] On Rozmirovich, see T. F. Avramenko and M. N. Simoian, "Elena Fedorovna Rozmirovich," *Voprosy istorii KPSS*, no. 3 (1966): 101. On Iakovleva, see Robert C. Tucker and Stephen F. Cohen, *The Great Purge Trial* (New York, 1965), 397–413. On Karaseva, see Institut istorii partii MGK i MK KPSS, Filial instituta Marksizma-Leninizma pri TsK KPSS, *Soratniki* (Moscow, 1985), 194–95.

Table 29 *Government office-holding by Bolshevichki, November 1917–December 1921*

Offices	Old Bolshevichki	Civil war joiners
Government departments		
Narkompros		
Library head	1	—
City deputy department head	1	—
City department head	2	2
City deputy head	—	1
City head	1	2
Guberniia deputy department head	1	—
Guberniia department head	1	2
Republican head	2	—
Central deputy department head	1	—
Central department head	5	—
Collegium member	1	—
Other government departments		
City department head	6	2
Guberniia deputy department head	—	1
Republican head	—	1
Central deputy department head	2	—
Central department head	5	—
Collegium member	1	—
Journalism		
Editor, local paper	4	2
Editor, national paper	3	1
Military		
City military-revolutionary committee	2	4
Republican military-revolutionary committee	1	—
Political officer	15	17
Central staff, army	2	1
Miscellaneous		
Ambassador	1	—
Factory department head	1	—
Factory director	—	1
Hospital director	1	—
Police, courts		
City Cheka	1	—
City judge	3	—
Soviets		
Raion, uezd		
Delegate	1	3
Executive committee	2	—
Secretary	2	—
Department head	1	1
City		
Delegate	6	2
Executive committee	1	—

Secretary	1	—
Deputy department head	1	—
Department head	2	2
Guberniia		
Delegate	—	1
Executive committee	1	—
Secretary	2	1
Deputy chair	1	—
Chair	1	—
Department head	2	—
Republican		
Delegate	1	—
All-Russian Central Executive Committee	2	—
Council of People's Commissars	1	—
Trade unions		
City		
Committee	2	2
Secretary	3	—
Deputy chair	1	—
Chair	1	—
Central committee	2	—
Guberniia committee	1	—
Republican committee	—	1
Central		
Department head	1	—
Chair	1	—
None[a]	193 (60.7 %)	176 (77.5%)
Unknown	21	1
Total	318	227

Note: The highest office held by each woman was coded.
[a]Positions lower-ranking than those on the list were coded as "none."

Table 30 *Distribution of Bolshevichki's government office-holding during the civil war*

Field in which held office	Old Bolshevichki (%)	Civil war joiners (%)
Journalism	6.8 (7)	6.0 (3)
Military	19.4 (20)	44.0 (22)
Narkompros	15.5 (16)	14.0 (7)
Other government	16.5 (17)	10.0 (5)
Police, courts	3.9 (4)	—
Soviets	26.2 (27)	20.0 (10)
Trade unions	11.7 (12)	6.0 (3)
Total	100.0 (103)	100.0 (50)

Note: The figures in parentheses are base Ns for the adjacent percentages.

before joining the party in 1903. In 1921 she held the post of head of the department of maternity and child protection for the Crimea. Praskovia Vishniakova, the daughter of railroad workers, chaired a soviet in the Kuban region in 1919.[55] Some of these jobs were very temporary. Vishniakova, for example, left the Kuban in 1920 to spend a few months in Moscow as an instructor in the Commissariat of Labor. Furthermore, the difficulties confronting every individual who sought to institute programs of any sort were formidable. Chronic, severe shortages of personnel and material resources, the ordeal of simply fending off hunger and cold for another day, disrupted communications – all made it very difficult for Soviet planners to do much more than draw up grand designs.

Yet despite the obstacles, the Bolshevichki could find reasons to believe that the work they were doing was worthwhile. Krupskaia sketched out ideas for a comprehensive national system of adult education accessible to all citizens. Lebedeva worked to establish clinics that would deliver high-quality prenatal care. Krupskaia and Lebedeva and all the other Bolshevichki working away in soviets and commissariats believed that, in redesigning medicine, education, transportation, industrial management, and food supply, they were laying the foundations for a socialist society. And indeed they were. The Soviet system was beginning to take shape during the civil war years. Furthermore, the very presence of the Bolshevichki in governing institutions that had hitherto been closed to people from the lower ranks of society and to all women was a sign of the revolutionary process underway. So even in the midst of the civil war, the utopian hopes that had always been a central part of their collective identity sustained the Bolshevichki, making it easier for them to disregard the menace posed by the developing party autocracy.[56]

The Zhenotdel

Another event nourishing the optimism of some Bolshevichki during the civil war was the establishment of the Department for Work Among Women, better known by its acronym, Zhenotdel. The Zhenotdel was the crowning achievement of that group of Bolshevichki – Inessa, Kollontai, Samoilova, Nikolaeva, and Krupskaia – that had launched the party's

---

[55] RTsKhIDNI, f. 124, op. 1, d. 654, ll. 1–4; and d. 377, ll. 3–8.
[56] On Krupskaia's activities, see Robert H. McNeal, *Bride of the Revolution: Krupskaia and Lenin* (Ann Arbor, Mich., 1972), 183–214. On Lebedeva, see V. P. Lebedeva, "Zabota o rostkakh kommunizma," in *Oktiabriem mobilizovannye. Zhenshchin-kommunistki v bor'be za pobedu sotsialisticheskoi revoliutsii* (Moscow, 1987), 197–208.

earliest efforts to cultivate a female following in the prerevolutionary years. Their diligent lobbying persuaded the party leadership that a department specializing in reaching out to working-class women could contribute to the war effort.

The Zhenotdel grew out of more limited projects that had yielded modest successes, and which thus made it possible for the feminists to ask for authorization to do more. The first such project was *Rabotnitsa*, the newspaper which enjoyed considerable success in 1917 but was discontinued in January 1918 when the party cut back on publishing because of shortages of newsprint and ink. Thereafter the leading Bolshevik feminists scattered to other projects, and work among women dwindled to the activities of a few local committees, primarily those in Moscow and Petrograd. In the fall of 1918, however, Inessa, Kollontai, Samoilova, and Nikolaeva got together again to organize a meeting they grandly titled "The First All-Russian Congress of Working-Class and Peasant Women."

It met in November. More than one thousand delegates traveled to Moscow to hear rousing speeches from Inessa, Kollontai, and Samoilova, as well as testimonials from their own ranks on the importance of organizing working-class women. The message of the conference – that a pool of support existed among women, waiting only to be tapped – got through to the party leadership, particularly to Sverdlov and Lenin, both of whom attended the meeting. Shortly thereafter, Sverdlov authorized the establishment of committees for work among women in all city party organizations.[57]

Creation of these committees was easier decreed than accomplished, however. Communists working in the cities were already stretched to the limits of their energy and funding by the demands of the civil war, and so were not eager to assign people to a project the worth of which they questioned. Where activists were already set up, as in Moscow and Petrograd, the work proceeded. Where they were not, it languished. Throughout 1919 Inessa and Samoilova, the Bolshevik feminists who had the best access to the party leadership, argued that only a national department could ensure an effective campaign to mobilize women. Inessa repeatedly declared that working-class women, if approached properly, would be a powerful resource for the beleaguered party; if ignored, they would oppose the Bolsheviks and undermine the party's appeal among men as well.[58]

This argument, fashioned by the Bolshevik feminists before the revol-

---

[57] Barbara Evans Clements, *Bolshevik Feminist: The Life of Aleksandra Kollontai* (Bloomington, Ind., 1979), 154–57.

[58] On Inessa's work in establishing the Zhenotdel, see R. C. Elwood, *Inessa Armand* (Cambridge, 1992), 231–61.

Plate 19. The First All-Russian Women's Congress in session,
November 1918. On the podium the four figures seated in the center are,
from left to right, Alexandria Kollontai, Klavdiia Nikolaeva, Inessa
Armand (facing into the camera), and Konkordiia Samoilova.

ution, then shaped by them to fit the civil war, played on the party's
apprehensive sense of the generally negative influences of proletarian and
peasant women as well as on the evidence of the times. Working women
had been active participants in the upheavals of 1917. They constituted a
growing percentage of the factory labor force as more men were drawn
away to war, and they might provide tens of thousands of volunteers to
participate in a whole series of projects, from street-cleaning to working in
hospitals. But many of them were very critical of the Bolsheviks for not
alleviating the hardships in their lives. "Women workers have endured
disappointments and accuse Soviet power of not keeping its promises, of
not giving land and bread," Samoilova wrote in September 1918.[59] As the
civil war emergency deepened in 1919, the party leaders became persuaded that a department charged with persuading dubious women to
support the Red cause might not be such a bad idea. In the fall of that year
they authorized the creation of a department at the party's center to lead
work among women, and named Inessa to be its head.

[59] K. Samoilova, "Mezhraionoe soveshchanie rabotnits," *Petrogradskaia pravda*, 15 September 1918, 2.

Since returning to Russia in 1917, Inessa had spent most of her time in Moscow. After the Bolsheviks seized power she accepted an important appointment as chair of the Moscow guberniia soviet's economic council, an organization that was supposed to establish economic management of the region. In this post she proved herself to be a hard-working and competent administrator. In early January 1919 she was appointed to head the newly authorized commissions for work among women, but rather than pursue that endeavor, she left Russia to go to France in early February. There she worked for three months as member of a Soviet delegation in Paris to organize the repatriation of Russian POWs and to establish covert contacts with pro-Bolshevik French socialists. The mission, as she later described it, was basically a waste of time. When she returned to Moscow in May 1919 she settled down to concentrate on work with women. In the fall, she was appointed to head the Zhenotdel.[60]

Inessa brought all her considerable intelligence, diligence, and ability to work with others to the task of creating the department. Her headquarters in Moscow was staffed by twenty-two women, mostly from the new generation of Bolshevichki, and presided over by an unofficial governing board made up of veteran Bolshevik feminists – most importantly, Krupskaia, Stal, Samoilova, Nikolaeva, and Kollontai. Inessa and Krupskaia edited the department's magazine, *Kommunistka*, the first issues of which appeared in 1920. Nikolaeva headed the Zhenotdel in Petrograd; Sofia Smidovich ran the office for the Moscow region. Samoilova was an organizer who traveled throughout Russia and Ukraine, advising local committees. In 1919 Kollontai divided her time between assignments as an agitator at the front and minor posts in the Central Zhenotdel; in 1920 she returned to Moscow permanently to work on the central staff.

The initial work of the Zhenotdel consisted of drafting guidelines for the operation of departments at lower levels of the party hierarchy, planning periodic conferences of Zhenotdel workers, organizing meetings of working-class women, and setting up the publication of books, pamphlets, and periodicals. Throughout the first year of the department's existence, Inessa spent some of her time lobbying the party leadership for more funding. She also had to call on the leadership periodically to issue circular letters to local committees instructing them to give the Zhenotdel their support, for as the word of the establishment of the department spread down through the ranks of the party, the usual complaints surfaced that work with women in such times of crisis was a foolish diversion that might stir up feminism. Local party leaders who held such ideas often refused to cooperate with Zhenotdel workers.[61]

[60] Elwood, *Inessa Armand*, 214–30.
[61] On Inessa's work as leader of the Zhenotdel, see ibid., 240–61.

A goodly number of the older Bolshevichki shared many of these doubts, as they always had, and as a result very few of them participated in the department's activities. In a letter to Samoilova in 1921 Kollontai described one such Bolshevichka as behaving as though the "cause" of reaching out to poor women was "alien" to her. Samoilova put the case more directly in a pamphlet published in 1920: "They don't work among women because they consider this work beneath their dignity and declare that the organizing of women workers is feminism." Such Bolshevichki held fast to their beliefs that propagandizing women was a lesser activity and that anyone who spent most of her time on it was probably a feminist and therefore suspect as a person who put the interests of her gender ahead of the general good of the party and the working class. They also continued to share the general skepticism that prevailed in the party about the worth of devoting resources to working-class and peasant women.

Older Bolshevichki may also have feared that being associated with work among women would diminish their standing among men. Stasova implied as much in her memoirs when she wrote that she had declined an assignment in the Zhenotdel after being fired as party secretary. Samoilova hinted at the existence of such attitudes when she criticized those Bolshevichki who thought such work was "beneath their dignity." In 1922, A. Komarova, a Siberian Zhenotdel worker, was much more forthright, accusing Bolshevichki who refused to work in the Zhenotdel of identifying with men and scorning their own sex. "There has always been an affectation among these women, wanting to shine among men," she wrote in the newspaper *Krasnaia sibiriachka*. "They prefer the society of men, say 'my friends are only men, I can't tolerate the company of women.'" A more charitable and objective interpretation is that such attitudes expressed the insecurities of these Bolshevichki and their heartfelt desire to be accepted by their male comrades. Such identifications with the dominant group are commonplace among minority members of all sorts of institutions, from political parties to professions. It was also quite reasonable for Bolshevichki to fear the consequences of association with the Zhenotdel, not only because it was a women's organization, but also because it had always been suspected of harboring feminist ideas.[62]

---

[62] RTsKhIDNI, f. 148, op. 1, d. 3, l. 31.05; K. Samoilova, *Organizatsionnye zadachi otdelov rabotnits* (Moscow, 1920), 12; *Krasnaia sibiriachka*, no. 1 (1922), as quoted by Anne Rassweiler, "The Sibiriachka Encounters Revolution," paper presented at the annual meeting of the American Association for the Advancement of Slavic Studies, Washington, D. C., October 1995, 11. For an interesting discussion of the ways in which being identified with women's groups diminished the standing of female trade unionists in the United States in the early twentieth century, see Ruth Milkman, "Gender and Trade

The Bolshevik feminists who refused to bow to such fears and the eager young protégés they recruited made the Zhenotdel into a place where more positive attitudes toward women were nurtured. In the major cities the department instructed its teenaged recruits in Marxist feminism, encouraged them to believe in their abilities, and generally provided them a warm welcome to the party. Life for Zhenotdel workers in the provinces was more difficult, since there they worked as small teams in isolation, often with little support from the local party committee. Many were pressured to concentrate on the more important tasks that should properly engage all good communists; some were harassed verbally and physically. It is a sign of the appeal of the Zhenotdel that despite the difficulties surrounding it, thousands of young women signed up to work for the department during the civil war years.[63]

The Zhenotdel's success derived in no small measure from its effectiveness in disseminating an appealing message. Propaganda was its central task, the reason for which it had been created. Under Inessa's leadership the Zhenotdel published pamphlets and the journal *Kommunistka*, which built on the earlier work of *Rabotnitsa* and of weekly columns for women that had appeared in the major newspapers in 1918 and 1919. All these publications reiterated the general party line on why women should participate in the civil war. The Communist Party, Zhenotdel propagandists declared, had emancipated women from the legal and political inequality of the tsarist regime, was working to ensure them equal educational and employment opportunities, social services to ease their domestic labor, and good medical care, and was seeking more generally to liberate all the people of the nation. But these efforts had been cruelly hampered by the Whites, who had attacked the Reds in order to bring back the old regime. So working-class women must support the war effort in order to promote their own emancipation as well as the creation of a just new world. A meeting of female printers in Petrograd in 1919 summed up this message succinctly in a resolution: "Sending our husbands and brothers to the front, we ourselves will remain in our places and carry to a conclusion the cause of the liberation of the working class and the emancipation of women."[64]

That women should join men in building a righteous society had long been an important message of the Bolshevik feminists. Old Bolshevichki working for the Zhenotdel continued to be careful to reassure the party that they were not feminists seeking to separate women from men. Inessa

Unionism in Historical Perspective," in Louise A. Tilly and Patricia Gurin, eds., *Women, Politics, and Change* (New York, 1990), 102–03.
[63] The best collection of memoirs by Zhenotdel workers is *Bez nikh my ne pobedili by*.
[64] *Petrogradskaia pravda*, 17 May 1919, 4.

wrote in 1919: "All the interests of women workers, all the conditions for their emancipation are inseparably connected to the victory of the proletariat, are unthinkable without it. But this victory is unthinkable without their participation, without their struggle."[65] At the same time a more assertively feminist interpretation of Marxist ideas, first evident in *Rabotnitsa* in 1917, continued to develop in the civil war years. Explicit criticism of patriarchal attitudes among men and demands that women achieve their own personal, individual liberation from the ties of tradition, particularly from marital ties, appeared regularly in articles written by younger, less cautious Bolshevichki. Such authors abandoned the reassuring pledges of solidarity with men that had become the stock-in-trade of the older generation and called for the emancipation of women from all social constraints, save those of their own accepting.

An early example of the new thrust of Bolshevik feminism appeared in *Petrogradskaia pravda* in December 1918, signed by a woman who identified herself only as Anna. The revolution, Anna argued, had brought women the possibility of becoming "strong and free citizens, not inferior to men in anything." They had gained political rights and were "free economically" because they were now working in the paid-labor force. But they still returned home every night to a "medieval household." They were prevented from achieving full independence by the "social slavery" of traditional ideas, enforced by men who had learned from the bourgeoisie to treat their wives as property. To be fully free, Anna argued, a woman must be able to take her children and leave such a "slave master" without being punished by "the people's court" of public opinion. She concluded by calling for the appointment of female judges. Their understanding of "a woman's soul" would enable them to rule fairly in divorce cases.[66]

Anna's condemnation of men's treatment of their wives was similar to that which Lenin himself would express to Zetkin in his 1920 interview. He too would characterize marriage as "slavery." He too believed, as did many Marxists and other socialists throughout Europe, that the family was a bastion of patriarchal attitudes. But there was a significant difference of emphasis between Anna and the leader of her party. He sketched the same picture of conjugal oppression, but his solution was for the party to raise the consciousness of men and women. "We must root out the old slave-owner's point of view, both in the party and among the

[65] VKP(b), TsK, Otdel po rabote sredi zhenshchin, *Kommunisticheskaia partiia i organizatsiia rabotnits*, 16.
[66] Anna, "K tovarishcham rabotnitsam-kommunistam," *Petrogradskaia pravda*, 31 December 1918, 2.

masses," he told Zetkin. "That is one of our political tasks, a task just as urgently necessary as the formation of a staff composed of comrades, men and women, with thorough theoretical and practical training for party work among working women."[67] Lenin stuck to the classic Bolshevik prescription in which enlightened men and women brought freedom to the benighted. Anna proposed a different course, that women strike out on their own.

This vision of emancipation, in which women freed themselves, had long been a central component of feminism. For that very reason, Bolshevichki such as Inessa and Samoilova had avoided proclaiming it. But now, in the civil war, when resources were in desperately short supply but belief in utopian possibilities was rampant, Bolshevichki, including Inessa and Samoilova, began to call on women to make their own personal liberation. The idea suffused the speeches at the 1918 women's congress, letters and articles in newspaper columns, and the pages of *Kommunistka.* "The victory of socialism is turning the woman worker, like the man, into the conscious creator of her own life!," exulted an unsigned article in *Petrogradskaia pravda* in 1919.[68] From the days of the woman's congress onward, the discussion of how women should create their own lives kept returning, as Anna had, to the question of how they could extricate themselves from oppressive family ties. Anna proposed appointing female judges in order to facilitate divorce. Other Bolshevichki, particularly those from the younger generation, went further and argued that women should abandon marriage and family altogether.

In an article in *Kommunistka* in 1920, a 21-year-old Zhenotdel worker, Rakhil Kovnator, expressed the very radical ideas about revolutionized womanhood then circulating in the department. Kovnator was an agitator whose career typified those of the new generation of Bolshevichki that the Zhenotdel had recruited. A university student in Petrograd who joined the party in 1917, she had served as secretary of her raion party committee and delegate to the Petrograd soviet before moving to Moscow in the spring of 1918 to work as a raion secretary there. She joined the Moscow committee of the Zhenotdel in 1919, became a frequent contributor to the department's publications, and also worked as an agitator traveling around Russia to set up Zhenotdel departments.[69]

The theme of Kovnator's 1920 article was "the new woman" in

---

[67] Lenin, *The Emancipation of Women*, 115.   [68] *Petrogradskaia pravda*, 17 May 1919, 1.
[69] R. Kovnator, "Novaia zhenshchina v revoliutsionnoi literature," *Kommunistka*, no. 5 (1920): 32–35; Kovnator, "Vo imia prekrasnoi pory," in *Zhenshchiny rasskazyvaiut. Vospominaniia, stat'i, 1918–1959* (Smolensk, 1959), 40–42.

Russian literature. "The new woman" was a commonly used term first coined by the English feminist novelist Sarah Grand in 1894. Typically it referred to emancipated women such as the feminists and to their literary reflections, female characters in novels who were independent and self-defining, particularly in their love lives. Henrik Ibsen's Nora in *The Doll's House* and Thomas Hardy's Sue in *Jude the Obscure* are perhaps the best-known examples. In her article, Kovnator proclaimed that a "new woman" was emerging in Russia in fiction and in reality. The "new woman" was, first and foremost, a social activist, and her unconventional choice of lifestyle drew down upon her social condemnation. "When a woman gives up everything for a man, that's natural," Kovnator wrote, "but when she wants to dedicate herself to a cause, people bring up her duty as a mother." The new woman did not confine herself to service, however. Rather, she demanded "the right to a free, independent attitude in her personal life." From time to time she entered "a free union with her heart's choice." The "fulfillment of her 'female ego'" in love affairs was an optional complement to the primary duty of her life, her public service to her "cause."[70]

Kovnator's article raised issues that European radicals had been discussing for decades. Whenever they considered liberating women from the constraints of marriage, sexuality quickly became an issue. How was a woman who had chosen not to marry to live her intimate life? Many of the female activists of the second half of the nineteenth century, Florence Nightingale for instance, or, in the United States, Jane Addams, attempted to reassure society of their moral rectitude by resolving very publicly to remain celibate. This posture accorded well with long-established European acceptance of the chaste single woman who renounced her domestic vocation for a social one. Other prominent women, the novelist George Sand being one of the earliest and most famous, challenged the dominant belief that sexuality should be tied exclusively to marriage. They called instead for full freedom of sexual expression for women as well as for men.

Marxism committed itself to such a vision of individual freedom, but postponed its realization to the future. Marx and Engels argued that the forms of sexual expression were customs determined (as were all customs) by property arrangements. The economic dependence of women on men under capitalism made marriage yet another form of slavery, but it could be fundamentally transformed only when private property had been abolished. In his classic study *The Origin of the Family, Private Property, and the State* (1884), Engels declared that in the socialist future people

---

[70] Kovnator, "Novaia zhenshchina v revoliutsionnoi literature."

would satisfy "the impulse of individual sexual love" as they chose, without social regulation or interference. He implied that they would choose heterosexual relationships based on romantic love and terminable when that love faded. But he was happy to grant that the emancipated builders of socialism would arrange their lives however they wished. "That will be settled," he wrote, "after a new generation has grown up, a generation of men who never in all their lives have had occasion to purchase a woman's surrender either with money or any other means of social power; and a race of women who have never been obliged to surrender to any man out of any consideration other than that of real love, or to refrain from giving themselves to their lovers for fear of the economic consequences."[71]

Engels and the other great Marxist commentator on the family, August Bebel, did not consider female sexual emancipation to be a pressing current issue, for they believed that the resolution of all derivative social problems could only occur after revolution had destroyed private property. Bebel declared in his very influential *Woman Under Socialism* (1883) that "The complete emancipation of woman, and her equality with man, is the final goal of our social development . . . and this realization is possible only by a social change that shall abolish the rule of man over man – hence also of capitalism over the workingman."[72]

Some Marxist feminists were not willing to wait for a liberation so eventual. They understood that a woman who sought to escape the domestic sphere confronted immediately the issue of how to live her sexual life. Among the Germans, Lily Braun discussed the question in articles published in the Social-Democratic press and in her best-selling study of women in the labor force, *The Woman Question, Its Historical Development, and Economic Aspects* (1901). Influenced by Braun and by the work of Swedish feminist Ellen Key, Kollontai became the first Russian Social Democrat to analyze the relationship between woman's liberation and her sexuality. She published several articles between 1911 and 1913, in which she argued that patriarchal ideas of male superiority and female subordination affected the love affairs of even the most independent women. Men treated women as possessions, disregarding their sexual needs as well as their desires for emotional intimacy. Women knew no other way to relate to lovers than submission. The "new woman," as Kollontai understood her, was an exception to this general rule, because she had liberated herself from her conditioning. She gave

---

[71] Friedrich Engels, *The Origin of the Family, Private Property, and the State* (New York, 1940), 68.
[72] August Bebel, *Woman Under Socialism*, trans. from the 33rd ed. by Daniel De Leon (New York, 1904), 349.

herself to her work, but she also engaged in love affairs periodically. "She holds out her hand to her chosen one and goes away for several weeks to drink from the cup of love's joy, however deep it is, and to satisfy herself," Kollontai wrote in 1913. "When the cup is empty, she throws it away without regret and bitterness. And again to work."[73]

Such mechanistic and unsentimental reflections help to explain why many of the Old Bolsheviks considered Kollontai a feminist and a libertine. Their collective identity, built on disciplined, collectivist virtues, did not readily accommodate private pleasures or individual satisfactions, except those gained from service to the cause. Of course there were Bolsheviks who went away for several weeks, or longer, to pursue love affairs, but most followed the masters of their ideology in believing that such matters should not be elevated to the level of theoretical discussion. Only artists and intellectuals, that is, decadent dilettanti, occupied their minds with sex. The leaders of the Bolsheviks believed that paying attention to the subject would encourage narcissistic self-indulgence, rather than disciplined group effort. Lenin put the common view to Klara Zetkin in 1920: "I'm an old man and I do not like it. I may be a morose ascetic, but quite often this so-called 'new sex life' of young people – and frequently of the adults too – seems to me purely bourgeois and simply an extension of the good old bourgeois brothel."[74]

Rakhil Kovnator, twenty-one when she wrote her discussion of female independence, turned for guidance on such matters to Kollontai, not Lenin. She knew Kollontai was right to argue that women had to find means to sexual expression that did not tie them to subordinated relationships with men and subsequently to family responsibilities that demanded more of them than of men. Kovnator also accepted Kollontai's assertion that a woman had a right to individual fulfillment, sexual and spiritual. These ideas ran in direct opposition to the Old Bolshevichki's collective identity, with its stress on women's joining with men to serve the cause together. Kovnator also believed in the importance of the cause, but she saw it not simply as a means to social emancipation but also to the individual emancipation of the Bolshevichka as well. The older Bolshevichki may always have cherished the same need for personal freedom, but they had not been bold enough to lay claims in print to personal satisfaction or to emancipation from marriage and family.

[73] A. M. Kollontai, *Novaia moral' i rabochii klass* (Moscow, 1918), 9. On Lily Braun's discussions of sexuality, see Alfred G. Meyer, *The Feminism and Socialism of Lily Braun* (Bloomington, Ind., 1985), esp. 113–23.
[74] Lenin, *The Emancipation of Women*, 106.

Samoilova and the building of the Zhenotdel

The Zhenotdel quickly became an all-female world that encouraged emancipatory thinking among young women such as Rakhil Kovnator, but its central mission remained persuading working-class and peasant women to support the Bolsheviks. To that end, Zhenotdel staffers took to the railroads and dirt roads of Russia in 1919 and 1920 to spread the department's message. Of all these peripatetic Zhenotdel staffers, the most important was Konkordiia Samoilova. The organizer of the first Woman's Day celebration and founding editor of both incarnations of *Rabotnitsa*, Samoilova stayed away from the capital cities during the civil war years to concentrate on building work among women in provincial Russia and Ukraine.

Samoilova decided not to work at the central office of the Zhenotdel because of tragedies in her personal life. She spent 1917 and 1918 in Petrograd and Moscow, doing the sort of work she had done before the revolution – journalism and agitation among factory women. In the division of labor that developed between the three principal leaders of the feminist Bolsheviks – Kollontai, Inessa, and Samoilova – Samoilova chose to concentrate on the nuts-and-bolts mechanics of cultivating support among women. Kollontai and Inessa wrote analyses of the current situation and prophecies of the future which were anchored in Marxist feminism. Samoilova discussed current problems and their solution. She also worked on recruiting Zhenotdel staff, particularly from among working-class women, and spent a good deal of time meeting with small groups of factory workers.[75]

In early 1918 Samoilova's husband, the lawyer and Bolshevik Arkadii Samoilov, returned to Petrograd from military service. Theirs was a very close marriage that had survived long periods of separation when she was in exile and he was in the army. During the underground years Samoilova had lost touch with her own family, even with her sister Kaleriia with whom she had gone so many years before to study in the Bestuzhevskii courses. Arkadii and his sister had become her closest friends. It was a great sorrow to her, therefore, when he fell ill in the summer of 1918 with a recurrence of tuberculosis. They decided that he should head south, where the warmer climate might revive him, so in the autumn he

---

[75] This division of labor was particularly apparent at the women's congress in 1918, but is also documented in Samoilova's writings. For the congress see *Pervyi vserossiiskii s"ezd rabotnits* (Kharkov, 1920). Representative pieces by Samoilova are "Rabotnitsy i professional'nye soiuzy," *Rabotnitsa*, 30 May 1917, 6–7; Samoilova, "Neotlozhnaia zadacha (k organizatsii rabotnits)," *Petrogradskaia pravda*, 26 July 1918, 1–2; and Samoilova, *Organizatsionnye zadachi otdelov rabotnits*.

obtained an assignment in Astrakhan, working with Shliapnikov and Bosh.[76]

The move south proved not salubrious, but fatal. Instead of growing stronger, Samoilov was soon sick with dysentery; in the hospital to recover from that illness, he contracted typhus. He and Samoilova stayed in touch by mail, and on 22 December 1918 he wrote to reassure her: "My darling, I implore you, don't despair. Be kind and calm. You have a strong spirit, after all. Hope; everything will be fine. Just give me time. Wishing you good health. Many kisses. Keep writing and waiting for news from me." Shortly after he mailed the letter Arkadii Samoilov's health took a turn for the worse and within a few days he died of typhus.[77]

When she learned of her husband's death in January 1919, Samoilova decided that she must leave Petrograd, his birthplace and the city where they had spent their happiest times together. She could have gone to Moscow to work on setting up the committees that were the precursors to the Zhenotdel. There were rumors that the leadership thought so highly of her organizational skills that they preferred her to Inessa to head work on women at the national level. But in 1919 Samoilova did not want to settle in Moscow. "I have two children – Piter [Petrograd] and Ukraine – whom I love equally and in whose lives I am equally interested," she declared.[78] Too wounded to stay in Petrograd, she went to Ukraine and devoted herself to building the Zhenotdel from the ground up.

Based in Kharkov, Samoilova traveled thousands of miles helping young women organize Zhenotdel sections. She advised them on recruiting staff for the department, publishing columns in the local newspapers, and holding meetings. She was well suited to such work, for she was a kind person who knew how to speak to the uneducated in simple, direct, unpatronizing language that did not alienate them. She was thus able to bridge the enormous gap that separated the privileged from the poor in Russia. The working-class women with whom she surrounded herself perceived her as an authority figure, but a benevolent one. "We always knew very well what a big person Comrade Samoilova was," wrote Prokhorova, one of the contributors to *Rabotnitsa*, "but we never felt too

[76] G. Shidlovskii, "Pamiati dvukh starykh pravdistov," *Katorga i ssylka*, no. 10 (1931): 172–78; *Revoliutsionnaia deiatel'nost'* Konkordii Nikolaevny Samoilovoi. Sbornik vospominanii (Moscow, 1922), 59–62.

[77] RTsKhIDNI, f. 148, op. 1, d. 3, l. 53. For his letters to her in the fall of 1918, see ll. 68, 53–54, 78, 77, 80–81, 55–56, 79, 67, 82, 76, 51–52, 84. They are listed here in chronological order.

[78] Quoted in S. V. Karavashkova and L. D. Diuzheva, *Konkordiia Nikolaevna Samoilova* (Moscow, 1979), 52. On Samoilova's attitudes toward Petrograd, see RTsKhIDNI, f. 148, op. 1, d. 3, ll. 1–4, 60, 12. On the party leadership's attitude toward her, see B. Breslav, *Konkordiia Nikolaevna Samoilova* (Moscow and Leningrad, 1926), 15.

Plate 20. Konkordiia Samoilova, circa 1920.

small.''[79] Samoilova's communication skills also came out in dozens of speeches and pamphlets that offered straightforward arguments couched in simple language ornamented with folk expressions.[80]

Of course Samoilova did not win over all, or even most, of the women she sought out. Some avoided her. Absorbed in the continual struggle to survive the civil war, they had no time for meetings. Some distrusted her, for they had heard that Bolsheviks were godless ruffians who wanted to steal babies away from their mothers. Some women were actively hostile, blaming the Bolsheviks for all the difficulties of their lives. They would

[79] *Revoliutsionnaia deiatel'nost'* . . . *Samoilovoi*, 40. For other comments on her by co-workers, see ibid., 38; *Zhenshchiny v revoliutsii* (Moscow, 1959), 192; Klavdiia Nikolaeva, "Pamiati dorogogo bortsa, liubimogo druga Konkordii Samoilovoi," *Kommunistka*, no. 12–13 (1921): 8–9.

[80] *Revoliutsionnaia deiatel'nost'* . . . *Samoilovoi*, 40–44, 48–50, 62–64; *Bez nikh my ne pobedili by*, 251. For an example of her pamphlets, see K. Samoilova, *Krest'ianka i sovetskaia vlast'* (Moscow, 1921).

show up at meetings to jeer, shout complaints, and make such a commotion that the speaker had to retreat from the podium. More than once Samoilova was silenced in this way. But there were also women who applauded, who came to see Samoilova after a speech to tell her how much they had learned from her, and who gave her presents and appreciative notes as she left.

Thirty-two of these notes remain among her personal papers to provide a glimpse into the reactions of ordinary women to a Zhenotdel leader. "Comrade Samoilova," wrote one female railroad worker, "today is the last day of our meetings with you. You've put so much into our dark souls about that radiant life that we didn't and wouldn't understand. We women workers are sorry that our meetings were so brief, but they will leave a deep mark of consciousness about the building [of socialism]."[81] The submissive language this writer employed was typical of the way the poor, male as well as female, addressed the powerful in Russia. Samoilova might consider herself a revolutionary dedicated to social leveling, but this woman, and many more besides, saw her as one of a new generation of rulers whose good will could be cultivated by emphasizing their greatness and the supplicants' humility.

Samoilova's fans often confessed their ignorance, their "darkness." This word referred not only to their lack of schooling, but also to the fact that they lived in rural places far from the enlightened urban world. One peasant wrote, "You have shown to us dark and blind ones the way to create a free Russia and Soviet republic. Your speech removed a blindfold from the eyes of a dark and blind peasant woman. When I return home I'll try to impress upon our still dark peasant women everything you said and to persuade them to sympathize with and promote the cause of freedom for peasant women."[82]

These workers and peasants praised Samoilova in glowing terms that contrasted their darkness to her saintly illumination. Several emphasized how beautiful she was, both spiritually and physically. "You're a wonderful, rare woman, the likes of whom I've never seen before. If only I could learn a great deal from you," wrote one admirer. Another declared her to be "the first decent woman," making the point that a woman could be liberated from normal social constraints, as they perceived Samoilova to be, and yet not be sexually licentious. Individual admirers requested photographs of her. One group of workers offered to pay her to have her picture taken with them. "We'll look at the picture as if it were a ray of light shining on our poor hut," they wrote.[83]

By endowing this revolutionary woman with the quasi-religious female

[81] RTsKhIDNI, f. 148, op. 1, d. 9, l. 2.   [82] Ibid., l. 20.   [83] Ibid., l. 8.

virtues inherited from former times, Samoilova's humble admirers made sense of her. They contrasted themselves – ignorant, backward peasant women – to her, the "decent," "beautiful," inspirational presence. They denied that she was a devil or a prostitute (charges peasants commonly leveled at Bolshevichki). Instead she figured as a radiant example of womanhood, who made them proud. Exaggerating Samoilova's virtues, her admirers bore witness to the fact that they were impressed to see a woman on a podium, speaking directly to them. On a more personal level they expressed concerns for her health, urging her to dress warmly and take care of herself. For her part, Samoilova no doubt found proposals to turn her into an icon somewhat embarrassing; but they probably also kept her going through all the weeks when more critical women only came to meetings to scream insults. Treasuring her admirers' notes, she kept them and carried them along with her on her travels.

The end of the civil war

In the late summer of 1920, while Samoilova crisscrossed Ukraine, Bosh recuperated in Moscow, Zemliachka terrorized the Crimea, Stasova settled in Tbilisi, and Inessa and Kollontai worked at the Zhenotdel, the Red Army was winning the civil war. The conflict had taken a heavy toll on the Bolshevichki, particularly those of the older generation. They had come to the revolution of 1917 weakened by the stresses of life in the underground and had then endured malnutrition, disease, and extraordinary emotional pressures for three years more. They coped as they had done in the underground: they marshaled their *tverdost*, reaffirmed their commitment to the collective identity, and relied on their friends. Many of them also worked twelve- to fourteen-hour days for weeks on end, not just to win the war but to forge a new Russia from the wreck of the old one. As historian Robert H. McNeal has written of Krupskaia during this time: "Despite chronic ill health, she hurled herself at a furious pace into the impossible task of designing and constructing a humane, cultivated, socialist system of education in a country that was economically ruined."[84]

The strain wore down the health and the spirits of many Bolshevichki, the younger as well as the older. Kollontai had a heart attack in 1919, Bosh's heart disease disabled her the same year, and Stasova suffered a recurrence of tuberculosis in 1920. Most of the individuals of the younger and older generations fell ill at some point during the war years, a few so seriously that they retired permanently. Still others succumbed altogether. Thirteen percent of the Old Bolshevichki and 8 percent of the civil

[84] McNeal, *Bride of the Revolution*, 188.

war generation died between 1917 and 1921, most of infectious diseases such as cholera, typhus, and influenza.

Inessa was one casualty whose decline is well documented. Liudmila Stal remembered noticing in 1919 that Inessa, who had once been so beautiful and elegant, now dressed carelessly in tattered clothes. Throughout the winter of 1919–20, as she drove herself relentlessly to establish the Zhenotdel, she grew more haggard. "She withered before our eyes," wrote Polina Vinogradskaia, a staffer at the Zhenotdel. Worried about her when she did not come to work one cold day in February 1920, Vinogradskaia sought Inessa out at home, only to discover that her boss was living in an unheated apartment, with no food or even fuel to boil water for tea. She was also running a temperature of over 100 —F. As soon as Lenin learned of his friend's illness he wrote anxious letters urging her to take care of herself, but Inessa disregarded his advice and soon contracted pneumonia. She recovered when spring came, at which point she went back to working fourteen-hour days. By mid-summer she was exhausted again. In August 1920, when her sixteen-year-old son Andrei also became ill, Inessa finally agreed to take a vacation on the grounds that she had to look after Andrei. Lenin arranged for them both to stay in a resort hotel in the Caucasus. He also urged her to go on from there to an extended visit in Paris, where she could recover fully.[85]

Inessa and Andrei spent several weeks in Kislovodsk, in a dreary, run-down country house that local party officials had converted into a sanitarium for recuperating Bolsheviks. Avoiding the other guests, even her old friend Liudmila Stal, Inessa tended to her son, went on long walks in the surrounding mountains, and confided in her diary. The first entry, dated 1 September, confessed the toll the war had taken on her:

Passionate feelings remain only for the children and V. I. [Lenin]. It's as if my heart had died to all other relationships. As if having given all my strength, all my passion to V. I. and the cause of work, all the well-springs of love, of feeling for people, which were once so deep, have been drained. I don't have any more personal relationships with people, except for V. I. and my children, only work ones. And people feel this deathliness in me, and they repay me with the same mercenary indifference or even antipathy (and before they loved me). I am a living corpse and this is horrible![86]

[85] The quotation from Vinogradskaia and the observation by Stal appeared in N. K. Krupskaia, ed., *Pamiati Inessy Armand* (Moscow, 1926), 59, 44–45. On her living conditions, see Vinogradskaia, *Pamiatnye vstrechi*, 191–92; Krupskaia, *Pamiati Inessy Armand*, 61–62. On relations with her son Andrei, see the reference in I. F. Armand, *Stat'i, rechi, pis'ma* (Moscow, 1975), 253. For Lenin's letters, see *PSS*, vol. LI, 261, 262, 265, 273.
[86] Quoted in Dmitrii Volkogonov, *Lenin. Politicheskii portret*, 2 vols. (Moscow, 1994), vol. II, 310. Volkogonov was the first to gain access to a few pages of this diary in Inessa's papers at the former Central Party Archives in Moscow (RTsKhIDNI, f. 127). He believes that

Inessa's overwhelming sense of emotional deadness is one of the defining symptoms of depression. Like Stasova after the loss of her father or Bosh at the end of her first military campaign, Inessa felt isolated, distanced from comrades on whom she relied for support. She did not have a psychologist's understanding that depression always creates such aloneness, so she believed that she had become "a living corpse" because she had chosen to dedicate herself completely to the cause. She blamed that absorption in work for stunting the loving side of her nature. "Our life now is a continuous death," she mourned to her diary. "There is no personal life because all time and strength are given to the general cause." She also mourned the fact that she had not spent enough time with her children. "I have gotten weaker about these relationships," she wrote. "I am not at all like the Roman matron who easily sacrificed her children to the interests of the revolution. I cannot." In letters to her daughter Inna written two years earlier, she had confessed that there was strain in her relations with her daughter Varvara and her two sons Fedor and Andrei. They were rebellious adolescents; she was the stern, judgmental mother whom they had seen very little as they were growing up. Now she blamed herself for having neglected them.[87]

The diary also suggests that Inessa was experiencing some sort of crisis in her relationship with Lenin. On 9 September she declared that she had to continue to hide her "secret." On 11 September she wrote, "In my life, love now occupies a large place, forces me to suffer greatly, actually occupies all my thoughts." What had happened between them remains a secret today. All that is certain is that she was once again a frequent guest of Lenin's and Krupskaia's in the winter of 1919–20 and that Lenin wrote her affectionate, gentle letters whenever he learned that she was ill. He had also suggested, as he had done once before, that she leave the place where they had been living in close proximity to one another and go to Paris for a while. Perhaps Inessa once again felt that he had rejected her, this time because of the toll the war had taken on her. She mournfully wrote in her diary: "Since I can't give any more warmth, since I don't radiate this warmth anymore, I cannot give anyone happiness anymore."[88]

Sunk in depression in dismal Kislovodsk, Inessa questioned, but did not renounce, the choices she had made in her life. She confessed feeling

some of it is missing and may have been destroyed. An eyewitness who confirms that Inessa avoided all the other Bolsheviks in the hotel is G. N. Kotov, "Iz vospominanii o t. Inesse i t. Arteme," *Proletarskaia revoliutsiia*, no. 2 (1921): 116.

[87] Volkogonov, *Lenin*, vol. II, 311. For the letters to Inna, see Armand, *Stat'i*, 253–57.

[88] Quoted in Volkogonov, *Lenin*, vol. II, 312. Inessa's Soviet biographer, Pavel Podliashuk, quotes from Lenin's 1920 letters to Inessa in *Tovarishch Inessa*, 3rd ed. (Moscow, 1973), 198–200. On Inessa's frequent visits, see N. K. Krupskaia, *Reminiscences of Lenin*, trans. Bernard Isaacs (New York, 1970), 539.

great guilt because she had put the cause ahead of her children, but then condemned such feelings as a sign of her own "weakness." She affirmed that she still loved Lenin with great "passion," but then, in the last entry she wrote in her diary, on 11 September, she belittled the importance of her desire. "The meaning of love in comparison to a life dedicated to society is very small, not bearing any comparison with a social cause. But this doesn't stop me for a minute from recognizing that however painful it is to me, love, personal attachments, are nothing in comparison with the needs of the battle."[89] These declarations were more than a pathetic attempt to reconcile herself to her situation; they were the credo by which she, and many other Bolshevichki, had lived their lives.

Resting in Kislovodsk, Inessa did not realize that she had very little time left for anguish or regrets. In mid-September a White army neared the town and anxious Bolshevik commanders urged her to leave the area immediately. She bridled at offers of special treatment. They nonetheless insisted, and after a few days she agreed to go with Andrei and several ill patients who had to be evacuated. Traveling in a railway car attached to the train of Bolshevik commander Davydov, the little party spent several days searching for another place in which to settle. They ended up in the town of Nalchik on 21 September. Late that night Inessa came down with cholera, probably contracted from some of the other travelers that she had encountered on her journey; two days later she died.

Perhaps it would have pleased Inessa to know that when her remains were returned to Moscow for internment, Lenin's rectitude deserted him and he let his feelings for her show. He stood at her funeral on Red Square on 11 October 1920, wrapped in a heavy winter coat despite the warmth of the autumn sun, looking so anguished that Kollontai feared he would collapse and embarrass Krupskaia, who stood beside him. His beautiful lover was laid to rest in front of the Kremlin Wall, in the place of highest honor for fallen Bolsheviks.[90]

Eight months later cholera also struck Samoilova. In the spring of 1921 a friend, K. S. Eremeev, asked her to join him on the *Red Star*, an "agitboat" sailing up and down the Volga. The agitators on board stopped off at towns and villages en route to distribute a newspaper they wrote themselves, give speeches, and hold "spectacles" – playlets that dramatized the evils of the old regime and the virtues of the Bolsheviks. Eremeev had just received an important charge – to go south to the mouth of the

---

[89] Quoted in Volkogonov, *Lenin*, vol. II, 312.
[90] Elwood, *Inessa Armand*, 264–66; Marcel Body, "Alexandra Kollontai," *Preuves*, no. 14 (April 1952), 17. This journal, in which for the first time in the West speculation about Lenin's relationship with Inessa was publicized, was a CIA-financed, anti-Soviet publication. See Walter Hixson, *Parting the Curtain: Propaganda, Culture, and the Cold War, 1945–1961* (New York, forthcoming).

river and raise the morale of fishery workers operating there. Food supplies were critically low in the spring of 1921 and it was essential that the catch from the Volga's bountiful waters be preserved quickly for shipment north.

Samoilova did not really want to undertake another difficult journey into a region that was low on food and brimming with epidemic diseases. She had already put in a tour on the *Red Star* in the fall of 1920. Since then, her health weakening, she had decided that she needed to return to a more settled life, and she had applied for reassignment to the Central Zhenotdel. "If you come, it will be wonderful!," a delighted Kollontai wrote back to her in late March 1921. "Then we'll talk about your job . . . I miss you badly in many aspects of the work . . . Waiting for you!"[91] In April Eremeev managed to prevail on Samoilova to postpone her departure from Ukraine for a couple of months so that she could make one more trip on the *Red Star*.

Although they had been told that conditions in the Volga delta were bad, Samoilova and her comrades were not prepared for what they found. Every spring, when sturgeon, pike, bream, vobly, and perch were running in the river, workers cleaned, salted, and packed fish into wooden barrels. Like migrant laborers everywhere, fishery workers in Russia had always been subjected to long hours, low pay, and primitive housing. But the economic collapse of the civil war had made their situation even more wretched. "The revolution, rushing in like a wave of neglect, destroyed the bits of comfort that had existed," wrote L. Katasheva, one of Samoilova's staffers on the *Red Star*. Now most of the fishery workers were desperate peasant women who had fled south with their children to find relief from the famine that was rising upriver. They worked just as long and hard as their predecessors, but on very low food rations. Their famished children passed their days in the filth of ramshackle barracks. Typhus, cholera, dysentery, and pneumonia were rampant. The local Communist Party leaders and soviet officials had thrown up their hands and declared themselves powerless to help.[92]

Samoilova was horrified by what she saw. A year later her colleague Eremeev remembered her distress: "More than once she took me by the hand and led me aside, so the others wouldn't notice, and said 'Konstantin Sergeevich, this is awful! What are they doing? Where's our party?'" She was also very troubled by having to make speeches lauding Bolshevik

---

[91] RTsKhIDNI, f. 148, op. 1, d. 3, ll. 30–31.05. The letter is undated, but internal evidence suggests it was written in late March or April 1921.

[92] L. Katasheva, *Natasha: A Bolshevik Woman Organiser* (London, 193?), 29; Katasheva, "Posledniaia rabota tovarishcha Konkordii Nikolaevny Samoilovoi," *Kommunistka*, no. 14–15 (1921): 28–29; *Revoliutsionnaia deiatel'nost' . . . Samoilovoi*, 30–31.

Plate 21. Peasants assembled to hear a lecture on the agitboat *Red Rose*, 1920. These are the sorts of meetings that Samoilova orgainzed during her trips on the *Red Star*.

accomplishments, but she tried to keep these feelings to herself. "As we left one of the plants," Eremeev wrote, "Konkordiia led me aside and wanted to say something, but tears filled her eyes, and shaking her hands, swallowing her sobs, she kept silent. 'I am . . . going . . . to the ship.' That evening after the meeting and the spectacle, she came up to me and said, 'Well, I've gotten control of myself. I didn't want anyone to notice.' "[93] Somehow she had resumed her hardness, or the appearance of it.

To assuage her distress, Samoilova poured out a series of articles for the ship's newspaper, proposing improvements and calling on local officials to clean up the decay around them. Women workers did not always find this a sufficient response. On 31 May one crowd shouted their anger back at her. Women also poured on board the ship to tell her their personal horror stories and beg for her help.[94] From one of these women, or perhaps from the ship's laundress, Samoilova contracted cholera.

She fell ill on 31 May. Eremeev immediately ordered the boat back to Astrakhan where there were doctors, but Samoilova was too worn down

[93] *Revoliutsionnaia deiatel'nost'* . . . *Samoilovoi*, 31, 32.
[94] Katasheva, "Poslednaia rabota tovarishcha . . . Samoilovoi," 29–30.

by years of overwork to resist the deadly disease. Soon she lapsed into a coma. Two days later she died, murmuring phrases from her speeches: "Red Petrograd, Red Petrograd. The organizational tasks of the department of working women . . . A great book has been closed." Samoilova was buried in Astrakhan on 3 June, in the same grave as her husband.[95]

Samoilova died after the civil war had been won, but during a terrible spring when famine and disease were stalking city and countryside alike. Her despair was widely shared, for the continuing hardships of a nation devastated by six years of war bred a deep pessimism even as the war ended. Many Bolshevichki felt Inessa's depression over the personal costs of the conflict and Samoilova's horror at their inability to end the suffering. Furthermore, the Bolsheviks' hold on power was still tenuous, the tasks before them enormous, and they had given themselves over to arguing about what they should do next.

Many of their arguments concerned the emergence of the party dictatorship, another source of discontent for some Bolshevichki. From the time of the Brest-Litovsk Treaty on, small but vocal opposition groups had coalesced within the party around such issues as the employment of "bourgeois specialists" in the new regime, the presence of tsarist officers in the Red Army, and the erosion of inner-party democracy. Bolshevik leaders usually responded by promising to make reforms and urging the discontented to get back to work for the cause. In the fall of 1920 yet another faction, this one calling itself the Workers' Opposition, originated among Bolsheviks with close ties to the metalworkers', miners', and textile-workers' unions. One of its main leaders was Alexander Shliapnikov, Kollontai's close friend and Bosh's ally in the conflict in Astrakhan. The Workers' Opposition came together to protest what the group perceived as the party leadership's high-handed treatment of the trade unions, and, by extension, of the working class itself. To remedy this situation Shliapnikov proposed a tripartite division of power in which the unions would run industry, the soviets would administer the government, and the party would coordinate their interactions and provide ideological guidance.[96]

As the Workers' Opposition organized in the fall of 1920, Kollontai was named to head the Zhenotdel, succeeding Inessa. Kollontai quickly proved herself, as many had predicted, a less diplomatic leader than her predecessor. Rather than continually reassure the party that she had no separatist intentions, Kollontai proclaimed that the department was going

---

[95] *Revoliutsionnaia deiatel'nost'. . . Samoilovoi*, 36–37; G. Mishkevich, *Konkordiia Nikolaevna Samoilova* (Leningrad, 1947), 41.

[96] On the Workers' Opposition, see Larry E. Holmes, *The Workers' Opposition*, Carl Beck Papers (Pittsburgh, 1990).

Plate 22. From left to right, Klara Zetkin, Klavdiia Nikolaeva, an
unidentified Zhenotdel staffer (standing), and Alexandra Kollontai.
This photograph was probably taken in the summer of 1920, during the
Second Comintern Congress.

to be a women's lobby. Zhenotdel sections, she wrote in *Kommunistka* in
November 1920, "should preserve their independence in bringing cre-
ative tasks to the party; they should set themselves the goal of genuine and
full emancipation of women, while defending their interests as representatives of the sex that is largely responsible for the health and vitality of
future generations." Intent on setting an example of such advocacy,
Kollontai appeared at soviet congresses to decry the paucity of women
among the delegates, protested the fact that there were so few women on
trade union boards, and urged Zhenotdel workers to rally women to set up
daycare centers and public dining rooms on their own.[97]

Kollontai also began to publicize the most controversial ideas of
Marxist feminism, particularly the liberating changes in the structure and
values of the family that would come with the creation of socialism.
Marxists since the founding fathers had argued that revolution would
radically alter the family just as it destroyed property and patriarchy.

[97] A. M. Kollontai, "Zadachi otdelov po rabote sredi zhenshchin," *Kommunistka*, no. 6
(November 1920): 3. On Kollontai's work in the Zhenotdel in the fall of 1920, see
Clements, *Bolshevik Feminist*, 163–77.

When Kollontai declared that the alteration had already begun, she was making no great theoretical or feminist leap. But cautious Bolshevichki – for example, Inessa, Samoilova, and Krupskaia – had always avoided discussing change in the family, because they knew that the topic would stir up angry misunderstandings among rank-and-file communists. Kollontai flung caution to the winds and rhapsodized about a coming world in which everyone would live in communes, women would be free to choose whatever sorts of romantic relationships met their needs, and dedication to the "great laboring family" of the collective would be more important than "ties to relatives."[98] This vision appealed enormously to young Bolshevichki such as Rakhil Kovnator, for it proposed a communal answer to the question of how women could have an unfettered intimate life and still participate in the public world. It annoyed more conventional Bolsheviks, who thought it was silly, if not immoral, even as it provided the Bolsheviks' enemies with more evidence that the Reds intended to destroy civilization itself.

Strengthening the Zhenotdel was Kollontai's primary concern in the fall and early winter of 1920, but she decided to lend her support also to the Workers' Opposition because she was very concerned that the emerging party dictatorship was alienating the working class on which the Bolsheviks and the revolution itself depended. Mobilizing all her formidable powers as a propagandist, Kollontai made a number of stirring speeches and wrote a pamphlet, *The Workers' Opposition*, that eloquently voiced the group's demand for more democracy within and outside the party. She and Shliapnikov then acted as the faction's chief representatives at the Tenth Party Congress in March 1921. But the great majority of the delegates to that assembly, anxious about the party's hold on power, were easily persuaded to support the leadership that had piloted them successfully through the civil war. They voted overwhelmingly for resolutions drafted by Lenin that condemned the proposals of the Workers' Opposition as "anarcho-syndicalist" and rebuked the faction for undermining the unity the party must have to weather the current crisis.[99]

Kollontai returned to the Zhenotdel battered but not broken, even though the attack on her at the Tenth Congress had been unusually demeaning. The Russian Social Democrats' polemics against one another had always been sharp, and had frequently been laced with nasty *ad hominem*s. But when they criticized Kollontai at the party congress, Lenin and Bukharin stooped lower than usual. They insinuated that her criticism of the party's shortcomings did not deserve serious consideration because

[98] A. M. Kollontai, "Sem'ia i kommunizm," *Kommunistka*, no. 7 (December 1920): 19.
[99] On Kollontai's participation in the Workers' Opposition, see Clements, *Bolshevik Feminist*, 178–201.

she was a befuddled, emotional female. Lenin made leering allusions to the fact that Kollontai and Shliapnikov had once been lovers. Bukharin, who must not have read her articles about the family under communism, dismissed Kollontai as a woman given to writing "disgusting, sentimental, Catholic banalities." In a letter to Samoilova shortly after the congress, Kollontai noted how unpleasant these attacks had been. But she remained defiant. "You will hear," she wrote, "how much stir has been made by the Workers' Opposition and by my pamphlet, harshly criticized by Lenin, who threw thunder and lightning at it. But such struggle, even when it takes the ugly form of personal attacks, always inspires me, especially when you are fighting for something you strongly believe in." Rather than anger or humiliation, she felt sadness. "I'm grieved by something else: the general aggravating atmosphere and the sad story of Kronstadt, which we could have prevented but never did, thanks to our [illegible word] unwillingness to take the sentiment of the masses into account. All around the atmosphere is depressing. There are splits in the party that are growing ever wider. All this is extremely difficult."[100]

Unlike Stasova after political defeat, Kollontai did not flee to the Caucasus. Unlike Bosh, she did not retreat into retirement. She did scale back her public advocacy for the Workers' Opposition after the Tenth Party Congress so as to concentrate on being a forceful leader of the Zhenotdel in the fall. She had to spend considerable time in an effort fighting to save the department; party leaders in the provinces were transferring its staff to other assignments, and many Zhenotdel workers had become so demoralized by the difficulties of their work that they were ready to quit it altogether.[101]

As Kollontai struggled to rally her troops, Lenin continued his efforts to destroy the Workers' Opposition. He concentrated his fire on the male leaders of the faction. Kollontai, as he knew, had never been a member of the inner circle of this group of unionists, and she had not been involved in the politics that sustained it. However, his tolerance toward her ended when, in early 1922, the news arrived that she had sent her pamphlet, *The Workers' Opposition*, abroad to be published by socialists critical of the Bolsheviks. In late January or early February 1922 Kollontai received the news that she had been removed as head of the Zhenotdel. She then flung herself back into supporting the Workers' Opposition, defending it and demanding reform in the party at a meeting of the Comintern Executive

---

[100] RTsKhIDNI, f. 148, op. 1, d. 3, ll. 30.05–31. Bukharin's attack on Kollontai is recorded in KPSS, *Desiatyi s"ezd RKP(b). Stenograficheskii otchet* (Moscow, 1963), 325; Lenin's is in *PSS*, vol. XLIII, 34–50. An uprising against the Bolsheviks took place in February 1921 at the Baltic naval base of Kronstadt.
[101] Clements, *Bolshevik Feminist*, 202–13.

Committee in late February and at the Eleventh Party Congress in March. In both forums the Workers' Opposition was rebuked for breaking the rules against factionalism that had been passed by the Tenth Congress the year before. Lenin attempted to get Shliapnikov and Kollontai expelled from the party, the most drastic punishment he could impose on them, but the delegates to the Eleventh Congress would agree only to put the two Old Bolsheviks on notice that should they engage in factional activities again, they would be expelled.[102]

Thus when spring came in 1922, Kollontai found herself without a job and shunned by her comrades. Her defiance at last began to ebb. "Expulsion from the collective has always been and remains the harshest and most terrible punishment for a person," she wrote mournfully in an article published in September 1922. She attempted to take refuge in her personal life, traveling to Odessa to see her estranged husband, Pavel Dybenko, but there she found that he was living happily with another woman. In mid-summer Kollontai wrote to Stalin, now party secretary, to request a new assignment. He replied he would find her a post in the Soviet foreign service. It was a banishment, although one less humiliating than that meted out to Stasova two years before. In early October Kollontai, having received an appointment to a Soviet trade delegation to Norway, headed off to begin a long and distinguished diplomatic career.[103]

By the time Kollontai left Russia for Norway, most of the prominent Old Bolshevichki had faded from public view. Inessa and Samoilova were dead. Krupskaia was still with Lenin, but she was living on an estate outside Moscow, nursing her husband through his recovery from the first of a series of strokes that would lead to his death in 1924. Stasova was in Berlin, working with German communists. Bosh was recuperating in Italy. Only Zemliachka, once more a leader in the Moscow party organization, was prospering. Unlike the exiled Bolshevichki, Zemliachka knew how to cultivate male allies, and she was an enthusiastic defender of the party's autocratic tendencies.

It would be a mistake, however, to see Kollontai, Stasova, or even Zemliachka as representative of the entire brigade of Bolshevichki at the end of the civil war. Alexandra Artiukhina and Klavdiia Nikolaeva, the textile worker and the printer, were in fact more typical of the older generation. In 1922 Artiukhina was in Tver, heading the Zhenotdel in that city. She had spent the civil war in various posts as she moved with her husband, Mikhail Artiukhin, from one front to another. Nikolaeva had

[102] Ibid., 205–20.
[103] A. Kollontai, "Pis'ma k triudiashcheisia molodezhi. Pis'mo vtoroe: Moral', kak orudie klassovogo gospodstva i klassovoi bor'by," *Molodaia gvardiia*, no. 6–7 (1922): 132; Clements, *Bolshevik Feminist*, 221–24.

remained in Petrograd throughout the war, working primarily on organizing women. She was the original leader of the Zhenotdel in that city and had made it, by 1922, one of the largest, most activist, and most successful of the regional departments. Unlike Stasova, Zemliachka, and Bosh, Artiukhina and Nikolaeva had not aspired to national leadership and had not taken up the cause of any opposition group. Rather, they had worked hard, changed their perceptions and values in tune with the collective identity as it twisted and turned through the civil war, and hoped for better times.[104]

Those times appeared to be coming as 1922 drew to an end. With the war over, the political and economic situation in Russia began to improve. At the Tenth Congress the party had inaugurated a series of taxation measures, known collectively as the New Economic Policy, that permitted a limited free market in grain. Because the government thereby eased pressures on the peasants and because the war was now at an end, the food supply improved. Reconstruction of damaged factories and railways also began, and the crisis atmosphere eased. If the illusions the older generation had once cherished about itself as a happy band of brothers and hard sisters, leading an appreciative working class, had begun to seem somewhat naive, there were new satisfactions to be derived from being the powerful leaders of a monumental experiment in social engineering. Furthermore, the revolution and the civil war had intensified the Bolshevichki's commitment to the "great stern family" of the party by strengthening the bonds of shared belief and experience, the sense of embattlement, and the faith in their own righteousness that lay at the core of their collective identity. It was, more than anything else, this martial ethos that the younger generation imbibed in their formative years as communists.

In 1922 the personal prospects of those Bolshevichki who still had their health and who accepted the party's growing power shone brightly. Women of the older generation could seek out important but far less taxing jobs. Those of the younger could explore their opportunities for education and valuable work. As Stasova, Bosh, and Kollontai retreated from the "collective," the "great stern family" with which they had quarreled, tens of thousands of Bolshevichki of less disputatious and independent temper set to work to build a new social order. To those who would subscribe to the collective identity and conform to the general will, the future promised great rewards.

[104] On Artiukhina, see *Oktiabriem mobilizovannye*, 117–19. On Nikolaeva, see *Zhenshchiny russkoi revoliutsii*, 302.

5 The ruling class

When the civil war ended, the Bolshevichki could turn their attention to building socialism. Many of them, especially the younger generation, set about it with great enthusiasm. The 1920s, christened the NEP decade after the New Economic Policy introduced at the Tenth Party Congress in 1921, was a time of experiments inspired by the utopian prospects the revolution had opened. Young people organized communes; artists, filmmakers, architects, and designers created a vibrant avant garde; workers and peasants flocked into the schools and into white-collar jobs; pilots flew Soviet aircraft through the skies, and Soviet explorers mushed toward the North Pole. In all these many pioneering ventures, women, particularly the women of the Communist Party, were heavily involved. Their personal successes supported their belief that they were building a bright new world.

Some of the veterans of the underground, Kollontai, Bosh, and Stasova for example, were not so sanguine. They saw the new world as already deeply compromised by party policies that they regarded as corrupted by craven concessions to the peasantry and bourgeoisie. NEP did work; it encouraged the peasants to rebuild agriculture and permitted the existence of small businesses (such as restaurants) so as to restore the consumer economy. But more radical, irreconcilable Bolsheviks, Bosh for example, considered both the grain policy and the legalization of private enterprise to be betrayals of sacred socialist principles. Equally galling to Stasova and Kollontai was the fact that the government, now their government, was still staffed by many of the people who had worked in the tsar's bureaucracy. In the view of leftist Bolsheviks, all these holdovers from the old regime were making the new Soviet government just as intrusive, cumbersome, and witlessly inefficient as its Russian predecessors. Meanwhile, the workers were suffering. Throughout the mid-1920s there were more of them looking for work than there was work to be had, so unemployed people walked the streets of Petrograd and Moscow just as they did those of London and Rome, while the bureaucrats scuttled off to do whatever they did in their paper-filled offices.

Nor did changes within their own movement give disillusioned Bolshe-vichki much cause for hope. The party spent the years 1922 to 1928 locked in a conflict orchestrated by its leaders. Outwardly at issue were economic policy and party government, but behind the discussions of how to industrialize Soviet Russia and run the party, a struggle for personal power was going on in the Politburo. Stalin, Bukharin, and their supporters advocated a gradualist approach to the construction of socialism, while the opposition, a shifting coalition led by Trotsky and belatedly joined by Zinoviev and Kamenev, favored more rapid industrialization. The opposi-tion also took up the charge that the party was excessively centralized and bureaucratized. These debates were fought in typically Bolshevik fashion, with no-holds-barred polemic, but now polemic could be joined to attacks more materially damaging in the sense that they might result in the transfer, demotion, or firing of functionaries who took minority positions. As Stalin's supporters used these means to consolidate their power in the mid-and late 1920s, they consolidated as well the party's dictatorship over its own members. From Moscow to the extreme perimeters of the country, submission to the authority of one's superiors became the order of the day. The political police (which changed its name from Cheka to OGPU) participated enthusiastically in enforcing obedience, extending its man-date to include keeping an eye on communists.

These developments did not make the party into the highly disciplined army that its propagandists conjured up with martial metaphors in the press of the 1920s. Rather, it remained a congeries of cells, committees, and bureaus, unified formally by hierarchical principles of organization and by a multitude of ritualized displays of obedience, but bound together as well, as it had always been and as most political groups are, by alliances based on shared interests, kinship, and friendship. Officials in provinces and cities set themselves up as powerful figures in their own bailiwicks and then dealt with their superiors by supporting, advising, cajoling, deceiving, or avoiding them. Recently, critics have likened the Soviet Communist Party to the Sicilian mafia, for they see both as built on family ties and naked self-interest ruthlessly pursued. The party bore still greater similarity to the regime of the tsars, for it too was becoming in the 1920s a powerful autocracy obeyed, supplicated, and manipulated by its subjects. The tsarist and the Soviet regimes were likewise capable and willing, when roused, of striking at the people they ruled with lethal effect. This Communist Party at the head of this sort of state was very far from the vision of the post-revolutionary world Stasova and Bosh had long cherished.[1]

[1] Much has been written about the power struggles of the 1920s, but the classic remains Robert Vincent Daniels, *The Conscience of the Revolution: Communist Opposition in Soviet Russia*, reprint ed. (Boulder, Colo., 1988).

Of course the collective identity changed along with the party, enabling people more reconcilable than Bosh to adjust their understandings to the new realities. The egalitarian ways of the underground, fashioned in opposition to autocracy, had been shoved aside by more martial mores during the civil war. The elements of the old identity that remained strong into the 1920s were primarily definitions of personal revolutionary integrity: dedication to the cause; scorn for the pursuit of individual advancement and material gain; respect for intellectual accomplishment, particularly in Marxist theory; openmindedness with regard to personal life; and experimental attitudes toward social engineering and cultural expression. All these were still honored Bolshevik ideals, although during the 1920s many younger communists came to see them as quaint and increasingly irrelevant characteristics of an older generation. Late in the 1920s, as party harassment of the intelligentsia escalated into persecution, official definitions of the collective identity depreciated still further the older ideals of personal character once sprung from the intelligentsia. Instead, they emphasized ever more the hard virtues which had always coexisted with the others, particularly dedication, subordination, and renunciation of the individual will.

Scholars, viewing these developments from a distance, have suggested that they were virtually inevitable, given the circumstances of the 1920s. A poorly educated new elite, largely drawn from the ranks of the working class and the peasantry, was bound to fall back on conformity, indoctrination, and coercion. Scholars have also pointed to the fact that adjustments of underground values are inevitable when any political movement gains power, and that such adjustments will most probably involve a diminution of democracy, even in movements more democratic than the Bolsheviks had ever been. It remains to be noted that such changes, when they occur in organizations full of inexperienced people operating in nations with long histories of autocratic politics, are particularly ominous for women, since authoritarianism has been aligned with patriarchalism everywhere in human history. The more stress there was on hierarchy and order in the party, the more certain it was that notions about women's equality would suffer. That process had already begun during the Russian civil war. It would continue, indeed accelerate, in the 1920s and 1930s.[2]

Bolshevichki such as Stasova and Kollontai found the alteration of the movement they had once idealized profoundly depressing. Instead of readily accepting the revised version of the collective identity that

---

[2] For recent discussions of the relationship between party and society in the 1920s, see Lewis H. Siegelbaum, *Soviet State and Society Between Revolutions, 1918–1929* (Cambridge, 1992), and Sheila Fitzpatrick, Alexander Rabinowitch, and Richard Stites, eds., *Russia in the Era of NEP* (Bloomington, Ind., 1991).

validated the new order, they and many other Old Bolsheviks looked to their long-held Marxist beliefs for reassuring explanations of the train of events. History moved relentlessly, they told themselves, driven forward by the behavior of the masses. The party was an epiphenomenon, a world-historical means to an end, history's current driver. A bad driver might cause an automobile to career down a road, but his incompetence did not mean that the car itself was defective – to borrow a metaphor that Bukharin employed in the late 1920s. Nor did it mean that the car's passengers were on the wrong road. Of course, the driver might smash up both car and passengers by plowing into a ditch; but Bukharin, Kollontai, Stasova, and many other Bolsheviks believed that the growth of the Soviet Union in the 1920s showed that history was not heading for a ditch but was instead pointing toward the communist future, despite some veering around en route. Kollontai rued the development of the party dictatorship, but she laid its origins to the dictatorial temperaments of all the party leaders, and to the still more powerful fact that the revolution had occurred in a country with a long history of autocracy and a great mass of traditionalist peasants. These realities had to have their effect, she argued; but the revolution had been made not by the leaders but by the workers, and, despite all obstacles, they were busy building a new world even while their leaders squabbled. History would eventually make everything right. It is probable that Stasova shared many of these thoughts, although we do not know it because as usual she kept her critical thoughts discreetly to herself. Both Kollontai and Stasova, having felt the wrath of the Politburo in the early 1920s, gave the controversies of a few years later a wide berth.[3]

Bolshevichki in the power struggle

At the lower ranks of the party, most Bolshevichki were probably as uninvolved in the infighting that absorbed the new party hierarchy as were Stasova and Kollontai, but they did participate in the public displays of the struggle, that is, in the denunciations that formalized the rout of the oppositionists. The great majority of Bolshevichki working in the party during the 1920s were in agitprop jobs, so it fell to them to organize meetings at which the opposition was excoriated. "I led various lectures and discussions during the time of the Trotskyite bloc and the right deviations," remembered Anna Bits, a one-time brewery worker who was

---

[3] On Kollontai, see Barbara Evans Clements, *Bolshevik Feminist: The Life of Aleksandra Kollontai* (Bloomington, Ind., 1979), 247–48. Bukharin made his observation about cars and drivers to Abdurakhman Avtorkhanov in 1928. See Avtorkhanov's *Stalin and the Soviet Communist Party: A Study in the Technology of Power* (New York, 1959), 210–11.

a factory librarian in the late 1920s.[4] Bolshevichki also served on party control commissions and purge commissions, bodies that investigated charges against those accused of opposition activities. Any participation in a group critical of party policies could be construed as a violation of the ban on forming factions, a disciplinary infraction that warranted expulsion from the party. Bolshevichki seem to have participated quite substantially as members of the control commissions: 46 percent of the older generation did such work in the 1920s and early 1930s. They probably did not determine who would be punished, those decisions having already been made by the party bosses, but they did attend the services of excommunication.

How many Bolshevichki participated in the opposition and what happened to them as a result are very difficult to determine. Much of the history of the political battles of the 1920s, particularly in local party organizations, has yet to be written because the necessary archival records have been inaccessible until recently. Scattered evidence suggests that women who publicly supported the opposition were subject to the penalty most commonly meted out to men, that is, they were fired from their jobs. For example, Olga Shatunovskaia, a Bolshevichka since 1916 who was stationed in Azerbaidzhan in the late 1920s, drew Stalin's fire for an article in which she praised an Azeri communist whom Stalin considered an enemy. The General Secretary ordered Molotov to see that she was transferred back to Moscow. More prominent cases include that of Klavdiia Nikolaeva, the printer from Petrograd, who was removed from the headship of the Zhenotdel in 1925, probably because she supported Zinoviev, under whom she had worked in the Petrograd party organization. Another well-known Bolshevichka, Varvara Iakovleva, a Moscow communist, lost her post as deputy commissar of education in 1929 because she had backed Bukharin in his struggles with Stalin in the late 1920s.[5]

The passages through the power struggles of the 1920s of three of the most prominent Bolshevichki – Krupskaia, Bosh, and Zemliachka – are more fully documented. These three, unlike Stasova and Kollontai, did not avoid the conflict but instead plunged into it. Their instincts and their principles led them, however, onto very different paths, with the consequence that two of them ended their political careers forever, while one emerged victorious to join the ranks of Stalin's leadership.

[4] RTsKhIDNI, f. 124, op. 1, d. 195, l. 4.
[5] On Shatunovskaia, see Lars T. Lih, Oleg V. Naumov, and Oleg V. Khlevniuk, eds., *Stalin's Letters to Molotov, 1925–1936* (New Haven, Conn., 1995), 167–68. On Nikolaeva, see *Slavnye bol'shevichki* (Moscow, 1958), 236. On Iakovleva, see Roy Medvedev, *Let History Judge*, eds. David Joravsky and Georges Haupt, trans. Colleen Taylor (New York, 1973), 292.

Bosh returned to Moscow in the late winter of 1923, her heart disease in abeyance after treatment in Germany and rest in the warmth of Italy and Greece. Hoping to go back to Ukraine, she requested an assignment in the countryside, working with the peasants. While she waited for a response from the Secretariat, she moved in with her daughters Olga and Mariia in Moscow and began writing a history of 1917 in Kiev. Bosh's attitudes toward the developments within the party and the nation had not been softened by her sojourn abroad. Within a few months, she had again made common cause with her old friend Iurii Piatakov.[6]

In October 1923, Bosh signed the "Petition of the Forty-Six," a manifesto drafted by Piatakov and his friend Evgenii Preobrazhenskii, the leftist communist who had been one of Stasova's three successors as party secretaries. The petitioners criticized the party leadership, then in the hands of Zinoviev, Kamenev, Stalin, and Bukharin, for pursuing inept economic policies while stifling inner-party debate. "Under the external form of official unity," they wrote, "a narrow circle" was making all decisions. Consequently, "free discussion within the party in fact has disappeared." The petition called for a party conference to discuss issues more openly. It also espoused systematic economic planning, implied that more attention should be paid to the industrial workers and less to the peasants, and criticized the leadership for fostering bureaucracy and stifling the independence of lower-ranking communists. It was signed by forty-six members from the Bolshevik old guard, an assortment of people who had differed politically in the past but now agreed on the need for democratization. The two female signatories were Bosh and Varvara Iakovleva.[7]

After she signed, Bosh withdrew, but this time less completely than she had done in the past. She did not join Piatakov or Preobrazhenskii in writing articles or making speeches critical of Zinoviev, Kamenev, or Stalin, but she did remain in the debate in a way that was discreet but unmistakable. She began to publish a history of events in Ukraine in the period 1917–18 which argued that the Bolsheviks of the south had been defeated because of their leaders' incompetence. In a series of articles published in 1924, Bosh portrayed the Kiev party committee and the commanders in Antonov-Ovseenko's army as ignorant, irresolute to the point of cowardice, and distrustful of the working class. She also portrayed them as obsessed with their feuds with one another; those who held some power quickly became puffed up by their own authority and grabbed onto

---

[6] E. Preobrazhenskii, "Evgeniia Bogdanovna Bosh," *Proletarskaia revoliutsiia*, no. 2 (1925): 14.

[7] Trotsky Archive, Houghton Library, Harvard University, T-802. This is a typescript of the petition.

Plate 23. Evgeniia Bosh, early 1925. A picture of Lenin hangs on the wall behind her.

the trappings of officialdom, piling arrogance onto all their other inadequacies.[8]

Bosh told story after damning story to illustrate her thesis. Particularly effective was her account of her interview with a Red Army colonel whose train pulled into her headquarters town one day in March 1918. The Germans were advancing; Bosh was trying to hold her dispirited troops together. The colonel, resplendent in a bright new uniform, had come to receive a report from her on the situation in her sector and, she hoped, to tell her when she could expect supplies and reinforcements. He ushered her into his railroad car, which, Bosh declared, looked like "a lady's boudoir," complete with red velvet settees. The place reeked of cologne. The colonel, "a former SR," apologized for the smell, then confided that

[8] Bosh wrote a book, *God bor'by*, excerpts from which she then published as E. Bosh, "Oblastnoi partiinyi komitet s.-d. (bol'shevikov) Iugo-Zapadnogo kraia, 1917 g.," *Proletarskaia revoliutsiia*, no. 5 (1924): 128–49; Bosh, "Oktiabr'skie dni v Kievskoi oblasti," *Proletarskaia revoliutsiia*, no. 11 (1923): 52–67. She also wrote two articles about her participation in antiwar activities during World War I: Bosh, "Vospominaniia uchastnikov Bernskoi konferentsii," *Proletarskaia revoliutsiia*, no. 5 (1925): 179–93; Bosh, "Vstrechi i besedy s Vladimirom Il'ichem," *Proletarskaia revoliutsiia*, no. 3 (1924): 155–73. In these latter pieces she argues that she had never had serious disagreements with Lenin. *God bor'by* was published in Moscow in 1925.

he was using it to block out the odors emanating from the enlisted men billeted in the next car. He also told her that she could expect neither supplies nor reinforcements. Then he ushered her out of his velvet room and chugged away.[9]

The criticism Bosh leveled against the Bolshevik leaders of the civil war era was, of course, the same criticism she was making of the Bolshevik leaders of NEP. She believed that they too were out of touch with the people, self-interested, and excessively eager to fatten on the perquisites of office. She did not make these connections explicitly in her work, but she knew that any informed reader would do so. Hashing over others' mistakes in the past in order to discredit them in the present was an oft-used weapon in the feuding leaders' arsenals. Zinoviev and Trotsky were dueling through alternative accounts of party history at the same time. Bosh made a strong case for the proposition that the communists had been prone to the very sins five years earlier that were leading them into present-day corruption. The book that was the final product of her study, *God bor'by*, was also a serious work of historical scholarship that remains an important source on the revolution in Ukraine today.

Bosh's mood in all her writings was dark, brooding, Cassandra-like; her withering critique of Bolshevik mistakes was unrelieved by any rays of hope that the failings she enumerated would be remedied. As the opposition, a minority even within the party leadership, fought its losing battles in 1924, her depression deepened. Furthermore, the assignment she had requested from the Secretariat was not forthcoming, undoubtedly because of her affiliation with the opposition. By early 1925 Bosh had not held a meaningful job in five years, and she could see no prospects ahead that the situation would ever improve, unless she took what she saw as the hypocrite's course, recanted her criticism, and endorsed the Stalin–Bukharin leadership. That she was unwilling to do. In January 1925, Trotsky was forced to resign from his position at the head of the Red Army, a particularly humiliating surrender that demonstrated the rising power of Stalin. Shortly after she heard that news, Bosh decided to withdraw once and for all from party politics. She committed suicide.

The major newspapers took little notice of her death, but Evgenii Preobrazhenskii published a long obituary in the journal *Proletarskaia revoliutsiia* in which he praised Bosh as one of the heroes of the revolution. "In her character she was made of that steel that is broken but not bent," Preobrazhenskii wrote, "but all these virtues were not cheap. She had to

[9] The account of the perfumed colonel is in Bosh, *God bor'by*, 207. A group of Bosh's comrades from Ukraine published this book after her death.

pay dearly, pay with her peace of mind, her health, and her life. Her health was weak and she paid to the full, with her life."[10]

Preobrazhenskii's reference to steel when eulogizing Bosh had special meaning. Steel had become a symbol of modernity in the late nineteenth century, for the metal was not only vital materially to the building of modern factories and war machines, it also possessed all the qualities admired by "modern" people, among whom the Bolsheviks enthusiastically numbered themselves. Steel was strong and durable, that is, hard, but it was also, unlike the iron from which it was crafted, extremely malleable. Steel's shining qualities had obvious appeal to the Bolsheviks, who prided themselves on being both hard and flexible. It had so appealed to young Iosif Dzhugashvili that he made himself a grandiloquent underground alias from it, Stalin, meaning, in Russian, the Man of Steel. Preobrazhenskii was indirectly alluding to Stalin when he wrote that Bosh was also steel, but that she did not bend. There was, he implied in an obvious reference to the General Secretary, a kind of steel that could be too readily shaped to the possibilities of the moment.

Krupskaia had always been more flexible than Bosh, and so she managed to survive her despair. It was easier for her to countenance developments that drove Bosh to depression because she had not opposed the growing power of the party and, within it, the Politburo during the civil war. Instead, Krupskaia had seen the power of the center as necessary to the success of the revolution. She shared Lenin's views, as she had always done. Indeed, supporting Lenin became the chief mission of Krupskaia's life in the 1920s. When he suffered his first stroke in 1922, she left her work at Narkompros to nurse him on an estate outside Moscow. It was a sad duty, for over the next two years her husband was never well again. A series of additional strokes left him progressively more incapacitated until finally he died in January 1924.

Krupskaia took on herself the duty of tending to Lenin as well as mediating his contact with the other members of the Politburo, among whom Stalin was coming to rank ever higher. She did not like Stalin, in no small measure because he treated her dismissively, refusing to honor her as a revolutionary who had been at the center of party life when he was still a seminarian in Georgia. For his part Stalin suspected Krupskaia of plotting against him. She probably did not do so during Lenin's illness, for she had never been a plotter and was too absorbed in trying to keep her

---

[10] Preobrazhenskii, "Bosh," 16. That Bosh had committed suicide was widely known, despite the fact that it was not officially announced in the press. See Victor Serge and Natalia Sedova Trotsky, *The Life and Death of Leon Trotsky*, trans. Arnold J. Pomerans (New York, 1975), 132; Alexander Solzhenitsyn, *The Gulag Archipelago*, trans. Thomas P. Whitney, 3 vols. (New York, 1975), vol. II, 680.

Plate 24. Nadezhda Krupskaia in the 1920s.

husband alive to bother about much else. But she knew better than anyone that Lenin had grown very critical of Stalin in his last days. When Lenin died, Krupskaia became one of the keepers of his memory, a person who could speak with his voice, should she choose to.[11]

She did so reluctantly and cautiously. Krupskaia was fifty-five years old in 1924, exhausted by her vigil at Lenin's bedside and bereft without him. Her own health had not been good for years, for she suffered from chronic thyroid disease. She did not want to get involved in the leadership's fights; that had never been her preference even in the underground, where she had often played the role of reconciler. In 1924 she wanted to go back to her work at Narkompros, and that is basically what she did, although she publicly expressed support for her old friends Zinoviev and Kamenev both before and after Lenin's death. She also tried, somewhat naively, again to be a peacemaker, urging the party's leaders to resolve their quarrels.

But Krupskaia, like Stasova and Kollontai, was concerned about the

[11] Robert H. McNeal, *Bride of the Revolution: Krupskaia and Lenin* (Ann Arbor, Mich., 1972), 218–28.

power Stalin was gathering to himself, and so when the alliance between him and Zinoviev came apart in 1925, she stepped more resolutely forward to support Zinoviev. She was also motivated by her concern that the agricultural policies promoted by Stalin's new ally, Bukharin, would unnecessarily delay progress in industrialization. For ten months Krupskaia argued for more inner-party democracy and against the current economic decisions, bolstering her case by invoking Lenin's authority. The Politburo retaliated with the same treatment meted out to other oppositionists – shunning and heckling, and polemics in the press and at party meetings. Someone also began a whispering campaign about Lenin's marital infidelities in which Stasova, Zemliachka, Artiukhina, and, of course, Inessa, were named as his lovers. Stalin had often snidely commented about Krupskaia, remarking, for example, that "sleeping with Lenin doesn't mean you understand Leninism." Now he and his supporters were suggesting that Krupskaia was not the only woman who had shared the bed of the dead hero.[12]

One cannot help noting that, once again, references to a Bolshevichka's sexuality were being employed to delegitimate her political criticism. At the Tenth Party Congress, Lenin had referred sneeringly to Kollontai's relationship with Shliapnikov and indirectly to her reputation as a beautiful woman who had led an active sex life. Now other Old Bolsheviks, perhaps Stalin and Bukharin themselves, were denigrating Krupskaia by implying that her husband had been unfaithful. If Lenin and Krupskaia had not been a particularly close couple, then her claims to understand how he would have reacted to current developments were bogus. The rumors also suggested that Krupskaia, a woman who was not beautiful, had not had the sexual power to keep her husband interested in her. It was a time-honored strategy to strike at a woman by pointing out transgressions or shortcomings in her sexuality. By contrast, criticisms of male oppositionists went to the wrongheadedness of their ideas and their political mistakes in the past. Stalin and Bukharin did not stoop to trample upon Zinoviev's sexual prowess, or lack thereof.

Krupskaia remained defiant despite the attempts to humiliate her, but by the fall of 1926 she had come to realize that the opposition was being beaten into submission. In November she announced that she was withdrawing her support from it. She never recanted her criticism, however, unlike other prominent oppositionists, probably because Stalin could only bring limited pressure to bear on her. She was, after all, the revered Lenin's widow. Stalin probably also knew quite well that Krupskaia was not a threat to him. Molotov summed up the attitude of the men

---

[12] Feliks Chuev, *Sto sorok besed s Molotovym* (Moscow, 1991), 212.

around Stalin when he told an interviewer decades later, "Krupskaia followed Lenin around her entire life, before the revolution and afterwards, and in fact she didn't understand politics." The truth was that she had never liked politics and was always relieved to withdraw from it. Krupskaia went back to Narkompros, where she worked for another eleven years to build a socialist educational system.[13]

Zemliachka was Stalin's kind of steel. Like him, she emerged from the power struggles of the 1920s neither beaten nor bowed. Back in Moscow in 1921, Zemliachka secured an appointment as secretary of the party committee in the Zamoskvoretskii raion of the city. She worked there for a year or so, then went off to the northern Caucasus, where she became a propagandist in a provincial committee. From this assignment she moved on to the Urals, to serve there as a propagandist. All these posts were extensions of her civil war work into the peacetime situation: Zemliachka was responsible for training subordinates, supervising the production of pamphlets, and holding lectures and classes among factory workers. It was work typically given to Bolshevichki in the 1920s, and Zemliachka was unusually successful, winning promotion after promotion.[14]

One secret of her success was that she became a stalwart backer of the party leadership. Indeed, she built a reputation as one of the most unbending of all the hard Bolsheviks who came to power under Stalin. In the 1920s, Zemliachka applied her propaganda skills to rallying party members and factory workers to denounce the opposition. She summarized the results of one of her campaigns with great satisfaction in an undated report from 1926 or 1927: "During the discussion the opposition got only one vote from a member of a Soviet cell. Last summer the party organization unanimously moved to expel Trotsky from the party."[15]

Zemliachka's decision to join the party majority, although very advantageous to her personally, did not spring from simple opportunism. She had always been the sort of Bolshevik to whom Stalin appealed because she shared his Manichean view of the world as a place of deadly struggle between allies and enemies. She thrived on confrontation, and she had little taste for compromise. The feuding within the party had bothered her before the revolution, but mostly because she saw her comrades as too indecisive and accommodating. Zemliachka thus took readily to the world

---

[13] McNeal, *Bride of the Revolution*, 237–64. Molotov is quoted in Chuev, *Sto sorok besed s Molotovym*, 211.
[14] *Slavnye bol'shevichki*, 147–48.
[15] R. S. Zemliachka, "Kak otnosiatsia opozittsiiami partiinye i bezpartiinye massy," RTsKhIDNI, f. 90, op. 1, d. 98, ll. 1–24.

conjured up by the new leaders, a world of mortal combat in which enemies lurked within as well as outside the party.

That the party had to become more like an army, hierarchical and autocratic, in order to fight this war bothered Zemliachka not at all. She accepted the mission of building an organization honed to military sharpness in order to fulfill its historical mission, and she rose in the command structure. In 1927, two years after Bosh's death, less than a year after Krupskaia's withdrawal from the opposition, Zemliachka left the Urals to take an appointment in the Central Control Commission, a party agency charged with maintaining discipline and investigating complaints of dereliction of duty. In the late 1920s the control commissions were rooting out oppositionists, so Zemliachka's promotion to department head in that organization meant that she had achieved the rank of senior enforcer of party discipline. It was a role she would continue to play for the rest of her career, one that would keep her near the top of the organization and win her eventually the distinction of being the only woman to serve on the Council of People's Commissars under Stalin.[16]

Bosh and Krupskaia, who had always participated in party politics, engaged with greater or less enthusiasm in the power struggles of the 1920s. Bolshevichki who usually had shrunk from such engagement withdrew, with Stasova and Kollontai, into acquiescence. Others, like Zemliachka, supported the new leadership. Such support was probably stronger in the younger generation of Bolshevichki, for they had been brought up in a party far more autocratic than the underground one had been. For communists in their twenties in the 1920s, the party leaders were not men whose deficiencies they had come to know through years of close association; rather, they were distant, powerful figures whom the young were taught to follow unquestioningly. Most of the party's spokespeople urged that Stalin and his various allies were reasonable leaders who understood how to build socialism in Russia. The very real, very rapid changes occurring in the new society buttressed this argument.

Bolshevichki in the new regime

The party's messengers and the evidence before their own eyes persuaded many Bolshevichki to take a view of Soviet society in the 1920s that was very different from Bosh's unmitigated gloom or Stasova's private doubts. For every Kollontai who deplored the changes in the party, there were many younger women who believed that all that they had done so quickly

---

[16] Zemliachka's attitudes in the late 1920s are expressed in an unpublished article, "Vospominanie o vtorom s"ezde i biuro komiteta bol'shinstva," RTsKhIDNI, f. 90, op. 1, d. 123, ll. 1–6. Internal evidence suggests the article was written in 1927 or 1928.

– the opening up of education to the lower classes, the promoting of working-class and peasant people into positions of authority, the assault on the influence of the Church and traditional customs, the creation of radically new artistic ideas – showed that the USSR was leading the world toward a future of plenty and justice. The extraordinary progress women themselves had made was another sign, a very important one to young Bolshevichki. In a poem entitled "Our Joy," published in *Rabotnitsa* in 1926, Elena Chernysheva praised in ecstatic tones the liberation women were enjoying:

> At times you don't believe your eyes.
> Is this a dream? What is this?
> A woman worker, and in the prosecutor's office,
> A charwoman, and in a *rabfak*.[17]

Earlier generations of young people living in revolutionary times had also rhapsodized about their feeling of being present at the creation of a new world. Wordsworth had spoken for all of them when he had written of the days of the French Revolution, "Bliss was it in that dawn to be alive, / But to be young was very Heaven!"[18] Chernysheva shared this buoyant sense of limitless possibilities; she ended her poem with the happy thought, "This is only our morning of the communist day."

Chernysheva believed differently from Bosh because she was too young to feel nostalgia for the Bolsheviks' lost innocence. Her unjaundiced eyes looked past the bureaucrats, laid-off workers, and OGPU agents that crowded Moscow's dirty streets and saw instead that women were living under a government that offered them more liberation than any other on earth. In only a few years they had left behind an old world in which they could not divorce, were barred from many jobs, had only the most limited access to education, and were enjoined to be submissive. They had entered a new world in which the government called on them to go to school, learn new trades, and participate in politics. "Here is yesterday's day laborer," Chernysheva wrote, "Our young woman of letters." They were also able to order their private lives with very little regulation from the state (divorce and abortion had been legalized in 1918 and 1920 respectively). Historian Sheila Fitzpatrick has argued that the Bolsheviks succeeded in establishing an enduring regime in part because they promoted social mobility, creating opportunities for advancement that people from the lower classes would never have known under the tsars. This advancement extended to women as well, and given the fact that

---

[17] A *rabfak* was a school for workers held in factories.
[18] E. Chernysheva, "Nasha radost'," *Rabotnitsa*, no. 16 (1926): 9. Wordsworth's lines are from *The Prelude*, Book XI (*The Norton Anthology of English Literature*, vol. 2 [New York, 1962], 166).

women were able to breach both class and gender barriers, they had strong reasons to believe in the new order.[19]

No women in Soviet Russia in the 1920s had more reason for such belief than the Bolshevichki of both generations, for they, the women of the Communist Party, became the vanguard of the Soviet female labor force, the administrators, managers, doctors, lawyers, judges, professors, editors, teachers, archivists, librarians, and engineers who participated in the construction of the new government and the socialized economy. Of the women in the data base who were still alive in 1921, 84 percent of the older generation and 88 percent of the younger were employed full-time; the remainder had retired because of ill health. Seventy-three percent of the older generation and 85 percent of the younger worked on into the 1930s. The Bolshevichki were very mobile workers, changing fields of employment several times, holding many different jobs within one field, and often, particularly in the 1920s, carrying more than one assignment at a time. Only 21 percent of the older generation and 20 percent of the younger stayed in one type of employment throughout their working lives in the Soviet period. (See tables 31 and 32.)

Paulina Bertse had a typically diversified employment history. A Latvian shepherd before the revolution, Bertse was working in Pskov in 1921 as secretary of the local party committee. At the same time, she held a government job, head of the city committee charged with organizing daycare centers and helping to equip and staff elementary schools. In 1923 she also took on the leadership of the local Zhenotdel. In 1927 she became the chief administrator of a nursery. Throughout this period she continued to serve on the party committee and the local party control committee. In 1930 she moved to Moscow, where she found a position in the city government's department of preschool education. In 1931 she left that work to become the secretary of a party cell in a factory in Moscow's Bauman raion.[20]

As did Bertse, many Bolshevichki in the 1920s divided their time between government and party assignments. Forty-four percent of the older generation in the data base and 58 percent of the younger held full-time party jobs in the 1920s, while 71 percent and 47 percent respectively worked in government, broadly construed to include both the commissariats and the professions that labored under the supervision of those commissariats. Party work will receive fuller consideration below (pp. 257–61). In government, the Bolshevichki occupied the Soviet equivalent of middle and lower management; they were again, so to speak, "red lieutenants." They also worked in the professions, particularly

---

[19] Sheila Fitzpatrick, *The Russian Revolution*, 2nd ed. (New York, 1994), 144–47.
[20] RTsKhIDNI, f. 124, op. 1, d. 177, l. 4.

Table 31 *Bolshevichki's occupations, 1921–1941*

Occupation	Old Bolshevichki (%) $(N=205)$[a]	Civil war joiners (%) $(N=160)$[b]
Agronomist	—	0.6 (1)
Archivist, librarian, museum worker	16.1 (33)	5.0 (8)
Artist	0.5 (1)	—
Chemical engineer	—	0.6 (1)
Clerk	2.9 (6)	0.6 (1)
Dentist	0.5 (1)	—
Diplomatic staff	2.0 (4)	1.9 (3)
Economist	1.0 (2)	1.9 (3)
Editor, journalist	21.5 (44)	20.6 (33)
Electrical engineer	0.5 (1)	0.6 (1)
Engineer (unclassified)	—	3.1 (5)
Factory administrator	1.5 (3)	4.4 (7)
Factory director	3.4 (7)	3.1 (5)
Factory worker	3.9 (8)	1.3 (2)
Faculty member, administrator in higher education	12.2 (25)	15.6 (25)
Government civil servant	19.5 (40)	20.6 (33)
Hospital administrator	0.5 (1)	—
Hospital director	2.0 (4)	0.6 (1)
Judge	2.0 (4)	1.9 (3)
Local soviet official	10.2 (21)	3.8 (6)
Museum director	0.5 (1)	—
Nurse	0.5 (1)	—
Party worker	36.1 (74)	58.1 (93)
Physician	2.9 (6)	0.6 (1)
Procurator	1.0 (2)	1.3 (2)
School director	1.0 (2)	2.5 (4)
Sovkhoz[c] director	—	0.6 (1)
Statistician	1.0 (2)	—
Student	4.4 (9)	11.3 (18)
Teacher	1.5 (3)	1.9 (3)
Telephone operator	0.5 (1)	—
Trade union official	6.3 (13)	11.3 (18)
Voluntary association official	4.4 (9)	3.8 (6)

Note: All occupations were recorded. For those individuals who held several different posts in the same occupation (e.g., director at three factories), only one instance was counted. The percentages indicate the percentage of the total N of Bolshevichki on whom information is available.

[a] Old Bolshevichki on whom information about occupations available.
[b] Members of civil war generation on whom information about occupations available.
[c] A large agricultural enterprise, also known as a "state farm."

Table 32 *Bolshevichki remaining within one field of employment until retirement*

Field	Old Bolshevichki (%) (N = 52)[a]	Civil war joiners (%) (N = 26)[b]
Arts	1	—
Clerical work	1	1
Economic management	7	1
Education	15	15
Factory work	1	2
Journalism, editing	6	1
Judiciary	1	—
Library work	4	1
Medicine	15	5
Trade union administration	1	—
Total	52	26

[a] This N constitutes 21 percent of the Old Bolshevichki in the labor force, 1921–28.
[b] This N constitutes 15 percent of the civil war joiners in the labor force, 1921–28.

journalism, editing and publishing, medicine, and education (a category constructed here to include teaching and educational administration as well as work in libraries, archives, and museums). Members of the older generation, as befitted people with higher levels of education and longer party service, were more likely to work in the professions and in the middle and upper ranks of Narkompros and other government ministries. The younger spent more time in the 1920s in lower-ranking party jobs and in schooling. According to the very fragmentary statistics available, 31 percent of the civil war generation attended institutions of higher education after 1921. (See tables 33, 34, and 35.)

The patterns of labor-force participation established by the Bolshevichki in the 1920s became those of white-collar female workers throughout the Soviet period. Simply holding white-collar jobs made the Bolshevichki elite, for the great majority of Soviet women doing non-agricultural work before World War II were employed in manual labor. Among the women in the data base, only four of the ninety-four Old Bolshevichki who had worked in the factories or fields before 1917 and one of the sixty-two such women in the civil war generation remained at their blue-collar jobs in the 1920s. Nor were the Bolshevichki restricted to clerical work, the white-collar field most open to women elsewhere in the European world. They moved into fields as varied and important as electrical engineering, law, and medicine.

Klavdiia Kovshalova-Teslenko is a good example. She had been born

Table 33 *Fields of employment of Old Bolshevichki after 1921*

| Fields | Old Bolshevichki in the labor force | | | |
	1921–1928 (%) (N=249)	1929–1941 (%) (N=214)	1941–1945 (%) (N=78)	1946–1955 (%) (N=73)
Arts	0.4 (1)	1.4 (3)	—	—
Economy	8.8 (22)	12.6 (27)	7.7 (6)	4.1 (3)
Education	24.9 (62)	25.2 (54)	17.9 (14)	20.5 (15)
Journalism, publishing	8.8 (22)	9.3 (20)	2.6 (2)	1.4 (1)
Medicine	5.2 (13)	5.1 (11)	10.3 (8)	9.6 (7)
Miscellaneous government[a]	15.3 (38)	17.3 (37)	1.3 (1)	1.4 (1)
Party (excluding the Zhenotdel)	31.7 (79)	20.6 (44)	6.4 (5)	4.1 (3)
Police, courts	3.6 (9)	1.4 (3)	—	—
Social welfare	4.4 (11)	2.3 (5)	—	—
Trade unions	8.4 (21)4.7 (10)	1.3 (1)	—	
Zhenotdel	12.4 (31)	0.9 (2)	—	—

Note: All instances of types of work were coded. The percentages represent the percentage of the total *N* working at any time in the period.
[a] Work for government agencies not included under the other categories in the table.

Table 34 *Fields of employment of civil war joiners after 1921*

| Fields | Civil war joiners in the labor force | | | |
	1921–1928 (%) (N=172)	1929–1941 (%) (N=170)	1941–1945 (%) (N=133)	1946–1955 (N=122)
Arts	—	0.6 (1)	—	—
Economy	10.5 (18)	20.0 (34)	15.0 % (20)	15.6 % (19)
Education	16.3 (28)	28.2 (48)	28.6 (38)	32.8 (40)
Journalism, publishing	5.2 (9)	6.5 (11)	6.8 (9)	8.2 (10)
Medicine	3.5 (6)	2.9 (5)	3.8 (5)	3.3 (4)
Miscellaneous government[a]	8.1 (14)	10.6 (18)	6.8 (9)	7.4 (9)
Party (excluding the Zhenotdel)	25.0 (43)	22.9 (39)	10.5 (14)	7.4 (9)
Police, courts	3.5 (6)	4.1 (7)	1.5 (2)	1.6 (2)
Social welfare	1.7 (3)	0.6 (1)	0.8 (1)	0.8 (1)
Trade unions	9.3 (16)	7.1 (12)	—	—
Zhenotdel	33.1 (57)	2.4 (4)	—	—

Note: All instances of types of work were recorded. The percentages represent the percentage of the total *N* working in the period.
[a] Work for government agencies not included under the other categories in the table.

Table 35 *Social origins of Bolshevichki and fields of employment, 1921–1941*

Field	Old Bolshevichki			
	Nobility (%) (N = 24)	Middle[a] (%) (N = 65)	Workers (%) (N = 72)	Peasants (%) (N = 32)
Economy	12.5 (3)	15.4 (10)	34.7 (25)	12.5 (4)
Education	62.5 (15)	33.8 (22)	29.2 (21)	40.6 (13)
Journalism, publishing	33.3 (8)	21.5 (14)	9.7 (7)	3.1 (1)
Medicine	4.2 (1)	10.8 (7)	2.8 (2)	3.1 (1)
Miscellaneous government[b]	16.7 (4)	13.8 (9)	18.1 (13)	12.5 (4)
Party (excluding the Zhenotdel)	29.2 (7)	53.8 (35)	52.8 (38)	46.9 (15)
Police, courts	8.3 (2)	—	9.7 (7)	9.4 (3)
Social welfare	—	6.2 (4)	6.9 (5)	18.8 (6)
Trade unions	—	6.2 (4)	18.1 (13)	15.6 (5)
Zhenotdel	20.8 (5)	4.6 (3)	23.6 (17)	31.3 (10)

Field	Civil war joiners			
	Nobility (%) (N = 5)	Middle[a] (%) (N = 20)	Workers (%) (N = 70)	Peasants (%) (N = 16)
Economy	20.0 (1)	20.0 (4)	34.3 (24)	37.5 (6)
Education	80.0 (4)	45.0 (9)	15.7 (11)	43.8 (7)
Journalism, publishing	40.0 (2)	30.0 (6)	14.3 (10)	6.3 (1)
Medicine	—	10.0 (2)	4.3 (3)	6.3 (1)
Miscellaneous government[b]	20.0 (1)	15.0 (3)	14.3 (10)	—
Party (excluding the Zhenotdel)	40.0 (2)	20.0 (4)	50.0 (35)	56.3 (9)
Police, courts	20.0 (1)	—	5.7 (4)	12.5 (2)
Social welfare	—	—	5.7 (4)	6.3 (1)
Trade unions	—	15.0 (3)	20.0 (14)	18.8 (3)
Zhenotdel	20.0 (1)	35.0 (7)	42.9 (30)	18.7 (3)

Note: All instances of types of work were coded. Percentages represent the percentage of the total *N* working in the period.

[a] Intelligentsia, *sluzhashchie*, *meshchanstvo*.

[b] Work for government agencies not included under the other categories in the table.

in 1897 in a village in the Urals, the daughter of a family of factory workers. Her father was a "master," or skilled worker, so the family could afford for Kovshalova-Teslenko to go to school. She finished gymnasium in 1915 and became a teacher. In 1918 she joined the party. She spent the civil war in her hometown of Ufa, working as secretary of the city's party committee. In 1922 she moved to Moscow to become a political instructor, teaching Marxism and the current party line. Kovshalova-Teslenko moved up in the hierarchy of propagandists throughout the decade. In the early 1930s she spent two years at the Institute of Red Professors, studying economics. In 1935 she became a member of the plenum, or board of judges, at the Supreme Court of the Russian Republic.[21]

There are many other examples. Anna Pankratova, a village teacher, became an academic historian. Mariia Shustova, a textile worker, served as head of the department of children's institutions of the Moscow city Department of Health. Polina Sorokina, also a textile worker, rose to be a factory director. Mariia Meshkova-Lapshina, a peasant by birth, was dean of faculty at the Stalin Trade Academy. Their progress from daughters of factory workers to members of the Soviet government illustrates the extraordinary social mobility the party was encouraging. Nowhere else in the European world were there so many female lawyers, professors, scientists, and artists, as well as judges and party secretaries, as there were in the Soviet Union by 1930. This change was sweeping and extraordinarily rapid, particularly when set in the context of a decade in which feminism was in retreat throughout Europe and North America.

For the most part, the Bolshevichki appear to have sought work in fields in which they were personally interested and in which they had prior experience. Fifty-five percent of the older generation in the data base worked primarily in specialties in which they had been trained before 1917, that is, education, journalism, editing, and medicine. Krupskaia is the most famous former teacher who returned to education after the revolution, but many other Bolshevichki less well known made the same choice. In a regime desperately short of skilled people, it made sense to assign those available to the management of fields in which they had already received some relevant training.

The civil war generation of Bolshevichki was more positively affected than the older one by the party's policy of breaking down barriers erected by gender assumptions. Most of the younger generation received training in the 1920s and early 1930s; consequently, fewer of the younger Bolshevichki went into medicine and education. More of them (20 percent as opposed to 13 percent of the older generation) worked in the rapidly expanding fields of engineering and economic management after 1928. Bolshevichki who had been factory workers were most likely to take this course. Typically they became involved in the trade unions while working as organizers for the local party committee, then moved into

[21] TsGAORSS Moskvy, f. 2948, op. 1. d. 9, l. 1.

managerial positions in the factories with the huge expansion in industry that began in the late 1920s. By contrast, those older Bolshevichki of proletarian backgrounds and those women of the younger generation who did not have experience in the factories were more inclined to specialize in education and journalism.

Members of both generations changed occupations in the 1930s. Both did more work in the economy after 1928 than before, although the shift was greater for the younger Bolshevichki. Significant numbers of the younger generation also moved into education in the 1930s, after having studied for that career in the late 1920s. For both generations there was less job mobility in 1930s and thereafter than before, a sign of the settling of the system and perhaps of their aging, too.

The optimism of a young women such as the poet Chernysheva was inspired by the rapid expansion of opportunities for women that was going on all around her. In her delight, Chernysheva did not note that the majority of Bolshevichki of both generations were at the bottom of the white-collar hierarchy, or that they tended to concentrate in general-practice medicine, elementary and secondary-school teaching, copy-editing, and clerical work. Nor could she know that the bottom was where the great majority of women would remain throughout the Soviet period, for the party, even while it was breaking down traditional patriarchal barriers, was erecting new ones of its own. The party had a long history of involving women in unconventional activities. Sending them to engineering classes was not an extraordinary step for a movement that had employed them as bomb-makers or machine-gunners in the recent past. Promoting them into decision-making ranks was something else again. Despite the fact that upwards of 85 percent of the Bolshevichki of both generations was gainfully employed during the 1920s and 1930s, the percentages of women in middle and upper management of the new government changed very little over what they had been during the civil war. Of the Old Bolsheviks in the data base, 31 percent held government office between 1918 and 1921; 33 percent did so afterward. The civil war joiners experienced greater opportunities, although fewer than one would expect. During the civil war, 25 percent held government office (a testimony to the desperate need for staff in that emergency) and 33 percent did so thereafter. (See tables 36, 37, and 38.)

Those Bolshevichki who did hold government office appear to have earned their promotions by dint of personal ability, qualifications, and ambition. There is very little evidence in the data that the party was promoting people on the basis of class origins, despite its professed desire to fill its new government with workers. This was particularly true of the Old Bolshevichki. Figures for the younger generation are fragmentary, but they

Table 36 *Social origins of Bolshevichki and office-holding after 1921*

| | Old Bolshevichki | | |
Social origins	Of entire group (%) (N = 318)	Of those in government office (%) (N = 110)	Of those in party office (%) (N = 86)
Nobility	9.4	14.5	12.8
Intelligentsia	10.4	11.8	13.9
Sluzhashchie	6.0	7.3	5.8
Meshchanstvo	11.3	8.2	10.5
Workers	26.4	30.0	31.4
Peasantry	10.4	11.8	12.8
Clergy	1.6	1.8	2.3
Unknown	24.5	14.5	10.5
Total	100.0	99.9	100.0

| | Civil war joiners | | |
Social origins	Of entire group (%) (N = 227)	Of those in government office (%) (N = 75)	Of those in party office (%) (N = 86)
Nobility	3.5	2.7	2.3
Intelligentsia	4.8	4.0	4.6
Sluzhashchie	3.5	8.0	3.5
Meshchanstvo	1.3	1.3	2.3
Workers	36.6	45.3	43.0
Peasantry	9.2	8.0	7.0
Clergy	—	—	—
Unknown	41.0	30.7	37.2
Total	99.9	100.0	99.9

suggest some advantage being given to working-class Bolshevichki. Among women of all classes, education remained a far more important prerequisite than social origins for higher-ranking government positions. Women of both generations held office in those areas where there were the most female employees, primarily in the soviets (where they had been a presence during the civil war) and in Narkompros. Some civil war joiners rose in economic positions, primarily as factory managers or trade union officials.

The upward mobility of the Bolshevichki within the government, limited from the earliest days of the NEP, became even more circumscribed in the 1930s. The great majority of the promotions that Bolshevichki received came before the mid-1930s. (See figure 3.) The experiences of the two generations in this regard are, again, similar. Most women

Table 37 *Education and office-holding by Bolshevichki after 1921*

Education before 1917	Of entire group (%)	Of those who held government office (%)	Of those who held party office (%)
Old Bolshevichki			
None	3.2 (7)	—	—
Primary	21.9 (48)	25.8 (8)	45.0 (18)
Secondary	42.0 (92)	32.3 (10)	25.0 (10)
Higher	32.9 (72)	41.9 (13)	30.0 (12)
Total	100.0 (219)	100.0 (31)	100.0 (40)
Civil war joiners			
None	1.2 (1)	—	—
Primary	15.1 (13)	25.0 (2)	30.4 (7)
Secondary	61.6 (53)	37.5 (3)	56.5 (13)
Higher	22.1 (19)	37.5 (3)	13.0 (3)
Total	100.0 (86)	100.0 (8)	99.9 (23)

Note: Figures in parentheses are base *N*s for the adjacent percentages.

achieved their highest positions when the demand for skilled people was the greatest, during the fever of the First Five Year Plan (1928–32). There were additional but far smaller spates of promotion during the party purges in the late 1930s and during World War II.

To a certain extent, this stagnation resulted from choices women themselves made. Some limited their career options in order to move with their husbands as they were transferred from job to job. Others shrank from seeking high-ranking positions because they doubted their own abilities. A few left the labor force altogether: 8 percent of the Old Bolshevichki retired in the 1920s, and a handful more did so in the early 1930s. But Bolshevichki had made these choices even in the underground, so by itself the lack of ambition shown by some women cannot fully account for the fact that most women did not continue to advance in their careers in the 1930s. That fact can only be explained by the continuing expansion of male control over powerful offices in the new Soviet regime. The first glass ceiling barring women from entering the upper reaches of a managerial hierarchy was put up in the Soviet Union at the beginning of Stalin's rule.

From the earliest days of the prerevolutionary movement, women's fortunes had been advanced by the party's commitment to their liberation

Table 38 *Highest government offices held by Bolshevichki after 1921*

Offices	Old Bolshevichki	Civil war joiners
Academia		
Institute		
Senior scientific worker	—	3
Deputy department head	—	1
Department head	3	3
Deputy head	1	1
Head	3	2
University		
Department head	—	1
Akademiia nauk		
Senior scientific worker	—	4
Deputy department head	1	1
Economic management		
Factory		
Department head	1	3
Deputy director	—	1
Director	4	6
State Bank		
Republican deputy head	1	—
Machine Tractor Station		
Political officer	1	—
State Farm		
Director	—	1
Trust		
Deputy head	—	1
Head	—	1
Government departments		
Commissariat of Enlightenment (Narkompros)		
School director	1	1
Library		
Deputy head	—	1
Head	1	1
City level of Narkompros administration		
Department head	1	2
Deputy head	1	1
Head	1	—
Oblast level of Narkompros administration		
Head	1	1
Republican level of Narkompros administration		
Deputy department head	1	—
Head	1	—
Central administration		
Deputy department head	2	—
Department head	6	1
Deputy head	2	—
Collegium member	1	—

Other government departments
  City
    Deputy department head   1   —

Other government departments		
City		
Deputy department head	1	—
Department head	3	1
Oblast		
Deputy department head	4	—
Department head	1	1
Republic		
Department head	3	—
Deputy head	1	—
Head	1	—
Central		
Deputy department head	1	1
Department head	4	2
Deputy head	—	1
Collegium member	1	—
Journalism, publishing		
Local newspaper		
Editor	—	1
Local press		
Editor	—	1
National newspaper		
Editor	1	—
Secretary	1	—
National press		
Department head	1	—
Deputy editor	1	—
Editor	5	6
Head	1	—
Medicine		
Hospital director	1	—
Miscellaneous		
Deputy ambassador	1	—
Ambassador	1	—
Police, courts		
Local		
City police deputy department head	—	1
Oblast		
Judge	1	1
Central		
Cheka	—	1
Prosecutor	1	—
Judge	1	2
Soviets		
Raion, uezd		
Delegate	1	—
Department head	1	—
Chair	1	1
City		
Delegate	11	1
Deputy department head	1	—

Table 38 *(cont.)*

Offices	Old Bolshevichki	Civil war joiners
Soviets *(cont)*		
Oblast		
Delegate	1	—
Department head	1	—
Republic		
Secretary	—	1
Executive committee	—	2
Supreme Soviet		
Department head	1	—
Executive committee	—	2
All-Russian Central Executive Committee (VTsIK)	4	—
Council of People's Commissars	1	—
Trade unions		
Factory		
Secretary	1	1
Raion, uezd		
Committee member	1	—
Chair	—	1
City		
Committee member	1	2
Secretary	—	1
Chair	1	—
Oblast		
Committee member	1	—
Secretary	—	1
Chair	1	3
Central		
Committee member	1	1
Secretary	2	—
Voluntary organizations		
Executive committee member	1	1
Chair	2	—
None[a]	162 (50.9%)	111 (48.9%)
Unknown	51 (16.0%)	42 (18.5%)
Total	318	227

Note: The highest office held by each woman was coded.
[a] Jobs lower-ranking than those on the list were coded as "none."

and by its urgent desire to enlist skilled, hard-working people in its service. In the 1920s there were few signs that the ideological commitment was weakening. Widespread consensus existed within the upper reaches of the party and among the revolutionary intelligentsia that women's equality was an important goal; the government made substantial advances in promoting education and job-training programs, as well as in establishing social services to assist women entering the paid-labor force. The party's liberationist message went out to millions of citizens. And Bolshevichki came to occupy positions in government monopolized everywhere else in the world by men.

Nor did the sense of urgency diminish perceptibly, despite the end of the civil war. Instead, it persisted in the atmosphere for decades, through the power struggles of the 1920s, the turmoil of collectivization and the First and Second Five Year Plans, the terror of the mass arrests of the 1930s, World War II, and the era of postwar reconstruction and of the onset of the Cold War. Emergency became the prevailing condition of party life, and danger was ambient; the need for skilled people who would dedicate themselves to the collective enterprise persisted.

But now that the Bolsheviks had ceased to be an underground community and had become instead a government, their sense of beleaguerment strengthened not their egalitarian tendencies but their autocratic ones. Hierarchy joined discipline as central Bolshevik ideals. In practice, the party functioned through the continuous crises by building and then rebuilding clientage and patronage relationships between men. Both the ideals of order and the realities of power excluded women, for both continued to be pervaded by the ancient belief that politics was the business of men working in teams.

Bolshevichki in the party

The consequences of these developments are apparent in the patterns of women's participation in government, but they affected even more strongly their status in the party. During the civil war, 43 percent of the older generation and 39 percent of the younger had worked in full-time party jobs. In the NEP years, those figures fell to 32 percent and 25 percent respectively (outside that small but all-female department, the Zhenotdel). At the same time, the numbers of women holding party office declined dramatically. In 1928, women were 13 percent of communists but only 3 percent of cell secretaries (this was one of the lowest offices). None was serving in that year at the higher rank of secretary of a provincial committee.[22] Most of the Bolshevichki in the data base had held the highest office they would ever hold in the party by the late 1920s, several years earlier than women in government reached their highest ranks (see figure 4), and almost all the offices these Bolshevichki did occupy were at

---

[22] P. M. Chirkov, *Reshenie zhenskogo voprosa v SSSR, 1917–1937 gg.* (Moscow, 1978), 171.

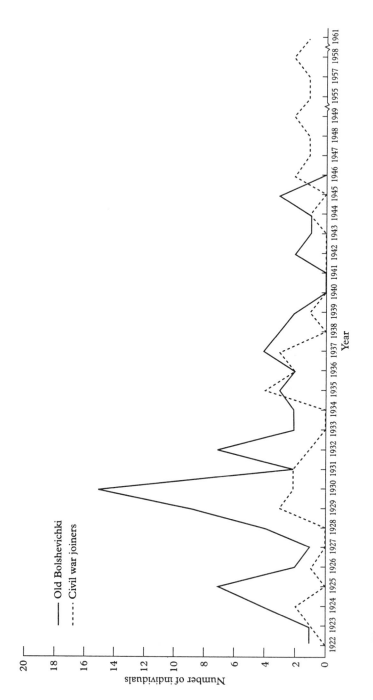

Figure 3. Years in which Bolshevichki held highest government office

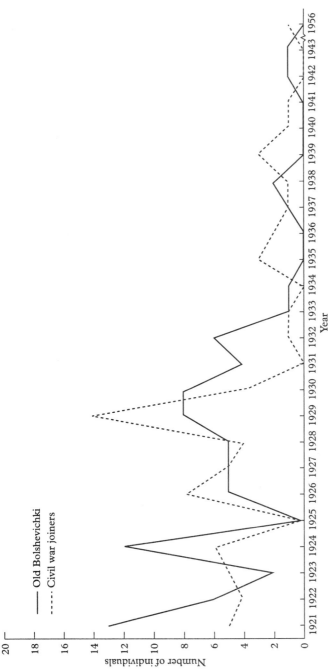

Figure 4. Years in which Bolshevichki held highest party office

Table 39 *Party office-holding by Bolshevichki during the civil war and thereafter*

Level of office held	Old Bolshevichki		Civil war joiners	
	1918–1921 (%)	After 1921 (%)	1918–1921 (%)	After 1921 (%)
Cell	0.6 (2)	5.7 (18)	2.2 (5)	0.9 (2)
Raion, uezd	6.6 (21)	3.8 (12)	5.3 (12)	6.6 (15)
City	6.0 (19)	3.1 (10)	5.3 (12)	6.2 (14)
Oblast	6.9 (22)	3.5 (11)	3.5 (8)	2.2 (5)
Republic	0.9 (3)	1.9 (6)	—	2.2 (5)
Central Committee	0.9 (3)	2.5 (8)	—	1.3 (3)
Party congress delegate	0.9 (3)	1.3 (4)	1.3 (3)	0.4 (1)
Zhenotdel	2.5 (8)	4.1 (13)	12.8 (29)	17.6 (40)
Held no office	69.5 (221)	65.1 (207)	69.2 (157)	55.9 (127)
Unknown	5.0 (16)	9.1 (29)	0.4 (1)	6.6 (15)
Total	99.8 (318)	100.1 (318)	100.0 (227)	99.9 (227)

Note: Figures in parentheses are base Ns for the adjacent percentages.

Table 40 *Prior office-holding by Bolshevichki who held party office in the 1920s*

Prior office-holding	Old Bolshevichki (%) ($N = 65$)	Civil war joiners (%) ($N = 73$)
Before 1917 only	3.1 (2)	—
In 1917 only	4.6 (3)	—
During civil war only	15.4 (10)	23.3 (17)
Before 1917, and in 1917	—	—
Before 1917, in 1917, and during civil war	21.5 (14)	—
Before 1917, and during civil war	7.7 (5)	—
In 1917, and during civil war	30.8 (20)	6.9 (5)
None	13.9 (9)	28.8 (21)
None (held office only in Zhenotdel in the 1920s)	3.1 (2)	41.1 (30)
Total	100.1 (65)	100.1 (73)

Note: Figures in parentheses are base Ns for the adjacent percentages.

the very lowest levels of the party. The younger generation had experienced even less success. The statistics show that women who became Bolshevichki during the civil war increased their office-holding in the 1920s mainly because of promotions within the Zhenotdel. By the beginning of the 1930s the Bolshevichki, with a very few exceptions (Zemliachka was one), had simply disappeared from the ranks of the leadership. (See table 39.)

The criteria by which Bolshevichki were selected for party office changed as well in the 1920s. Class origins began to figure more heavily than they had in the past, with the working class being favored. Seniority became an important qualification as well; Bolshevichki of the older generation who had held office earlier, particularly during the civil war, were more likely to be party officials in the 1920s than those who had not. Seniority was less important for the younger generation, who, of course, had had less opportunity to accumulate it, but even among them, civil war experience was correlated with office-holding in the 1920s. The younger generation also had some success using office-holding in the Zhenotdel as a stepping stone to offices elsewhere in the party. The older generation, most of whom were still loathe to work in the Zhenotdel, refused to pursue this path to higher rank. (See tables 36, 37, and 40.)

The type of work the Bolshevichki did in the party also altered in the 1920s, when increasingly they concentrated on agitation and propaganda. Seventy-two percent of the older generation and 85 percent of the younger now did such work. These figures are inflated by the existence of that great agitprop center for women, the Zhenotdel, but 60 percent of the older generation and 52.5 percent of the younger also worked in agitprop outside the Zhenotdel. Again, the experience of the Bolshevichki in the 1920s set the pattern for future Soviet communist women; bearing the party's messages became the chief assignment of female communists throughout Soviet history. This had, of course, been one of their primary functions in the prerevolutionary era, but at that time some Bolshevichki had also participated in decision-making and party management. With power, management became a prerogative of male leaders, clerical work was turned over to female secretaries far removed in authority from the technical secretaries of the underground, and the majority of the Bolshevichki who stayed in party work moved into agitation and propaganda. Agitprop was not an utterly powerless place to be, as Zemliachka proved, but it was considered ancillary, support work.[23]

---

[23] For an analysis of the later involvement of women in agitprop and the low status accorded such work, see Joel C. Moses, "Women in Political Roles," in Dorothy Atkinson, Alexander Dallin, and Gail Warshofsky Lapidus, eds., *Women in Russia* (Stanford, 1977), 340–48.

The Zhenotdel

The Zhenotdel was the only party arena in which the Bolshevichki scored great successes in the 1920s. Under the leadership of Sofia Smidovich (1922–24), Klavdiia Nikolaeva (1924–25), and Alexandra Artiukhina (1925–30), the department accomplished many of the goals set for it by its creators. It became an energetic, effective propagandist among lower-class women, drawing tens of thousands to conferences and reaching many more with huge printings of pamphlets and magazines. Zhenotdel leaders also educated what they called a *zhenskii aktiv*, cadres of activist women spread throughout the Soviet system who lobbied for attention to be paid to women's needs. Alexandra Artiukhina proudly told a meeting of the Moscow city party committee in 1930: "You know, we can't show up anywhere without hearing, 'Well, Artiukhina or Goreva [one of her staffers] is going to be here; that means there'll be discussion of nurseries, kindergartens, and such.'" A voice from the audience called out, "That's not a bad thing." "No," Artiukhina shot back, "that's not a bad thing, dealing with those tasks that Lenin spoke about – women's emancipation."[24]

The Zhenotdel also became a major recruiter of women into volunteer activities and into the party itself. Most commonly, the department led factory and office workers in setting up daycare centers and lunch rooms, but there were also women's purchasing cooperatives and even a few well-publicized collective farms established in the countryside by widows and other women displaced from their villages by the long years of war. Tens of thousands of those who took part in all these projects joined the party and served their first assignment in the Zhenotdel before moving on to other work. Like women's colleges or other such women-only organizations, the Zhenotdel taught its recruits the skills they needed in a sheltered environment in which they could build their self-confidence with the support of more experienced women, who also served as role models.[25]

The women's department reached its largest audience through its publications, chief among them the widely distributed monthly magazines *Kommunistka* (*Communist Woman*), *Krestianka* (*Woman Peasant*), and *Rabotnitsa* (*Woman Worker*). *Kommunistka*, an informational journal for the department's own workers, consisted mostly of instructions to

24 "Za sotsialisticheskuiu peredelku byta," *Rabotnitsa*, no. 4 (1930): 3. On the ethos of the Zhenotdel, see Barbara Evans Clements, "The Utopianism of the Zhenotdel," *Slavic Review* 51 (Fall 1992): 485–96.
25 The most comprehensive study of the Zhenotdel to date is Carol Eubanks Hayden, "Feminism and Bolshevism: The Zhenotdel and the Politics of Women's Emancipation in the USSR, 1917–1930," Ph.D. dissertation, University of California, Berkeley, 1979.

Plate 25. Zhenotdel workers of the Tver guberniia committee, 1922.

lower-ranking operatives and reports on national and regional activities. The other two magazines, aimed at general audiences and modeled on the earlier *Rabotnitsa*, carried articles on Zhenotdel projects and recent party decisions, features on women breaking down traditional barriers, particularly in the workplace, columns on various subjects such as women's legal rights and the problems of daily life, letters to the editors, short stories, and poetry. *Krestianka* was the more simply written of the two, and its avowals of Marxist feminism were more muted, so as not to alienate suspicious peasants. *Rabotnitsa* was once again, as it had been in its earlier incarnations, the voice of Bolshevik feminism.

Rabotnitsa's editors remained true to the principles developed by Inessa, Kollontai, Samoilova, and their collaborators. They called on women to work with men, now in the construction of socialism, so as to advance their personal liberation while participating in the liberation of all society. They stressed the great achievements of the Soviet system to date and the shining future that lay ahead. They held fast to the proposition that women's emancipation could only be realized in a communalized society, so they praised experiments in redesigning family life, such as group-living arrangements or the collective farms run by women, and criticized proposals that, in their analysis, would contribute to the preservation of the traditional division of labor within the family. In 1926 and 1930, *Rabotnitsa* ran articles arguing that Soviet architects should not copy western European housing designs. Kitchens and bathrooms in every apartment (the Western model) would keep women tied down, cooking and cleaning for their families.[26]

Zhenotdel leaders also used *Rabotnitsa* to propagate their analysis of the most pressing problems confronting Soviet women in the 1920s. Deploring the unequal treatment of female workers, they identified as the worst abuses wage differentials between women and men, discrimination in hiring, sexual harassment, layoffs of women first in times of economic contraction, and the refusal of factory managers to allocate funds for cafeterias and on-site daycare. They called for an ambitious program of affirmative action, arguing that issues of greatest consequence to women would not be addressed until women served on trade-union boards and in factory management and until the government established training programs that would enable women to qualify for high-paying jobs.

Rabotnitsa's editors also argued strenuously that domestic life had to be transformed, not just by building social services designed to relieve the burdens of housework, but also through raising the consciousness of men. They targeted as problems of particular concern male alcoholism and wife-battering. A regular column on the legal code urged women to divorce men who abused them or refused to permit them to take advantage of the new opportunities. *Rabotnitsa*'s editors made their often pointed commentary on the difficulties in women's lives more palatable by blaming all the problems on economic hardship and the lingering influence of patriarchy. Their criticism still sounds remarkably fresh today, for most of the issues the magazine raised persist across the European world.[27]

The Bolshevik feminism of the 1920s was imaginative, lively, and self-confident. It was also, as Bolshevik feminism had always been, a minority position fundamentally at odds with the party majority's under-

---

[26] S. Radieva, "Rabotnitsa i zhilishchnoe stroitel'stvo," *Rabotnitsa*, no. 3 (1926): 9–10; A. Tatarova, "Gde vy khotite zhit'?," *Rabotnitsa*, no. 8 (1930): 19–20. The issue of housing designs that perpetuated the nuclear family was one hotly debated by architects as well. See Hugh D. Hudson, Jr., "'The Social Condenser of Our Epoch': The Association of Contemporary Architects and the Creation of a New Way of Life in Revolutionary Russia," *Jührbucher für Geschichte Osteuropas* 34 (1986): 562–66, 569–74. For an article on an all-female collective farm, see "Istoriia odnoi kommuny," *Rabotnitsa*, no. 8 (1930): 24.

[27] For an example of articles from *Rabotnitsa* on the theme of discrimination against women in the workplace, see "Mozhet li byt' zhenshchina slesarem," *Rabotnitsa*, no. 8 (1926): 20; no. 11: 17; no. 13: 14. For articles on family life, see "Byt rabotnitsy po ikh pis'mam," *Rabotnitsa*, no. 1 (1926): 15–17.

standing of the "woman question." As we have seen, the leadership had long believed that women's general role was to be supportive, that is, women were to help the men who led the process that would emancipate women. In the 1920s, when vague utopian promises about a future of liberty began to yield to hard choices between goals and the policies necessary to achieve them, Bolshevik leaders applied their assumptions to the new situation and argued that women should still support the leaders' efforts, now directed not at overthrowing a tsar but building an industrialized economy. If women found that programs beneficial to them, such as daycare centers, were low on the government's priority list, they should accept this fact as an unpleasant but temporary necessity. The harder they worked, the more they would hasten the coming of that time when their needs too could be met. Many years later, Sofia Pavlova, a Zhenotdel staffer, described the role of the Zhenotdel as many communists had understood it in the 1920s: "We assembled women, we told them what Soviet power was, what it did. If some concrete task stood before us, such as collecting dried bread, we called on them to do that. If it was necessary to collect donations, we called on them to do that. Thus we had concrete tasks and concrete goals, which we summoned women to perform, in addition to our general propaganda work." As Pavlova remembered it, the Zhenotdel was simply a wing of the party that told women what needed to be done to help out.[28]

Such conceptualizations of women's participation in the political process have been common among European reformers of all political stripes since the Enlightenment. Most of them have believed, according to political scientist Anna Jönasdóttir, that "women's essence as well as existence *was in the world to be used* by the new state-society in general and by men in particular."[29] Women's liberation was a question of social utility. Reformers throughout the nineteenth century, including many feminists, played to this idea when they declared that women's emancipation from traditional constraints was justifiable because it would permit women to serve some "greater good." "Educated women will be better mothers" ran one familiar call for admission to higher education. If women have the vote, they will clean up corrupt politics, the suffragists asserted. Bolshevik

---

[28] Typescript interview conducted with Sofia Pavlova by Anastasia Posadskaia and made available to me by Barbara Alpern Engel, 21–22. This interview will be forthcoming as chapter 2 of *A Revolution of Their Own: Voices of Women in Soviet History*, ed. Barbara Alpern Engel and Anastasia Posadskaia (Boulder, Colo., 1997). I would like to thank Barbara Engel for sharing the interview with me. It will be deposited at the Hoover Institution, Stanford, Calif. The scholar who first analyzed this shift in party perceptions was Gail Warshofsky Lapidus, *Women in Soviet Society* (Berkeley, 1978), esp. 95–122.

[29] Anna G. Jönasdóttir, *Why Women Are Oppressed* (Philadelphia, 1994), 197. Italics in the original.

feminists, as eager for arguments that would win them support as were feminists elsewhere, proffered the same appeals to social utility, even while they asserted the importance of women's emancipation as a goal in itself. Party leaders paid lip service to the latter sentiment, but were willing to offer real support only when persuaded that women could be useful to the cause.

The party's ordering of priorities derived, then, from ideas widely accepted far beyond the radical wing of socialism. The same values and logic affected the situation of the Zhenotdel within the party. History shows that female groups in predominantly male organizations – the women's branch of a political party, the women's caucus in a legislature, the women's auxiliary of a trade union or a social or professional organization – have often been hobbled by their dependence on a male leadership that assumes the rightfulness of their subordination. For Bolshevik feminists, this predicament was aggravated by the party's autocracy. They were not to cultivate an independent base of support beyond the party's ranks, and they could not criticize party policies or the top leadership.

The dependency of the Zhenotdel was reflected in its organizational status within the party. Although it reported directly to the Central Committee, the department had less autonomy than other departments equal to it in the hierarchy. It did not receive its funding directly from the Central Committee, but rather was paid through circuitous channels that sent appropriations to the Department for Agitation and Propaganda (Agitprop) as well as to local and regional party committees. Zhenotdel operatives at all levels of the hierarchy reported to the Zhenotdel officials above them, but they were also under the jurisdiction of the party committee in the region where they worked. As a result, they were plagued by divided loyalties and conflicting demands. Denying to the Zhenotdel primary control over its appropriations and its staff sent a clear message, of course, not only to the department itself but also to the larger party membership, that the leadership intended to keep a tight rein on the department's feminist proclivities. Zhenotdel leaders fought back with lobbying efforts, but they never managed to achieve any lasting improvement in the department's institutionalized weakness.

The Zhenotdel's leaders resorted instead to a tactic common among feminists: they ran their operations with very little money and a lot of volunteers. It is ironic that an organization often portrayed in the contemporary Western press as dangerously revolutionary resembled so closely far more politically mainstream women's organizations throughout the European world. Like the Women's Christian Temperance Union in the United States and the Women's Social and Political Union in Britain, the Zhenotdel took its message to tens of thousands of people and effected real change, especially on the local level, but like them it had very little consistent support even from its political sponsors, and relied heavily on volunteer labor. Zhenotdel leaders made the best of their threadbare situation by arguing that volunteering would promote women's self-confidence, but they knew that having to rely on volunteers was yet another sign of the department's weakness.[30]

Artiukhina and the Zhenotdel

Alexandra Artiukhina, head of the Zhenotdel from 1925 to 1930, coped as effectively as any of the department's leaders with all these difficulties. She was the Bolshevichka who had begun her working life in St. Petersburg sewing collars on shirts. As had her mother, she became active in the textile workers' union and then in 1910 joined the Social-Democratic Party. A charter member of the community of Bolshevik feminists, Artiukhina was an editor of the first *Rabotnitsa*. She spent the years of World War I on the run from the police. After the February Revolution she returned to her old neighborhood in Petrograd, where she went to work as secretary of the raion party committee. She also renewed her friendships with Samoilova and Klavdiia Nikolaeva, and shortly thereafter became a staffer at the revived *Rabotnitsa*. During the civil war she and her husband, Bolshevik Mikhail Artiukhin, served in Ukraine as political officers. Artiukhina began working for the Zhenotdel in Tver in 1923. The next year, she and her husband applied for jobs in Moscow. She was appointed to the Central Zhenotdel. In 1925 she was made its head, replacing Klavdiia Nikolaeva.[31]

Artiukhina succeeded two colleagues who had not been particularly strong leaders of the department. Sofia Smidovich, although she was the head of the Moscow Zhenotdel during the civil war and thereafter, had never played a prominent role among the Bolshevik feminists. Rather, she had divided her time between work with women, various projects with her husband, the well-respected Bolshevik P. G. Smidovich, and their family life. Appointed to succeed Kollontai in 1922, Smidovich was at pains to distance the department from Kollontai's flamboyant advocacy and radical feminism. In *Kommunistka* in 1923 she announced that the journal would print no more theoretical discussions of women's emancipation.

---

[30] On the importance of voluntarism as a method of female political participation in the United States, see Suzanne Lebsock, "Women and American Politics, 1880–1920," in Louise A. Tilly and Patricia Gurin, eds., *Women, Politics, and Change* (New York, 1990), 35–62. Diane Koenker refers to the participation of female printers in voluntary organizations in "Men Against Women on the Shop Floor in Early Soviet Russia," *American Historical Review* 100 (December 1995): 1443.

[31] RTsKhIDNI, f. 124, op. 1, d. 83, ll. 13–14.

This disavowal was tactical, for Smidovich was a staunch Bolshevik feminist who supported the mission of the department as framed by her predecessors. She concentrated on expanding programs and increasing funding, with some success, for she proved able to argue persuasively for the Zhenotdel before the Central Committee. But her personal reticence and understandable caution made her a less dynamic leader than either Kollontai or Inessa.[32]

Smidovich remained in her post only two years. The reasons for her resignation are unclear, although the pressures of the job and her health, weakened by long years in the underground, were probably important factors. She was succeeded in 1924 by Klavdiia Nikolaeva, the printer from St. Petersburg who had been active in women's affairs since the first *Rabotnitsa*. Smidovich remained a prominent, respected contributor to *Kommunistka* thereafter, and in that capacity she played an important role in reaffirming the basic principles of Bolshevik feminism throughout the 1920s.[33]

Nikolaeva had once been Kollontai's protégé: recruited into the party by Kollontai, she had followed her as well into specializing on work among women. From the earliest days of the Zhenotdel, Nikolaeva had served as head of the department in St. Petersburg. There she had built the Zhenotdel's most activist, feminist, and successful outpost. Although neither a prominent orator nor a prolific writer on the women question, Nikolaeva proved to be an able administrator as well as a person who communicated well with female factory workers.[34]

Nikolaeva might have become a more vocal spokesperson for the Zhenotdel than Smidovich, for she did not suffer from the noble origins that may have inhibited Smidovich – upper-class women were always more readily suspected of feminism than proletarian ones. Nikolaeva had also served a long, honorable tenure in the party, she had amassed much experience in working with women, and she was a strong believer in Bolshevik feminism. But she survived in the headship less than one year, because she followed her long-time boss Zinoviev into the opposition. In the widespread demotions of his Petersburg allies that occurred in 1925, Nikolaeva was removed from the Zhenotdel.[35]

---

[32] Her renunciation of theoretical discussions is S. Smidovich, "Znachenie 'Kommunistki' dlia raboty sredi zhenshchin," *Kommunistka*, no. 7 (1923): 7–9. For examples of her advocacy for the Zhenotdel, see KPSS, *Odinnadtsatyi s"ezd RKP(b). Stenograficheskii otchet* (Moscow, 1961), 456–58.

[33] For an example of her continuing advocacy for Bolshevik feminism after she left the headship of the Zhenotdel, see S. Smidovich, "Reorganizatsiia byta za 10 let proletarskoi revoliutsii," *Kommunistka*, no. 10 (1927): 77.

[34] On Nikolaeva, see *Slavnye bol'shevichki*, 236–37. For examples of her work with women in Petrograd, see *Petrogradskaia pravda*, 8 March 1919, 4.

[35] *Slavnye bol'shevichki*, 237, asserts that Nikolaeva supported the opposition. It is my

Plate 26. Klavdiia Nikolaeva, probably in the 1920s.

Artiukhina became the leader that Nikolaeva could not. Of all the leading Bolshevik feminists, she was most like Samoilova – firm, determined, politically astute, and outspoken in the cause of women's issues. Like Samoilova, she was able to call for attention to women's problems without stirring up suspicions that she was a feminist. Also like Samoilova, she knew when to be careful. Therefore she stayed away from the opposition and made sure that the publications under her control hewed to the party line, wherever it went.[36]

Artiukhina's political agility enabled her to declaim the premises of Bolshevik feminism as ardently and insistently as Kollontai had done. She pursued an active speaking schedule at party meetings and Zhenotdel conferences, where she reiterated the importance of emancipating women from domestic burdens as well as creating opportunities for them to find

supposition that she lost her position at the Zhenotdel because of her participation.

[36] As an example, see A. Artiukhina, "Zapomni, rabotnitsa. Ob osnovnykh piatnadtsatoi partkonferentsii," *Rabotnitsa*, no. 22 (1926): 1–2.

good jobs. She demanded that women be included among those designing the new society, both because they would raise their own consciousness thereby and because they would give a higher priority to their own emancipation than men would. She called for fidelity to the socialist vision of a communalized society where the nuclear family and the subordination of wives that attended it would have disappeared. And she deduced from these general principles very specific policy recommendations. Artiukhina proposed that trade unions improve training programs for women and that the government include women on the budget committees of every department. She also demanded that all the many plans for socialist construction being proposed in the late 1920s be considered in the light of how they would advance or retard women's emancipation. In 1930 Artiukhina rejected proposals to manufacture electrical appliances in the Soviet Union in an acerbic tone typical of her:

Our task is to build a socialized life. It is better to suffer now with old dishrags, flat irons, and frying pans in order to have the means and strength to throw into the construction of socialized institutions – cafeterias, nurseries, kindergartens, and laundries.

We are making giant steps on the road to socialist construction. Why should we copy the bourgeoisie, who with these same dishrags and saucepans enslave women workers still more and draw them into the kitchen? *Lenin didn't teach us this.*[37]

Under Artiukhina's leadership, the department reached a greater audience than ever before. In 1926–27, 620,000 women attended the delegate conferences held by the Zhenotdel across the Soviet Union.[38] Many thousands more people read its publications; by 1930 *Rabotnitsa* was being published bimonthly in press runs of 265,000 copies. Hundreds of Zhenotdel workers preached the visions of Kollontai and Inessa and Samoilova from Leningrad to Kiev to Omsk. They also scraped together the money for daycare centers or cafeterias with little help from the local party organizations and sometimes in the face of active opposition. At worst, the projects languished after a few months. At best, they won support from factory managers or government agencies and became institutionalized public facilities.

Despite these successes, Artiukhina could not save the Zhenotdel. She must have feared that it was coming to the end of its short life on the day in August 1928 when Joseph Stalin walked unannounced into her office.

[37] "Za sotsialisticheskuiu peredelku byta," *Rabotnitsa*, 3. Italics in the original. An example of her approach to trade unions is A. Artiukhina, "Sorok protsentov vsekh bezrabotnykh na birzhakh truda – zhenshchiny," *Rabotnitsa*, no. 21 (1926): 3. For an analysis of the importance of women being involved in leadership, see Artiukhina, "Rabota sredi zhenshchin – na vysshuiu stupen'," *Rabotnitsa*, no. 5 (1930): 4–6.

[38] F. Rizel', "Sostav delegatskikh sobranii sozyva 1926/27 g.," *Kommunistka*, no. 9 (September 1927): 27.

The party's General Secretary told her that the Central Committee, responding to her complaints that there were too few women holding office, had just passed a resolution urging that women be promoted. Stalin had therefore come to ask Artiukhina for a list of people willing and able to take on greater responsibilities. Artiukhina, somewhat nonplussed, replied that it would take her a few days to compile such a list. Stalin did not like that answer, so he asked her the name of her staffers. Advising her on his way out to order up replacements from local Zhenotdel departments, he left. Within weeks, the most experienced people in the Central Zhenotdel had been transferred to other posts.[39]

The Central Committee decree that had sent Stalin to see Artiukhina was no answer to her prayers, as she well knew. It was instead a refusal to defend the Zhenotdel at an hour of very grave need. Ever since its creation, Zhenotdel leaders had fought the attempts of local and regional party officials to abolish the department. Such people had complained continually that the Zhenotdel was a waste of resources. They had criticized the department's workers as poorly trained, and they had accused them of vices commonly attributed to women, that is, incompetence, laziness, and frivolousness. The harassment such men routinely visited on Zhenotdel workers had driven many of them to quit the work over the years. The complainants also sent a stream of petitions up the party hierarchy, calling for the Zhenotdel's elimination. Until 1928 the Zhenotdel's leaders had beaten back these attacks by rallying the Central Committee to reaffirm its support and instruct local communists to cooperate.

In the fall of 1927, the party leaders began to waver. Responding to complaints from Agitprop that the Zhenotdel duplicated its work, the Central Committee authorized the creation of "rationalization committees" to investigate overlap between the two departments. Agitprop had long been seeking to get work among women put clearly under its purview. Armed by the Central Committee decree, its leaders managed to persuade the rationalization committees to abolish one Zhenotdel section after another in the provinces.[40]

Consequently, when Stalin walked into her office that August day in 1928, he encountered a woman who had been trying for months to save the department. Artiukhina could not have been encouraged by the refusal of the party leaders to issue another of their customary reaffirmations of support. Rather, they offered her the sop that they would promote

[39] *Bez nikh my ne pobedili by. Vospominaniia zhenshchin-uchastnits Oktiabr'skoi revoliutsii, grazhdanskoi voiny, i sotsialisticheskogo stroitel'stva* (Moscow, 1975), 234.

[40] Wendy Z. Goldman, "Industrial Politics, Peasant Rebellion, and the Death of the Proletarian Women's Movement in the USSR," *Slavic Review* 55 (Spring 1996): 57. I am indebted to the author for making a copy of this article available to me prior to its publication.

large numbers of women into "leading positions in the Party, unions, and soviets."[41] On its face such a declaration was irrelevant to Artiukhina's problems, even before Stalin managed to turn it into a raid on the central department's staff.

Without Central Committee support, Artiukhina could not hope to succeed. She had no recourse but to beg the male leadership for help. But her standing with them in the summer of 1928 was probably not very high, because of the failure of a particular Zhenotdel scheme with which she was closely associated. Artiukhina had been a vocal advocate over the previous two years of efforts to liberate women in Central Asia, the region of the Soviet Union east of the Caspian Sea and north of the border with Afghanistan. Artiukhina had argued that the women of the area, Muslims who lived under very strict forms of patriarchy, were so downtrodden that they could serve as a "surrogate proletariat," a base of support for the party in an area that had seen virtually no industrialization and which therefore lacked a native working class. Women would come to Bolshevism if properly approached, the familiar argument ran. The party leadership had been persuaded by Artiukhina and others, and Zhenotdel workers had fanned out across the region to urge women to shed their veils and attend women's conferences. The result was a disastrous bloodbath that reached a horrifying climax in 1928. Enraged Muslim men struck back at those who were attempting to undermine their authority within their families, attacking women who cooperated with the Zhenotdel, Zhenotdel activists, and some supportive male communists. Between 1926 and 1928, more than 800 people died in this violent retaliation. In 1928 the Central Committee ordered the Zhenotdel and the local communist officials to discontinue the campaign. Artiukhina's reputation probably suffered as a consequence.[42]

It is doubtful, however, that any Bolshevichka, however unblemished her record, could have defended the Zhenotdel from the attack that intensified in the eighteen months following Stalin's visit to Artiukhina's office. Local party conferences across the Soviet Union voted to abolish the department, Agitprop kept up its efforts through the rationalization committees, and trade union officials dismantled their organizations' work among women. In June 1929, the Politburo, alarmed by reports that peasant women were leading resistance to the collectivization of agriculture in many provinces, finally issued a decree reaffirming the necessity for the Zhenotdel; the old theory that hostile and backward females could

[41] "O vydvizhenii zhenshchin kommunistok," *Kommunistka*, no. 8 (1928): 3, quoted in Goldman, "Industrial Politics, Peasant Rebellion, and the Death of the Proletarian Women's Movement in the USSR," 57.

[42] On the campaign in Central Asia, see Gregory Massell, *The Surrogate Proletariat: Moslem Women and Revolutionary Strategies in Soviet Central Asia, 1919–1929* (Princeton, 1974).

wreck the transformation of the country was still influential even at this date. Artiukhina worked hard in the months thereafter to defend the department at party conferences, but this time her advocacy was not enough. In January 1930 the Central Committee announced plans for a general party reorganization that included the transfer of the Zhenotdel's work to Agitprop. Finally the leadership in Moscow and in the provinces had agreed that a separate department for work among women was no longer necessary.[43]

Throughout 1930 Artiukhina tried to make the best of this decision by declaring that now all agitators, not just the *zhenskii aktiv*, the female cadres, would see it as their responsibility to reach out to women. She wrote article after article and appeared at meeting after meeting to urge Agitprop to take its new obligations seriously, but she did not succeed. As she herself had predicted, after the Zhenotdel was gone, Agitprop paid virtually no attention to the projects it had been instructed to continue. The lobby for women within the party, set up fifteen years before by Inessa, Krupskaia, Stal, Samoilova, and Kollontai, had been dissolved and the era of Bolshevik feminism had ended. Artiukhina went back to the textile mills she had left so many years before, to serve as a factory director.[44]

While it lasted, the Zhenotdel played a crucial role in disseminating ideas about women's emancipation to the party and the larger society. Nowhere in the European world was there an organization like it, a department in a ruling party that publicized the importance of women's emancipation from domestic as well as civic and economic inequality. The Zhenotdel brought to millions of women the message that they were valued members of the new society who no longer had to live in ignorance and subjection. Its lobbying efforts from the top to the bottom of Soviet society caused attention to be paid to women's problems, more attention than those problems would otherwise have gotten, particularly on the local level. The Zhenotdel was also the training ground for tens of thousands of Bolshevichki, who later looked back on their youth in the department with great pride.[45]

The onset of the Stalin era

The abolition of the Zhenotdel coincided with, indeed was a part of, the end of the NEP decade and the beginning of the Stalin era. The

---

[43] Goldman, "Industrial Politics, Peasant Rebellion, and the Death of the Proletarian Women's Movement in the USSR," 57–63.
[44] For Zhenotdel workers' reaction to the abolition of the department, see Clements, "The Utopianism of the Zhenotdel," 495–96; Goldman, "Industrial Politics, Peasant Rebellion, and the Death of the Proletarian Woman's Movement in the USSR," 63–72.
[45] The best single collection of Bolshevichki memoirs of the Zhenotdel is *Bez nikh my ne pobedili by.*

department was dissolved in 1930, a year of turmoil in the Soviet Union. Stalin's leadership, having decided to push the economy along rapidly toward industrialization, had undertaken the collectivization of agriculture in 1929. The peasants were now fighting back, so the countryside was once again plunged into violence. Meanwhile, the party was also supervising the implementation of the ambitious First Five Year Plan for building up heavy industry. The decision to do away with the Zhenotdel was closely connected with these initiatives. The leadership in Moscow needed a well-run Agitprop to deliver the calls for heroic effort to the masses, and it needed an obedient officialdom in the provinces to carry out orders. Not only did the Zhenotdel irritate both Agitprop and the local party leadership, it used up funds that could be spent more efficiently through one unified department for agitation. The Zhenotdel was not the only agency to fall victim to the argument that agitprop functions should be consolidated; in the same reorganization the Central Committee also abolished the Section for Jewish Affairs and the Department for Work in the Countryside.

The decision to abolish the Zhenotdel was taken, therefore, within the context of a party reorganization driven by the leaders' reading of the necessities of the moment. It also occurred within the much larger context of the creation of a new, Soviet system of values. The party leaders sought to control this process, but they were unable to. In truth, they could not even fully comprehend it. A vast array of interactions between communists of all ranks and the multitudes of the nation resulted in the blending of radical socialist visions, liberal ideals long current in Russia's cities, and traditional beliefs and customs into an official Soviet culture to which the party gave its blessings in the 1930s. Such accommodations between revolutionary leaderships and the people they lead have occurred in many places, from eighteenth-century France to twentieth-century China, and they have often involved reconsideration and then repudiation of the radical attacks on patriarchy that marked the revolution's initial phase. In France, the demands of feminists such as Olympe de Gouges that women be granted the same liberties as men were denied even before Napoleon ended the revolution's most experimental period; de Gouges herself was sent to the guillotine. In China, efforts in the early 1950s to break up the traditional family by encouraging daughters-in-law to renounce publicly their mothers-in-law gave way in a few years to declarations of the importance of the family to the preservation of the social order.[46]

---

[46] On Olympe de Gouges, see Joan Landes, *Women and the Public Sphere in the Age of the French Revolution* (Ithaca, N. Y., 1988), 124–27. On the "speaking bitterness" campaign in China, see Kay Ann Johnson, *Women, the Family, and Peasant Revolution in China* (Chicago, 1983), 115–53.

The Zhenotdel's demise emerged from a similar transition in the Soviet Union. By the end of the 1920s, the party leadership had disavowed earlier proposals for free love, communal living, and collective childrearing, proposals that had always been dangerously unpopular with the Soviet people, particularly the peasants. Instead, the party endorsed premarital chastity and the pattern of a nuclear family bound together by love, respect, and fidelity between the spouses. This Soviet conceptualization of the family marked a compromise. It was not simply traditional, for the Russian traditional family had been extended rather than nuclear, and far more severely patriarchal. But neither did the new Soviet ideal go so far as Bolshevik feminists such as Kollontai and Inessa had wanted. Repudiated were their notions of intimate life transformed to promote individual sexual and emotional fulfillment. Instead, official spokespeople – propagandists and party leaders – endorsed long-term monogamy and extolled its value to the proper care of children. "To rear children, to set them on their own feet, requires a minimum of fifteen years," wrote Anatolii Lunarcharskii, head of Narkompros, in 1927. "That means marriage should be a long, companionate marriage."[47]

The editing of socialist ideals to make them fit with a modernized patriarchalism required that the Bolshevik vision of the emancipated woman be changed. The party never rejected its original conception, that women should be fully equal participants in society, but in the 1930s it adopted as well the notion that women should also find fulfillment in taking care of their families. Women were to be citizens, workers, housekeepers, wives, and mothers. They were to serve their families and their nation. Klavdiia Nikolaeva summed up this revised view of women's roles in a pamphlet published in 1940. "In the Soviet Union," she wrote, "a woman is active in politics and government and at the same time is a mother, whom our party and government take care of. This is a new woman, who participates actively in the governing of the state, in the governing of the economy, and in the cultural affairs of the country." The government had created social services that would permit women to enjoy both "beloved work" and "the joys of maternity," Nikolaeva declared. Women should work outside the home in order to be equal members of the new society, but they also had important childrearing obligations. It was their responsibility "to instill in their children a communist worldview, patriotism, heroism, and courage." "The strength, the unity of interests of the members of the Soviet family," Nikolaeva declared, "are most important factors in socialist construction."[48]

[47] V. Lunacharskii, *O byte* (Moscow and Leningrad, 1927), 202.
[48] K. Nikolaeva and L. Karaseva, *Zhenshchina v boiakh za kommunizm* (Moscow, 1940), 7, 23.

Such idealizations of conjugal love and parental responsibilities were not only more congenial to the great majority of Soviet citizens than visions of free love, they also served the purposes of the regime. The family, once denounced by Marxists even in its nuclear form as a bastion of oppressive ideas, was restored to its conventional role as the foundation of the social system. The family was thought of in the 1930s as the place where mothers taught patriotism to the new generation and ministered to the needs of men weary from the grueling labor of building industry. This conception grew from ideas far more deeply rooted than Marx's. The notion that women should inculcate civic values went back to the ancient past in Europe and had been reinforced throughout the modern period. It was a staple belief of bourgeois industrial society in the nineteenth century. The notion that women should build a home to shelter the children and to succor the men who toil in the urban jungle appeared first in industrializing Britain and has since traveled the world alongside industrialization. Both ideas anchor the social order in the family and then grant women's nurturance a key role in the family's preservation, and hence in the preservation of the social order. Both ideas represent adaptations of very old conceptions of the female to the urban world and to contemporary political forms, and they have appealed to politicians all over Europe in the twentieth century. Yet it is nonetheless deeply ironic that no European politicians joined in singing the praises of woman's domestic vocation more happily than the Soviet Communist Party leaders of the 1930s, as they sought to extend their control and cement their own status in the reordered national society. Stalin's men were happy to endorse a plan for Soviet society in which order radiated downward from Moscow through the ranks of male leaders and came to rest finally in a well-tended family of patriotic citizens.

At the center of the cult of domesticity was a new model of womanhood, the pattern of the supportive helpmeet to the elite man. By the mid-1930s the Soviet press was praising the wives of the high-achieving workers called Stakhanovites, the wives of professional men, particularly engineers, and the wives of party officials, for providing good homes for their busy husbands and beautifying their environment. Conferences of engineers' wives convened in the mid-1930s to plan volunteer activities (such as planting flower beds) and charity projects (such as collecting clothes for the needy) that would soften the harsh effects of rapid industrialization. Such developments bespoke the emergence of a new, Soviet elite, one in which women were scheduled to play not only the roles of comrade and worker, the Bolshevichka's roles, but also the more familiar part as symbols of and supporters of male achievement. The ideal Soviet wife was almost the polar opposite of the hard Bolshevichka, for not only did she confine herself to hearth and home, she was warmly maternal. A subordinate to her husband, the idealized Soviet wife was committed to the private life the Bolshevichki were supposed to have left behind.[49]

The available evidence does not permit us to probe very deeply into the responses of the Bolshevichki to these new ideas. The pressure to keep criticism to themselves mounted during the Stalin years, muzzling all but the most incautious of people. The feminists, Kollontai, Artiukhina, Sofia Smidovich, and their disciples, were undoubtedly deeply disappointed. No one understood better than they how unequal Soviet women still were. They knew as well that women's inequality was deeply rooted in those very interpretations of domestic life that were now receiving official blessing. On simply a practical level, maintaining the family nest meant doing a huge amount of labor above and beyond that in the workplace, labor that the government had once pledged to transfer to public institutions. When homemaking was declared to be a part of woman's natural vocation, it became all the easier to postpone socializing it.

The Bolshevichki who had always held feminism at arm's length probably interpreted the rising importance accorded domesticity rather differently. The ethos of the female revolutionary had devalued private life by calling on women to devote themselves exclusively to the public cause and to public work. But many Bolshevichki, unable or unwilling to order their priorities accordingly, had in fact already made their families central to their lives. They had given their husbands' work assignments precedence over their own, and they had agonized over neglecting their children while they pursued their party duties. In her last days, Inessa had borne witness to how difficult it was, even for the hardest of Bolshevichki, to keep the conflicting political and familial loyalties in balance. She and other Bolshevichki had long hoped for a future in which the nuclear family would be not abolished but reformed into an institution founded on "love and friendship, common labor in rearing children, and common work in communist construction," to borrow Nikolaeva's words.[50] For the present, the new conception of Soviet motherhood provided a way to reconcile the tugs of family with political commitments, for it declared that the Bolshevichka was contributing to the cause by inculcating "the communist worldview" in her children.

There were many other reasons for Bolshevichki to accept the new

---

[49] This analysis is also developed in Barbara Evans Clements, *Daughters of Revolution: A History of Women in the USSR* (Arlington Heights, Ill., 1994), 67–76. For a memoir by a party official's wife that expresses these values, see E. E. Vesnik, "Nepartiinye bol'shevichki," in *Uchastnitsy velikogo sozidaniia* (Moscow, 1962), 214–22. On Stakhanovite wives, see Lewis H. Siegelbaum, *Stakhanovism and the Politics of Productivity in the USSR, 1935–1941* (Cambridge, 1988). The seminal study of the domestic values of the Stalin regime is Vera Dunham, *In Stalin's Time: Middle-class Values in Soviet Fiction* (Cambridge, 1976).

[50] Nikolaeva and Karaseva, *Zhenshchina v boiakh za kommunizm*, 21.

regime in the early 1930s, despite its shortcomings. The factories, so long the repositories of Bolshevik hopes, were humming. Social progress was everywhere: the schools had been thrown open to students from all classes and ethnicities; health care was publicly funded; day-care centers and cafeterias were springing up in neighborhoods and workplaces. Newspapers, magazines, radio, and movies lauded the present and confidently predicted a glorious future of social justice and material plenty. Socialists from all over the world flocked to the Soviet Union to observe at first hand the brave new world. The cost to the country of the party's autocratic leadership, which included the deaths of millions in collectivization, did not make it into the newspapers to raise doubts in the minds of those who wanted, as the Bolshevichki wanted, to believe in the system's fundamental merits.

The Bolshevichki also had reason for hope because they were benefiting quite considerably in the present. They were the new elite, blessed with status and privilege. Those who were connected to high-ranking men had comfortable apartments staffed with cooks and nannies. They enjoyed cars and radios and vacations on the Black Sea. Most Bolshevichki possessed far fewer luxuries, but nonetheless the majority had higher standards of living than those Soviet citizens who were not communists. They also were honored members of the new order, for a well-established mythology, drawn from the Bolshevichki's own collective identity, portrayed them as stern, ascetic, dedicated, formidable heroes of the Revolution. They took their honors as a due recognition of this role in leading the greatest social transformation in history, but they did not join the engineers' wives in volunteer work. Rather, the Bolshevichki stayed true to their own heritage and identity, working at their jobs as long as their health would permit it.[51]

By the middle of the 1930s the two founding generations of communist women were entering middle, even old, age. Those who had been born in the 1870s were already in their sixties. Those of the younger generation were well into their thirties. Their lives were set into established patterns of home life and professional work. Many of them probably expected that the privileges and status they had earned as creators of the revolution would endure, as would the successes of the society they had helped to build. There had been difficulties and mistakes all along the way, but the

---

[51] For three very different portraits of elite women in the 1930s, see Elena Bonner, *Mothers and Daughters*, trans. Antonina W. Bouis (New York, 1992); Lidiia Shatunovskaia, *Zhizn' v Kremle* (New York, 1982); and Margaret Wettlin, *Fifty Russian Winters* (New York, 1992), esp. 49–73. On the self-definition of Bolshevichki in the 1930s, see any of the many memoir collections. Especially enlightening because they include women from provincial areas are *Kaluzhskie bol'shevichki* (Kaluga, 1960), and A. Pomelova, *Slovo o zhenshchinakh severa* (n.p., 1968).

tightening controls over public discussion made these ever harder to assess, even with friends. The prisons were still full of Mensheviks and SRs as well as engineers and miscellaneous other professionals, people who, according to the state-controlled press, were guilty of plotting against the government. There had been horrors committed against the peasants during the collectivization of agriculture, although the scope of the catastrophe was not clear and few people spoke openly about it. Some Bolshevichki undoubtedly nourished doubts about Stalin and other top leaders, but most had probably long since ceased to question the rightfulness of the party's control over society. This seemed justified by the USSR's many accomplishments. Any deficiencies would work themselves out as the system matured.

The Purges

And then, in the second half of the 1930s, the Communist Party began to visit on its own members the brutal persecution it had hitherto meted out to its opponents. The mass arrests carried out by the NKVD (the new acronym for the political police) between 1937 and 1939 are often referred to as the Purges, because one of their purposes was to purge and clear out the membership of the Communist Party itself so as to make it fully amenable to control by Stalin's dictatorship. The Purges were only one of the many assaults Stalin's government perpetrated against the Soviet people, but they constituted the first great attack on the party itself. Between 1936 and 1939 the NKVD arrested millions of communists, usually on fabricated charges of conspiracy and treason. Tens of thousands of party members were executed, and many more were sent off to hard-labor camps spread across the Soviet Union. Scholars hotly debate the total number of the victims of the Purges, but whatever the extent of the carnage, there is no question that the party leadership ordered the NKVD to attack the party and to pay particularly aggressive attention to high-ranking officials. According to figures released in 1956 by Nikita Khrushchev, 56 percent of the delegates to the Seventeenth Party Congress in 1934 had been arrested by 1939; and 70 percent of the members of the Central Committee elected by that congress had been executed.[52]

Assessing the effects of the Purges on the Bolshevichki is difficult, for the necessary statistics are only beginning to become available. The evidence that currently exists does establish that the NKVD arrested, imprisoned, and executed far more men than women. Women were 11

[52] Nikita S. Khrushchev, *The Crimes of the Stalin Era*, annotated by Boris I. Nikolaevsky (New York, 1962), 520–21.

percent of all of those prosecuted formally by the legal system in the late 1930s; in 1940 they made up 8 percent of the prison population. Men also died in greater numbers than women, a fact confirmed by the death dates of male and female Bolsheviks in the data bases.[53] (See figure 5.) But moving from general statistics to estimate the numbers of Bolshevichki actually arrested is extremely difficult because the creators and curators of the records of these women's lives deliberately covered up the effects of the Purges. They did not, for the most part, write about women who had perished, and they ordinarily did not mention the prison sentences of those who survived to be rehabilitated later. Yet even the sanitized documents that Soviet memoirists and biographers produced yield the fact that perhaps as many as 14 percent of the women in the data base were arrested, and 5 percent were executed. Both the statistics that are available on arrests, and a comparison of the death dates of the Bolshevichki of both generations, suggest that more Old Bolsheviks fell victim than did civil war joiners, a situation the reverse of that which prevailed among communist men. (See figure 6.) Yet it should be cautioned that this disparity may be an illusion arising from imperfect documentation, for the information generally available on the female civil war joiners is in several respects less complete than that on older women. One should add also that it is likely that more Bolshevichki of both generations were arrested than the data base suggests, because the data base was necessarily built primarily from sources that did not include purge victims. (See table 41.)

Women who were arrested fell into the NKVD's net for many of the same reasons as men. Bolshevichki who held important positions in economic management, who were the subordinates or superiors or friends of persons who had been arrested, who had been members of any opposition faction, who had once been Mensheviks or SRs, who had come from the upper classes, or who possessed any combination of these characteristics were likely to fall under suspicion.

Women were also subject to a charge seldom leveled against men. They could be accused of being "a member of the family of an enemy of the people." The NKVD, acting in accord with the new patriarchal ideas of the Stalin regime, took away women married to suspect men and passed over many of those who, like Stasova and Kollontai, had once been powerful in their own right but were now simply ageing women on their own. The

---

[53] J. Arch Getty, Gábor T. Rittersporn, and Viktor N. Zemskov, "Victims of the Soviet Penal System in the Pre-War Years: A First Approach on the Basis of Archival Evidence," *American Historical Review* 98 (October 1993): 1025; J. Arch Getty and Roberta T. Manning, eds., *Stalinist Terror: New Perspectives* (New York, 1993), esp. 165–66, 217–21, 225–46.

Table 41 *Estimates of effects of 1936–1939 Purges on Bolshevichki*

	Old Bolshevichki (%) (N = 267)	Civil war joiners (%) (N = 204)
A. Bolshevichki arrested and imprisoned	5.2 (14)	3.9 (8)
Of the imprisoned, those married to a man who was also purged	85.7 (12)	25.0 (2)
B. Bolshevichki executed	2.6 (7)	1.5 (3)[a]
C. Bolshevichki who died, 1936–39, causes unspecified in sources	3.7 (10)	1.5 (3)
Possible death toll (B + C)	6.4 (17)	2.9 (6)
D. Bolshevichki whose work records end in id-1930s, causes unspecified	7.5 (20)	5.4 (11)
Possible arrest toll (A + C + D)	16.5 (44)	10.8 (22)

[a] Included here is Romana Volf, who committed suicide shortly before being arrested.

enforcers who had hunted witches in the European past had sought out solitary old women, because they feared the power of females who were not tied to families. The NKVD did not fear single women, but it believed in the power of wives. So many wives of fallen Bolsheviks were arrested in 1937 that the prison administration was forced to create special camps to hold them.[54] Among the Old Bolsheviks in the data base, twelve out of the fourteen who were imprisoned were married to imprisoned men.

Those Bolshevichki arrested because they were "wives of enemies of the people" were usually charged with participation in treasonous activities, either with their husbands or independently of them.[55] The accusations were fabricated; there was no great network of traitors operating within the Soviet Union. But in a terror that fed on guilt by association, those closest of associates, wives, were natural suspects. This perverse reasoning could take ludicrous forms. Feodosiia Drabkina, the stalwart Bolshevichka who had once smeared mustard on her daughter Elizaveta's tongue to teach her discretion, was arrested along with her daughter in 1937 or 1938 after her husband Sergei Gusev was expelled from the party *posthumously* (he had died of natural causes in 1933).[56]

Some wives may have been arrested chiefly to keep them quiet. Others

[54] Anna Larina, *This I Cannot Forget: The Memoirs of Nikolai Bukharin's Widow*, intro. Stephen F. Cohen, trans. Gary Kern (New York, 1993), 42.

[55] Both Anna Larina and Evgeniia Ginzburg were accused of belonging to such groups. See ibid., and Eugenia Ginzburg, *Journey into the Whirlwind*, trans. Paul Stevenson and Max Hayward (New York, 1967), 50.

[56] Roy Medvedev, *Let History Judge*, rev. ed., ed. and trans. George Shriver (New York, 1989), 409.

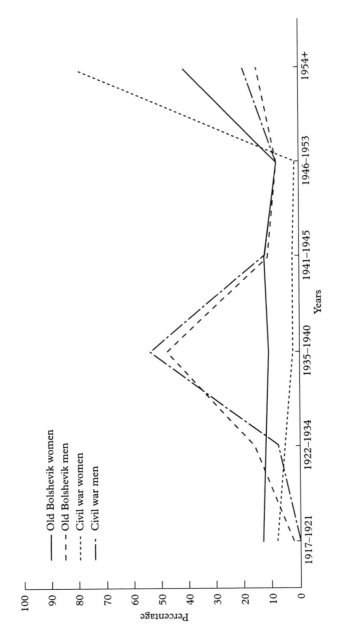

Figure 5. Death dates of male and female Bolsheviks

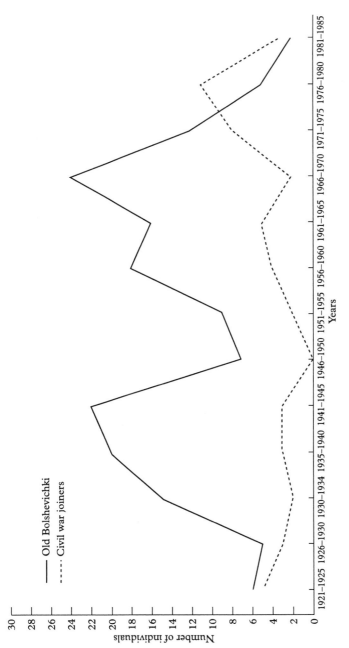

Figure 6. Death dates of Bolshevichki

may have been detained in order to intimidate and silence those who were not. Viacheslav Molotov, Stalin's lieutenant and the co-signer with him of many execution orders, claimed much later that wives of purged men had to be "isolated" from the general population because they spread "complaints" and "discontent."[57] The truth is that many wives knew that their husbands were completely innocent of the crimes of which they were accused. Wives were also likely to be privy to information that might prove embarrassing to those who had profited from their husbands' fall. Liudmila Shaposhnikova, for example, was married to Mikhail Chudov, the second secretary of the Leningrad city committee. She was the model Bolshevichka, a textile worker who had grown up in St. Petersburg, joined the party in 1917 when she was twenty-two, and spent the 1920s running a perfume-manufacturing enterprise. Her husband had hitched his fortunes to those of Sergei Kirov, who rose to head the party organization in Leningrad after Zinoviev's ouster in 1925. By the early 1930s, Shaposh-nikova was firmly (or so she thought) ensconced in the Soviet Union's new elite. She even went to the United States to study merchandising techniques with Polina Zemchuzhina, another civil war joiner who was Molotov's wife. Shaposhnikova's success ended in 1937, when first her husband and then she herself were arrested. She was sent to a camp reserved for wives of prominent Bolsheviks in Tomsk. There she became a leader among the prisoners, but she held out little hope for her future. She told fellow inmate Anna Larina, Bukharin's wife, that she knew too much about Stalin's involvement in Kirov's assassination in 1934. Before the year was out Shaposhnikova was taken back to Moscow and executed.[58]

Women who were married to prominent Bolsheviks and who had their own history of party service, such as Shaposhnikova, may have been particularly vulnerable. Varvara Iakovleva and Anna Reiman are two other cases in point. Born in 1884 into a family of rich merchants, Iakovleva worked in the party underground in Moscow from 1904 on. Like Bosh and Zemliachka, Iakovleva sought out political leadership during the civil war years; she was a member of the Moscow party committee, leader of the Left Communist protest over the Treaty of Brest-Litovsk, and, in 1919, head of the Cheka in Petrograd, where she earned the sobriquet "Bloody Iakovleva." She also joined Bosh in signing the Petition of the Forty-Six in 1924. Thereafter she became a supporter of Bukharin and of his accommodationist approach to the peasantry.

Iakovleva worked through the 1920s as a deputy commissar in Narkom-pros, but with the onset of the First Five Year Plan she was transferred to a lesser post in the Commissariat of Finance. Her demotion was probably

---

[57] Chuev, *Sto sorok besed s Molotovym*, 415.   [58] Larina, *This I Cannot Forget*, 41, 45–47.

connected to the political disgrace of Bukharin in the late 1920s. In 1933 Iakovleva's husband, I. N. Smirnov, commissar of mail and telegraph in the 1920s and once a close friend of Trotsky, was arrested for conspiring against Stalin; in 1936 he was tried with Zinoviev and Kamenev in the first of the three extraordinary "show trials" (public pseudojudicial exhibitions) of the purges. All the defendants were found guilty of treason and executed shortly thereafter; Iakovleva was arrested a few months later. She testified against Bukharin at his trial in March 1938 and later either was executed or died in the camps.[59]

Anna Reiman was a lower-ranking communist than Iakovleva, but she too sprang from middle-class origins, acquired a job in the economic sector, and married a man who was later purged. The daughter of a Latvian miller, Reiman had been a clerk and tutor before the revolution. In 1919 she joined the party. She worked in trade union organizations in Moscow throughout the 1920s and early 1930s, then earned a degree in engineering and became an expert in workplace safety. In 1936 she was denounced as an "enemy of the people," fired from her job, and expelled from the party. Reiman was apparently not arrested, and she was able to appeal her expulsion successfully. Early in 1938 she was restored to party membership, but then, on 12 March of that year, her husband, Alexander Putyn, was arrested. Ten days later Reiman was once again expelled from the party. Arrested this time, she was soon sentenced to eight years' imprisonment, the standard term for "wives of enemies of the people." She served less than a year in a camp; thereafter she was sent as a captive laborer to an asphalt factory in Siberia, where she worked as an engineer. She was released from this assignment in 1946, and received an official rehabilitation in 1955. Reiman probably experienced an easier fate than Iakovleva because she was not so prominent, but like Iakovleva she possessed the dangerous combination of middle-class origins, a career in the economic sector, and an arrested husband.[60]

Old Bolshevichki and the Purges

Most Bolshevichki managed to escape arrest during the Purges. Some, especially from the civil war generation, prospered during the late 1930s,

[59] V. Iakovleva, "Partiinaia rabota v Moskovskoi oblasti v period fevral'–oktiabr' 1917 g.," *Proletarskaia revoliutsiia*, no. 3 (1923): 196–204; Iakovleva, "Podgotovka oktiabr'skogo vosstaniia v Moskovskoi oblasti," *Proletarskaia revoliutsiia*, no. 10 (1922): 302–06; Ronald I. Kowalski, *The Bolshevik Party in Conflict: The Left Communist Opposition of 1918* (London, 1991), 21, 148; Medvedev, *Let History Judge*, 1st ed., 292; Robert C. Tucker and Stephen F. Cohen, eds., *The Great Purge Trial* (New York, 1965), 397–413.

[60] GARF, f. 7920, op. 2, d. 1, ll. 1–3.

for they received promotions into the many vacancies the purges created. Some Bolshevichki also collaborated in the process by denouncing co-workers to the police. And a few worked with the NKVD. Of these, Rozaliia Zemliachka may have been the most successful; she was certainly the highest ranking.

In the midst of all the suffering, Zemliachka flourished. She continued throughout the 1930s to hold office in the party's Central Control Commission; at the Seventeenth Party Congress in 1934, she was also elected to the Commission of Soviet Control, a watch-dog organization that investigated infractions by government employees. The distinctions between the party and government control commissions were more bureaucratic than real. In each post, Zemliachka was an investigator and enforcer. Her reputation as a merciless inquisitor spread. *Pravda* described her in 1936 as "the kind of person who is either loved or hated." Poet Demian Bedny intended to compliment the unappealing photograph of her that hung in the waiting room at her office when he wrote, "This is only a portrait of Zemliachka / The original is one hundred times more terrible!"[61]

There is no question that Zemliachka worked closely with the NKVD. Her jobs required that she turn over reports of infractions to them. Moreover, it is likely that she was their willing ally. For at least a decade, if not longer, she had shared the unhealthy Manicheanism that prevailed among party leaders close to Stalin and that blossomed in the 1930s into full-blown paranoia. A believer in the plots alleged to be menacing the party, Zemliachka became an adroit participant in destroying them. She also managed to protect herself from the Purges that swept through the ranks of the NKVD itself in 1938 and 1939. Instead of falling victim, Zemliachka won promotions. In September 1936 she was awarded the highest Soviet civilian decoration, the Order of Lenin. In 1937 she was elected a delegate to the Supreme Soviet. In May of 1939 she became chair of the Commission of Soviet Control, and that same year she became the only woman since Kollontai to serve on the Council of People's Commissars.[62]

If Zemliachka ever questioned the justice of what was going on all around her, she did so very privately. Her archives contain virtually nothing from this period. Such lacunae occur quite often in the sources on the 1930s; the testimony of the victims and a few of the bystanders has been recorded, but very few documents have turned up as yet to shed light on the thoughts of those who ran the terror. Their attitudes are expressed

---

[61] Both the *Pravda* article and the Bedny poem are quoted in *Geroi Oktiabria. Kniga o uchastnikakh Velikoi Oktiabr'skoi sotsialisticheskoi revoliutsii v Moskve* (Moscow, 1967), 35.
[62] *Slavnye bol'shevichki*, 152–53.

primarily in the official record of press pronouncements and Central Committee meetings, where they declaim, in the slogans and overheated rhetoric of the time, that the Purges are rooting out deadly enemies of the Soviet system. Perhaps this absurdity was in fact what people such as Zemliachka believed. Perhaps she sat in her dismal office under pictures of Lenin and Stalin and called down doom upon people whom she believed to be despicable traitors. If she had doubts, she may have done as Bukharin did and taken comfort from her Marxist faith that the socialist system itself would prosper despite the errors individuals made along the way. Perhaps occasionally she tried to save some of the innocent. Perhaps she was intent, mainly, on looking out for herself. Whatever her thoughts, she kept her place in the pack of leaders. By 1940 Zemliachka, the hardest of the hard Bolshevichki, was the only woman at the top of Stalin's government.[63]

Many Bolshevichki, perhaps the majority, hunkered down while the storm passed over them. Krupskaia continued her work in education. She tried several times to intercede with Stalin for accused comrades in 1936 and 1937, with some limited success. In 1939 she died of natural causes. Artiukhina managed to hold on to her job as director in a Moscow textile factory. Her friend Klavdiia Nikolaeva fared well also, despite her earlier association with Zinoviev. In the late 1920s Nikolaeva had worked as an agitator in the Caucasus, a position from which she had been promoted in the early 1930s, first to an Agitprop job in Moscow, then to an assistant secretaryship in an oblast committee, and then in 1936 to an administrative position in the national trade union organization. Bosh's sister Elena Rozmirovich, wife of the purged Nikolai Krylenko, appears to have survived the Purges while working in the party archives. Klavdiia Novgorodtseva, Stasova's friend and Sverdlov's wife, became an editor, while one of her sons, Andrei Sverdlov, made an evil reputation as an NKVD agent.[64]

Other Bolshevichki endured years of harassment, but avoided arrest. Of these the most important were the most famous women of Lenin's government, Kollontai and Stasova. Kollontai, who served as ambassador

---

[63] The best source to date on the mindset of top Stalinists is Chuev, *Sto sorok besed s Molotovym*. On the general acceptance by Soviet citizens of the threat of internal enemies, see Gábor T. Rittersporn, "The Omnipresent Conspiracy: On Soviet Imagery of Politics and Social Relations in the 1930s," in Getty and Manning, *Stalinist Terror*, 99–115. On Bukharin, see Larina, *This I Cannot Forget*.

[64] On Krupskaia, see McNeal, *Bride of the Revolution*, 291–92; Medvedev, *Let History Judge*, rev. ed., 403–04. On Artiukhina, see *Uchastnitsy velikogo sozidaniia*, 21; on Nikolaeva, *Slavnye bol'shevichki*, 236–38; on Rozmirovich, *Zhenshchiny russkoi revoliutsii* (Moscow, 1968), 567–68; on Novgorotseva, ibid., 317–18. Anna Larina, Bukharin's wife, revealed that the junior Sverdlov had worked for the NKVD; he was her interrogator (*This I Cannot Forget*, 240–41).

to Sweden throughout the purge years, had to return to Moscow every summer for consultations. In 1937 and 1938 she feared that she would be arrested, but she was not. Her grandson, Vladimir Kollontai, has speculated that Stalin left her free because she was the only female ambassador in Europe and therefore made good press for the Soviet Union. Molotov told an interviewer that there was no reason to arrest Kollontai since "she wasn't dangerous to us." Perhaps she had simply been away too long for Stalin's lieutenants to pay much attention to her. Perhaps the NKVD knew she was no threat because in fact they kept a very close eye on her. Like all Soviet diplomats, Kollontai was under the surveillance of agents in her embassy.[65]

Stasova settled into a far less glamorous and prestigious career than Kollontai's. After she returned from Germany in 1925, she worked for two years in the Central Committee Information Bureau. Then she became deputy head and, in 1928, head of MOPR, the International Organization for Help to Revolutionaries. MOPR provided financial and moral support to imprisoned radicals throughout the world, publicized human rights abuses in capitalist countries, and praised the achievements of the Soviet system at home and abroad. A large volunteer organization with chapters all over the USSR, MOPR also assisted refugees who had come to the Soviet Union; among its projects were schools for the children of foreign communists resident in Moscow in the early 1930s.

Stasova was not paid for her work at MOPR, but she seems to have devoted a considerable amount of time to it and to have taken considerable pride in the organization's accomplishments. She probably derived some spiritual sustenance in her work from the constant reminders of how revolutionaries and oppressed people were persecuted abroad. Perhaps immersing herself in the evils of capitalism assuaged any doubts she had about the evils of Stalinist socialism. Her work at MOPR also brought her into the lively community of exiled communists living in Moscow. They greatly admired her and through them she stayed in touch with the world of revolutionaries.[66]

---

[65] Vladimir Kollontai's remarks on his grandmother are contained in a documentary film, *A Wave of Passion*, prod. Kevin M. Mulhern, Kevin M. Mulhern Productions, 1994, videocassette. Molotov's remark about Kollontai is in Chuev, *Sto sorok besed s Molotovym*, 189. See also Clements, *Bolshevik Feminist*, 252–57.

[66] On Stasova's work in MOPR, see E. D. Stasova, *Vospominaniia* (Moscow, 1969), 185–209; S. M. Levidova and E. G. Salita, *Elena Dmitrievna Stasova. Biograficheskii ocherk* (Leningrad, 1969), 307–15; Pavel Podliashuk, *Bogatyrskaia simfoniia. Dokumental'-naia povest' o E. D. Stasovoi* (Moscow, 1977), 218–23; S. Chernomordik, "K desiatiletiiu MOPR," *Katorga i ssylka*, no. 95 (1932): 12–19; Stasova, *MOPR's Banners Abroad: Report to the Third MOPR Congress of the Soviet Union* (Moscow, 1931); Stasova, *Za edinyi front solidarnosti i pomoshchi. Doklad na IV plenume TsK MOPR SSSR, 17 noiabria 1935 g.* (Moscow, 1935).

Plate 27. Elena Stasova, date unknown.

That was a world she still cherished, as did her old comrade, Kollontai. In 1932, on the occasion of her sixtieth birthday, Stasova received a letter from Kollontai, one of the few the two ever exchanged. They had known one another since girlhood; their families were friends, and they had even had the same tutor, Mariia Strakhova, who had inspired both of them with her erudition and deep commitment to social reform. But they had never been friends because they were so different temperamentally – Kollontai was the warm one, expansive and emotional, while Stasova was composed and austere. In 1932 Kollontai broke the silence between them to write, "You know very well, Leilushka [an affectionate nickname for Elena], that I have always had not only warm feelings toward you, an attachment from our youth, but also, and above all, great respect and admiration for your character. I haven't kept such feelings for many people," Kollontai added, in a pointed reference to what she saw as the decay of moral standards in the Stalin era.

"Have you heard," Kollontai continued, "that Mariia Ivanovna [Strakhova, their tutor] died a year ago? She had been a ghost of the past for us for a long time, and yet, when I heard that Mariia Ivanovna was no more, I had a moment of sadness. A great deal of me was connected with her." Stasova wrote back that she too had heard of their teacher's death: "You're right; she is a ghost of the past, but for me, as for you, so much was connected with her from the time of our youth. A *Sturm-und-Drang* period, when so much formed, took shape, a dear time and irretrievable. It was a good time!"[67]

Stasova's nostalgia for their lost innocence and, perhaps, integrity did not prevent her from publicly defending the Soviet regime. In the early 1930s, when critics abroad charged Moscow with persecuting its political opposition, Stasova stoutly declared that there were no political prisoners in her country. The Mensheviks and SRs who languished in Soviet jails were guilty of the charges of counter-revolutionary activities preferred against them, she maintained. But Stasova, even then, may have known better. In 1934, perhaps as an act of mercy or of justice, she sent a colleague from MOPR, the Italian communist Vittorio Vidali, on a mission abroad when she picked up rumors that he was about to be arrested. In 1935 and through the first half of 1936 she served on various party control commissions and purge committees, signing her name to documents that declared people guilty of offenses that could result in their deaths. Probably she continued to tell herself that the accused had deserved their fate, but in the summer of 1936 she herself was denounced as a Trotskyite. Then the walls she had carefully erected to keep her from seeing the abuses committed by her own party crumbled.[68]

Stasova extricated herself from the charges leveled against her in 1936 and continued to head MOPR until 1938, while the Purges rumbled through the ranks of the foreigners gathered around MOPR. People she knew disappeared daily. The Dom pravitelstva, the apartment building for the privileged in which Stasova lived, became a house of doom, so many were the arrests of its residents in 1937 and 1938. Stasova herself was investigated more than once by the NKVD. Her secretary, Elizaveta Sheveleva, was sent to the camps. In 1938 Stasova finally left the decimated MOPR and sought refuge instead in an editorial job at the magazine *Internatsionalnaia literatura* (*International Literature*).[69]

[67] Quoted in Podliashuk, *Bogatyrskaia simfoniia*, 13–14.
[68] Stasova, *MOPR's Banners Abroad*, 37; Stasova, *Protiv belogo terrora* (Moscow, 1934), 24; Vittorio Vidali, *Diary of the Twentieth Congress of the Communist Party of the Soviet Union*, trans. Nell Amter Cattonar and A. M. Elliot (Westport, Conn., 1984), 36, 17; Podliashuk, *Bogatyrskaia simfoniia*, 229.
[69] On arrests in the Dom pravitel'stva, see Shatunovskaia, *Zhizn' v Kremle*, 99–106. Denunciations of Stasova are reported by Medvedev, *Let History Judge*, 1st ed., 308; and Vidali, *Diary of the Twentieth Congress*, 17. The arrest of Stasova's secretary is reported in Ginzburg, *Journey into the Whirlwind*, 342; and Vidali, *Diary of the Twentieth Congress*, 131.

It is a sign of the capriciousness of the terror that *Internatsionalnaia literatura* existed at all. This journal published foreign literature in Russian translation at a time when the daily press was shrieking about the dangers of foreign influences. It also gave work to poverty-stricken writers who would not or could not work within the controls of Soviet censorship. Boris Pasternak was one of its most famous contributors. Stasova must have worked with Pasternak from time to time, for she became the head of the department that dealt with English and French literature. Perhaps both of them attended the reception in 1939 held at the Institute of World Literature to celebrate the 375th anniversary of Shakespeare's birth – Pasternak because he was one of the most noted translators of the English poet, and Stasova because she was one of the organizers of the commemoration. Perhaps Stasova told herself as she circulated through the crowd of writers and editors that she was helping to preserve that Russian culture to which her beloved family had dedicated itself. The gathering had some special meaning to her, for she kept the beautifully printed invitation to Shakespeare's Moscow birthday party in her desk for the rest of her life.[70]

Stasova's formidable powers of self-control, honed earlier under such different circumstances, enabled her to retain her public composure through the Purges. She looked as much the Victorian schoolteacher as ever, her white hair coiled into a tight bun on the top of her head, her pince-nez wedged firmly onto her long nose, her blue eyes sharp and intimidating. She was a demanding boss to the editors and translators working under her, and they were awed by her severity, her aloofness, and the strength of her intellect. Hiding behind a facade of imperturbability, quietly, surreptitiously, Stasova also tried to help some of the victims of the Purges. She continued to warn her foreign comrades when arrest threatened. She collected money and clothes to give to the families of men who had disappeared. Occasionally she contacted Stalin or Molotov to plead the innocence of someone who had been arrested. (Krupskaia did the same.)[71]

Perhaps Stasova, like Kollontai, managed to ride out the storm because she was considered too harmless to arrest. By the late 1930s she had not held party office for more than fifteen years. She had never been an

---

[70] The invitation is in a file containing some of the contents of Stasova's desk (RTsKhIDNI, f. 356, d. 13).

[71] Subordinates testified to Stasova's demeanor in these years. See A. A. Isbakh, *Tovarishch Absoliut* (Moscow, 1963), 85–86; Lidiia Bat', "Absoliut," in her *Nezabyvaemye vstrechi* (Moscow, 1970), 11–28. Stasova's appeals for arrested people are mentioned in Levidova and Salita, *Stasova*, 327–28, and discussed in Vidali, *Diary of the Twentieth Congress*, 17, 133–34. On Krupskaia's attempts to free the accused, see Medvedev, *Let History Judge*, rev. ed., 403–04.

oppositionist, she had no husband, and she was always available to be trotted out on ceremonial occasions as one of Lenin's old guard. The ranks of those so available were now thinning drastically. Periodic reminders – the arrest of someone close to her, the news that someone had denounced her – brought home to her the importance of maintaining her spotless record. Stasova ended the 1930s in a small, spartan apartment in the center of Moscow, within sight of the Kremlin's red brick walls. There she drew the shades tight at night and tried not to hear the noises echoing down the hallways.[72]

The numbers of arrests diminished in 1939. Although episodes of renewed terror occurred throughout the rest of Stalin's long reign, never again did communists come under such wholesale assault from within their own ranks. In 1941, the USSR was pulled into World War II, a horrendous conflict in which many more millions died, but at least one in which the enemies were again clearly discernible and the crimes with which they were charged were real. The purges had no such clear-cut lines of definition, although there were Bolshevichki such as Zemliachka who benefited by convincing themselves to the contrary. Those Bolshevichki who had the honesty and courage to see the truth, who had been awakened by the attacks on innocents within their own movement to the possible innocence of all those others who had been persecuted over the years – peasants, intellectuals, members of rival political parties – must have ended the 1930s with their faith in all that they had once believed deeply shaken.

---

[72] Roy Medvedev names Stasova as one of those toothless old communists left alive to demonstrate that Stalin had not killed the entire old guard (*Let History Judge*, 1st ed., 308).

6   Recessional

In October 1961, the Twenty-Second Congress of the Communist Party of the Soviet Union convened in Moscow. Elena Stasova was then eighty-eight years old. Her eyesight was failing, her white hair was thin, and her fair skin stretched tightly across the long bones of her face. But Stasova was still strong enough to attend the congress. It was a happy occasion for her. On 17 October she heard the party's pudgy first secretary, Nikita Khrushchev, laud the accomplishments of the system she had helped create. "Our Soviet homeland," Khrushchev declared at the beginning of his very long report to the congress, "has entered the period of the full-scale construction of communism along the entire broad front of giant undertakings." Soviet cosmonauts were flying in space, communist parties were ruling the majority of the world's peoples, the economy of the USSR was more prosperous than ever before, and progress was to be seen everywhere in the world's socialist camp. Capitalism was obviously weakening. Later in the day, Khrushchev introduced a new party platform that laid out "a concrete, scientifically motivated program for the building of communism," to be realized by 1980.[1] He then described the future toward which his country was rapidly moving:

Communism is a classless social system with one single form of public ownership of the means of production and full social equality of all members of society; under it, the all-round development of people will be accompanied by the growth of the productive forces through continuous progress in science and technology; all sources of public wealth will gush forth abundantly, and the great principle "From each according to his ability, to each according to his needs" will be implemented. Communism is a highly organized society of free, socially conscious working people in which public self-government will be established, a society in which labor for the good of society will become the prime, vital requirement for everyone, a necessity recognized by one and all, and the ability of each person will be employed to the greatest benefit of the people.[2]

---

[1] *Documents of the 22nd Congress of the CPSU*, 2 vols. (New York, 1961), vol. I, 5; vol. II, 28. In the original this entire passage is italicized.
[2] Ibid., 34. Entire passage italicized in the original.

Stasova, one of the few remaining veterans of Lenin's old guard, glowed at this reaffirmation of her life's credo. The congress became an occasion for her to celebrate the successes of the Soviet Union. She chatted during breaks in the sessions with foreign communists come to admire the world's most powerful socialist country and was particularly impressed with Vietnamese leader Ho Chi Minh. Stasova also met cosmonaut G. S. Titov, at the meeting to publicize the Soviet Union's victories in its "space race" with the United States. In a photograph taken of the two of them, Stasova is standing straight and tall, despite her eighty-eight years, and staring intently into the face of the young man who had orbited the earth.

Stasova was no more a fool in 1961 than she had ever been, and she had now spent more than four decades listening to Soviet leaders proclaim half-truths and outright lies. She knew that Khrushchev's laudatory report was exaggerated, that the communist world itself was split by the deep rift between the Soviets and the Chinese, that agriculture in her own country was in crisis because of the First Secretary's bumbling inability to overhaul it. Stasova also knew that many Soviet citizens, particularly the peasants, still lived in great hardship. But she could believe Khrushchev when he said that the USSR had made enormous progress in the previous two decades, and this conviction gave her great satisfaction as she assessed the state of her nation in 1961.

First had come the colossal victory in World War II. Faced with the largest military invasion in history, the party and government had held together, and the nation had prevailed. It did so in no small part because more than 800,000 women had served in the military, while millions more worked in every sector of the economy, from munitions manufacturing to agriculture. By the end of the war, women made up 80 percent of collective farm workers and 57 percent of the nonagricultural labor force.[3] The great majority of the Bolshevichki did not go to the front, for that was a place for younger women; rather, they remained in their civilian jobs. Older, more privileged Bolshevichki were evacuated from cities close to combat; Stasova, for example, went to Central Asia. A few, however, refused to leave the endangered capital. Zemliachka and Nikolaeva stayed in Moscow, enduring the German siege while they worked in departments managing military supplies. It seems curious that the great crisis of the war did not open up opportunities for many Bolshevichki to move into higher-ranking jobs. A few earned promotions, but most did not.

The defeat of Nazi Germany was one source of pride for Bolshevichki such as Stasova. Another was the enormous achievement of rebuilding the Soviet economy after the war. The entire western part of the nation, an

---

[3] Barbara Evans Clements, *Daughters of Revolution: A History of Women in the USSR* (Arlington Heights, Ill., 1994), 86.

Plate 28. Elena Stasova with the cosmonaut G. S. Titov in the Kremlin. Palace during a break at the Twenty-Second Party Congress, 1961.

area roughly equivalent in size to the United States from its Atlantic coastline to the Mississippi River, had been laid waste. Perhaps as many as 27 million people had died in the carnage, and millions more were wounded emotionally and physically. Long, lean years of struggle were required to restore the economy, but by the mid-1950s great progress had been made. Agriculture had managed to recover sufficiently to provide a reliable, albeit far from abundant, supply of food for the cities and countryside. Industry grew, particularly in military-related areas of munitions and rocketry, but resources were devoted as well to the consumer economy, with the result that by the end of the 1950s the general standard of living had improved considerably. Particularly in the major cities, new apartment blocks were rising. More clothing and appliances were available in the nation's stores. The triumphs of the Soviet space program, although economically insignificant, also testified to the growing technological mastery of the system.[4]

These achievements were accompanied by political improvements after Stalin's death in 1953. His successors quickly became involved in a power struggle from which Khrushchev emerged as a powerful First Secretary, but neither Khrushchev nor his successors were ever permitted to amass the authority Stalin had wielded. Instead, coalitions centered in the Politburo shared power. The new leadership also released most of Stalin's political prisoners from the labor camps and imposed greater accountability on the NKVD (later renamed MVD, then KGB). At the same time, the Politburo relaxed controls over Soviet society at large, bringing on a period christened "The Thaw" (after the novel by Ilia Ehrenberg) when writers, artists, and academics reached for greater freedom of expression. All these developments amounted to a partial renunciation of the brutal coercion that had so disfigured the Stalin era.

Stasova took pride also in the USSR's international position in the 1950s. With the other major European powers, Britain, France, and Germany, weakened by war and the postwar collapse of their colonial empires, her nation had emerged as a leader in world affairs. The Soviet Union, the ragged, disheveled veteran of civil strife and ferocious war, was now hailed as a superpower that confronted on equal terms the enormously powerful and far more prosperous United States of America. The USSR stood as a beacon of hope to all those millions of people around the world, from China to Cuba to Mozambique, who were devoting themselves to replacing their corrupt native rulers or colonial masters with communist governments. To old internationalists such as Stasova, the world revolution proclaimed by Marx appeared to be proceeding apace, with the Soviet Union as its leader.

The Bolshevichki write their memoirs

All this was enough to warm the last years of many of the surviving Bolshevichki. Thirty-seven percent of the older generation in the sample and 69 percent of the younger lived into the 1950s to become senior citizens of the Soviet Union. As venerable members of the ruling elite, most of them eased into honored retirements. Many (at least 50 percent of the remaining Old Bolsheviks and 67 percent of the civil war joiners) qualified for the pensions awarded to party members. They also enjoyed

---

[4] For an assessment of the Khrushchev years, see Martin McCauley, *Khrushchev and Khrushchevism* (Bloomington, Ind., 1987).

Plate 29. Photograph taken during a reunion in 1957 of delegates to the First All-Russion Women's Congress of 1918. Alexandria Artiukhina is in the center of those seated, wearing the light suit.

access to the other benefits accorded to the privileged in the Soviet system, such as higher-quality health care and consumer goods in short supply for ordinary folk. However, a woman's standard of living depended very much on where she lived and on what rank she and her family members had achieved. A Bolshevichka working as a librarian in Arkhangelsk had far fewer luxuries than one who was in Moscow, married to a party official.

The Bolshevichki also benefited from a campaign that began in the Khrushchev years to restore the reputation of the founding generations of the party. Under Stalin, particularly after 1945, very little attention had been publicly given to the party's founders, probably because those in charge of propaganda were loathe to mention, even indirectly, the people who had been ravaged by the purges, but also because honoring other Old Bolsheviks might steal luster from Stalin himself. As party publicists competed to coin ever more ridiculous encomiums to the General Secretary, the Genius of All Mankind, even Lenin was eclipsed. The party's founding generations returned to prominence only in the 1950s, when Stalin's successors denounced their former leader for creating a "cult of personality." They then permitted the publication of memoirs and biographies as well as articles, so-called "rehabilitations," which declared purge victims innocent of the crimes of which they had been accused. As a result, the standing of the other Old Bolsheviks rose even while that of the dead Georgian plummeted.

In this new climate the Bolshevichki could tell the stories of their lives. Over the next twenty-five years, dozens of books were published across the Soviet Union recording their accomplishments. Most of these were collections of autobiographical and biographical sketches, although there were also full-length biographies of the most prominent Bolshevichki – Krupskaia, Kollontai, Inessa, Samoilova, Smidovich. The resulting record contained a wealth of information about the women of both the prerevolutionary and civil war generations. It also captured their thoughts in old age, thus opening a window onto their recollections and reflections at the end of their lives.[5]

It is necessarily a rather opaque window, as we have already seen. In writing their memoirs, the Bolshevichki were governed by officially approved interpretations of Soviet history as well as by the party's notions of what was appropriate in biography and autobiography. Since the days of the underground, communists had believed that they should portray themselves as dutiful, modest, faithful servants of the cause. In describing their lives they were to say very little about their families or their own personalities, for to do so would be an unseemly assertion of the importance of the individual. Rather, they should concentrate on what they had done to advance the cause.

In the context of the Khrushchev and the Brezhnev eras, such notions of literary propriety dictated that Old Bolsheviks and civil war veterans, male and female, should write about their participation in the great events of Soviet history – the revolutionary movement, the revolution itself, and the civil war, collectivization, and the Five Year Plans. They were to praise the cause of building a just society, laud the party that led the process, and blame any difficulties on the usual enemies – the Whites, nobles, priests, kulaks, recalcitrant members of the old intelligentsia, traditionalist males (usually peasants), and ignorant females (also usually peasants). They were to admit these people's opposition to communist government, as well as Russia's backwardness, and to recount the party's difficulties along the way, so as to chronicle the great sacrifices that had been made and the challenges that had been overcome. Their stories were always to end in the victory of the party, and of the people flourishing under its tutelage.

Rakhil Kovnator, the Zhenotdel worker who had written the piece

[5] The discussion that follows is based on all the works published, 1955–85, and listed in the bibliography of this book under the heading "Autobiographical and biographical sources on Bolshevichki."

praising the "new woman" discussed in chapter 4, published a typical article in 1975 in a collection entitled *Without Them We Would Not Have Won: Memoirs of Female Participants in the October Revolution, Civil War, and Socialist Construction*. Kovnator's piece discussed her experiences during the revolution and the civil war. She began with the year 1916, the date of her arrival in Petrograd as a seventeen-year-old girl come to study psychology at the Psychoneurological Institute. At the Institute, Kovnator met Bolsheviks who impressed her as "people of disinterested, selfless service to the social cause, of great revolutionary valor." She quickly became involved in strikes with her fellow students, and when the revolution began, she marched through the streets with the demonstrators, sharing in the general euphoria. Her closest friend from the Institute, a Bolshevichka named Mariia Avilova, enlisted her in party work that spring of 1917. Soon the headquarters of the raion party committee had become "my home," and Kovnator had become a Bolshevik.[6]

The young woman from Riga found her party colleagues to be a community of dedicated people who supported one another while they went about the great work of making revolution. "All my life I have kept feelings of the greatest respect for them," she wrote. Very quickly they promoted her to membership on the raion committee, where she worked closely with her friend Avilova. "I was then the youngest member of the party," Kovnator remembered, "but the comrades showed great faith in me." Thereafter in the article she portrayed herself as working within this supportive group as she proceeded along from assignment to assignment, momentous event to momentous event.[7]

The greatest Bolshevik of all, Lenin, figured prominently in Kovnator's story, as he did in the memoirs of all the Bolshevichki who had encountered him personally. Hewing to the prevailing idealization of the long-dead leader, Kovnator characterized him as a kind, approachable man of great intellect who dispensed fatherly guidance and almost priestly admonitions to his faithful subordinates. "We must understand and remember once and for all," she quoted Lenin as saying to a small group of attentive Bolsheviks in November 1917, "that those who believe in the people, who become immersed in the wellsprings of the living creativity of the people, will be victorious and hold power."[8] When on the podium at important meetings, however, Lenin shed this avuncular persona to become the great tribune of revolution, showing the righteous the path through the surrounding obstacles and heaping withering scorn on those

---

[6] R. A. Kovnator, "My postroim respubliku truda," *Bez nikh my ne pobedili by. Vospominaniia zhenshchin-uchastnits Oktiabr'skoi revoliutsii, grazhdanskoi voiny, i sotsialisticheskogo stroitel'stva* (Moscow, 1975), 13, 15.
[7] Ibid., 13, 19.   [8] Ibid., 21.

who disagreed with him. A devout recollection of his guiding presence permeates all of Kovnator's memoir.

Kovnator also sketched in loving detail the events of the revolution at which she had been privileged to assist. She remembered with great clarity a meeting she attended in October 1917 where Petrograd Bolsheviks discussed the decision to seize power. "It seemed that History herself had come into that small, dimly lit room to control the destiny of humankind in the name of Truth and Justice," she wrote.[9] The Eighth Party Congress of March 1918 also stood out in her memory because she had worked on it as one of the secretaries, taking the minutes of the contentious debate over ratification of the Brest-Litovsk Treaty. Kovnator also remembered fondly her attendance at the Ninth Party Congress, which had approved the establishment of work among women. After hearing another inspiring speech by Lenin, she and her comrades had returned to Smolensk with renewed vigor, to organize a campaign to staunch a typhus epidemic then ravaging the city.

Kovnator concluded her article with an affirmation of her party's successes that represented another common motif in the Bolshevichki's memoirs. "More than half a century has passed," she wrote. "The 1920s passed into legend long ago. The Soviet Union is now an invincible mighty rock, a great power, the socialist republic of labor that was dreamed of, that Lenin foretold. The immortal name, Lenin, rings out over the planet as a symbol of the liberty, hope, and friendship of emancipated peoples."[10]

The themes that suffused the memoirs of Bolshevichki such as Kovnator had grown out of the party's collective identity in a process very similar to that which gave rise to the hagiography of the medieval church. There was no single director, no compelling censor who sketched out the values the stories must teach. Rather, the writers refracted their own experiences through shared understandings. And similarities not only in values but in subject-matter linked the two hagiographical traditions. There were strong resemblances between the lives of female saints, as recounted by medieval Christians, and the lives of the Bolshevichki, as recounted by themselves and by their biographers. In both genres a young woman, living in a world of poverty, injustice, and sin, is taught the way to redemption, after which she devotes herself to the cause of righteousness and to its servant, the church in the case of the Christians, the party in the case of the Bolshevichki. She struggles, she confronts evil and her own inadequacies, but she remains steadfast. In Christian hagiography the earthly travails end in the saint's death and transportation into paradise; the Soviet variant usually concludes with a victory in whatever campaign – revolution, war, collectivization, factory-building – constitutes the central

[9] Ibid., 19–20.   [10] Ibid., 28.

event of the memoir. The virtues of the female saint are also close to those of the Bolshevichka. Both sets of women are characterized by modesty, devotion, and fidelity. They possess great courage, which enables them to rebel against the sin around them, but they also are utterly submissive to higher moral authority, that of God in the case of the saints, or that of the party in the case of the Bolshevichki.[11]

Kovnator had been born Jewish, and as a party member she was officially an atheist; so she would have been deeply offended by any comparison between her narrative and earlier stories of virtuous Christian women. But the parallels nonetheless exist, because Christian conceptions of righteous movements, and of the character of the members of such movements, had shaped the ethos of revolutionaries all over Europe. Russian Orthodoxy's hagiography had directly influenced the development of Russian revolutionaries' definitions of heroism in the nineteenth century, and those definitions in turn had been incorporated into the collective identity of the Social Democrats. The passage of decades of Soviet history had then strengthened the emphasis on the importance of devotion, modesty, and submission in communist women, for those virtues resonated with the more traditional notions about women that had gained official approval during the Stalin years. What the Bolshevichki, even erstwhile Zhenotdel activists such as Kovnator, downplayed in their memoirs was the *tverdost* which had once been the central element in their collective identity.[12]

The Bolshevichki did however, if only indirectly, affirm their *tverdost*, when they told, in appropriately modest tones, the stories of their accomplishments. One signal difference between the female saint and the Bolshevichka was the Bolshevichka's refusal to paint herself as a martyr to the sins of the world. Typically, medieval hagiographers portrayed the female saint as demonstrating her virtue by enduring horrible physical punishment at the hands of unbelievers or minions of the devil. She was an exemplar of suffering and victimization. The Bolshevichka, by contrast, showed herself to have been an activist, a fighter who, in close alliance with her comrades, participated in the construction of a virtuous society. Kovnator made it a point to say that women played an important part in controlling typhus in Smolensk when they voluntarily took on work that was filthy and dangerous. Other Bolshevichki recounted how they left young children to go to war, how they endured prison, combat, and hunger, how they conquered their fear, in order to contribute to the party's victories. They told such stories very matter-of-factly, for to draw

---

[11] On hagiography, see Renate Blumenfeld-Kosinski and Timea Szell, *Images of Sainthood in Medieval Europe* (Ithaca, N. Y., 1991), especially 199–287.

[12] On Russian hagiography's influence, see Margaret Ziolkowski, *Hagiography and Modern Russian Literature* (Princeton, 1988), esp. 250–54.

Plate 30. Photograph taken during a reunion of textile workers from Moscow's Zamoskvoretskii raion, 1957.

too much attention to their personal achievements would have been considered immodest. The laconic tone of Anna Nazarova's account of her encounter with White troops during the civil war is characteristic:

The enemy had already surrounded me. And so, when they stopped, I threw a grenade at them. This was also a signal of danger to my comrades. Running away a few steps, I threw a second grenade. It was successful. One was killed, one was wounded. The White Guards who were still alive lay down and returned fire. But obviously they still had not recovered from the confusion caused by the explosion of the grenades. Therefore their shots were not aimed and I succeeded in running away into the forest. Soon I met up with my comrades and that night we returned to our headquarters, supplied with valuable intelligence.[13]

By not commenting on the extraordinary quality of this scene – a teenaged girl attacking a unit of White troops on her own and then escaping in a hail of fire – Nazarova decorously reaffirms her *tverdost*. She did what she had to do, then rejoined her comrades. A similar tone of understatement, which has the effect of accentuating their heroism, pervades the accounts of those other Bolshevichki who wrote about their exploits at the front or in the factories and on the farms.

[13] *Bez nikh my ne pobedili by*, 71.

Only when describing group accomplishments – of a party committee, a work crew, or the masses of the people – did the Bolshevichki permit themselves to express pride. Vera Ulianovskaia, a former schoolteacher and Ph.D. in history, summarized the successes of her unit of political officers during the civil war with typical modesty and appropriately collectivist sentiments. "The most important thing," she wrote, "was the consciousness that we were doing necessary work. Before our eyes the Red Army soldiers, the majority of them completely illiterate, became not only literate but politically educated, conscious people. And we ourselves grew along with the soldiers." Alexandra Artiukhina, the former head of the Zhenotdel, published a number of articles in the late 1950s and early 1960s that stressed the contributions women had made to the growth of the Soviet system. "The intelligent, industrious women's hands, their minds and passionate hearts, have actively participated in the production of all the uncounted riches of our country," Artiukhina wrote in 1959. "Without the active participation of women the Soviet Union would not now have surpassed prerevolutionary Russia by thirty-five times in the production of industrial products."[14]

In their memoirs the Bolshevichki also made again the claims for inclusion central to their collective identity. Consistently they concentrated on their work for the cause, discussing their personal lives only in passing. Wholly subordinating the private to the public, they called the party their "home," their "family," the source of their emotional sustenance. Within this party, in their telling, women worked as men's equals and were almost always treated by the men as respected comrades. In portraying themselves as fully liberated and refusing even to discuss their married lives, the Bolshevichki rejected, albeit subtly, the domesticated femininity that had gained official favor in the 1930s. This implicit feminism was particularly characteristic of the memoirs published in the 1950s and 1960s. Collections of sketches of the Bolshevichki written not by them but by Soviet publicists much their juniors more often downplayed their independence and linked them more closely to domestic life, reinterpreting them in ways that they themselves refused to do when they wrote for themselves.[15]

[14] V. A. Ul'ianovskaia, "Moi iiunye gody," in *Kaluzhskie bol'shevichki* (Kaluga, 1960), 201; A. Artiukhina, "Nam Lenin put' ukazal," in *Zhenshchiny rasskazyvaiut. Vospominaniia, stat'i, 1918–1959* (Smolensk, 1959), 16. Artiukhina's other articles are the following: "Nas-polovina chelovechestva," in *Zhenshchiny goroda Lenina* (Leningrad, 1963), 383–93; "Nashi zavoevaniia," in *Uchastnitsy velikogo sozidaniia* (Moscow, 1962), 21–37; "Polveka," in *Oktiabriem rozhdennye* (Moscow, 1967), 12–25; "Proidennyi put'," in *Zhenshchiny v revoliutsii* (Moscow, 1959), 17–40.

[15] For an example of the more emancipated tone, see *Zhenshchiny russkoi revoliutsii* (Moscow, 1968). For the more domesticated presentation see *Docheri zemli Vladimirskoi* (Iaroslavl', 1982).

The canon of self-presentation to which the Bolshevichki subscribed grew out of the party's collective identity, its definition of itself. Far more directly imposed was the official interpretation of the specific events of Soviet history which appeared in the various memoirs. In their reminiscences the Bolshevichki repeated that interpretation obediently; indeed, had they not done so, their memoirs would not have been published. For example, Bolshevichki who wrote about collectivization reported that it had proceeded well, despite the continual opposition of the infamous kulaks. Discrimination against women was treated in a similar fashion, as an evil that had existed everywhere, inside the party as well as outside, but that had been progressively vanquished. The Bolshevichki recounted coping with sexism, but emphasized how they had gained acceptance by proving themselves to the soldiers, workers, or party officials who initially refused to work with them. Those women who had been Zhenotdel activists proudly recorded the struggles of that long-dead department, but always they presented gender discrimination as a relic of the old world, vanquished by the victorious Communist Party and Soviet people.[16]

Those events in Soviet history too dark to be construed as great victories simply were not discussed by the Bolshevichki or their biographers. The purges were mentioned only when absolutely necessary. An article on Latvian Evgeniia Egorova, who was executed in 1938, concluded this way: "In the period of the cult of personality, Evgeniia Nikolaevna Egorova was repressed without cause, but to the end of her life she remained a staunch Leninist, true to the cause of the party."[17] The great majority of biographical and autobiographical works were even more reticent, passing over the victims in silence. The Bolshevichki also talked very little about the dour days of the late 1940s, when the Soviet Union lay in ruins and the Stalin regime resumed its habits of persecution. Nor did they comment, except in passing, on the official denunciations of Stalin that began almost immediately after the dictator's death. Discussing any of these topics would have diminished, if not silenced, the triumphal tone of the memoirs. Nor could any Bolshevichka ever be sure that discussion of the violence of the Stalin era would be welcomed by the editors who were to publish the memoirs.

To understand precisely how the Bolshevichki interpreted the Stalinist horrors is difficult, therefore. They did know about the purges, for it was

---

[16] For an example of an article on collectivization, see M. O. Levkovich, "Kolkhoznaia nov'," in *Uchastnitsy velikogo sozidaniia*, 233–40. Stories about male harassment of Bolshevichki and male prejudice against women more generally appear throughout the memoirs. See ibid., and *Bez nikh my ne pobedili by*.

[17] *Zhenshchiny goroda Lenina*, 165.

impossible not to. Bolshevichki may have looked the other way when the government attacked peasants during collectivization in the early 1930s, or when, after World War II, it sent returning POWs off to the Gulag, deported entire ethnic groups, and arrested intellectuals. These were atrocities about which accurate information was impossible to obtain, and in any case the safest course was simply to believe what the newspapers said. But the Bolshevichki found it much more difficult to remain ignorant of the arrests of their own comrades. Nor could all of them have accepted at face value the official charges that the arrested were public enemies. Once Stalin was dead and revelation after revelation exposed the ghastly excesses of his government, how did the Bolshevichki feel? How did they reconcile these crimes with their hosannas to the Soviet Union's successes? How did they come to terms with the meaning of their own lives, since those who had remained outside the Gulag had at least stood by silently while their colleagues were dragged away, and some had collaborated in the destruction of people's lives?

In their memoirs the Bolshevichki stressed the positive. The censorship would not have allowed them to do otherwise, but they also had their own reasons to promote a rosy view of the past. After all, they had been personally very involved in that past and as communists were responsible for both its triumphs and its crimes. So they willingly emphasized the triumphs in their memoirs, and probably did so as well in their private moments of coming to terms with the meaning of their lives. As Marxists they were supposed to believe that history was shaped by great impersonal forces rather than by the actions of an individual or even of a dictatorship. Kollontai and Stasova had taken refuge in these ideas in the 1920s. Their comrades later had even better reasons to believe that the violence of the Stalin regime was redeemed by the achievements of the great masses of the people and the party. The historically significant events of the 1930s were not, in this view, the arrests of millions of people, but the efforts of millions more to industrialize the Soviet Union. That achievement had then made it possible for the nation to win World War II in Europe. Defeating Nazi Germany had saved an entire continent from an evil greater than the Gulag. Once Stalin was dead, the new leaders had executed Beria, the head of the NKVD from 1939 to 1953, and renounced terror. They had then led the nation to unprecedented international prestige and rising prosperity at home. The Bolshevichki had every reason to believe that the future held still greater triumphs. Thus they could argue that their memoirs, which stressed the accomplishments of Soviet history, were a true statement of the ultimate meaning of the Bolshevik Revolution.

Stasova in old age

Many of these thoughts buoyed the aged Stasova as she sat listening at the Twenty-Second Party Congress while Khrushchev proclaimed that the achievement of a perfected society lay only twenty years in the future. Stasova was then deeply engaged in writing the second edition of her memoirs, as well as a series of articles on Lenin, all of which recorded her efforts to come to terms with the meaning of her own life and of the system she had helped to build. The usual characteristics of Bolshevichki memoirs were there in Stasova's – the self-effacement, the dedication to the cause, the veneration of Lenin, the glorification of the people's progress, and the great omissions. But Stasova also left a small but telling record of her private thoughts on the horrors of the Stalin regime that revealed a crisis through which she had passed before she told the glowing story of Soviet achievements in her memoirs.

In the late 1930s, while on the run from the purges, Stasova had found refuge within the vulnerable but enduring world of the intelligentsia. There she managed to remain for the rest of her life. After retiring from *Internatsionalnaia literatura* in 1946, she began working on a multi-volume edition of the letters of her uncle, V. V. Stasov, the eminent St. Petersburg musicologist and critic whose championing of Russian composers in the late nineteenth century had made him a positive figure to the Soviet musical establishment. Some communists accused Stasova of immodesty in puffing the reputation of a relative, but she responded that reading about Vladimir Stasov would teach Soviet citizens to appreciate good music. Although she would not admit it publicly, she also knew quite well that the volumes she published between 1953 and 1962 were a tribute to the entire nineteenth-century intelligentsia, among whom her family had played so prominent a part. The letters were also connected to a larger effort then in progress within the Soviet intelligentsia to reaffirm its connections to Russia's prerevolutionary culture. Her co-editors on the project later wrote that the three volumes would never have seen the light of day had not the venerated Old Bolshevichka used her influence to win approval of the project.[18]

Publicly in the mid-1950s Stasova was the much esteemed veteran of the party's heroic past. She bore the nickname "The White Dove of the Revolution," in tribute to her unblemished reputation, and communists and schoolchildren from around the world wrote her letters expressing their admiration for her long service to communism.[19] Her serene image

---

[18] On Stasova's role in editing her uncle's letters, see Sim Freiden, *Muzyka – revoliutsii*, 2nd ed. (Moscow, 1970), 506–08. The letters themselves were published as V. V. Stasov, *Pis'ma k rodnym*, ed. E. D. Stasova, 3 vols. (Moscow, 1953–62).

[19] On her correspondence in the 1950s, see RTsKhIDNI, f. 356, op. 1, d. 137, 126, 119, 120, 121, 155, 174. For a folder containing invitations to party functions, see ibid., d. 13.

masked deep, but private, anguish and anger. Stasova was gratified by the return from the Gulag of people she knew, and she continued to give money and clothes to the families of those who had yet to come back, but she was also tormented by the fragmentary information filtering through about the enormous scale of the purges. At the Twentieth Party Congress in February 1956, the rumors were finally given flesh by Khrushchev, who made the famous "Secret Speech" attacking Stalin and making the first official accounting of the purges to the party. Khrushchev reported the numbers of Central Committee members and top military officers who had been arrested and executed. He also declared that the victims had not been guilty of the crimes of which they had been accused. Stasova responded by letting her guard down, and her reactions were recorded in a diary kept during the congress by an old comrade, Italian communist Vittorio Vidali.

Vidali and Stasova had not seen one another for more than twenty years when they met in February 1956. He was many years her junior, but they had become friends when he worked with her in MOPR in the 1930s. In 1934 Vidali left Moscow to fight in the Spanish Civil War, and on Stasova's advice he had not returned thereafter to the Soviet Union. After World War II he became one of the leaders of the Italian Communist Party.[20]

In Moscow in 1956 to represent his party at the congress, Vidali was not the docile and admiring foreign communist that the Soviet party wanted in attendance at its meetings. The deaths of many of his friends from MOPR in the Gulag had made Vidali bitterly critical of the Stalin leadership and deeply suspicious of its successors – too many of whom, in his view, had served Stalin. But Vidali did still cherish fond memories of Stasova, who, he believed, had saved him more than once from arrest in the 1930s. When he ran into her outside the congress hall, therefore, he quickly steered her to an out-of-the-way corner so that they could talk.

After the two old friends had exchanged their initial pleasantries, Vidali began to question Stasova about the purges. Khrushchev had not yet made the Secret Speech, but the Italian had heard talk that a powerful revelation of Stalin's crimes was imminent. He wanted Stasova to tell him which of their former comrades had died, and to explain to him what had happened in those awful years. Perhaps the general atmosphere encouraged Stasova to talk frankly to her old friend. Perhaps she was simply happy to meet again a comrade from MOPR. Whatever her motivation, Stasova unburdened herself to Vidali in a way few Soviet communists ever did to foreigners. She gave him details on the fate of their colleagues, on the use of torture to extract confessions, and on the ways in which the

[20] Vittorio Vidali, *Diary of the Twentieth Congress of the Communist Party of the Soviet Union*, trans. Nell Amter Cattonar and A. M. Elliot (Westport, Conn., 1984), vii–xviii.

families of the accused had been victimized. "Yelena told me about thirty-eight people who had been friends of mine – and had not come back. All of them are dead . . . and rehabilitated. I was speechless, horrified," Vidali wrote later that day in his diary.[21]

Their conversation was interrupted by Polina Zemchuzhina, Molotov's wife, who came by to say hello to Stasova. As she walked away, Stasova told Vidali that Zemchuzhina had spent years in the Gulag, jailed on Stalin's order, while Molotov, still on the Politburo, had continued to do his master's bidding. Then she confided with satisfaction that Zemchuzhina was now refusing to reconcile with her husband, because she thought he had been too cowardly to plead for her release. Evil men such as Molotov, Stasova continued bitterly, and Beria, and Malenkov (the last recently defeated by Khrushchev in the power struggle among Stalin's heirs) had brought about the purges. Just then the congress session resumed, and the two friends returned to the hall.[22]

In the days that followed, Vidali continued to seek out Stasova during breaks in the meeting, and she continued to speak quite freely with him. On 15 February she told him that she had been a member of the honor guard called to Leningrad in 1933 for the funeral of Sergei Kirov, the head of the Leningrad party organization who had been assassinated by a disgruntled communist. Everyone else who stood with her around the coffin had been arrested, she said, and all of them were innocent of the crimes of which they were accused. Her mood was angry, but she also emphasized to Vidali that she continued to believe in the righteousness of the cause and of the party that was its champion. She even continued her efforts to shift some responsibility from Stalin to Beria, telling Vidali the next day that the General Secretary had turned against Beria toward the end of his life.[23]

On 24 February, Khrushchev delivered the Secret Speech to a session from which visitors, including Vidali, were barred. As the First Secretary documented the massive scale of the purges, recited the names of prominent Bolsheviks who had been innocent of the crimes of which they were accused, and laid the responsibility for all these evils directly on Stalin himself, Stasova was reduced to tears. She was particularly pained when she heard that her good friend Sergo Ordzhonikidze, who had given her refuge in 1920 in Tbilisi after she had been fired as party secretary, had killed himself in 1937 rather than undergo arrest. So stricken was she that she went home after the speech and took to her bed to nurse a cold. She did not return to the congress thereafter.[24]

---

[21] Ibid., 18.   [22] Ibid., 17–18.   [23] Ibid., 27, 59, 60.

[24] The information that Stasova was particularly pained by the news of Sergo's suicide is reported by Anton Antonov-Ovseenko, *The Time of Stalin*, trans. George Saunders (New York, 1981), 314.

When Vidali visited Stasova in her apartment on 27 February, he found her weak but still angry. She told him about how the families of purge victims had been persecuted, and how she herself had been denounced. "Now everybody is being rehabilitated," she declared bitterly, "but now they are dead!" Beria was responsible, she fumed; he was the evil genius behind all the horror. Vidali responded with equal candor. He denounced the entire congress as "an assembly of functionaries and bureaucrats" who were refusing to admit their own complicity in Stalin's crimes. Why had they not permitted foreign communists to hear the speech, Vidali asked. Everyone should be allowed to know what had happened, and those responsible, including those still in the leadership, should be brought to justice. Stasova lay in bed, listening and now silent. Vidali saw that her lips were trembling as she looked up at him, but she refused to agree with his blanket indictment of her party. "I stood up and touched her cold, bony, and feather-light hands," he wrote in his diary. " 'Come and see me before you leave,' she whispered. Her eyes were tired, gentle."[25]

In the years that followed the Twentieth Party Congress, Stasova recovered her strength and her equilibrium. Then she set to work to rebuild the reputations of her dead comrades. Sitting in her tiny study, before a wall hung with pictures of her uncle, her father, her husband, Sergei Kirov, Lenin, and Stalin, she wrote letters to the Politburo appealing for the rehabilitation of prominent Bolsheviks who had not yet been exonerated. She was particularly interested in obtaining forgiveness for Bukharin, to whom she had never been personally close but whose moderate policies on industrialization had appealed to her.[26]

Stasova also wrote her own rehabilitation of the Old Bolsheviks into her memoirs. A series of articles as well as several editions of her memoirs (the first of which appeared in 1957) told the story of her party career in extraordinary detail, naming comrades by the dozens, many of them purge victims, with whom she had worked. Ever careful, she did as Kovnator would also do and made Lenin the main hero of her story. Stasova praised his integrity, his collegial style of leadership, and his devotion to inner-party democracy. The Lenin of Stasova's reminiscences was far more saintly than she herself had known him to be, but no doubt the passage of time had blurred and illuminated her memories of him. In

---

[25] Vidali, *Diary of the Twentieth Congress*, 27, 59, 92–94.

[26] On Stasova signing appeals for rehabilitations, see ibid., 93, 327; A. A. Isbakh, *Tovarishch Absoliut* (Moscow, 1963), 89; Roy Medvedev, *Let History Judge*, 1st ed., ed. David Joravsky and Georges Haupt, trans. Colleen Taylor (New York, 1973), 184–85. For a letter she wrote to the son of Evgeniia Egorova, her one-time comrade on the Petersburg committee who had died in the purges, see Elena Vechtomova, *Tovarishch Zhenia* (Moscow, 1975), 108.

sanctifying Lenin, however, Stasova intended more than simply another hymn to the party's founder. She was attempting to rebuild the reputation of the entire generation of the Old Bolsheviks, in order to recall to prominence the values they had once professed, particularly their concept of revolutionary integrity.[27]

"A communist is an active soldier of the party," Stasova wrote in one article on Lenin, "a crystal clean, idealistic and principled fighter for communism, for the people's happiness, and there cannot be any indulgence here. Communists don't have any special privileges, except one – to be first, to be an example and model always and in everything. The thousands of Leninists – Babushkin and Bauman, Olminskii and Spandarian, Dzerzhinskii and Ordzhonikidze, Sverdlov and Tsiurupa – were so ardent, principled, disciplined to the end."[28] Stasova was particularly anxious that the younger generation of communists hear such messages, for she believed that they were too easily corrupted by careerist ambitions and material gain. Communists of less savory reputations, particularly Stalin, she simply did not discuss.

Decorously to affirm the antique ideals of an organization which now, even in the eyes of its own members, stood accused of appalling crimes struck many observers as cowardly, if not viciously immoral. Anton Antonov-Ovseenko, whose father, Bosh's old adversary, had been executed, wrote in his exposé of the purges that Stasova should have done more than weep when she heard Khrushchev declare that Ordzhonikidze had killed himself. "She didn't have the nerve to stand up and call for the accomplices in Sergo's murder to be brought to justice," Antonov-Ovseenko declared. And he was right. Stasova lay silently in bed as Vidali condemned those guilty of great crimes who still served in the party leadership. She knew how many such people there were, despite her efforts to blame the purges on Beria. But as she thought it over afterwards, in the years before the Twenty-Second Congress, she decided that it was not wise to publicize the party's sins because she believed that knowing the

---

[27] This work is, by order of publication date: E. D. Stasova, ed., *Iz istorii nelegal'nykh bibliotek revoliutsionnykh organizatsii v tsarskoi Rossii* (Moscow, 1956); Stasova, *Stranitsy zhizni i bor'by*, 1st ed. (Moscow, 1957); Stasova, "Zhenshchiny sem'i Ul'ianovykh," *Slavnye bol'shevichki* (Moscow, 1958), 9–15; Stasova, *Stranitsy zhizni i bor'by*, 2nd ed. (Moscow, 1960); Stasova, "U istokov bor'by," in Institut istorii partii, *V edinom stroiu* (Moscow, 1960), 11–24; Stasova, ed., *V kol'tse frontov. Molodezh' v gody grazhdanskoi voiny* ([Moscow], 1963); Stasova, "Znamenostsy Il'icha," in *U istokov partii* (Moscow, 1963), 5–8; Stasova, "Pravda bol'shoi zhizni," in *Bol'shevik-pravdist. Vospominaniia o K. S. Eremeeve* (Moscow, 1965), 19–20; Stasova, "Vvedenie," in *Vladimir Il'ich Lenin v proizvedeniiakh sovetskikh khudozhnikov* (Moscow, [1967]), 7–9; Stasova, "Schast'e byt' pervymi," *Leningradki. Vospominaniia, ocherki, dokumenty* ([Leningrad], 1968), 5–9; Stasova, *Vospominaniia* (Moscow, 1969); Stasova, *Uchitel' i drug* (Moscow, 1972).
[28] Stasova, *Uchitel' i drug*, 24.

Plate 31. Elena Stasova in 1963.

horrors of the Stalin era would disillusion young people about communism.[29]

Stasova thus used her position as aged grandmother of Bolshevism to
reaffirm her Bolshevik credo. Everyone must go back, she argued, to the
ideals that had inspired the party before the nightmare set in. She praised
Lenin, inner-party democracy, and people of integrity. At public gatherings she had her photograph taken with contemporary heroes, Ho Chi
Minh and the Soviet cosmonaut G. S. Titov. She listened happily when
Khrushchev proclaimed that communism was within sight. And she
hailed all the accomplishments of the Soviet system, "the truly legendary
exploits of the people, of the party during industrialization, collectivization, the cultural revolution, in the terrible time of the Great Fatherland
War."[30]

[29] Antonov-Ovseenko, *The Time of Stalin*, 314–15. She expressed her doubts about
disillusioning the young in *Vospominaniia*, 27.
[30] Stasova, *Vospominaniia*, 226. For her references to the new party platform, see ibid., 217;
Stasova, "Znamenostsy Il'icha," 7.

It is impossible to say how many Bolshevichki reconciled themselves to Soviet reality as Stasova did, for few left as full a record of their later years. Probably many felt redeemed by the successes of the Soviet system and by the honors heaped on Old Bolsheviks after Stalin's death. The only spiritual recourse such women had, if they were to remain communists, was to cling to their faith that the regime they had built would ultimately prove itself by making the lives of the people better. Under Khrushchev's ebullient leadership and the dour but initially competent rule of his successors, the Soviet Union did move ahead. Very few Bolshevichki survived to see it falter, then collapse in the last two decades of the twentieth century.

The Bolshevichki in history

Recent history has not been as easy on the Bolshevichki as they were on themselves. The relaxation of controls by Mikhail Gorbachev's government let loose what became in the late 1980s a thorough reevaluation of the Soviet past. By the early 1990s the Communist Party had fallen into disgrace, dragging down with it the reputations even of its most illustrious founders. Female communists descended into a special sort of obloquy, for they were accused of having been the handmaidens of a corrupt regime. Such accusations derived chiefly from the politics and contemporary affairs of the 1980s, but inevitably they spread into general appraisals and understandings of the entire historic relationship between communist women, the Communist Party, and the Soviet people. Such women, it was believed, powerless in their own right, had supported a party that was bent on exploiting the women of the nation for its own purposes, even while it proclaimed that it had liberated them. When Russian feminist thought began to flourish in the newly liberated intelligentsia in the 1990s, Bolshevik feminists such as Kollontai came to be seen in a somewhat kinder light, but they too were criticized for their willingness to subordinate the welfare of women to the controls of a power-hungry regime.[31]

There had been some truth in the hagiography of the Soviet regime; there was truth as well in the blanket condemnations of the Bolshevichki. Obviously they were an extraordinary group of women. Their history lends itself to hyperbole. Defying the conventions of their age, they became revolutionaries and went on to assist in the creation of one of the most powerful political edifices of the twentieth century. Assimilationists,

---

[31] For recent Russian feminist discussions of the Soviet program of women's emancipation, in which the work of the Bolshevik feminists is treated sympathetically, see Anastasia Posadskaia, ed., *Women in Russia: A New Era in Russian Feminism*, trans. Kate Clark (London, 1994), esp. 8–10, 37–56.

they sought acceptance by adapting themselves to the definitions of virtue and the expectations for meritorious conduct that prevailed within their party. This suppleness made it possible for them to be Bolsheviks, but it also made it impossible for most of them to formulate or support a critique of Bolshevism's failings, even when these were connected with the abandonment of many of its promises to women.

Most Bolshevichki seem to have accepted the limits placed on them. Their acquiescence was easier because those limits had insensibly crept into place over a period of many years, in conditions of emergency, where calls for loyalty to the movement were exceptionally compelling. The party dictatorship and the relegation of women to subordinate positions grew together, as twin deformities of Soviet history. The Bolshevichki responded by supporting the dictatorship, coping with gender inequality, and attending to the daily struggle. Like many other twentieth-century women who rejected traditional frameworks of life, the Bolshevichki practiced audacity and timidity in varying degrees, and divided themselves among conflicting obligations. Throughout their lives, however, they retained a more emancipated attitude toward women's role in the new society than that held by many of their male comrades.

Bolshevichki contributed to the party as members of the rank and file and to the Soviet Union as the vanguard of the female labor force. Before the revolution they performed the same conspiratorial tasks in the underground as men; large numbers of them also held party office. During the revolution and the civil war they continued to serve as officials, broadening their assignments to include military commands. After the war, as Soviet society stabilized, they increasingly found themselves marginalized within the party, though they labored successfully in government, the professions, and the economy. In large numbers they entered fields where women were more readily accepted – education, social services, health care, journalism, and publishing – and they also pioneered the employment of women in occupations such as engineering and law that were still closed to them elsewhere.

The Bolshevichki's most distinctive accomplishments were the formulation of a Marxist variant of feminism and the institution of programs for women's emancipation that came to be enacted not only in the Soviet Union but also in all those countries from China to Cuba that adopted Soviet-style socialism. Eschewing reformist solutions, the Bolshevichki sought emancipation through the radical reconstruction of all society. They did not fully achieve that emancipation, but they did craft a program that provided more substantial solutions to a broader range of problems than did the reformist feminism of their time. After the Zhenotdel was abolished their program for women ossified into a set of policies shaped more to fit the needs of the regime than to promote the welfare of women. This deterioration was part of a more general corruption that spread throughout the Soviet system as egalitarian principles gave way to autocratic realities.

Stasova's death

Stasova, who lived longer than most of the communist women of her generation, survived the fall of Khrushchev in 1964 and carried on into the early Brezhnev years. By then she had become an icon of Bolshevik probity and a relic of the party's golden age. Born in 1873, she was, in 1966, ninety-three. She was nearly blind, as her father had been in his old age, and she had difficulty walking, but she still sat down every morning with her secretary to work in her study. In the fall of 1966 she began to plan articles commemorating the upcoming fiftieth anniversary of the revolution.[32]

But she did not live to enjoy the celebration. On New Year's Eve 1966, Anastas Mikoian, one of the few Old Bolsheviks whom she still considered a friend, came to visit her in the Kremlin hospital. They had known each other since 1919, and he called on her regularly in her later years. That New Year's evening he found her unconscious and struggling for breath. Mikoian rushed to get a doctor, but Stasova's heart stopped despite their efforts. It was just six weeks short of fifty years since she had led a frightened group of women out of a jail in St. Petersburg and into the Russian Revolution.[33]

Stasova was buried with full party honors. After a ceremonial lying-in-state in the House of the Soviet Army, her remains were interred in the Kremlin Wall, beside those of other highest-ranking Bolshevik luminaries. But this most venerated of all Soviet resting places was not what Stasova had requested. In a letter to the party secretariat in 1963 she had asked to be buried near her uncle Vladimir in the Tikhvinskii Cemetery in Leningrad. Her father, aunts, and mother had all been laid to rest there, but their graves had been removed during remodeling after the revolution. Only her grandfather and uncle still reposed in an honored spot near the graves of Peter Tchaikovsky, Modest Mussorgsky, and other luminaries from the cream of St. Petersburg's nineteenth-century intelligentsia. There Stasova wanted to be buried. Her request was denied, possibly because the cemetery was very crowded. Perhaps someone also decided

---

[32] On Stasova in her last years, see Lidiia Bat', "Absoliut," in her *Nezabyvaemye vstrechi* (Moscow, 1970), 11–28; Pavel Podliashuk, *Bogatyrskaia simfoniia. Dokumental'naia povest' o E. D. Stasovoi* (Moscow, 1977), 247–49.

[33] Stasova, *Vospominaniia*, 11.

that one of the female saints of Bolshevism should not lie too near to these remains of the tsarist past.[34]

In a short, simple will, written in January 1966, Stasova disposed of her worldly goods. Her household possessions were to go to a long-time female companion, her pictures to various friends, her personal papers to the party archives, her books to the Saltykov–Shchedrin Library in Leningrad. Stasova left the contents of her savings account to her niece and nephews. And she left her brain to the Brain Institute in Moscow, where slices of Lenin's brain were also on file. "I think it will be of interest since I am distinguished by my memory and I have an excellent ability with languages," she declared.[35]

Stasova had written her own epitaph in 1963, when she had received the Soviet Union's highest civilian medal, the Order of Lenin, for the fifth time. "I was and I shall remain to the end of my life a soldier in the great Leninist party. I am committed to it with all my being and I put above all else the fulfilling of my duty to it."[36] If she ever thought that her faith had been misplaced, if she ever wondered whether the revolution they had made had gone terribly wrong, if she ever considered that the system they had built was doomed by its inefficiencies and its authoritarianism, she never said so publicly. Indeed, if she ever had such thoughts, she may have confided them to no one. What seems certain is that the old Marxist devotee of material progress saw her loyalties validated in every shining Soviet spacecraft and towering new apartment block.

Stasova's ashes are in the Kremlin Wall. Nearby are Inessa's, there since 1921, Krupskaia's, there since 1939, and Zemliachka's, there since 1947. Kollontai died in 1953, but she had not earned her spot on Red Square. When she died the reputation of a lady-feminist still hung over her; and she had lived away from the Soviet Union for a long time while she served as Soviet ambassador to Sweden. So Kollontai was interred in Moscow's Novodevichy Cemetery, a honorable resting place for the lesser lights of the Communist Party. Her grave is decorated with a splendid statue of her in white marble, donated by admirers. The remains of Alexandra Artiukhina, who died in 1969, are in Novodevichy too, beside her daughter's, under a large marble headstone. The remains of Samoilova, Bosh, Nikolaeva, and the tens of thousands of other Bolshevichki now repose in graveyards all across the lands that once were the Soviet Union. They lie in large cemeteries beside great churches, in small plots tended by relatives, and in unmarked wastes at the edge of fearsome places hedged with rusting wire.

---

[34] RTsKhIDNI, f. 356, op. 1, d. 19, l. 1.   [35] Ibid., l. 2.
[36] Podliashuk, *Bogatyrskaia simfoniia*, 248.

Appendix

Notes on the data bases

Much of the statistical material in this book was derived from two data bases. *The Soviet Data Bank*, compiled by William Chase and J. Arch Getty (Version 1.0, 1986), contains records on approximately 28,000 individuals, filed according to category of work (e.g., education, imprisonment, activity in 1917). For the most part, this information was taken from government and party documents of the 1920s and 1930s. I disaggregated the data by sex, using names as my method of distinguishing men from women. Then I analyzed the resulting files on men. They were very useful for the period 1900–21, less so for the 1920s and 1930s, primarily because the information provided by *The Soviet Data Bank* on employment after 1921 was too general to compare meaningfully to the more specific information I had compiled on Bolshevichki.

The data base that I constructed consists of information on 545 Bolshevichki, 318 of whom joined the party before 1917 and the remaining 227 of whom joined between 1917 and 1921. The sources were memoirs, biographies, periodical articles, histories, and document collections, the great majority of them published in the Soviet period, as well as archival holdings. The most valuable of the archival materials were the files of the Society of Old Bolsheviks, an organization founded in the 1920s and disbanded in 1934, which counted among its members only people who had joined the party before 1917. To apply for membership, a communist had to file with the society a statement on her background and party service, that is, she had to write an autobiographical sketch. More than three thousand of these sketches remain in fond 124 in the Rossiiskii tsentr khraneniia i izucheniia dokumentov noveishei istorii (the former party archives) in Moscow; of the 3,000, 326 are by women. All were written between 1932 and 1934. I sampled them by dividing them into two categories, those by Bolshevichki on whom I already had information (78 individuals) and those by women new to me (248). I then sampled the two groups by selecting roughly one-third of each randomly. This process yielded material on 91 individuals, 22 of whom were already in the data base, 79 of whom were not.

I constructed the data base using categories modeled, roughly, on those employed in *The Soviet Data Bank*, with one significant difference. My data were arranged longitudinally, by individual Bolshevichka, making it possible to follow an individual through her life. I then ran a variety of calculations comparing the information I had gleaned from published sources with that coming from the files of the Society of Old Bolsheviks. I determined that the Bolshevichki included in the Society's files were as a group more proletarian, less well educated, and less prominent in the party than those who had been the subject of published works. This was not an astonishing finding, but it suggested that incorporation of the archival material into the data base had made it more representative of the Old Bolshevichki as a whole.

The shortcomings of the evidence from the data base have been apparent throughout this study. It is tantalizingly incomplete, particularly where politically sensitive matters and private lives are concerned. It contains more information about women of the party elite and the Old Bolsheviks than about lower-ranking people in general and the civil war generation in particular. It is fuller in its descriptions of the period 1900–21 than of later decades. Because of all these deficiencies, more advanced statistical correlations proved impossible to make. But what can be gleaned from the material is a good deal of descriptive information from a fairly representative sample.

There follows here a list of the names of the women in the data base. The selected bibliography thereafter includes the major sources consulted in the course of the research, particularly those from which the data base was built. Readers seeking references to sources relied on less heavily are urged to consult the notes.

BOLSHEVICHKI IN THE DATA BASE

OLD BOLSHEVICHKI

Abolina, M. I.; Adamovich; Adamovich, E. N.; Afanas'eva, A. S.; Afanas'eva, S. N.; Agadzhanova, N. F.; Agrinskaia-Romanenko, E. K.; Aladzhalova, N. N.; Aleksandrova-Riazanova, N. A.; Alekseeva, A. F.; Alekseeva, E. A.; Allilueva, O. E.; Andreeva, E. I.; Andreeva, M. F.; Anson, E. P.; Antonova; Arbuzova, A. E.; Armand, I. F.; Artiukhina, A. V.; Aurin-Urvatsan, O. A.; Avaliani-Shiriraeva, E. E.; Aveide, M. O.; Babeva, A. A.; Babushkina, M. M.; Baiaf, L. M.; Barkhatova, L. N.; Baskir, R. V.; Bazanova, M. V.; Belokonskaia, L. M.; Belova, O. A.; Belova-Gavrilova, O. A.; Bertse, P. I.; Berzin, E. L.; Birgel', A. I.; Bits, A. I.; Blum, L. I.; Bobrovskaia, Ts. S.; Bochagova, A. I.; Bogorad, M. L.; Bogrova, V. L.; Boikova, L. I.; Boimenblit, A. E.; Borisova, P. B.; Borman, P. F.; Bosh, E. B.; Brodskaia, S. A.; Bronshtein, V. S.; Brusilovskaia, M. V.; Brutser-Pel'she, L. I.; Budnitskaia, A. E.; Buiko, A. M.; Bukharina-Lukina, N. M.; Bychkova, A. N.; Bychkova, M. N.; Chachina, O. I.; Cherniak, M. I.; Cherniak, R. I.; Chuchina, A. V.; Chudak, B. M.; Chudinova, K. P.; Dargol'ts, Ts. I.; Denisova, E. S.; Deriabina, S. I.; Derman-Dal'naia, S. Ia.; Dilevskaia, O. A.; Dilevskaia, V. A.; Dimant, R. Ia.; Dodonova, A. A.; Doronina, S. P.; Drabkina, F. I.; Dvoires, D. I.; Dvortsova-Babushkina, L. D.; Dzerzhinskaia, S. S.; Efremova, S. V.; Elagina-Khrushcheva, A. A.; Elizarova, A. I.; Emelianova, N. K.; Esaeva, A. V.; Essen, M. M.; Fedorova, E. N.; Fedorova, E. S.; Fedorova-Suvorova, M. A.; Fel'dman, R. A.; Fisher, L. V.; Fotieva, L. A.; Frishman, S. I.; Galkina, L. I.; Gavrilova, K. N.; Genkina, O. M.; German, O. F.; Gobi, L. Kh.; Golikova, E. V.; Golubeva, E. K.; Golubeva, M. P.; Golubiatkaia-Mal'kind, S. V.; Goncharskaia, S. S.; Gopner, S. I.; Goriacheva, E. S.; Gorshkova, A. N.; Grishfel'd, O. S.; Gromozova, L. K.; Gurevich, A. Ia.; Iakovleva, V. N.; Ianysheva, A. A.;

Ikrianistova, M. F.; Imbovits, A. F.; Ivanova, A. I.; Ivanova, A. M.; Kadik, M. A.; Kalantyrskaia, M. G.; Kalygina, A. S.; Kalyrina, A. S.; Kameneva, N. I.; Kameneva, O. D.; Karaseva, I. U.; Karavaikova, V. A.; Karmanova, A. G.; Katsnel'son, B. A.; Kharitonova, R. B.; Khavkina, S. L.; Khazan, D.; Khosudov-skaia, S. B.; Khutulashvili, D. A.; Kirsanova, K. I.; Knipovich, L. M.; Kogan, E. S.; Kolesnikova, N. N.; Kollontai, A. M.; Konstantinovich, A. E.; Korovaikova, V. A.; Korzheva-Portnova, A. I.; Kostelovskaia, M. M.; Kotliar-Voitsinskaia, E.; Kovalenko, E. G.; Kozhevnikova, V. F.; Krasnova, V. D.; Kravchenko, A. G.; Kravchenko, E. K.; Kristovkaia, I. I.; Kruglova, A. I.; Krupskaia, N. K.; Krymkok, M. O.; Krzhanovskaia, Z. P.; Kudelli, P. F.; Kulagina-Chaichenko, P. M.; Kuliabko, P. I.; Kurskaia, A. S.; Lagutina, S. V.; Lapteva, O. M.; Lashadze-Bochoridze, B. G.; Lazurkina, D. A.; Lebedeva, M. A.; Lebedeva, V. P.; Leitman, E. Ia.; Leman, M. N.; Lepeshinskaia, O. B.; Levenson, T. M.; Levitskaia, E. G.; Levitskaia-Aristarkova, S. L.; Levitskaia-Loznetskaia, Z. N.; Lezhava-Chichinadze, E. M.; Liepin, E.; Lifshits, O. G.; Lilina, Z. I.; Lisinova, L. A.; Listova-Lisbaron, V. M.; Liudvinskaia, T. F.; Lobova, V. N.; Malinovskaia, E. K.; Malova, E. M.; Mandel'shtam, L. P.; Mariusia; Mar'tianova, M. A.; Matinson, A. M.; Melent'eva, S. V.; Mendeleva, I. A.; Menzhinskaia, L. R.; Menzhinskaia, V. R.; Mikhailova, N. I.; Minchina-Kleitman, O. I.; Mitkevich, O. A.; Mukhina-Zavadskaia, M. V.; Muralova, S. I.; Myralova, S. I.; Nagurskaia, E. V.; Nevel'son, S. A.; Nevzorova, A. P.; Nevzorova, S. P.; Nikiforova, A. N.; Nikiforova, M.; Nikolaeva, K. I.; Nogina, O. P.; Novgorodtseva, K. T.; Novik-Kondrateva, V. R.; Novikova, D. A.; Novikova, E. A.; Novikova, P. A.; Okulova-Teodorovich, G. I.; Orakhelashvili-Mikeladze, M. P.; Ovvian, A. S.; Ozol, E. D.; Pavlova, M. G.; Perfil'eva, N. S.; Pervykhina, A. N.; Petrova, A. P.; Pilatskaia, O. V.; Piskunova, E. I.; Plaksina, E. D.; Pliusnina, N. I.; Podvoiskaia, N. A.; Poldushkina, P. F.; Poliakova, E. M.; Pomerantseva, A. V.; Popova, E. I.; Popova, E. N.; Pozner, A. G.; Pozner, S. M.; Prokhorova, A. O.; Prokhorova-Bugrova, A. I.; Pulatskaia, O. V.; Puskupova, E. I.; Raeva, A. I.; Rastopchina, M. A.; Ratner, B. A.; Ravich, S. N.; Razumova, M. N.; Riazanova-Gol'dendakh, A. L.; Rivlina-Obraztsova, R. S.; Rozenbaum, S. M.; Rozmirovich, E. F.; Ruben, E. P.; Rudnitskii, M. I.; Rumba, E. Kh.; Runina, A. M.; Ryzhanskaia, E. M.; Sakharova, P. F.; Samoilova, K. N.; Sapozhnikova, M.; Sapozhnikova, V. A.; Saraeva-Zubkova, M. S.; Savchenko, M. G.; Savel'eva, A. V.; Sedova, N. I.; Sedugina, A. N.; Sergeeva, E. L.; Shalaginova, E. P.; Shapovalova, L. P.; Shillert-Ponomareva, E. F.; Shlikhter, E. S.; Shnitnikova, L. Kh.; Shoikhet, M. E.; Shteiner, E. O.; Shulga, S. I.; Shul'gina, I. N.; Shveitser, V. L.; Simanovskaia, M. A.; Sirota-Nakoriakova, A. I.; Skrovna, R. A.; Skrypnik, M. N.; Slavinskaia, A. A.; Slutskaia, V. K.; Smidovich, S. N.; Smitten, E. G.; Sokolova-Solov'eva, N. V.; Sokolovskaia, E. K.; Sokolov-skaia, S.; Solin, E. A.; Solomakha, T. G.; Solovei, E. M.; Stal', L. N.; Stankina, B. Z.; Starikova, T. I.; Stasova, E. D.; Stepanova, P. S.; Stoklitskaia, M. M.; Strashnova, E. M.; Strievskaia, S. I.; Subbotina, L. I.; Sulimova, M. L.; Sverdlova, M. G.; Sveshnikova-Vydrina, M. N.; Sycheva, T. I.; Taraeva, A. M.; Tarasova, E. P.; Tikhomirova, M. V.; Tille, A. M.; Tokareva, A. N.; Torsueva-Rezanova, E. V.; Trelina, V. I.; Tret'iakova, N. V.; Troitskaia, E. I.; Ul'ianova, M. I.; Uvarova, E. N.; Varentsova, O. A.; Vasil'eva, A. P.; Vasil'eva, E. A.; Vasil'eva, V. A.; Vavlentsova, P. I.; Velichkina, V. M.; Vetoshkina, A. I.; Vinogradova, O. I.;

Vinokurova, P. I.; Vishniakova, P. I.; Vladimirova, V. F.; Voinova, K. I.; Volkonskaia, S. N.; Voloshina, E. N.; Zagainaia, S. K.; Zagumennykh, M. M.; Zakharova, V. V.; Zaslavskaia, A. N.; Zavadskaia, E. V.; Zav'ialova, K. G.; Zemel', I. E.; Zemliachka, R. S.; Zemlianitskaia, S. L.; Zenkevich, Z. A.; Zhilevich, Iu. I.

CIVIL WAR GENERATION

Afanas'eva, E. T.; Alekseeva, A. A.; Allilueva, N. S.; Anikst, O. G.; Apukhtina, F. M.; Aristova, P. M.; Armand, I. A.; Astankova, E. V.; Babeva, P. A.; Barg, P.; Barinova, A. G.; Barmashikhova, F. M.; Bashakova, S. M.; Baturina, K. S.; Belova, M. I.; Belova, P. P.; Berdnikova, A. V.; Bil'shai, V. L.; Bogacheva, N. M.; Bogolepova, L. S.; Bondarenko, M. I.; Bulycheva, Z. G.; Burtseva, S. V.; Butuzova, E. V.; Chaadaeva, O. N.; Chernysheva, O.; Dagaeva, E. M.; Dolinina, V. I.; Drabkina, E. I.; Dridzo, V. S.; Dukhanina, K. I.; Dvoretskaia, M. P.; Efimova, T.; Egorova, I. I.; Egorova, O. A.; El'kina, D. I.; Fofanova, M. V.; Frolova, E. O.; Frumkina, Ts. E.; Gagarina, Z. N.; Gatovskaia, P. V.; Ge, K.; Gerr, E.; Giliarova, E. A.; Ginzburg, V. G.; Glazer, E. M.; Glizer, P. S.; Golik, L. A.; Goreva, E. G.; Graf, T. I.; Gribova, E. N.; Gurevich, E. S.; Gutman, E. I.; Ianova, A. M.; Ianovskaia, S. A.; Iarovaia, E. P.; Ignat'eva, P. S.; Ignatova, I. M.; Il'ina, O. F.; Isaicheva, V.; Ishkova, K.; Itkina, A. M.; Iusupova, L. I.; Ivanitskaia, M. P.; Ivanova, A. V.; Kalacheva-Golikova, K. A.; Kalinina, E. I.; Kalmykova, P. I.; Kaptel'tseva, N. D.; Karaseva, L. E.; Karklin, E. M.; Karneeva-Glebova, N. S.; Kasperovich, A. G.; Kazantseva, M. N.; Khaldina, A. N.; Khliupsheva, A. I.; Khor'kova, N. P.; Kniazeva, E. A.; Kniazeva, E. V.; Kogan, Z. N.; Kogan-Pismanik, E. I.; Koledova, A. I.; Koliabskaia, M. S.; Kolokolova, E. P.; Kondrashova, T. A.; Konstantinova, A. S.; Korunova, A. E.; Kostianovskaia, M.; Kovalchuk, E. B.; Kovaleva, E. F.; Kovnator, R. A.; Kovrigina, A. N.; Kovshalova-Teslenko, K. D.; Kozhina, K. K.; Kuropatkova, A.; Kuzheleva, E. M.; Kuznetsova, L.; Kuznetsova, M.; Kuznetsova, N. A.; Lapenina, E. I.; Lavinskaia, N. P.; Lebedeva, E. I.; Legon'kaia-Kholodnova, Z.; Levikova, R. I.; Levina, A. A.; Levkovich, M. O.; Litveiko, A. I.; Liubarskaia, D.; Liubimova, S. T.; Lysova, M. D.; Mamaeva, A. Kh.; Maslikhina, O. M.; Mastiukova, G. I.; Mekhonoshina, M. A.; Meshkova-Lapshina, M. I.; Miliutina, N. S.; Mil'kina, M. L.; Mitina, E. P.; Moirova, V. A.; Mokievskaia-Zubok, L.; Monina, O. M.; Morkina, M. A.; Muratova, M. F.; Nagradova, E. V.; Nikandrova, Z. B.; Nikiforova, A. G.; Nikolaeva, V. N.; Novikova, A. I.; Ogladnikova, M. F.; Okulova, E. I.; Orlova, R. E.; Orlova, V. A.; Osodoeva, F. M.; Pankova, S.; Pankratova, A. M.; Parviainen, L. P.; Pernovskaia, A. M.; Petrova, V. I.; Platonova, A. F.; Platonova-Shakova, M. P.; Podchufarova, E. I.; Podsotskaia, A. I.; Poliakova, E. I.; Poliakova, M. F.; Pomelova, A. N.; Popova, E. A.; Postolovskaia, K. S.; Potapova-Gabysheva, M.; Prianishnikova, A. I.; Prokina, O. N.; Pylaeva, E.; Razumova, M. I.; Reiman, A. V.; Reisner, L. M.; Reshetnikova, M. V.; Rezakova, T.; Riazhentseva, A.; Rodionova, A. I.; Ross, E. A.; Rozen, O. B.; Sapun, A. P.; Semenova, K. M.; Shablievskaia, L. R.; Shaburova, M. A.; Shagaeva, F. S.; Shaposhnikova, L. K.; Shekun, O. A.; Shimchenko-Ksendzova, P. M.; Shornikova, G.; Shustova, M. A.; Sinitsyna, T. A.; Sirota, V. M.; Slonimskaia, V. G.; Smorodkina, A. F.; Sobol, T. A.; Soboleva, I. G.; Soboleva, M. A.; Sokolova,

A. M.; Sokolova, O. N.; Sokolova-Sarafannikova, A. D.; Solunova, S. S.; Sorokina, A. E.; Sorokina, E. A.; Sorokina, P. D.; Sorokova-Tselenko, R. I.; Stasevich, E. T.; Stashevskaia, P. P.; Strievskaia, N. I.; Strukova, E. A.; Sukhareva-Klochkova, N. M.; Surnova, E. K.; Suzdal'tseva, V. I.; Tachalova, V. P.; Tarantaeva, M. V.; Tenikhina, A. S.; Terent'eva, A. N.; Tetina, O. D.; Tiurikova, V. S.; Toporovskaia, Kh. S.; Troitskaia, Kh. S.; Turkina, R. I.; Ul'ianovskaia, V. A.; Uspenskaia, A. V.; Uvarova, E. I.; Vaichus, T. I.; Vantorina, E. I.; Vasil'eva, E. I.; Vasil'eva, E. R.; Vasil'kova, A. I.; Ventskovich-Ligeti, S.; Verevkina, E. V.; Vinogradova, R. N.; Vinogradskaia, P. S.; Vinokurova, E. A.; Vol'f, E. D.; Vol'f, R. D.; Volkova, M.; Voronova, P. I.; Zakharova, Z. M.; Zalivina, N. T.; Zamogil'naia, P. G.; Zapevalova, E. E.; Zelenskaia, E. F.; Zelikson, R. S.; Zhirkova, D. S.; Zlobinskaia, G. D.; Zorina, Ts. V.

Select bibliography

ARCHIVES

Gosudarstvennyi arkhiv Rossiiskoi federatsii (GARF).
Okhrana Archives, Hoover Institution on War, Revolution, and Peace, Stanford, Calif.
Rossiiskii tsentr khraneniia i izucheniia dokumentov noveishei istorii, Moscow (RTsKhIDNI).
Trotsky Archive, Houghton Library, Harvard University, Cambridge, Mass.
Tsentral'nyi gosudarstvennyi arkhiv Oktiabr'skoi revoliutsii i sotsialisticheskogo stroitel'stva Moskvy, Moscow (TsGAORSS Moskvy).

AUTOBIOGRAPHICAL AND BIOGRAPHICAL SOURCES ON BOLSHEVICHKI

Arenshtein, A. *Rannim moskovskim utrom*. Moscow, 1967.
Armand, I. F. *Stat'i, rechi, pis'ma*. Moscow, 1975.
Artiukhina, A. "Nas-polovina chelovechestva." In *Zhenshchiny goroda Lenina*, 383–93.
  "Nashi zavoevaniia." In *Uchastnitsy velikogo sozidaniia*, 21–37.
  "Polveka." In *Oktiabriem rozhdennye*, 12–25.
  "Proidennyi put'." In *Zhenshchiny v revoliutsii*, 17–40.
  "Rabota sredi zhenshchin – na vyshuiu stupen'." *Rabotnitsa*, no. 5 (1930): 4–6.
  "Sorok protsentov vsekh bezrabotnykh na birzhakh truda – zhenshchiny." *Rabotnitsa*, no. 21 (1926): 3.
  "Zapomni, rabotnitsa (Ob osnovnykh piatnadtsatoi partkonferentsii)." *Rabotnitsa*, no. 22 (1926): 1–2.
Avramenko, T. F., and M. N. Simoian. "Elena Fedorovna Rozmirovich." *Voprosy istorii KPSS*, no. 3 (1966): 98–102.
Bat', Lidiia. *Nezabyvaemye vstrechi*. Moscow, 1970.
Belen'kaia, Aniuta. "O rabote Kievskoi organizatsii v 1905 g." *Proletarskaia revoliutsiia*, no. 2 (1926): 259–64.
Berdnikova, A. V., ed. *Zhenshchiny v revoliutsii*. Novosibirsk, 1968.
Bez nikh my ne pobedili by. Vospominaniia zhenshchin-uchastnits Oktiabr'skoi revoliutsii, grazhdanskoi voiny, i sotsialisticheskogo stroitel'stva. Moscow, 1975.

Bobrovskaia, Cecelia. *Twenty Years in Underground Russia*. New York, 1934.

Bochkareva, E., and S. Liubimova. *Svetlyi put'*. Moscow, 1967.

Bonner, Elena. *Mothers and Daughters*. Trans. Antonina V. Bouis. New York, 1992.

Bosh, E. B. *God bor'by*. Moscow, 1925.

"Neskol'ko zamechanii o knige V. A. Antonov-Ovseenko ('Zapiski o grazhdanskoi voine')." *Proletarskaia revoliutsiia*, no. 12 (1924): 318–23.

"Oblastnoi partiinyi komitet s.-d. (bol'shevikov) Iugo-Zapadnogo kraia, 1917 g." *Proletarskaia revoliutsiia*, no. 5 (1924): 128–49.

"Oktiabr'skie dni v Kievskoi oblasti." *Proletarskaia revoliutsiia*, no. 11 (1923): 52–67.

"Pis'mo k redaktsiiu." *Proletarskaia revoliutsiia*, no. 11 (1924): 269–70.

"Vospominaniia uchastnikov Bernskoi konferentsii." *Proletarskaia revoliutsiia*, no. 5 (1925): 179–93.

"Vstrechi i besedy s Vladimirom Il'ichem." *Proletarskaia revoliutsiia*, no. 3 (1924): 155–73.

Breslav, B. *Konkordiia Nikolaevna Samoilova*. Moscow and Leningrad, 1926.

Broido, Eva. *Memoirs of a Revolutionary*. Trans. and ed. Vera Broido. London, 1967.

Docheri zemli Vladimirskoi. Iaroslavl', 1982.

"Elena Fedorovna Rozmirovich." *Voprosy istorii KPSS*, no. 3 (1966): 98–102.

Essen, M. M. *Pervoi shturm*. Moscow, 1957.

Freiden, Sim. *Muzyka – revoliutsii*. 2nd ed. Moscow, 1970.

Frid, D. "Taganroz'ka Narada." *Litopys revoliutsii*, no. 4 (1928): 25–43.

Geroi Oktiabria. Kniga o uchastnikakh Velikoi Oktiabr'skoi sotsialisticheskoi revoliutsii v Moskve. Moscow, 1967.

Ginzburg, Eugenia. *Journey into the Whirlwind*. Trans. Paul Stevenson and Max Hayward. New York, 1967.

Haimson, Leopold H., ed. *The Making of Three Russian Revolutionaries*. Cambridge, 1987.

Iakovleva, V. "Partiinaia rabota v Moskovskoi oblasti v period fevral'–oktiabr' 1917 g." *Proletarskaia revoliutsiia*, no. 3 (1923): 196–204.

"Podgotovka oktiabr'skogo vosstaniia v Moskovskoi oblasti." *Proletarskaia revoliutsiia*, no. 10 (1922): 302–06.

Institut istorii partii. *V edinom stroiu*. Moscow, 1960.

Institut istorii partii MGK i MK KPSS, Filial instituta Marksizma-Leninizma pri TsK KPSS. *Soratniki*. Moscow, 1985.

Institut istorii partii pri TsK KP Belorussii, Filial instituta Marksizma-Leninizma pri TsK KPSS, *Pod krasnym znamenem oktiabria*. Minsk, 1987.

V bor'be i trude. 3rd ed. Minsk, 1985.

Institut Marksizma-Leninizma pri TsK KPSS, Nauchno-metodicheskii kabinet. *Revoliutsionerki Rossii*. Moscow, 1983.

Isbakh, A. A. *Tovarishch Absoliut*. Moscow, 1963.

Itkina, A. M. *Revoliutsioner, tribun, diplomat. Stranitsy zhizni Aleksandry Mikhailovny Kollontai*. 2nd ed. Moscow, 1970.

Kakhovskaia, I. "Iz vospominanii o zhenskom katorga." *Katorga i ssylka*, no. 22 (1926): 145–62; no. 23 (1926): 170–85.

Kaluzhskie bol'shevichki. Kaluga, 1960.

Karavashkova, S. V. *Publitsisticheskaia deiatel' nost' A. M. Kollontai, I. F. Armand, K. N. Samoilovoi.* Moscow, 1979.

Karavashkova, S. V., and L. D. Diuzheva. *Konkordiia Nikolaevna Samoilova.* Moscow, 1979.

Katasheva, L. *Natasha: A Bolshevik Woman Organiser.* London, 193?.

"Poslednaia rabota tovarishcha Konkordii Nikolaevny Samoilovoi." *Kommunistka*, no. 14–15 (1921): 28–30.

Klapina, Z. "Zhenshchiny katorzhanki v Butyrkakh." *Katorga i ssylka*, no. 4 (1922): 148–53.

Kolesnikova, N. N. *Po dorogam podpol'ia. Iz vospominanii.* Baku, 1973.

Kollontai, A. M. *Iz moei zhizni i raboty.* Moscow, 1974.

"Iz vospominanii." *Oktiabr'*, no. 9 (1945): 59–89.

Izbrannye stat'i i rechi. Moscow, 1972.

Konstantinov, M. M., ed. *Na zhenskom katorge.* 2nd ed. Moscow, 1932.

Kovnator, R. "'My postroim respubliku truda.'" In *Bez nikh my ne pobedili by*, 13–28.

"Novaia zhenshchina v revoliutsionnoi literature." *Kommunistka*, no. 5 (1920): 32–35.

"Vo imia prekrasnoi pory." In *Zhenshchiny rasskazyvaiut*, 40–42.

Krasnye kosynki. Rostov, 1971.

Krovitskii, G. A. *Put' starogo bol'shevika. K shestidesiatiletiiu E. D. Stasovoi.* Moscow, 1933.

Krupskaia, N. K., ed. *Pamiati Inessy Armand.* Moscow, 1926.

Pedagogicheskie sochineniia. 11 vols. Moscow, 1963.

Reminiscences of Lenin. Trans. Bernard Isaacs. New York, 1970.

Kuznetskaia, L. I. *Krupskaia.* Moscow, 1973.

Larina, Anna. *This I Cannot Forget: The Memoirs of Nikolai Bukharin's Widow.* Intro. Stephen F. Cohen. Trans. Gary Kern. New York, 1993.

Leningradki. Vospominaniia, ocherki, dokumenty. [Leningrad], 1968.

Levidova, S. M., and E. G. Salita. *Elena Dmitrievna Stasova. Biograficheskii ocherk.* Leningrad, 1969.

Levitskaia, Evg. "Iz zhizni odesskogo pod'polia." *Proletarskaia revoliutsiia*, no. 6 (1922): 135–57.

"Pamiati starogo druga." *Proletarskaia revoliutsiia*, no. 8 (1922): 3–7.

"Stranichka iz dnevnika." *Proletarskaia revoliutsiia*, no. 1 (1923): 256–58.

Liudvinskaia, T. F. *Nas Leninskaia partiia vela. Vospominaniia.* Moscow, 1976.

Maiorov, M. "Na putiakh k I s"ezdu KP(b)U." *Litopys revoliutsii*, no. 4 (1928): 7–24.

Mar, Evgenii. *Nezakonechnoe pis'mo.* Moscow, 1970.

Mints, I. I., and A. P. Nenarokov, eds. *Zhenshchiny – revoliutsionery i uchenye.* Moscow, 1982.

Mishkevich, G. *Konkordiia Nikolaevna Samoilova.* Leningrad, 1947.

Nikolaeva, Klavdiia. "Pamiati dorogogo bortsa, liubimogo druga Konkordii Samoilovoi." *Kommunistka*, no. 12–13 (1921): 8–9.

Nikolaeva, K., and L. Karaseva. *Zhenshchina v boiakh za kommunizm.* Moscow, 1940.

O Nadezhdoi Krupskoi. Vospominaniia, ocherki, stat'i sovremennikov. Moscow, 1988.

Oichkin, G. D. *Nadezhda Konstantinovna Krupskaia.* 2nd ed. Moscow, 1988.

Oktiabriem mobilizovannye. Zhenshchiny-kommunistki v bor'be za pobedu sotsialis-ticheskoi revoliutsii. Moscow, 1987.

Oktiabriem rozhdennye. Moscow, 1967.

Olesin, Mikhail. *Pervaia v mire. Biograficheskii ocherk ob A. M. Kollontai.* Moscow, 1990.

Palant, M. *Kursant Ania.* Moscow, 1985.

Petropavlovskaia, L. *Liusik Lisinova.* Moscow, 1968.

Podliashuk, Pavel. *Bogatyrskaia simfoniia. Dokumental'naia povest' o E. D. Stasovoi.* Moscow, 1977.

Tovarishch Inessa. 3rd ed. Moscow, 1973.

Pomelova, A. *Slovo o zhenshchinakh severa.* N.p., 1968.

Pravda stavshaia legendoi. Moscow, 1964.

Preobrazhenskii, E. "Evgeniia Bogdanovna Bosh." *Proletarskaia revoliutsiia,* no. 2 (1925): 5–16.

Revoliutsionnaia deiatel'nost' Konkordii Nikolaevny Samoilovoi. Sbornik vospominanii. Moscow, 1922.

Rosnovskii, A. "Iz epokhi 'Zvezdy' i 'Pravdy' v Kieve." *Litopys revoliutsii,* no. 6 (1926): 101–42.

Ruganov, S., and S. Negrinskii. *Krupskaia v Peterburge–Leningrade.* Leningrad, 1975.

Samoilova, K. "Avgust Bebel i zhenskii vopros." *Rabotnitsa,* 23 February 1914, 9–10.

"K mezhdunarodnomu dniu zhenshchin-rabotnits." *Put' pravdy,* 29 January 1914, 2.

"Konferentsiia rabotnits i organizatsionnaia rabota." *Pravda,* 9 December 1917, 3.

Krest'ianka i sovetskaia vlast'. Moscow, 1921.

"Neotlozhnaia zadacha (k organizatsii rabotnits)." *Petrogradskaia pravda,* 26 July 1918, 1–2.

Organizatsionnye zadachi otdelov rabotnits. Moscow, 1920.

"Pamiati tovarishch Very (Bronislavy Klement'evny Slutskoi)." *Rabotnitsa,* 8 December 1917, 4–6.

"Rabotnitsy i professional'nye soiuzy." *Rabotnitsa,* 30 May 1917, 6–7.

Serge, Victor, and Natalia Sedova Trotsky. *The Life and Death of Leon Trotsky.* Trans. Arnold J. Pomerans. New York, 1975.

Shatunovskaia, Lidiia. *Zhizn' v Kremle.* New York, 1982.

Sheinis, Zinovii. *Put k vershine. Stranitsy zhizni A. M. Kollontai.* Moscow, 1984.

Shidlovskii, G. "Pamiati dvukh starykh pravdistov." *Katorga i ssylka,* no. 10 (1931): 172–78.

Shvarts, A. [Shvartsman, D. M.]. "Kievskaia partorganizatsiia v 1911–1912 gg." *Litopys revoliutsii,* no. 4 (1928): 148–53.

"Iz revoliutsionnogo proshlogo." *Voprosy istorii KPSS,* no. 1 (1967): 115–20.

Slavnye bol'shevichki. Moscow, 1958.

Smirnova, A. I. *Plammenye revoliutsionerki.* Barnaul, 1960.

Vospitannitsy partii. Delegatki 20-kh godov. Barnaul, 1967.

Stasov, V. V. *Pis'ma k rodnym.* Ed. E. D. Stasova. 3 vols. Moscow, 1953–62.

Stasova, E. D. "Iakov Mikhailovich Sverdlov." In *Rasskazy o Sverdlove. Sbornik vospominanii* (Moscow, 1962), 114–21.

"Iz vospominanii o partiinoi rabote do revoliutsii 1917 g." *Proletarskaia revoliutsiia*, no. 12 (1927): 186–202.

MOPR's Banners Abroad: Report to the Third MOPR Congress of the Soviet Union. Moscow, 1931.

"Pravda bol'shoi zhizni." In *Bol'shevik-pravdist. Vospominaniia o K. S. Eremeeve* (Moscow, 1965), 19–20.

Protiv belogo terrora. Moscow, 1934.

"Schast'e byt' pervymi." In *Leningradki*, 5–9.

Stranitsy zhizni i bor'by. 1st ed. Moscow, 1957. 2nd ed. Moscow, 1960.

"U istokov bor'by." In Institut istorii partii, *V edinom stroiu*, 11–24.

Uchitel' i drug. Moscow, 1972.

Vospominaniia. Moscow, 1969.

"Vvedenie." In *Vladimir Il'ich Lenin v proizvedeniiakh sovetskikh khudozhnikov* (Moscow, [1967]), 7–9.

Za edinyi front solidarnosti i pomoshchi. Doklad na IV plenume TsK MOPR SSSR, 17 noiabria 1935 g. Moscow, 1935.

"Zhenshchiny sem'i Ul'ianovykh." In *Slavnye bol'shevichki*, 9–15.

"Znamenostsy Il'icha." In *U istokov partii* (Moscow, 1963), 5–8.

Stasova, E. D., ed. *Iz istorii nelegal'nykh bibliotek revoliutsionnykh organizatsii v tsarskoi Rossii.* Moscow, 1956.

V kol'tse frontov. Molodezh' v gody grazhdanskoi voiny. [Moscow], 1963.

Steinberg, Isaac. *Spiridonova, Revolutionary Terrorist.* Trans. and ed. Gwenda David and Eric Mosbacher. Intro. Henry W. Nevinson. Originally published 1935. Freeport, N. Y., 1971.

Sverdlov, Ia. M. *Izbrannye proizvedeniia.* 3 vols. Moscow, 1960.

Uchastnitsy velikogo sozidaniia. Moscow, 1962.

Vechtomova, Elena. *Tovarishch Zhenia.* Moscow, 1975.

Vidali, Vittorio. *Diary of the Twentieth Congress of the Communist Party of the Soviet Union.* Trans. Nell Amter Cattonar and A. M. Elliot. Westport, Conn., 1984.

Vinogradskaia, Polina. *Pamiatnye vstrechi.* 2nd ed. Moscow, 1972.

Volkogonov, Dmitrii. *Lenin. Politicheskii portret.* 2 vols. Moscow, 1994.

Vol'shtein, Liza. "Zapiski fabrichnoi rabotnitsy." *Proletarskaia revoliutsiia*, no. 9 (1922): 160–81.

Vsegda s vami. Sbornik posviashchennyi 50-letiiu zhurnala "Rabotnitsa." Moscow, 1964.

Wettlin, Margaret. *Fifty Russian Winters.* New York, 1992.

Zhenshchina v grazhdanskoi voine. Epizody bor'by na severnom kavkaze v 1917–1920 gg. Moscow, 1937.

Zhenshchiny v grazhdanskoi voine. Epizody bor'by na severnom kavkaze v 1917–1920 gg. Moscow, 1938.

Zhenshchiny goroda Lenina. Leningrad, 1963.

Zhenshchiny rasskazyvaiut. Vospominaniia, stat'i, 1918–1959. Smolensk, 1959.

Zhenshchiny russkoi revoliutsii. Moscow, 1968.

Zhenshchiny v revoliutsii. Moscow, 1959.

Zil'berblat, Ida. "Vilenskaia katorga, 1910–1914 gg." *Katorga i ssylka*, no. 65 (1930): 149–67; no. 66 (1930): 148–59.

DATA BASES

Chase, William, and J. Arch Getty. *The Soviet Data Bank*. Version 1.0. 1986.

DOCUMENTS

Institut istorii partii Leningradskogo obkoma KPSS, Filial instituta Marksizma-Leninizma pri TsK KPSS. *Peterburgskii komitet RSDRP. Protokoly i materialy zasedanii, iiul' 1902–fevral' 1917*. Leningrad, 1986.

Institut Marksizma-Leninizma pri TsK KPSS. *Tretii s"ezd RSDRP, aprel'–mai 1905 goda. Protokoly*. Moscow, 1959.

Vtoroi s"ezd RSDRP, iiul'–avgust 1903 goda. Protokoly. Moscow, 1959.

"Iz perepiski E. D. Stasovoi i K. T. Novgorodtsevoi (Sverdlovoi), mart–dekabr' 1918 g." *Voprosy istorii*, no. 10 (1956): 85–101.

"K otchetu o I vseukrainskom s"ezde sovetov RS i KD." *Litopys revoliutsii*, no. 1 (1928): 257–66.

KPSS. *Desiatyi s"ezd RKP(b). Stenograficheskii otchet*. Moscow, 1963.

Deviataia konferentsiia RKP(b), sentiabr' 1920 goda. Protokoly. Moscow, 1972.

Odinnadtsatyi s"ezd RKP(b). Stenograficheskii otchet. Moscow, 1961.

Vos'maia konferentsiia RKP(b), dekabr' 1919 goda. Protokoly. Moscow, 1961.

Lenin, V. I. *Polnoe sobranie sochinenii*. 5th ed. 56 vols. Moscow, 1958–66. Cited as *PSS*.

Meijer, Jan. M., ed. *The Trotsky Papers, 1917–1922*. 2 vols. The Hague, 1964.

Moscow, Institut Marksa–Engelsa–Lenina. *Partiia i revoliutsii 1905 goda. Dokumenty k istorii partii v 1905 godu*. [Moscow], 1934.

"Perepiska V. I. Lenina i N. K. Krupskoi s Peterburgskoi organizatsiei." *Proletarskaia revoliutsiia*, no. 3 (1925): 9–45; no. 4 (1925): 14–40.

Perepiska V. I. Lenina i redaktsii gazety "Iskra" s sotsial-demokraticheskimi organizatsiiami v Rossii, 1900–1903 gg. 3 vols. Moscow, 1969.

Perepiska V. I. Lenina i rukovodimykh im uchrezhdenii RSDRP s partiinymi organizatsiiami, 1905–1907 gg. 3 vols. Moscow, 1982–86.

Pervyi vserossiiskii s"ezd rabotnits. Kharkov, 1920.

"Protokoly i rezoliutsii Biuro TsK RSDRP(b), mart 1917 g." *Voprosy istorii KPSS*, no. 3 (1962): 134–57.

"Protokoly pervogo legal'nogo Peterburgskogo komiteta bol'shevikov i ispol'nitel'noi komissii za period s 15 marta po 7 aprelia (s 2 po 25 marta) 1917 g." *Proletarskaia revoliutsiia*, no. 3 (1927): 317–83.

"Protokoly pervoi (Moskovskoi) oblastnoi konferentsii tsentral'nogo-promyshlennogo raiona RSDRP(b) proiskhodivshei v g. Moskve (2–4 maia) 19–21 aprelia 1917 g." *Proletarskaia revoliutsiia*, no. 10 (1929): 129–94.

"Protokoly Tsentral'nogo komiteta RSDRP(b), avgust–sentiabr' 1917 g." *Proletarskaia revoliutsiia*, no. 8 (1927): 322–51.

"Protokoly Tsentral'nogo komiteta RSDRP(b), noiabr' 1917 g." *Proletarskaia revoliutsiia*, no. 11 (1927): 202–14.

"Protokoly Tsentral'nogo komiteta RSDRP(b), sentiabr'–oktiabr' 1917 g." *Proletarskaia revoliutsiia*, no. 10 (1927): 246–98.

"Protokoly TsK RSDRP(b) perioda Brestskikh peregovorov, fevral' 1918 g." *Proletarskaia revoliutsiia*, no. 2 (1928): 132–69.

RSDRP, TsK. *Perepiska sekretariata TsK RKP(b) s mestnymi partiinymi organiza-tsiiami, aprel'–mai 1919 g.* Moscow, 1972.

Perepiska sekretariata TsK RKP(b) s mestnymi partiinymi organizatsiiami, av-gust–oktiabr' 1918 g. Moscow, 1969.

Perepiska sekretariata TsK RKP(b) s mestnymi partiinymi organizatsiiami, ian-var'–mart 1919 g. Moscow, 1971.

Perepiska sekretariata TsK RKP(b) s mestnymi partiinymi organizatsiiami, iiun'–iiul' 1919 g. Moscow, 1974.

Perepiska sekretariata TsK RKP(b) s mestnymi partiinymi organizatsii, noiabr'–dekabr' 1918 g. Moscow, 1970.

VKP(b), TsK, Otdel po rabote sredi zhenshchin. *Kommunisticheskaia partiia i organizatsiia rabotnits.* Moscow, 1919.

Sbornik instruktsii otdela TsK RKP(b) po rabote sredi zhenshchin. Moscow, 1920.

ADDITIONAL ENGLISH-LANGUAGE MATERIALS

Bebel, August. *Woman Under Socialism.* Trans. from the 33rd ed. by Daniel De Leon. New York, 1904.

Borys, Jurij. *The Russian Communist Party and the Sovietization of Ukraine.* Stockholm, 1960.

Brittan, Arthur. *Masculinity and Power.* New York, 1989.

Clements, Barbara Evans. *Bolshevik Feminist: The Life of Aleksandra Kollontai.* Bloomington, Ind., 1979.

Daughters of Revolution: A History of Women in the USSR. Arlington Heights, Ill., 1994.

"The Utopianism of the Zhenotdel." *Slavic Review* 51 (Fall 1992): 485–96.

Elwood, R. C. *Inessa Armand.* Cambridge, 1992.

Russian Social Democracy in the Underground. Assen, Netherlands, 1974.

Engel, Barbara Alpern. *Mothers and Daughters: Women of the Intelligentsia in Nineteenth-Century Russia.* Cambridge, 1983.

Engels, Friedrich. *The Origin of the Family, Private Property, and the State.* New York, 1940.

Farnsworth, Beatrice. *Alexandra Kollontai: Socialism, Feminism, and the Bolshevik Revolution.* Stanford, 1980.

Fieseler, Beate. "The Making of Russian Female Social Democrats, 1890–1917." *International Review of Social History* 34 (1989): 193–226.

Fitzpatrick, Sheila. *The Russian Revolution.* 2nd ed. New York, 1994.

Getty, J. Arch, and Roberta T. Manning, eds. *Stalinist Terror: New Perspectives.* New York, 1993.

Getty, J. Arch, Gábor T. Rittersporn, and Viktor N. Zemskov. "Victims of the Soviet Penal System in the Pre-War Years: A First Approach on the Basis of Archival Evidence." *American Historical Review* 98 (October 1993): 1017–49.

Glickman, Rose. *Russian Factory Women.* Berkeley, 1984.

Goldman, Wendy Z. "Industrial Politics, Peasant Rebellion, and the Death of the Proletarian Women's Movement in the USSR." *Slavic Review* 55 (Spring 1996): 46–77.

von Hagen, Mark. *Soldiers in the Proletarian Dictatorship.* Ithaca, N. Y., 1990.

Higgonet, Margaret Randolph, and Jane Jenson, eds. *Behind the Lines: Gender and the Two World Wars*. New Haven, Conn., 1987.

Jönasdöttir, Anna G. *Why Women Are Oppressed*. Philadelphia, 1994.

Kowalski, Ronald I. *The Bolshevik Party in Conflict: The Left Communist Opposition of 1918*. London, 1991.

Lane, David. *The Roots of Russian Communism*. Assen, Netherlands, 1969.

Lapidus, Gail Warshofsky. *Women in Soviet Society*. Berkeley, 1978.

Laraña, Enrique, Hank Johnston, and Joseph R. Gusfield, eds. *New Social Movements*. Philadelphia, 1994.

Lenin, V. I. *The Emancipation of Women: From the Writings of V. I. Lenin*. New York, 1966.

Lih, Lars T., Oleg V. Naumov, and Oleg V. Khlevniuk, eds. *Stalin's Letters to Molotov, 1925–1936*. New Haven, Conn., 1995.

Macdonald, Sharon, Pat Holden, and Shirley Ardener, eds. *Images of Women in Peace and War: Cross-Cultural and Historical Perspectives*. Madison, Wis., 1988.

McNeal, Robert H. *Bride of the Revolution: Krupskaia and Lenin*. Ann Arbor, Mich., 1972.

Maxwell, Margaret. *Narodniki Women: Russian Women Who Sacrificed Themselves for the Dream of Freedom*. New York, 1990.

Medvedev, Roy. *Let History Judge*. Ed. David Joravsky and Georges Haupt. Trans. Colleen Taylor. New York, 1973. Rev. ed. Ed. and trans. George Shriver. New York, 1989.

Meyer, Alfred G. *The Feminism and Socialism of Lily Braun*. Bloomington, Ind., 1985.

Morris, Aldon D., and Carol McClurg Mueller, eds. *Frontiers in Social Movement Theory*. New Haven, Conn., 1992.

Norton, Barbara T. "The Making of a Female Marxist: E. D. Kuskova's Conversion to Russian Social Democracy." *International Review of Social History* 34 (1989): 227–50.

Perrie, Maureen. "The Social Composition and Structure of the Socialist-Revolutionary Party Before 1917." *Soviet Studies* 24 (October 1972): 223–50.

Rabinowitch, Alexander. *The Bolsheviks Come to Power: The Revolution of 1917 in Petrograd*. New York, 1978.

  Prelude to Revolution: The Petrograd Bolsheviks and the July 1917 Uprising. Bloomington, Ind., 1968.

Raleigh, Donald J. *Revolution on the Volga: 1917 in Saratov*. Ithaca, N. Y., 1986.

Rigby, T. H. *Communist Party Membership in the USSR, 1917–1967*. Princeton, 1968.

Service, Robert. *The Bolshevik Party in Revolution: A Study in Organisational Change, 1917–1923*. New York, 1979.

  Lenin: A Political Life. Vol. II, *Worlds in Collision*. Bloomington, Ind., 1991.

Stites, Richard. *The Women's Liberation Movement in Russia: Feminism, Nihilism, and Bolshevism, 1860–1930*. Princeton, 1978.

Tilly, Louise A., and Patricia Gurin, eds. *Women, Politics, and Change*. New York, 1990.

Wildman, Allan K. *The End of the Russian Imperial Army*. 2 vols. Princeton, 1980–87.
The Making of a Workers' Revolution: Russian Social Democracy, 1891–1903. Chicago, 1967.

ADDITIONAL RUSSIAN-LANGUAGE MATERIALS

Bochkareva, E., and S. Liubimova. *Svetlyi put'*. Moscow, 1967.
Bondarevskaia, T. P. *Peterburgskii komitet RSDRP v revoliutsii, 1905–1907 gg.* Leningrad, 1975.
Chernysheva, E. "Nasha radost'." *Rabotnitsa*, no. 16 (1926): 9.
Chirkov, P. M. *Reshenie zhenskogo voprosa v SSSR, 1917–1937 gg.* Moscow, 1978.
Chuev, Feliks. *Sto sorok besed s Molotovym*. Moscow, 1991.
Igumnova, Z. *Zhenshchiny Moskvy v gody grazhdanskoi voiny*. Moscow, 1958.
Institut istorii partii pri TsK Kompartii Ukrainy. *Bol'sheviki vo glave trudiashchikhsia v period bor'by za ustanovlenie sovetskoi vlasti na Ukraine, oktiabr' 1917 g.–fevral' 1918 g.* Kiev, 1982.
Leikina, V. "Oktiabr' po Rossii. Chast' 2ia: Ukraina." *Proletarskaia revoliutsiia*, no. 12 (1926): 238–54.
Serditova, S. *Bol'sheviki v bor'be za zhenskie proletarskie massy, 1903 g.–fevral' 1917 g.* Moscow, 1959.
Smitten, E. "Zhenshchiny v RKP." *Kommunistka*, no. 1–2 (1923): 30–32; no. 4 (1924): 8–10.
Sverdlova, K. T. *Iakov Mikhailovich Sverdlov*. 1st ed. Moscow, 1957. 4th ed. Moscow, 1985.
Tsvetkov-Prosveshchenskii, A. "Eniseiskaia ssylka v tsifrakh." *Katorga i ssylka*, no. 87 (1932): 143–54.
"Vseukrainskii s'ezd sovetov." *Litopys revoliutsii*, no. 1 (1928): 267–92.

FILMS

A Wave of Passion. Prod. Kevin M. Mulhern. Kevin M. Mulhern Productions, 1994, videocassette.

PERIODICALS

Katorga i ssylka, 1921–35
Litopys revoliutsii, 1926–28
Petrogradskaia pravda, 1918–20
Pravda, 1912–14, 1917–21
Proletarskaia revoliutsiia, 1921–38
Rabotnitsa, 1914, 1917, 1921–30

Index